Jonny Muir is a writer, hill runner and English teacher. He is the author of three other books: *Heights of Madness*, *The UK's County Tops* and *Isles at the Edge of the Sea*. He lives in Edinburgh.

Alex Staniforth is an adventurer, author and motivational speaker.

THE MOUNTAINS ARE CALLING

Running in the High Places of Scotland

JONNY MUIR

Foreword by Alex Staniforth

SANDSTONE PRESS

First published in Great Britain by
Sandstone Press Ltd
Dochcarty Road
Dingwall
Ross-shire
IV15 9UG
Scotland

www.sandstonepress.com

This edition 2018

The publisher acknowledges subsidy from Creative Scotland
towards publication of this volume.

ISBN: 978-1-912240-63-0
ISBNHBK: 978-1-912240-10-4
ISBNe: 978-1-912240-11-1

Cover and plate sections design by Raspberry Creative Type, Edinburgh
Typeset by Iolaire Typography Ltd, Newtonmore
Printed and bound by Totem, Poland

For Fi, Arielle and Aphra

CONTENTS

LIST OF ILLUSTRATIONS

LIST OF MAPS

HILL RACES OF SCOTLAND

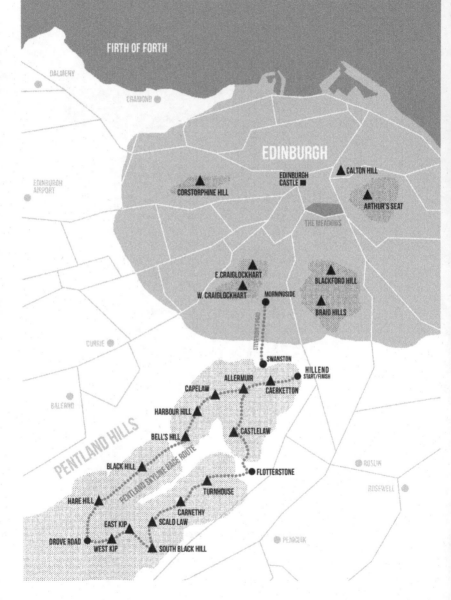

EDINBURGH AND LOTHIAN
PENTLAND HILLS AND PENTLAND SKYLINE RACE ROUTE

FIRTH OF FORTH

DALMENY

CRAMOND

EDINBURGH
AIRPORT

EDINBURGH

CORSTORPHINE HILL

EDINBURGH
CASTLE

CALTON HILL

ARTHUR'S SEAT

THE MEADOWS

E.CRAIGLOCKHART

W. CRAIGLOCKHART

MORNINGSIDE

BLACKFORD HILL

BRAID HILLS

STEWART ROAD

CURRIE

SWANSTON

ALLERMUIR

HILLEND
START/FINISH

CAPELAW

CAERKETTON

BALERNO

HARBOUR HILL

BELL'S HILL

CASTLELAW

PENTLAND HILLS

BLACK HILL

ROSLIN

PENTLAND SKYLINE RACE ROUTE

FLOTTERSTONE

ROSEWELL

HARE HILL

TURNHOUSE

EAST KIP

CARNETHY

DROVE ROAD

WEST KIP

SCALD LAW

SOUTH BLACK HILL

PENICUIK

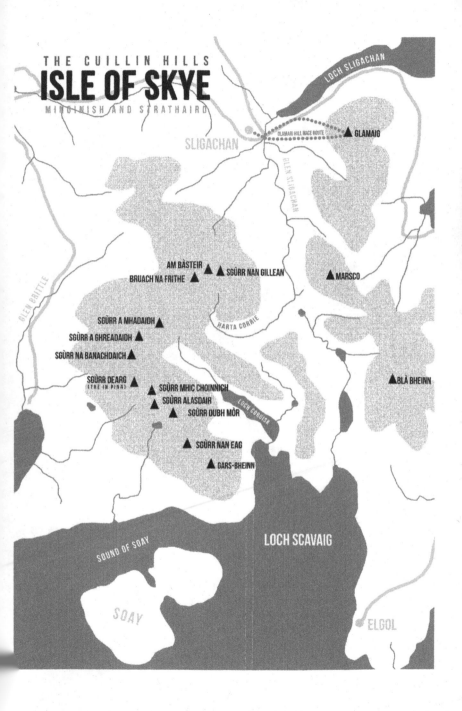

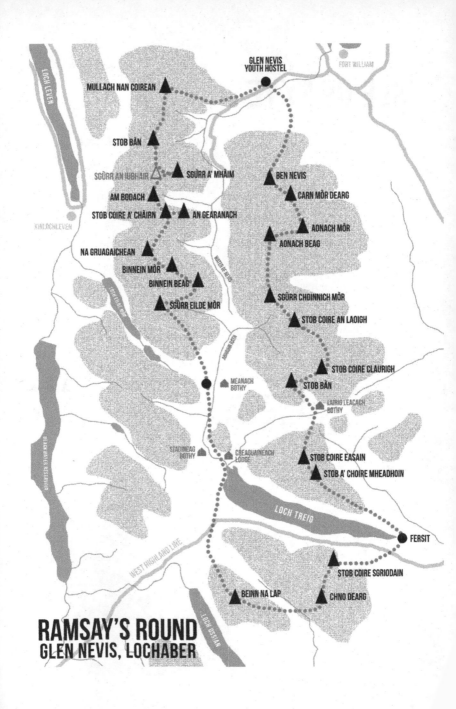

GLEN NEVIS
YOUTH HOSTEL

FORT WILLIAM

LOCH LEVEN

MULLACH NAN COIREAN

STOB BÀN

SGÙRR AN IUBHAIR   SGÙRR A' MHÀIM

BEN NEVIS

CARN MÒR DEARG

AM BODACH

STOB COIRE A' CHÀIRN   AN GEARANACH

AONACH MÒR

AONACH BEAG

KINLOCHLEVEN

NA GRUAGAICHEAN

BINNEIN MÒR

BINNEIN BEAG

SGÙRR CHOINNICH MÒR

SGÙRR EILDE MÒR

STOB COIRE AN LAOIGH

STOB COIRE CLAURIGH

STOB BÀN

MEANACH
BOTHY

LAIRIG LEACACH
BOTHY

WATER OF NEVIS

STAOINEAG
BOTHY

CREAGUAINEACH
LODGE

STOB COIRE EASAIN

STOB A' CHOIRE MHEADHOIN

BLACK WATER RESERVOIR

LOCH TREIG

FERSIT

WEST HIGHLAND LINE

STOB COIRE SGRIODAIN

BEINN NA LAP   CHNO DEARG

LOCH OSSIAN

RAMSAY'S ROUND
GLEN NEVIS, LOCHABER

FOREWORD

My first calling to Scotland was fairly unextraordinary. An impressionable child from Cheshire, I craned my neck at mountains like nothing I had seen before. From Loch Lomond to Fort William I pointed at these rocky shoulders with wide-eyed enthusiasm; asking whether they could be Ben Nevis, the mountain that had captured my imagination. Not much later, the nature of Scotland became etched in my memory after being almost snowed in as we crossed Rannoch Moor. This was not even in midwinter, but in March. A decade later, Scotland would call me back as the training camp for my Himalayan expeditions. As the old expression goes: 'Everest is great training for the Scottish winter!'

Anyone reading this book will have their own Everest – their ultimate goal – in life. Mine would be climbing the mountain itself, which I have attempted twice.

I can relate to the occasion in Glen Coe, when Jonny Muir lost his romantic view of running mountains. Similarly, I lost my calling to climb. Although I grew to hate the expression, it's true that the 'mountain will always be there'. For a while, Everest would remain an unanswered voicemail.

This realisation prompted me to seek a challenge closer to home, and it was while planning to link the highest points of all the United Kingdom counties, by cycling, running, walking and kayaking, that I discovered this amazing athlete and writer. My 5,000 mile journey, titled Climb The UK, was completed in July 2017, and he was the only person to have made an attempt before me.

In a world with so little uncharted and records set so high, it's thrilling to devise unique ideas that don't involve a chicken costume, and somehow reassuring to discover it has already been done by such a remarkable individual. Without a precedent it would be too easy to dismiss the idea as absurd and probably unachievable. Standing, exhausted, on Moel Famau, my final county top, I felt I had done well, but proof came when I was invited by my exemplar to write the foreword for the exceptional piece of writing that follows: *The Mountains are Calling*.

On four expeditions to the Himalayas, I have experienced altitude sickness, sleepless nights under the steam of breath, and –20 temperatures that left icicles in the stubble of my older colleagues, but it is still not an environment as unpredictable, character–building and enchanting as that of Scotland, whose bipolar tendencies can hit before the clouds roll off the hills. In contrast, the monsoon jetstream that knocks each Everest season on the head is forecast almost to the day. Predictable or otherwise, and be it Everest or Scotland's revered Chno Dearg, these mountains crush dreams without apology and can strike fear into the most robust of hearts.

On Ben More Assynt, to catch up on time, I was obliged to hop over boulders and run towards Conival, sliding down scree before reaching Inchnadamph. Like Jonny I received disapproving looks from hillwalkers who champion the slower approach, but I had sixty miles still to cycle and would have to be in the saddle before they reached the summit. At other times, running became a means of self–preservation; to generate heat, or simply to get me off the mountain before wind and rain could finish me off. I discovered how, in the space of a week, Scotland could add the danger of heatstroke to that of hypothermia; happily running through snow on Ben Macdui, sunburning in the Arrochar Alps.

Shivering in a phonebox at Braemore, south of Ullapool, I

took comfort in knowing that someone special had been here before me, when a ninety–mile day turned into an infuriating battle against headwinds, and the glens and blotted moorland, the chilly swathes of pine forest, had merged into one.

Arduous days of Himalayan climbing can start early in alpenglow, piercing blue skies. You can travel slowly, and finish early when the climbing day is short, with Sherpa hospitality and a mug of hot tea waiting. There was no hot tea in Glen Affric when I was benighted and deprived of a warm bed at the youth hostel, instead making an impromptu wild camp, scooping up dry protein powder with a toothbrush for dinner.

The tipping point came on Càrn Eighe the next day, when isolation drove me to converse with the sheep, and rain penetrated every seam of my clothing. False summits and lost paths all got too much and, in a weak moment, I crumbled into childish sobbing. The weight of the mountain seemed to sit on my shoulders, laughing in a booming cackle of wind. There was no option but to get back up and push on, though I had run out of ways to say: 'that was the worst day of my life'.

Whereas, a midge assault gave me good reason to run up Merrick with a fierce breeze tickling the hairs on my neck, and the sunset across Galloway cracking the sky into purple fire. Racing the daylight towards Durness, the otherworldly shadows of Assynt fell like dominoes behind me; the salty silence on the summit of Goatfell broken by the blast of ferry horns below; and the turquoise coasts of the Orkney Isles. In these moments the answer to the question 'why' was easy: being in places I had never known existed; free to do my own thing and step above the clouds. To think hill running was banned in Scotland in 1850! Can you imagine the lynch mob of X–Talons and hip belts if that happened today?

With the same passion and dedication he applies to his own training, Jonny Muir has gone the extra mile to gather a staggering wealth of insight. Reading about Finlay Wild in the Cuillin particularly fed my awe of the gnarly runners that Scotland has bred, whilst also sending shivers to my feet. It reminded me of a multi–day hike of the Skye Trail two years earlier in penetrating coastal rain. Sopping wet and squelching into Portree, we were apprehended by burly Highland workmen: 'Aye, lads, did you forget to take yer tablets this morning?'

These experiences raise our thresholds and make us more resilient to everyday life. It's hardly surprising that hill runners are so hard to break. We have a lot to thank these athletes for: superhuman feats that reset the bar and inspire apprentice runners. It's our white–haired heroes that dare us to dream that, yes, we really could join their exclusive company. We are hungry to learn their art.

When voices of reason tell us to turn back, we are reminded by what others have achieved; we groan, dig deep and push on because we want to be like them. Why are we drawn back, time and time again, hungry gluttons for punishment? This 'type–2' enjoyment that we find in the mountains is difficult to describe or explain. Outdoor writers have tried, and many can say what runners *do*, but these pages tell of the journey of *understanding*. In *The Mountains are Calling*, Jonny sums up these feelings to a tee. It's only by losing ourselves in these high places that we truly find ourselves.

After watching the sunset from 7,000 metres altitude, humbled by the grandeur of the Himalayas, I know nothing rubs away a longing for the familiar mountains on our doorstep that we know inside out, and love. The benefits of being outside for our physical and mental wellbeing cannot be overestimated.

At first, I wondered where I might fit into such a fascinating collection of perspectives; between the hill running wonders, the international champions, and satisfied Sunday plodders. From their banana bunches to Prosecco and playground hill reps, there seems to be no common factors beyond modesty and the simple desire to be out in the hills. This is what unifies us.

Runners are often asked: 'have you ever run a marathon?' as

mountaineers are somehow expected to have climbed Everest, but only a runner would ask: 'Have you completed Ramsay's Round?' Only a runner would understand. Maybe we don't need to be understood. Hopefully this community will remain mysterious for decades to come.

Reading Jonny Muir's book makes it apparent that animalistic capability and talent alone do not command the meaning we take from the mountains. Maybe it's not the battle of seconds and minutes, but the euphoria of owning a summit by the power of feet, grit and glycogen; the realisation of 'I've done it' is something we all relate to. Nothing else comes close. In its simplest form, running equates to survival: from prehistoric man chasing his dinner to city workers swapping briefcases for bothies and conference calls for checkpoints.

As recounted in the chapter *Ambushed by Chno Dearg*, some have risked the worst to run at their best, and drawn the short straw. Their legends still run today, if only through these pages and the hills they reigned over, but the biggest risk is in not doing what makes us feel so alive. Those who stay inside, warm and dry, can only be pitied – that's as alive as they're going to feel all day. We cannot run forever, though someone will probably try. The grasp of 'real life' pulls us back to *terra firma*, but soon enough the mountains will call us again. This is our way of life.

From the county tops to the Munros and the roof of the world, we all have our calling – and I'm certain these pages will inspire you to go outside and answer yours. Until then, I wish you as Jonny wished me – 'go well'.

Alex Staniforth
Endurance Adventurer, Motivational Speaker,
Ambassador and Fundraiser
Nepal 2017

1

RUNNING THROUGH TIME

Hearts bursting against ribs, two specks on a green-brown canvas reach for the sky. Plunging through the heather of a Scottish mountainside, the runners climb relentlessly, the gap between them and an exhausted chasing group widening with every ragged breath, nothing mattering but this and now.

Another runner, moving with the nonchalance of a mountain stag, is in pursuit, having started later than the rest.

'Let me run, let me run,' the kilted Highlander had begged.

'Go if you wish,' he was told, 'but you are too late.'

The crowd watched him clear the plain, then begin the ascent, clambering on hands and toes, grasping tresses of heather. He reached the end of the line of runners, now diminished to tiny, hunched figures, and began to pass them. He lifted his eyes to the mountaintop, lingering on the two distant bodies ahead, overcome by desire – desire to be the first to touch the sky.

'Look how he ascends!' exclaimed one of the onlookers. 'He will beat them all.'

The leaders, McGregor siblings, are approaching the brow of the final steep pull. Sensing a following presence, they look back in astonishment. The runner is their younger brother. McGregor leads McGregor from McGregor. 'Halves, brothers, and I'll stop,' the fledgling urges.

'No, never,' came the response.

An omniscient commentator seems to see them with the eye of a curious buzzard wheeling above: 'They felt their heads dizzy, their eyes dim and painful – the breath rolled quick through their nostrils like fire – their hearts beat louder than the sound of their footsteps – every muscle and sinew was tightened to breaking – the foam in their mouths seemed dried into sand – their bleeding lips, when closed, glued themselves together – the sweat pearled on their skin in cold drops – and their feet rose and fell mechanically more than otherwise.'

The finish line is in sight, the suffering nearly over. The brothers have never felt so alive, never felt so close to death. The junior McGregor, sensing he is strongest, surges ahead of his seniors. Fierce instinct rules their minds, overriding family obligation. Desperately, the oldest claws at his sibling, clutches his kilt, seizes hold and refuses to let go. With the middle brother gaining and the other clinging to a garment that is not his own, the impulse of the youngest emerges: he loosens the belt of his kilt and resigns it to his brother. 'I have yielded everything to you,' he declares, 'and I will that also.'

Dennisbell McGregor of Ballochbuie – the original mountain runner – runs on to victory.

It is the first Saturday in September. As 500 runners are gathering at the foot of Ben Nevis for the annual race up and down Britain's highest mountain, some seventy-five are back where a sport began: Braemar, the Aberdeenshire village that intrudes on the vast arctic wilderness of the Cairngorms.

We congregate on the turf of the games field, awaiting the crack of a gun. When it comes, as if a single entity, we launch ourselves forward. An elbow drives into my chest; my knees knock together. We are soon striding freely, parading around a track, then along the home straight, past the Royal Pavilion, and up and out of the stadium. At the end of a car park, we strike across a booby-trapped swathe of rough heather, disguising loose rocks and foot-sized holes.

I notice the silence first. There is sound – the rising of my own breath and the gurgle of feet on wet grass – but no noise. The suffering comes next: a trickle, then a seep, then a torrent. I do not fight it. It is why we are here. I am climbing steeply,

through a clutch of birch, then on the open heath of the mountain. I think of the McGregor siblings – their heads faint, their
sinews contracting, their gaping mouths dry. A millennium
lies between us and them. Everything has changed; nothing
has changed. We are running up a hill, a column of bodies
compelled to go higher, feeling the way three brothers once
felt. We are the same, for we long to touch the sky.

Running up hills has always been hard. With hill racing part
of a re-established Highland Gathering in Braemar in 1832,
McGregor's peak of Creag Choinnich, a hill that marks the
western conclusion of the Lochnagar massif, was the stage.
When Queen Victoria first came to the games in 1848, she
followed the progress of runners through Prince Albert's
telescope, while steadying herself on the shoulder of a general.
She was delighted when one of the Balmoral ghillies, Charles
Duncan – an 'active, good-looking young man' – won the race
in 1850. 'Eighteen or nineteen started,' Victoria observed,
'and it looked very pretty to see them run off in their different
coloured kilts.'

Spectating from the grounds of Braemar Castle, she watched
them scramble through woods of larch and pine, then climb
over heather and across boulders to the summit cairn, with
Duncan 'far before the others the whole way'. His victory
came at a price. 'He, like many others,' Victoria wrote, 'spit
blood after running the race up that steep hill in this short
space of time, and he has never been so strong since.' Victoria
put two and two together – in this case, upwards motion
and its perceived impact on a man's health – and decided,
however 'pretty' the sport might be, mountain running should
be abolished. 'The running up hill has in consequence been
discontinued,' she noted matter-of-factly in her diary.

It took another female monarch – and a gap of 129 years
– to overturn the prohibition. The permission of Elizabeth
II, Victoria's great-great-granddaughter, was gained to rein-
troduce a games race in 1979, with a midweek trial event
justifying its potential as a visual spectacle that even Victoria

with her spyglass would have appreciated. By the 1970s, the Gathering had switched to a permanent base to the south of Braemar, and rising above the Princess Royal and Duke of Fife Memorial Park was 859-metre Morrone. The new race had a new mountain, the mountain on which – to the naked eye of those below – I appear as a slow-moving red and yellow dot.

While the ethos of the Gathering – a spirit of toughness and tenacity – continues to be inspired by that first hill race, it is not easy to live up to such expectations. Right now, therefore, it is best to be glimpsed from afar. I stoop, hands on thighs, walking when the gradient steepens, willing my legs to run when it eases, even if the effort feels like I am pushing back an ocean. The games – now adrift beneath our feet – continue without us: the heats for the 220 yards race, the throwing of the 22-pound hammer, the local competition for the sword dance. Banchory Pipe Band provides the musical background that comes to us in whispers on the wind. The Cairngorms are spread on a painting of brown and green and grey, a realm of forest and mountain. I am clinging to a wave in a storm, with Morrone at the centre of a titanic sea. The sky, overweight with cloud, is hardened by a blue-black hue, as if rain could fall at any moment. This land is so familiar, yet it seems as if I am seeing mountains for the first time. As Nan Shepherd wrote of the Cairngorms in *The Living Mountain*: 'However often I walk on them, these hills hold astonishment for me. There is no getting accustomed to them.'

Time pauses again. The race over, the McGregors would have buried their faces in moist heather, panting furiously, light-headed from breathless exhilaration. Looking up, they would have seen what we saw, what Victoria observed on Ben Macdui, the crown of the Cairngorm plateau: a land possessed by a 'sublime and solemn effect, so wild, so solitary'.

We emerge suddenly into the consciousness of the crowd. A flare erupts, heralding the arrival of the first runner at the highest point. To those who glance up, I am still a red and yellow smear, only smaller, and doggedly sweating through heather. In time, I get there: a place where the gradient is momentarily gentler and the ground rockier. A line of cairn cones straddling the 730-metre contour marks our zenith. We go no further, for if we do, continuing perhaps to the summit of Morrone, we vanish from the view of the games field. The McGregors stopped at the top of a hill in 1064; in Europe, they still stop here; in Scotland today, we come up – and then we go down.

If there is something primeval about mountain running, then to run downhill is simply to answer instinct. For early man, running equated to survival – running to escape, running to eat, running to live and not die. We are destined to run – and perhaps it is running downhill that allies us most closely to our distant ancestors. After the suffocation of moving uphill, my legs – now descending more hurriedly than feels sensible – are stung into action. I dash across low heather, as if taking a direct bearing to Creag Choinnich, some two miles away, before swerving left to rejoin the path. I leave it almost immediately, following others who veer left again, as if we are a clutch of frightened deer, this time down a steep, slippery bank, ending a long way below at a fence. I lose height rapidly, first in a succession of leaps, lunges and slides, then in a seemingly uncontrollable set of bounds, arms flailing above my head, embroiled in euphoric terror. It is the closest a human can come to flight, and, as it was for the McGregors, life in these moments becomes only this. Runners are scattered below: a flash of yellow emerges from behind a knoll; a blue-green streak scales the deer fence like a ladder; a dash of white juxtaposes the green and brown of the moor. We are free; we go where we want. The summit is the only stipulation. How we get there – and back – is our concern.

As I cross the fence, I am disorientated for an instant. Everyone has gone. I skirt a hummock and climb a mound, pausing momentarily to glance about – then, like the skipping flicker of a lone doe, I glimpse a blue burst behind the bushes. I instinctively follow, finding the path and a familiar outcrop of rock. I retrace my steps, tiptoes on the way up, gallops now: back among the birches, across the field of tripwire, through the car park, down an angled slope of grass into the arena, accelerating towards the empty Royal Pavilion and the finish line. Elizabeth is not there; she would arrive in a blaze of pomp and pipes soon after. It was enough that she lets us be – and we all have our reasons for being.

McGregor was racing for the medieval equivalent of stardom. In the wild and uncertain world of eleventh century Scotland, his race was the decree of King Malcolm III to recruit the fastest runners to operate a post system across the clan lands. When one runner was exhausted, he would pass the literal baton, the fiery cross or *crann-tara*, on to the next. Made of two pieces of wood fashioned into a cross, one end alight, the other daubed in blood, the *crann-tara* would rouse the clans in a call that could not be ignored. 'Woe to the wretch who fails to rear / At this dread sign the ready spear!' wrote Sir Walter Scott centuries later. Every relay team needs its fabled last leg runner, its Usain Bolt – that was McGregor, a monarch among messengers.

Kris Jones, a Dundee-based Great Britain orienteer, was McGregor's twenty-first century equivalent. He would collect a purse of £300 for winning the race. Only the champion of the caber toss would take home more.

What about me? I finished a penniless nineteenth, seven minutes back from Jones. Why am I here?

The question implies a choice, like I could be somewhere else. As the environmental philosopher John Muir wrote in a letter to his sister in 1873: 'The mountains are calling and I must go.'

2

EPIPHANY

Frankie Miller is off. 'I don't know if you can see…' The setting is a crammed commuter train of indifferent Londoners. A caption offers exposition: 'London Underground, 8.15am.' The camera pauses on a tight-lipped, pensive hero, a suited man in his late-twenties. The train stutters into a station and freed passengers flood towards the exit. The protagonist emerges from this hellish cellar to its ground floor: street level in Central London. A cyclist ominously stretches a mask over his face; a moment later, an argument erupts between a lorry driver and a cabbie. We follow the man to his place of work: through the revolving door of a glass building and into a lift holding a dozen others. An identity badge hangs from his dark jacket. The camera craves another close-up: a rueful expression, a concealed sigh.

Miller, meanwhile, is getting ready for the chorus. As he cries the immortal words, 'Let me tell you that I love you, that I think about you all the time,' a lightning bolt of realisation flares. Suddenly, everything seems so simple.

Epiphany.

He steps out of the lift, tosses his badge to security guards and hurls his briefcase into the jaws of a bin lorry. There is a final sneer from a Londoner, then an instant after, a silhouetted Edinburgh Castle appears. Striding across Princes Street, tie discarded, pausing to buy *The Big Issue*, our hero has arrived. Next stop: the pub. The man, two mates, three pints of Tennent's. The utopian image becomes fixed, morphing into a photograph seen through the eyes of a woman travelling on the London Underground. *Join me*, it intimates.

Tennent's 1991 advertisement for its lager, complemented by the musical backdrop of *Caledonia*, celebrates epiphany in its simplest form: I am unhappy with my life; therefore, I am going to change my life.

There is a reason why epiphanies are the preserve of fiction: in reality, they rarely occur.

I had no need of Miller's romanticism as I climbed Geal-charn, the white peak, in the fading light of a late October evening. I had parked a car with my life packed in it by the rush of the A9 as it crests the Pass of Drumochter, crossed the train lines that link the central belt of Scotland to the Highlands, and passed deeper into a cooling valley. The sun was busy elsewhere, leaving the glen in shadow. A stony track succumbed to moor, and the way rose steadily up an innocuous spur. Rising to a peak of 917 metres above sea level with a starting point from the pass of 400 metres, Geal-charn is as straightforward as mountain-climbing gets. I trailed a jumper from my right hand. Presuming I would be back at the car in two hours, I took nothing else.

I was walking up, but also away – away from dissatisfaction. I had left an uninspiring job as a newspaper reporter in Cambridgeshire, assuming I would find better prospects in London. I sent out a flurry of hopeful emails and letters. Like scaling a mountain, it was not as easy as anticipated: false summit after false summit. After six weeks of rejection and diminishing hope, I temporarily abandoned the capital for the Alps, circumnavigating Europe's highest mountain on the Tour du Mont Blanc long-distance footpath as the first of the autumn snow swept across the cols. The night I arrived back in London, my girlfriend, Fi, ended our five-year relationship. I did not see the need, therefore, to begin what would also have been a difficult conversation: I had that week received two offers of interview at newspapers. One was in Ilford in East London; the other was in Aberdeen. Hundreds of miles apart, they were scheduled for the same day. I chose the high

road – and got the job: a reporter's post covering the Highlands of Scotland, working from a base in Inverness. I tossed
my figurative briefcase into the back of the bin lorry.

That is why I had driven up the A9, parked in a layby on the
Pass of Drumochter, and was walking up Geal-charn.

But that was not the epiphany.

I struggled to formulate words on the swathe of mountainside known as Geal-charn. The hill is not even unique in
name, with another three mountains of similar height bearing
the same moniker. I reached for adjectives, but they did not
inspire: lonely, barren, forgettable. It seems cruel to describe
a Scottish mountain in such a way. Yet it is possible to find
the extraordinary in the ordinary; it is there the extraordinary
is more likely to reside. As I passed the snow line on a stony
plateau, a bashful sun returned with a dazzling flash. The
snow was feeble at first, a scattering of frozen flakes deco-
rating the cake of the plateau. Gradually, as I gained altitude,
it was an inch thick, then thicker still, concealing the grey and
black beneath. I stopped to look back at my tracks – graffiti
in a sea of shimmering white. The road lay beyond, reduced to
a voiceless thread. The silence was vast, the stillness startling. A
shudder – a simultaneous tremble of trepidation, exultation
and relief – began in my shoulders, rolled down my body,
swayed through my limbs, touched my toes, mottled my skin
with goosebumps. Mountains would make me shudder like
this again: when immersed in the frigid waters of the Fairy
Pools on Skye, tracing the ferocious outline of the Black
Cuillin; when placing virgin footsteps on Moruisg on a flawless winter morning of deep snow; when glimpsing the Paps
of Jura from the motionless Minch. And more. So much more.

I was finally on the summit, sitting cross-legged on snow,
watching the sun melt over an unending dream of mountains.

That was the epiphany.

Tuesday was club night at Inverness Harriers. I still think of
them now, weekly at 7pm, shuffling away from the glaring

floodlights of an athletics track, edging along the Caledonian Canal and heading up Craig Dunain, a bobbing procession of head torches in the winter. For that hour or so, they leap into another world. Craig Dunain is a dot in the geography of the Highlands, a 288-metre lump at the end of a rolling ridge that garlands the western bank of Loch Ness. Yet I was captivated by that hill. Tuesday night was a given, but in the 18 months I would spend in Inverness I ran up and down and around Craig Dunain again and again. While those numerous expeditions inevitably blur into indistinguishable confusion, some recollections stand out as sharply as if I had run up Craig Dunain this morning.

There was the time David, Dougie and I set out on a freezing night in January, steaming breath illuminated by the glare of our lights as we passed quietly by the inky water of the canal. We turned up a ramp of gravel that became a muddy path under a canopy of tangled branches, smothering the stars. Once over the A82, the main road to Fort William, it seemed every pine had taken a step forward: we were enfolded in the ominous embrace of the forest. Out there, in the darkness, there was life: a pair of eyes, a rustling, a scuttling. As we climbed higher, a mist so clotted it seemed to bathe us swamped the hillside. I shuddered a Geal-charn shudder.

There was the time a pack of us on a spring evening ventured further south than usual, traversing a flank of Craig Dunain until we could see the brown water of a great loch below.

'What's that?' Gordie asked.

'Lock Ness,' I said triumphantly.

'It's loch, soft lad,' David roared, exaggerating the 'och'.

There was the time I ran alone on a benighted Craig Dunain. I climbed the hill on open grassland, knowing that entering the forest at some point was certain. What was benign by day was terrifying by night. As I hurried along pine avenues, never had I been so conscious of that I most take for granted: my beating heart. I stared into the abyss of the woods. There were no eyes tonight; nothing stirred and nothing sounded. As I looked up, the moon was a smear behind a bank of high cloud. The anticipation for something, anything, to happen was crushing. 'The stillness,' as John Muir once noted, was 'at once awful and sublime'.

I was a hill running Colin Smith, the reform school protagonist of Alan Sillitoe's *The Loneliness of the Long Distance Runner*: 'the first and last man on the world, both at once.' Smith's words offer the clearest rationalisation of running – any sort of running – I have found: 'So there I am, standing in the doorway in shimmy and shorts, not even a dry crust in my guts, looking out at frosty flowers on the ground. I suppose you think this is enough to make me cry? Not likely. Just because I feel like the first bloke in the world wouldn't make me bawl. It makes me feel fifty times better than when I'm cooped up in that dormitory with three hundred others.'

I touched the wire mesh that surrounds the telecommunications masts atop Craig Dunain and fled downhill, out of the forest, paradoxically back to the very thing I – and Smith – sought to escape.

The hill racing season in the Highlands commenced on Craig Dunain in March, with a short dash from canal to summit and back again. Wearing the mustard and maroon of Inverness Harriers for the first time in the hills, the experience extended to an alarmingly painful 37 minutes. 'Going up, I felt simply awful,' I wrote in a diary that evening – an evening of hobbling, walking sideways downstairs and intermittent groaning. I was terribly naive. Having raced a half-marathon on the roads of Inverness a fortnight earlier, I considered myself 'fit'. I had yet to learn that the 'simply awful' feeling was entirely normal, and that notions of 'fit' and fit-to-run-up-and-down-hills were radically different.

I thank my younger self for keeping journals, as the memories of the races I toiled through in that season of hill running baptism have congealed into a tussock of knotted scar tissue. Knockfarrel, on a course above the spa village of Strathpeffer, with a greater cumulative ascent than Craig Dunain, came next. I was ninth, I had noted, but my legs had been 'swimming in lactic'. Later that month was Cioch Mhòr, a nine-mile out-and-back race in the foothills of Ben Wyvis over far more committing terrain. 'Heavy underfoot and tired,' I recorded after labouring in heather and long grass, climbing through melting bands of snow, and twice wading a river.

Then there was Slioch: a daunting assignment on the Wester Ross Munro, seemingly on the cusp of toppling into Loch Maree at any moment, that made Cioch Mhòr resemble an amble down High Street in Inverness. There were fifty of us, none of whom seemed to do anything resembling a warm-up for a race of 12 miles with an overall ascent of almost 1,200 metres, on a day as hot and sunny as I can ever recall in Scotland. The route skirted the loch and its midges, before runners were catapulted into a wall of heather and loose rock on a towering protuberance known as Sgùrr Dubh. I had thought this might be 'it' – the summit of Slioch. It was not, of course. Really, I always knew the truth of the matter, but fervent hoping in hill running, I was learning, served the purpose of self-preservation.

When the weather is unfavourable on Slioch, the race organiser abandons the checkpoint on Sgùrr an Tuill Bhàin, the mountain's second summit; runners instead swoop immediately downhill to the glen. I could not imagine there ever being mist – or rain, or wind, or snow – such was the delicate exquisiteness of the minutes spent here. As I descended to the lower top, the giants of Torridon, the peaks of Fisherfield and rows of Fannichs, lining up from west to east, were grinning and waving.

'Head for the gully,' I was told by a marshal. I could not see a gully. I tumbled down a colossal mountainside riddled with tussocks, hoping to catch a glimpse of human life ahead, or to the right or left, or anywhere to at least give some confirmation that I was approximately in the correct place. I saw no-one, but eventually arrived at a gully – maybe *the* gully?

– where a rough track descended sharply to the glen. I drank the water from a burn with despotic resolve. The remaining four miles of stumbling, dizzying effort, back along the loch, back into the midges, were akin to struggling home after a long, late night of alcohol and pub brawling, ending with a series of drunken-like declarations of love as I passed runners in similarly wretched conditions.

Living in the Highlands, hill running felt like the natural thing to do – but that did not make it an easy thing to do. The road had been the home of my running for a decade. There is safety on asphalt; the next step mimics the last. After the initial shock of *racing* up a hill, I soon learnt I could drag my body skyward on the steepest of inclines; I could move over rough and uneven ground with relative adroitness; running downhill with grace and pace, I could not. Fear held me back, slowed me down, convincing me that a twist, a trip, a fall, would come in the next step. Rather than a dread or an I-cannot-do-this terror, the fear was a niggle, an irritation, an ever-present voice in my head whispering 'no' to the embrace of gravity. Instinct insisted that rapid downwards movement was not only wrong, it was tantamount to lunacy.

Years later, David Gallie – the runner who chastised my pronunciation on Craig Dunain – could not wait to tell me about what he had witnessed at Ben Nevis. His was a spectator's perspective, for David had at that point kept his promise to his mother never to race Ben Nevis again. In his last race on the Ben he had no memory of falling on the descent, but for a man with a fear of flying, he vividly recalled the moment he dismissed the potential of being airlifted to hospital. 'There was no way I was getting in a helicopter,' he said. 'I walked down.' The right side of his body bore the brunt of the fall: eight stitches to the head, missing skin off hip and shoulder. 'I've still got a piece of grit in my shoulder,' he announced happily, pulling on a sleeve to reveal the shrapnel. 'I was lucky. The doctor said she had been treating someone earlier who had broken his neck mountain biking.'

Luck: a subject David knew too much about. Iain Gallie, David's younger brother, sustained a life-changing brain injury in a car accident. 'I don't want two sons with head injuries,' David was instructed by his mother. He did as he was told.

David was waiting at the point where runners cross the tourist track after descending close to 700 vertical metres from the summit to reach a spate of scree above Red Burn. Rob Jebb, a British hill running champion and a four-time winner on the Ben, was predictably leading the race and dashed by the small crowd clustered on the path. David's eyes followed the line of Jebb's descent – down a steep grassy bank, angling towards a stream – then looked up the mountain again. 'Far above, as far as I could see, there was another runner,' he said. 'I glanced down to Rob Jebb for a few seconds, then back to the other runner. He was nearly at us. He flew past. He was flying – absolutely flying. I have never seen anyone descend like that. He was moving in a different gear to anyone else in the race, anyone I had ever seen on a hill.'

'He' was Finlay Wild. Five minutes adrift of Jebb at the top of the Ben, Wild – moving in a manner that seemed to belong to a mountain animal, not a human – won the race by 13 seconds.

To be Finlay Wild. To have grace and pace, and to be fearless. To be able to fly.

While I was reliant on diaries to piece together memories of racing, the recollections of simply being among mountains are fixed in my consciousness. The inevitable difficulties have been scratched away. The memories have been framed in perpetual perfection.

For years, I used roads to run and mountains to walk. I had only the haziest knowledge of hill or fell running being an offshoot of the more conventional foot-borne exercise. But very soon running and mountains were indivisible; there could not be one without the other. Running is prose. But hill running? This is poetry. Some years later, as I descended to the Nan Bield Pass in the Far Eastern Fells of the Lake District, a walker going up remarked: 'I don't know how you do it.' Encumbered by boots and bag, I wondered the same: *How do you do it?*

The early, innocent days are the most precious – and such were my wanderings through the Highlands. Late shifts in the newsroom permitted mornings for the hills. I went where the weather seemed best: to the wild reaches of the Monadhliath; to the Cairngorms; to the rough moors of Nairnshire where Inverness-bound planes rumbled overhead; to the Ben Wyvis massif; to the heath above Culloden. Early shifts in the spring and summer afforded similar opportunities at the other end of the day. It was after 10pm when Graham Bee, an Inverness clubmate, and I found ourselves descending the mossy ramp of Toll Creagach. We had climbed its neighbour, Tom a' Choinich, by a rocky ridge in the gloom of clag, but as we plunged off our second mountain, the mist was gone and the sun was boiling in the western sky, throwing flames across Glen Affric.

Not every mountain day was like that. Venturing west from Inverness to the Fannichs, Graham and I had no desire to vindicate the forecast. High winds and poor visibility were expected, while the Met Office had warned of heavy rain. Graham should have known better; at that time, I certainly did not. After slopping along sodden paths for an hour, we began climbing an incline to gain a bealach. We had been deceived by the mist-smothered mountains – we stood on the wrong pass. In a wild wind, we stubbornly pressed on, bent double on summits, committed to finishing what we had started.

As we left the final peak, Graham slipped awkwardly, skidding first, then landing hard on his back. With an apparent effortlessness in his stride, Graham was the runner I wanted to be. He was winning Craig Dunain in a course record when I still had a mile of the five-mile race to run. Seeing him fall was like watching a motor racing driver collide with a wall. There is a moment of shock, of agonised uncertainty, before you see a hand wave from the car. Graham was recumbent long enough for me to catch him up. He tentatively got back on his feet, muttered something about his shoes, and continued downhill with marginally less reckless abandon.

I was drawn to the Fannichs again a month later. Following a hydro-board track that weaves up a glen, I was running alone this time, my load lightened by a compass that remained in Inverness. I found Sgùrr Mòr, the highest of the range, easily enough, despite the presence of an inert clag. I blundered on, aiming for Beinn Liath Mhòr Fannaich. Where I went, I do not know. With visibility trimmed to about twenty metres, everything looked identical: a dismal world of boulders, grass and snippets of path that appeared and vanished. Beinn Liath Mhòr Fannaich, I decided, must be an elaborate ruse. It did not exist. At that point, two hours after departing Sgùrr Mòr, I was convinced that this mountain had also since vanished, as I could not find my way back there either. I seemed to have the hills exclusively when voices drifted through the murk and a party of six men emerged. Map in hand and scantily clad in shorts and a rapidly leaking waterproof, I calmly asked for clarification on where I was. 'Scotland,' came the reply.

In my year of hill running initiation, one of the dominant racing figures in the Highlands was Alec Keith. Consistency was his byword: a winner at Cioch Mhòr; runner-up at the brutal Isle of Jura fell race and at the Glenshee 9 – that is nine mountains, not nine miles; third at Glamaig on Skye and also at Knockfarrel. All this was despite Alec cutting an apparently harmless, even comical, figure on start lines; an unwashed, mud-spattered Inverness or brown Hunters Bog Trotters vest would invariably be worn inside out and adorned with a skewwhiff number. A fellow runner, Damon Rodwell, recalled meeting the 'illustrious' Alec crossing the bridge at Creaguaineach Lodge at the southern end of Loch Treig some years earlier. 'Alec is renowned for his holey, ragged running gear, and I noticed and commented that he was dressed in uncharacteristically natty attire. He admitted that the trousers were a present, the jacket a prize and the hat he had stolen. If I'd had my camera handy, you would have the pleasure of seeing Alec crossing the slippery, slime-covered wooden bridge in a 40-knot side wind on all fours.'

Now in his fifties, Alec will not get faster. His personal best of 35 minutes and 38 seconds for 10 kilometres on the road will undoubtedly prove a lifetime record. That mark, set in 2007 at a race in the Easter Ross village of Tain, did not even rank him among the top-250 men aged over 40 in the UK that year. But give him a mountain track, a peat hag, a maze of tussocks, a fence to cross, a river to ford, a summit to crest, scree to hurtle down – then you will see the real Alec Keith. He finished a little over a minute ahead of me in the Inverness half-marathon; at Cioch Mhòr six weeks later and four miles shorter, I was nine minutes back. His unerring ability in the Scottish mountains is not the outcome of overflowing natural ability. It is the product of decades of running thousands of miles over terrain most runners would baulk at, but it is also the product of love.

Alec was a seven-year-old schoolboy in north London when the mountains called. Opening a book on British geology, he was transfixed by a black and white image of a misty mountain in the Cairngorms, more than 500 miles north of where he sat, rising above a loch. 'It fascinated me then and still does,' Alec said. 'I'd never seen a real hill before but somehow this was for me.'

I called Alec from my then London home on the evening of the hottest July day on record. The temperature had reached 37 Celsius at Heathrow. The thermostat in my first-floor flat was telling its own horror story: 31 Celsius. Alec's wife answered: 'He's a bit mucky at the moment. He'll call you back.' When we finally spoke, Alec cheerfully announced he had been gutting drains, and I pictured him grinning.

I remembered Alec as an elusive figure. He rarely trained with Inverness and when he appeared at races, he was soon striding away into the distance, showing us only his back. As such, he became an athlete we mythologised. Alec was the runner whose idea of fun was to spend six hours wandering around the Cairngorms in vile weather. Alec was the runner who carried bunches of rapidly-mushed bananas to sustain himself on a day-long run in the mountains of Lochaber. Alec was the runner who ran England's Bob Graham Round on a family holiday having never encountered a step of the 66-mile route. An ascent route on Craig Dunain was named after Alec too. In a clearing of woodland dissected by electricity wires, a track zig-zags steeply up, hairpin upon hairpin; steeper still is a switchback-splitting path that goes straight through the middle of every bend. That was the Alec Keith route: the toughest way of all.

I was anxious when my phone rang – not because it was Alec, but because I wanted fable to be fact. I wanted to believe that fairy tales might be true.

Having served his mountain apprenticeship in the Cairngorms, by 1989 Alec felt ready to challenge Mel Edwards' decade-old fastest time of 4 hours and 34 minutes for the round of the quartet of the range's mountains – Braeriach, Cairn Toul, Ben Macdui and Cairn Gorm – that exceed 4,000 feet (1,219 metres). The 'fast hillwalker', by his own admission, set out from Glenmore Lodge in 'strange footwear, somewhere between boot, baffie and brothel-creeper', and returned 5 hours and 22 minutes later. 'The evidence of my human snowplough imitation descending Cairn Gorm remains etched into my right thigh and elbow,' he remarked.

The chasm between ambition and the record brought Alec his own epiphany: 'Having previously failed to see the point of hill running, I succumbed to the temptation it offered as a way of bypassing the duller bits of hillwalking and getting to the good bits. Running up hills is a relative concept: it's about getting up the ups as fast as you can.'

A new decade, the 1990s, arrived. The Soviet Union collapsed. The internet was unleashed. The Stone of Destiny returned to Scotland. Alec Keith 'just wanted to be in the hills' and by the end of the century would hold the record for the so-called Big Six – a longer round in the Cairngorms that includes the 4,000s, plus Beinn a' Bhuird and Ben Avon. Such feats do not occur by accident; they quite literally require trial and error. He gave the 4,000s another go in 1992, this time with more appropriate footwear, but again finished outside Mel Edwards' mark. It was later that same year that Alec discovered the Big Six – 'another thing to obsess over' – and persevered after failing to eclipse the record on a wind and rain-hampered first attempt.

Due some luck, Alec turned his gaze to the fabulous array of Lochaber mountains that square up on opposing sides of Glen Nevis. Here the roof-clipping brows and cascading slopes were imprinted with the sternest tales of endurance. Alec knew the magnitude of what he sought: to follow in the stud marks of a legend.

As the minutes ticked down to midday on 9 July, 1978, Charlie Ramsay tore down the lower slopes of Ben Nevis. He crossed a footbridge over the River Nevis and halted by the glen's youth hostel. The clock stopped. In the previous 23 hours and 58 minutes, Ramsay had passed over the summits of 23 Munros – Scottish mountains of at least 3,000 feet (914 metres) – in an immense loop, starting where he had finished. No-one had climbed so many Munros in a day; nor would anyone do so again for nine years. Scotland's classic 24-hour round – encompassing 60 miles of rough and wild mountain running, and an Everest-amount of ascending and descending – was born.

When Alec parked his car at Polldubh, deep in Glen Nevis, some 16 years later, only eleven others had demonstrated the endurance and mental stamina to match the deeds of Charlie Ramsay, with only a solitary success in the previous four years. Alec had every reason to doubt whether he could make it round within 24 hours. His preparation had been character-istically unconventional: he had not run for five days following a smash-and-grab ascent of the Jungfrau in Switzerland the previous weekend.

But Alec Keith is not a man to shirk a task: 'I was fit enough and strong enough, and I thought, when I get there, I will just get on with it. And I did.'

From Polldubh, he ran along the glen road he had driven minutes before. He passed the hostel, bridged the river, and began to climb Ben Nevis. It was not Alec's style to mimic the steps of another; he would run the circuit the other way around.

Up he went, alone and unsupported. Alec's method was that of the purist: 'I didn't want to say, "I need fifteen of you to help me to do this thing." I didn't want anyone to carry my rucksack. That's why I attempted unsupported. This would be my achievement, rather than the achievement of the people supporting me. That was my ethos. Everyone is entitled to do things as they want.' Alec's inimitable way of doing things extended to nutrition: 22 bananas, enough sachets of powder to make 26 pints of juice mixed with burn water, a packet of chocolate digestives and a small fruit cake. The bananas had been stuffed into a plastic box. 'I didn't think about dumping a bag of food,' he said. 'I could have left half of the bananas there. In this period, people were doing things in their own way – and doing extraordinary things. I was doing it my way.'

Mist enclosed the summit of Ben Nevis and the loose rock on the descent and ridge ahead forced caution, but the sky would lift. Under a grey roof, at least Alec could see where he was going: mountain after mountain after mountain. Eight hours had elapsed with ten peaks despatched when he descended to Loch Treig, a narrowing body of water that resembles a witch's digit, ran across the reservoir dam at its fingertip, and continued into the night.

By the first light of pre-dawn, with three further mountains climbed in darkness, he had begun the lengthy trudge back west, following the line of a river in a deserted glen. He was suffering: a cocktail of exhaustion and sleep deprivation. The mighty, bucking ridge of the Mamores, comprising another ten summits, plus the distance of 21 miles, still lay between the solo runner and Glen Nevis. 'The sun was blinding,' Alec remembered, 'and I thought, crikey, my head is aching. I should be happy, but I just feel awful.'

The undertaking could have then seemed insurmountable, but feeling 'awful' is not a reason to stop. Not for Alec Keith, anyway. He just got on with it. What else was there to do? He arrived on Mullach nan Coirean, the last top, after 23 hours had elapsed, knowing nonetheless that he was going to beat 24, and 'cruised along', finishing – in comparison to Charlie Ramsay – with a luxurious buffer of ten minutes to spare. He would become a statistic in a list of immortals: number 12.

Alec got in his car and started to drive home to Edinburgh. 'By the time I got to Tyndrum, I thought I must have something to eat. I opened the door and fell out sideways. My legs had seized up. I crawled to the Little Chef to put some food into myself.'

I could not sleep that night. It was not the heat. The same defiant words ran through my mind: 'When I get there, I will just get on with it. And I did.'

And, I thought, so will I.

3

THE MONARCH OF THE GLEN

Finlay Wild stood on the summit of Sgùrr nan Gillean, the northern culmination of the Black Cuillin of Skye. The scree fountain of Glamaig across the deep trough of Glen Sligachan gleamed in dazzling sunlight; islands punctuated the glittering glass of the Inner Sound; away in the east, Ben Nevis stared impassively. The transcendent world of the so-called Isle of Mist was at harmony. The runner was not. He looked back along the ridge he had just negotiated – an eight-mile scythe of alpine pinnacles and splintered crags, flanked by plunging gullies. There is no greater examination in British mountaineering; it is, as Sir Walter Scott noted, unrivalled in its 'desolate sublimity'. Finlay – a twenty-nine-year-old GP from Fort William, unknown outside the clique of hill running – had beaten the 'unbeatable', becoming the fastest to traverse the ridge, but something did not feel right. Doubt crowded his mind.

Starting from where it had all begun on Gars-bheinn, he traced the twisting blade of the ridge, silently counting mountains. His eyes lingered on Sgùrr Mhic Choinnich, the fourth of the eleven Munro summits. A surge of uncertainty. Finlay pulled out a flip book of summit diagrams, leafing through the pages until he located Sgùrr Mhic Choinnich. He looked hard at the drawing, then raised his eyes to gaze again at the mountain. A very simple question burst from his subconscious: had he touched the pile of stones on the 948-metre highest point? He had certainly climbed the peak; the spine of the central ridge made that unavoidable. The cairn though? Had he put his hand on it?

As Finlay descended, first to a road, then along a glen, the ridge now over his left shoulder, his mind dwelt on that airy crest. While he was unable to convince himself that he had touched the cairn, nor could he be sure he had not. His parents and a group of friends were waiting at Glenbrittle, ready to congratulate him. 'I wasn't, "yeah, I've done it",' Finlay remembered. 'I said that I've kind of done it, but I need to check something. Basically, I got away from there as soon as I could and walked back up to the summit. That gave me time to think: what will I do if I haven't touched it?'

Finlay clambered into the glaciated bowl of Coire Làgan, where vast chutes of scree cascade from a cirque of astonishing mountains. To the right was Sgùrr Alasdair, the acme of Skye; to the left, the shark's fin of the Inaccessible Pinnacle; between them was the steep sliver of Sgùrr Mhic Choinnich, its west face forming the gigantic headwall of Coire Làgan. Scrambling up West Buttress, he made directly for the summit. Once on the ridge, the vista opened: mountains were everywhere; Rum reared immaculate from the sea. It was the sort of day when you may have been able to glimpse the dark dots of the St Kilda archipelago, pitched some 100 miles to the west, jostled by the Atlantic swell.

Finlay was only looking to a summit of slabby rocks. Concreted to the cairn on Sgùrr Mhic Choinnich is a sixty-year-old plaque dedicated to climber Lewis Macdonald. Before it was shattered by lightning, a couplet read: 'To one whose hands these rocks has grasped, the joys of climbing unsurpassed.' Finlay knew before he got there. Unlike Macdonald, he had not grasped these rocks.

Desperately searching for a reason, Finlay began to piece together what had happened, why it had happened. He had approached the summit on a marginally different line to previous ascents – a common occurrence on the technical ground of the Cuillin. The newness must have momentarily disorientated him. Unconsciously, Finlay ran past the top, his mind already preparing for the difficulties ahead, principally the basalt-rudder of the Inaccessible Pinnacle and the six-storey down-climb from its top. The summit of Sgùrr Mhic Choinnich had been ten metres away, amounting to a single metre of height gain. 'Five seconds,' Finlay said ruefully.

The Alps were mastered a century before the Cuillin. While man summited Mont Blanc in 1786, the first documented ascent of Sgùrr Alasdair was by Sheriff Alexander Nicolson, Scotland's original mountain guide, in 1873. 'I have seen worse places,' Nicolson would report. As John Mackenzie, another Skye mountaineer, would give his name to Sgùrr Mhic Choinnich, Nicolson would lend his to Sgùrr Alasdair.

The apparently unreachable top of Sgùrr Dearg – known as the Inaccessible Pinnacle – would only be breached in 1880. It was as if the mountains of Skye were the personification of hostile beings, infuriated by the intrusion of man. Throwing down loose rock as they ascended the Inaccessible Pinnacle, Charles and Lawrence Pilkington, two brothers from Lancashire, said the 'very rock of the pinnacle itself seemed to vibrate with indignation at our rude onslaught'.

The world was preparing for the Great War when the first continuous traverse of the Cuillin ridge was accomplished by Leslie Shadbolt and Alastair McLaren in 1911. Starting at 3.30am on Gars-bheinn and pausing on Sgùrr Dearg to light their pipes, the crossing lasted 12 hours and 20 minutes, turning 'dreams of the winter fireside' into a scarcely believable reality. Howard Somerville completed a solo expedition in 10 hours three years later, inspiring a pattern of unaccompanied traverses that would extend into the twenty-first century. Mountaineers had nudged the record down to 6 hours and 45 minutes when, in the 1960s, the approach to the traverse was revolutionised by a hill runner. Born in Leeds, a school leaver at fourteen and not a runner until he was twenty-four, Eric Beard was absorbed in a prolific year of endurance mountain running when he came to Skye. In 1963, he established records for the Cairngorm 4,000s, the Arrochar Munros, the Welsh 3,000s and broke Alan Heaton's Lakeland 24-hour record, scaling 56 peaks. Employing the fast and light approach of the hill runner, Beard demolished the Cuillin ridge record too, slashing the benchmark to 4 hours and 9 minutes. Beardie, as he was known, was a one-off: an athlete fuelled by honey sandwiches who once connected the highest summits of Scotland, England and Wales in a ten-day run, and who was killed in a car accident at thirty-eight.

Fittingly, the record stood for nearly two decades, and when it was broken by Andy Hyslop, he could only shave off five minutes. Like Beard, Hyslop was a man of obsessional zeal. He would lower the time on two further occasions, spanning four months in 1994, with the second crossing only 35 seconds faster than the first, and in doing so enshrined, for himself and future contenders, what a traverse should constitute. According to Hyslop, not only must the route visit eleven Munros and two additional summits, but four main climbing sections should not be bypassed.

In the era when a traverse of the Cuillin had seemed as unfathomable as scaling the Inaccessible Pinnacle had once been, rock climbing pioneer George Abraham speculated on who could possibly achieve the feat: 'He would need to have exceptional physique and staying power,' as well as 'intimate knowledge of the entire range'. While Hyslop – who had spent part of the summer the year prior to his record climbing in California, notably conquering the formidable El Cap in a day – fitted the criteria, he lacked, by his own concession, the pure hill running ability of an 'elite' athlete.

Up stepped Es Tresidder, a climber and mountaineer, but also – having earned a Scotland vest in 2006 – an international-standard hill runner. In the style of Beard, he devoured the record, completing the traverse in what was considered to be an 'unbeatable' 3 hours and 17 minutes. Crossing the ridge in a cloud inversion and finishing above a brocken spectre,

Tresidder was 'running in heaven'. Asked if he knew anyone capable of an even faster time, he said: 'There aren't that many people with the right mixture of abilities, so I can't think of anyone at the moment.' It was May 2007, four months before Finlay Wild's fourth-placed finish at Ben Nevis as a twenty-two-year-old would announce his arrival at the top table of British hill running.

As he paused on the summit of Sgùrr Mhic Choinnich, 102 years after Shadbolt and McLaren's dreams were realised, Finlay's own dream hinged on a decision of conscience. 'The weird thing was that I knew I had done it, but at the same time, parallel to that, I knew I couldn't claim it the way I had done it,' he said. Finlay could have been excused for erring, for prevaricating. It was five seconds. The oversight was not deliberate. He had done everything else by the book: adhering to the Hyslop standards; taking splits at every summit on two watches. In races and mountain marathons there are marshals or checkpoints to ensure competitors do not – for want of a better word – cheat. 'No-one is policing this traverse,' Finlay said. 'These things are done on trust. It's totally on your own conscience.' Ultimately, there was no doubt, no debate. By strict definition, he had not summited Sgùrr Mhic Choinnich, and if he had not summited Sgùrr Mhic Choinnich, he had not traversed the ridge. There could be no record. Not today.

It was a gesture that symbolised the ethos of his sport: nothing was more important than doing things the right way.

Finlay was frustrated, of course, but the outlet for such emotions was obvious: he would do it again.

He did not wait long. The traverse-that-was-not had only to remain secret for an anxious week, for Finlay was back on the echoing mountain of Gars-bheinn the very next weekend, ready to climb again, in Nicolson's words, the 'peaks to the clouds that soar'. Such was Finlay's eagerness to bury the memory of that momentary lapse on Sgùrr Mhic Choinnich, he allowed optimism to rule his mind, deciding to attempt in inauspicious conditions: a ridge immersed in mist. Even at

Bruach na Frithe, the third from last summit, he was down on Tresidder's pace. Finlay rallied, stopping the clock on Sgùrr nan Gillean after 3 hours and 14 minutes. The record was his.

It did not end there.

What came next was not motivated by greed or foolish ambition. Finlay knew he could go faster, knew that perhaps he could close the gap to the 'fabled' three-hour barrier. So why not try again? This time he would wait for optimum weather.

The story of that next traverse was filmed by his father and mountain guide Roger Wild. First, on the day before, we see a car driven by Finlay approaching Sligachan. The Cuillin are silhouetted against a cloudless sky, while a glinting October sun throws shafts of low light across the island. Then, morning: Roger pans the camera around flawless mountains, before catching Finlay's slow trudge towards Gars-bheinn. Next, they are on the summit. Finlay, bare-footed, straps a bandage to his left foot, pulls on the sock, then the shoe. He takes a swig of water, then repeats the routine on the right.

'Rock looks dry,' Roger remarks. 'It's a nice cool wind, but not too cold.'

As he ties a lace, something on Finlay's wrist catches his attention. 'I've got a tick on me,' he says, plucking it off with a forefinger and thumb.

'It might be the fastest tick to ever do the traverse of the Cuillin ridge,' Roger quips.

As the minutes to midday go by, Finlay, in front of an extraordinary backdrop of mountains, islands and ocean, does a series of lunging stretches. He adjusts his shoes one final time. Roger steps back from the summit to film the departure. Finlay is outlined against the sea. With one hand on the cairn, he pushes off and is running.

'Have a good one,' his father calls after him.

Finlay's movements are less of a run, more of a leap. Like the monarch of the glen, he seems to belong in a high, wild world. The camera follows the initial minutes of the traverse,

watching the runner becoming ever smaller until he is swallowed by the monstrous enormity of the Cuillin. 'At times
the desolation of the Coolins is positively repellent,' the travel
writer Alasdair Alpin MacGregor noted in 1926. 'There is
nothing here but trackless wastes and a colossal welter of
rocks and mountains.' As for Finlay, he saw only the beauty
of opportunity.

By Sgùrr Mhic Choinnich, he was nine minutes up on his
schedule. He consciously touched the cairn and descended.
Two climbing sections, the Inaccessible Pinnacle and
Naismith's Route on the Bhàsteir Tooth, remained. Finlay's
familiarity with the ridge mitigated the potential for accident,
but he feared the things he could not control. If he were held
up or stopped by others on the technical parts of the ridge,
the attempt was over. Coincidentally, he knew a group of
friends were in Skye that weekend and as he approached the
Thearlaich-Dubh Gap – like a missing tooth, a sheer cleft in
the ridge – before Sgùrr Alasdair, he could see them ahead. 'I
got there just before they started abseiling,' Finlay recalled. 'If
I had been five minutes later, they would have been abseiling
where I needed to down-climb. To clear the area may have
taken an hour. I don't know what I would have done. I might
have stopped.' It was a good omen. To go faster than he or
anyone else had gone before demanded tens of thousands of
perfect moments: every foot strike of the rock, every handhold, every thought, be it cognisant or instinctive.

The perfect moments continued. Chain-eating jelly babies,
Finlay felt 'free and flying'. Not only was the record going
to fall, the runner sensed he could breach three hours for a
journey that was once deemed impossible and will still take a
confident scrambler two days of stupefying exposure split by
an overnight camp.

'For at least the last hour, I was chasing sub-three,' he said.
'Not in a crazed sprint but a persistent push. I had learnt this
over many hill races and thought I had enough fuel in the tank.
I got to the top of Am Bàsteir and had just over ten minutes to

do it. I could get there. Push. More jelly babies. My route up Sgùrr nan Gillean could have been ten seconds shorter but it was okay. Keep pushing. I was breathing hard and my knees were aching from all the high stepping. It didn't matter.' As the moments before three hours melted, he stepped onto the last summit. He had made it with 38 seconds to spare. 'I knew I had done it. No doubts about summits touched, or route taken,' he said. As he had done four months earlier, Finlay surveyed the ridge, counting off each top, but this time he 'did some shouting'.

Those almost-but-gloriously-not-quite-three halcyon hours on the Cuillin, the day Finlay Wild's stars aligned, loom large above everything else. 'Cuillin dreaming,' he calls it. For Finlay, the traverse provided the ultimate synthesis of mountaineering and running – his 'biggest strength as an outdoors person'. Going far beyond the physical, however, the ridge is an emblematic representation of his past, present and future. His first experience of the Cuillin – as part of Aberdeen University's Lairig Club – was characterised by 'bad weather, scrambles and *trying* to climb'. Later, when Finlay was twenty and working at Ellis Brigham in Fort William in the summer between his second and third years at university, a 'weather window' opened. Successfully begging time off, Roger and Finlay travelled to Skye, Motown music blaring from the car stereo. Up before dawn, father and son climbed Gars-bheinn by a direct route featuring a series of ledges. When Finlay emerged on the crest, he was 'blown away by how amazing it was. It remains my favourite view.' Eight hours later, they were on Sgùrr nan Gillean. They descended via Coire na Creiche, down which a crashing burn creates a series of deep, ice-cold baths known as the Fairy Pools. 'We swam in the pools, looking back at the Cuillin having completed this great mission,' Finlay said. 'I just felt privileged.'

Finlay went back, this time on his own, this time in five-and-a-half hours. He continued to visit, becoming increasingly accustomed to the mountains, even in mist, and got 'faster

and faster'. The Cuillin were no longer capricious protuberances of basalt and gabbro that sent compasses into a spin-
ning frenzy; they were tapestries of his knowhow and growing
expertise, with every excursion layering fresh appreciation
to his proficiency. He would traverse the ridge four times in
2013, culminating in his record, with a four-hour crossing
preceding his 'failed' attempt.

With Suzy, his girlfriend, he goes back every January, when
the Black Cuillin are white, to simply 'run about'. He will
always return: for pleasure, to breathe the spotless air of Skye,
to stare in wonder at the world, or perhaps if someone dare
take his record. And one day, just one day, he might stand at
Glenbrittle with his own children, and point to the mountains
that have 'no equal in the world'. He will identify the jagged
outline of Gars-bheinn. Then he will tell a story that will make
them quiver.

Positioned on opposite sides of Finlay's living room at his
home in Inverlochy (the interwar extension to Fort William
originally intended for workers at the town's aluminium
smelter, and less than two miles from the start of the pony
track to Ben Nevis) are two mountain paintings. On the left
is Stac Pollaidh, imagined as a blue-lipped silhouette against a
yellow sky. To the right is a deep blue Coire Mhic Fhearchair
on Beinn Eighe, framed by an orange firmament. The creator
of this 'psychedelic mountain art' is sitting before me. I had
previously seen the images on display at the John Muir Trust's
Wild Space Gallery in Pitlochry as part of an eight-week
exhibition called *Kaleidoscape*. 'His paintings feature Scottish
mountains – his first love as a mountaineer and hill runner
– which he depicts in stylised block colour using the energy
and passion he draws on when running,' the exhibition blurb
had explained. I had asked the woman staffing the gallery
how many pictures had been sold. 'One. Just one. If you ask
me,' she said, lowering her voice to a whisper, 'they are *quite*
expensive.' The two pictures in Finlay's living room were

priced at a combined cost of £1,500 – which goes a long way
to explaining why they are on his walls, not someone else's.

'I only sold one,' Finlay says. I feign surprise. 'I didn't want
them to all disappear, so I put the prices pretty high.' With
that reasoning, it is unsurprising that his top-valued painting
at £1,000 was of Bla Bheinn, a Skye mountain.

'The colours,' I ask, 'is that how you see the mountains?'
The question came with an unintended barb – a cruel inter-
rogation of a man of obvious modesty. After all, there have
been numerous occasions when I have seen hills dressed in
countless shades of humble green and brown. Just an hour
earlier, before a billion stars were pricking the sky over Glen
Nevis, I had seen Ben Nevis spotlighted in an auburn glow.
Finlay, on his cycle home from the medical practice where he
works as a GP, had noticed it too.

They are 'silly bright colours', he admits, 'but because I'm
not a traditional artist, it kind of frees me up to do what I
want – which is what the mountains are like, because you can
go and do whatever you want.'

The artwork treads a delicate balance between realism
and abstract. Some of the paintings are obscure; some more
obvious, perhaps most explicitly a dark blue Ben Nevis behind
a green Carn Mòr Dearg. The sky is on fire – a red and yellow
aether flecked with black and white. In another, the North
Face of the Ben is red and black, saturated with a demonic air.

Finlay could paint the Ben upside down and decorate it with
pink polka dots. He has earned the right, for this has become
his mountain, a mountain he first encountered aged eight.
Shortly after moving to Fort William, Finlay and a childhood
friend, under the auspices of Roger, spent a night at the Charles
Inglis Clark Memorial Hut, a brick building buried beneath
the sweep of the arête that connects Carn Mòr Dearg and
Ben Nevis. 'I remember it being so exciting because we were
staying in a mountain hut, then we weren't just going up the
tourist route, we were going up a climb,' Finlay says. The trio
would summit the Ben by Ledge Route, an easy scramble on a

north-east ridge. Some twenty-five years later, he might have imagined crossing the path of his eight-year-old self – wearing a thick knitted sweatshirt that made him feel 'like a real mountaineer' – on Ledge Route, as he plunged downhill on part of a route known as the Nevis Five Ridges. Beginning at sea level, Finlay ran into the shadow of the renowned North Face, and moved onto the prow of North East Buttress. From the top, he came down Tower Ridge, then up Observatory Ridge, down Ledge Route, and up Castle Ridge, before returning to the start. It was classic Finlay, existing in an intoxicating world between running, mountaineering and climbing, teetering on the edge of breathless risk, and, inevitably, doing it faster than anyone else.

Long before Finlay had scrambled up Ledge Route to gain Ben Nevis for the first time, he was absorbed by mountains. It was in the blood that pumped through his veins. His mother, Fiona Wild, won Yorkshire's Three Peaks Race in 1981, and back-to-back Carnethy 5 races in 1981 and 1982. Fiona, wearing the blue and white of Lochaber Athletic Club, was also twice second woman in the Ben Nevis Race, again in her peak years of 1981 and 1982. Finlay would be born at Thurso on a Saturday in 1984, a week after the Keswick fell runner Kenny Stuart set a course record at Ben Nevis.

There are photographs of Finlay in a baby carrier being lugged up hills on his father's back. When Roger was guiding in the Alps, the family would join him. 'I remember going to huts and holding an ice axe,' Finlay says. Back in Fort William, he attended a running club at school. Aged fifteen, Finlay asked Roger to teach him to lead rock climb – a 'terrifying prospect' for the father of a teenager, he remembers. A Lochaber childhood, for Finlay, meant a life in the outdoors. In the summer, he and his high school mates would ride their bikes up the glen, then camp under the gaze of Ben Nevis. When he was not on a hill or looking up at one from a saddle, he was sailing a dinghy on Loch Linnhe.

A seed was sown, but if there was to be a turning point, an

epiphany – a moment when passing interest became lifelong fascination – it came at the impressionable age of seventeen. As he had done many times before, Finlay went up Glen Nevis looking for adventure. Two mountains that rear above the glen, the Ramsay's Round peaks of Binnein Mòr and Binnein Beag, seemed to be calling. 'It wasn't particularly hard, but it was the first time I thought, I'm going to do this on my own. I just took to it.' Then, for someone with vaulting ambition in the mountains, running up them was the logical progression, enabling Finlay to go 'a bit further, a bit faster'.

He ran his first hill race in 2005, finishing tenth in Speyside whisky country at Ben Rinnes, some 17 minutes slower than the winner, far enough back to make the twenty-year-old's presence of little note.

'When did you realise you were good at this?' I ask.

Finlay paused for several seconds, searching for the right words. He was too polite to simply dismiss my questions. 'I don't think I ever felt like that,' he says.

An answer emerges, framed around a race on Morven, an Aberdeenshire mountain immortalised in verse by Lord Byron: 'When I rov'd a young Highlander o'er the dark heath, / And climb'd thy steep summit, oh Morven of snow.'

There was no snow that September, two years after his Ben Rinnes debut, but Finlay's prize for finishing third was a voucher. 'I got a book about the Cairngorms from some wee shop in Aboyne. It's up there,' he says, pointing to a shelf. 'I was dead chuffed with that.'

He was not a prolific racer in the early days, preferring 'big, hard days' of running and climbing, seemingly saving his all-out effort for Ben Nevis. As they warmed up for the Ben, English hill runners would tease Finlay about his lack of participation in the season's other races. He was 13th on his debut in 2006, fourth in 2007, fifth in 2009. The 2008 race – the only event Finlay had missed in eleven years – coincided with a post-university sabbatical of nine months in the west of Canada and the USA. It was a pilgrimage to the outdoors: he climbed at Yosemite, Lake Tahoe, Red Rocks and Squamish; he ice-climbed in Colorado and Wyoming; he ski-toured in the high mountains of the Rockies.

He had seen the world, but there was no place like Fort William, especially on the first Saturday in September. Finlay's Ben Nevis graduation, the beginning of the Wild dynasty, came on his fourth attempt in 2010. I was there that day. It would take me 1 hour and 19 minutes to reach the summit. I was only halfway. Finlay would finish the course in 1 hour and 34 minutes, which, by his future racing standards, was slow. My memories of Ben Nevis and the agony of it all have thankfully fogged. I recall sunshine and concentration and rocks and Finlay Wild. I was still some ten minutes from the summit when the race leader galloped downhill, stones flying around his ankles. In a moment, he was gone.

A period of domination unprecedented in such a major hill running race followed. Through a combination of luck – having never been injured pre-race or falling on a descent – and simple brilliance, he had won seven in a row. His success was built on an ability to descend faster than anyone else, even the cream of English fell racers who flock to the Ben every year, a trick stunningly exemplified in the 2014 race. It was what had got David Gallie so animated in an Inverness café – the day he had seen a human fly. Rob Jebb had accrued a seemingly unassailable lead, and as Finlay began the descent, he did not spare a thought for the leader; he was fixated on getting to the finish in the shortest possible time. If catching Jebb was a consequence, then so be it.

'I have always thought that it's a race against yourself,' Finlay says. 'At the top, you don't know how far ahead they are, you can't see them, you're not really thinking about them. You're thinking: I have to get down this hill as fast as I can. You're going as fast as you think is reasonable to sustain, but not hurt yourself.' He shrugs. 'I don't know why I'm good at running downhill. I haven't done downhill reps or anything. I think it's because I have always been in the hills, scrambling, on bikes, out in winter with a big bag, and by just being out in all these terrains, my body knows what to do. I can remember when I was about twenty or twenty-one doing the South Glen Shiel ridge with a friend and I was jumping between rocks, boulder-hopping, and loving it, and thinking, this is what it's all about. I enjoy that. You forget about the cardiovascular part of running and just have to concentrate on what you're doing.'

Perhaps Finlay could run the Cuillin ridge even faster? It would not matter, for his legend is built on Ben Nevis. The race is what he will always be known for. He will probably be turning on the Christmas lights in Fort William in 2040 to mark the thirtieth anniversary of his first win. He has raced all over Scotland, winning the races that ring with import – Glamaig, Isle of Jura, Stùc a' Chroin, Goatfell, Ben Rinnes (seven years after scraping into the top ten), and Slioch – and just about everything in the Lochaber postcode area. But it is Ben Nevis that casts the rest in shadow. As it should. Here is a context the non-hill runner can understand. Because of that, the race and the mountain – and therefore its hero – transcend a sport. Hundreds of thousands of people have journeyed up and down the Ben, each with their own motivation. They will have slogged up, along the seemingly endless zig-zags, into portentous mist, glimpsed the outline of the ruined observatory, then – at last – found the roof of a country. It will be several hours before they get back down. They might never exert themselves like this again. Tell these mortals that one of their own species, a man called Finlay, can match what they have done in 1 hour and 28 minutes, and they are slack-jawed in astonishment.

And so, every year, as September nears, at the approaching sight of Finlay, visitors to his surgery, acquaintances in the town's High Street and clubmates at Lochaber training sessions will have the words 'Ben' and 'Nevis' on their lips. 'I do other races as well, you know,' Finlay laughs. 'And I'm British champion – or I was.'

It takes Finlay fifteen minutes of easy running to get to the foot of Ben Nevis from his front door. Blaenau Ffestiniog in north-west Wales, the location of the first race in the 2015 British hill running championship, is seven hours by car and 400 miles from Inverlochy. Finlay had finished equal second – behind Rob Jebb – in 2013, while his tilt at the 2014 title ended in clag on Slieve Donard. First-hand experience of the mountains in Lochaber was key to his success locally, but a dearth of knowledge of courses in England, Wales and Northern Ireland was his undoing in previous championship assaults.

He arrived in Blaenau Ffestiniog early, giving him enough time for a 'good long look at the course' of Ras y Moelwyn. He deciphered the lines he would run, located the checkpoints, worked out the best way to cross the bands of slate. Finlay would win comfortably, more than three minutes ahead of his nearest rival. Such dominance might have prompted complacency, but on the long journey north, he left the M6 and set a course for the Lake District. The destination was Wasdale, the valley imbued by the spirit of England's greatest fell runner, a man dubbed 'Iron': Joss Naylor. The Scafell massif and Great Gable stand imperiously above Wasdale, but Lingmell, one of the 214 fells celebrated by Alfred Wainwright and the location of the third championship race, was his reason for being here. As he had done in Blaenau Ffestiniog, he ran the race route, committing to memory the unrelenting climb from valley to summit, and got back in his car. This time, nothing would be left to chance.

Durisdeer in the Borders came first. Knowing the amount of 'flat running' would not suit his strengths, Finlay relied on guile. On the descent from the first peak, when the leaders went one way, Finlay went another, the move propelling him from sixth to first. Tom Owens would win, but in the context of the championship, second place for Finlay would suffice. He celebrated in fine hill running tradition – with cake. 'There were angel cakes, rock cakes, fruit cakes, every type of cake,' Finlay remembers.

Back in Wasdale a month later, Finlay knew he could not let the fast ascenders get too far ahead before the fifteen-minute mad dash to lose 800 vertical metres. He had not had a straightforward build-up: the doctor had become a patient. A calf strain sustained ten days before the race resulted in Finlay 'frantically' calling on massage and physiotherapy. On race day, he wore an elasticated bandage stretching from foot to knee. The sight must have given a glimmer of hope to the others. Fifth at the summit, Finlay pushed downhill, overhauling everyone except Simon Bailey – a Mercia runner who was not a threat in the overall standings. The monarch of the glen was a champion. The champion would then meet another: Joss Naylor was handing out the prizes. 'I don't think he knew who I was,' Finlay admits.

The Seven Sevens in Northern Ireland was the final event of the championship series, but with only three finishes out of the four races to count, Finlay did not even need to go. Besides, the race was in mid-August, three weeks before Ben Nevis. He would save his legs.

'There's no training regime,' Finlay promised.

'None?'

'None.' I was disappointed. I was hoping he might whisper the secret of a British hill racing champion into my ear and I would be transported to a similar plateau of greatness.

'I'm pretty low-tech with my training. I go for long runs in the hills. I go mountain biking. I climb. I might do a jog with Suzy. Go for a walk. It all feeds in. I use running to switch off. At work, I'm thinking about complex, analytical problems. When I go running, I don't need to think.' He pauses. A *but* is coming. 'Arguably, I could be better.'

Malcolm Patterson, one of the selectors for the Scottish hill running teams, once told Finlay the Cuillin traverse was something he could do at 'any age', and that he should concentrate on running fast while he was young.

Finlay runs his fingers through his hair. 'I just don't feel that way. That is what I want to do, so why wouldn't I do it now?'

He works part-time, clocking in for three-and-a-half days. Why does he not work full-time?

He smiles incredulously. 'Why? So, I can do other stuff – like go running and go to the mountains. I'm lucky that money-wise, because of my job, I don't need to be full-time. Even before I went to medical school, going out in the mountains and having adventures was as important as doing medicine or any career aspirations.'

Finlay motions to a clutch of awards perched on top of a wardrobe. A trio of Ben trophies – first to the summit, first local, first place – are not among them. They are being looked after by Roger and Fiona who carried them home while Finlay celebrated yet another victory in Fort William. Apart from the silverware, there is little to identify Finlay's home as the resting place of a hill runner, let alone a champion – a line of running shoes by the front door excepted. There are shelves of books, many of them about running and climbing, but also the classics of English literature. Three guitars point to a musical streak: Finlay played the saxophone, electric guitar and viola at school. After making me a mug of tea, he asked if I wanted more, if I wanted water, if I wanted food. His phone repeatedly bleeped in our time together. He ignored it. There was no television. A wood burning stove stood where a set might.

I am standing to leave when he points to a quaich on the living room table. The bowl was a gift from Lundavra Primary, a newly-opened school in Fort William that was created out of the amalgamation of two primaries, Fort William, Finlay's old school, and Upper Achintore. At the opening ceremony, the pupils sang the school song, *Give it all you've got*. Finlay then ran a mile with the children as part of a national 'daily mile' initiative encouraging children to be more active. 'Everyone should do this,' Finlay enthuses. 'Change the Scottish couch potato reputation!'

I realise we have spoken predominately about records and

elitism, but the quaich seems to represent what really matters. In the words of the school song: 'Give it all you've got, 'cause you've really got a lot! Give it heart, give it mind, give it soul, don't stop!'

Being the fastest person up and down the Ben this century, being the swiftest to traverse the Cuillin ridge, being Scotland's pre-eminent hill runner – they were the consequence of the cocktail of heart, mind and soul and, perhaps most importantly, never stopping.

I sense he would swap it all simply to be able to go to the hills, to find a fundamental pleasure in high places.

Finlay was once running on Meall an t-Suidhe, a heathery lump overlooked by Ben Nevis, when he noticed pairs of stags and hinds, pacing across the hillside. The runner joined the dance. 'For a few seconds, it almost felt like I was running with them,' he says. 'I suppose that sums it up for me: to be a moving element within the landscape.'

We all have our place. This is the place of the monarch of the glen.

4

IMAGINATION

Philip Tranter's eyes snapped open. He had fallen asleep. Gazing around, he saw the sky and the rocks of a high mountain summit. Aonach Beag had been his rough bed. Slumber had snatched two hours. He rose to his feet, orientated himself, and staggered north to Aonach Mòr. Instinct told him one thing: keep moving.

Who could blame Tranter for falling asleep? He had walked longer and further than he had ever done before. His seminal expedition in the summer of 1964 – the year Tranter would become the first person to complete a second round of the Munros – had started 20 hours earlier. Wearing Spanish fell boots and gorging on cans of fruit, Tranter had started his journey in Glen Nevis. His first hill was Alec Keith's last, Mullach nan Coirean, the gateway to the Mamores. Ahead were a further ten mountaintops, two of them on the airy climaxes of narrow, scrambly, out-and-back ridges. One of those edges, leading to Sgùrr a' Mhaim, is ominously known as the Devil's Ridge, with the so-called Bad Step lying at its middle. Tranter climbed as high as 1,130 metres on Binnein Mòr before dropping from the final summit of the Mamores, Sgùrr Eilde Mòr, to the floor of the glen. He waded a river and climbed Stob Bàn, the first in the row of the quartzite-capped Grey Corries. Blyth Wright, his friend and companion from the beginning, said he could do no more and left Tranter to it. Tranter went on to Aonach Beag, his fifteenth Munro of the day, and lay down.

He woke to a living dream, a mountainous ecstasy. To the south were the Mamores, summit after summit stretching heavenward. To the east was the flickering line of the Grey Corries. To think he had voyaged to all these places. To the west a falling ridge of Carn Mòr Dearg met a slender rim that culminated in the colossal rump of Ben Nevis – where Tranter's destiny lay. The walker struggled on, exhausted by the rubble on the ascent of the Ben, driven half-mad by rampant thirst. He went as high as anyone can in these isles and descended, impelled by the lights of Fort William. Back in Glen Nevis, Tranter joined the strands of his epoch-making trek.

The route would become known as Tranter's Round, a journey of mind-boggling proportion: 36 miles, 6,000 metres of ascent, and 18 Munro summits amid Britain's superlative mountains – the roughest, the highest, the toughest. The benchmark for what was possible within a 24-hour period in the high places of Scotland was to be Tranter's legacy. Two years later, returning from a climbing trip in Turkey, he was killed in a car accident.

By 1977, Charlie Ramsay – a hill runner for only three years having switched from the road – had twice run Tranter's Round and, that year, became the 82nd person to formally complete the Bob Graham Round. Recruited to support an attempt by Chris Brasher – who co-founded the London Marathon four years later – Charlie continued when Brasher ended his effort at Wasdale. It was a round of the unexpected: starting from Keswick, Charlie had not anticipated even going beyond Skiddaw, the first summit of 42.

For a Scottish alternative to the classic 24-hour English round to be reality, logic pointed to two locations: the multitudinous mountains of Lochaber or the ridges either side of Glen Shiel. Both had precedent. Tranter's Round was established in Lochaber, while in 1977 Blyth Wright had walked 17 of the 20 Glen Shiel Munros in 23 hours, stopping for two pints of shandy at the Cluanie Inn.

The tested rounds – radical and exhausting undertakings

for walkers of any generation – were incomparable to the immensity of Bob Graham's original round of 1932. It was *too* easy for a competent hill runner to breach 24 hours to make the existing Scottish journeys viable day-long running challenges. Something further and harder was needed.

Imagination is not to be underestimated, but to act on imagination is the true measure of greatness. When Shane Ohly was plotting to become the first person to run a 24-hour Ramsay's Round in winter – thirty years after Charlie's inaugural summer effort – he did not celebrate Charlie's endurance or endeavour. He singled out the quality that came first: imagination. 'There would have been other people capable of running that distance in that time,' Ohly told *The Scotsman*, 'but (he had) the imagination to envisage the round, then to go and do it.' Charlie's imagination led him to the hills he knew best: the peaks of Lochaber, and notably to the five Munros surrounding Loch Treig to the east of the Grey Corries. There was a romantic logic in the apparent madness: five was inadvertently the magic number. After Sgùrr an Iubhair on the Mamores was elevated to Munro status in 1981, the additional five would take the Munro count to 24, and so, poetically, 24 Munros in 24 hours.

The extension of Tranter's original round brought the mileage and ascent on a par with the Bob Graham, but the numbers only tell half a story, for Charlie's route was indisputably more testing than travelling through the hills of the Lake District. The terrain, altitude and isolation of the Lochaber mountains made sure of that. Nonetheless, on paper, Charlie had created Scotland's answer to the Bob Graham: a round that was both plausible and implausible.

The five-Munro extension added a punishing complication: the distance between the tenth and eleventh Munros, before the runner has even reached the halfway point on an anticlockwise round, was vast. Some eight miles of remote and largely pathless country, including a potentially perilous river crossing of the Abhainn Rath, lay between Sgùrr Eilde

Mòr and Beinn na Lap. A Ramsayist will typically spend three hours running from summit to summit – three gaping hours to cover *just* eight miles, a period of time a competent club runner needs to complete a marathon – dwelling on the 13 Munros and the likely 12 hours to come. If it is to be much longer than three hours, the runner may as well stop, for they will not get back to Glen Nevis within 24 hours. That philosophy does not apply to all. When Glyn Jones undertook the round in the frozen depths of winter, his journey between the two Munros lasted a staggering eight hours. For some people and at some moments, time does not matter. For Charlie, it was everything.

Starting from the youth hostel in Glen Nevis and moving anticlockwise, just as Philip Tranter had done, Charlie ran the Mamores in mist and drizzle, descended Sgùrr Eilde Mòr, and continued along the faint paths that follow the Abhainn Rath to meet the southern reach of Loch Treig. There he stepped off the line of Tranter's Round – a moment he had meticulously prepared for. At lunchtimes, Charlie would leave his office at the Royal Commonwealth Pool in Edinburgh and be running on the lower slopes of Arthur's Seat within five minutes; in the evenings, he ventured from his then-home in Swanston to the north-eastern slopes of the Pentland Hills. For six months, he had dedicated himself to the cause, running and walking 1,600 miles, much during reconnaissance of the round, and climbing some 80,000 metres. He was undoubtedly able too. Running for Lochaber Athletic Club, he was 25th at the Ben Nevis Race in 1977, clocking a personal best of 1 hour and 41 minutes – a time that today would typically place a runner in the top ten.

Perhaps most importantly, Charlie adopted a mindset radically different to Tranter, Wright and other prolific walkers of the era. As Eric Beard had demonstrated on the Cuillin ridge, only the runner could do what Charlie intended. Borrowing the ideas of Bob Graham contenders, teams of supporters were employed to help with navigation and to carry food, water and kit. He arranged for the closest thing to road assistance on the route – at a pivotal time – by installing a crew at the northern end of Loch Treig in the middle of the night. The checkpoint was one of four, all manned by members of Lochaber Mountain Rescue, for which Charlie had raised £500 in sponsorship. Like the Lake District runners, Charlie would aim to move swiftly and travel unburdened, creating the sensation of urgency that comes with racing.

It was a high-risk strategy on an untested round. Charlie was not alone, however. Running alongside him was Bobby Shields, an athlete who was fifth in the same Ben Nevis Race, some nine minutes ahead of Charlie and just a minute behind Billy Bland, the man who would go on to record the fastest Bob Graham. The question was not whether Charlie and Bobby could run over 23 Munros. That was a given. But in 24 hours? That was the great unknown.

It was late evening when the pair reached the path that climbs away from Loch Treig, heading for a bridge that carries the West Highland Line in a sweeping curve to Fort William. The sprawling mass of the eleventh Munro lay ahead. Charlie was inevitably tiring. He looked up at the trap he had set himself – a snare in the form of Beinn na Lap, ironically the lowest summit of them all. There is scarcely a path now; in 1978, there would have been nothing – only a seemingly endless wave of grass and rock. 'This hill really got me down,' Charlie wrote in an article for *The Scotsman* marking the first anniversary of his round. 'The ridge, probably three miles, seemed to go on forever, and when we reached the summit of Beinn na Lap at 10.30pm, I was still in trouble. During the brief stop I felt really cold and put everything on.'

The blip passed, but several further hours of running in the darkness of a Scottish night beckoned. 'In theory, we were now on the home straight,' Charlie wrote. 'The excitement of reaching Stob Coire Sgriodain was intensified by the knowledge that on the other side there would be a change of clothes and refreshments.' The words 'on the other side' suggest a simplicity or inevitably. Nothing is simple here. 'We ran down over long grass with hidden boulders along the worst line downhill that I have ever taken,' he noted.

Charlie's kitchen window faces south, directly onto the Pentlands. A gloomy twilight of a February afternoon was gathering, the precursor to an Edinburgh haar, the sea-frets that clutch the east coast. Charlie, now in his seventies, described his round chronologically and without faltering, although the reflections of something that had occurred almost forty years earlier lacked the rawness of his words in *The Scotsman*. In those pages, his prose has echoes of Maurice Herzog in *Annapurna*. Like the Frenchman who would lead the first team to the summit of an 8,000-metre mountain, Charlie could be factual and pithy, but also romantic and bombastic. 'I would not stop or slow down,' he declared at one point. On his Ramsay's Round website, he notes how during the attempt his mind was 'possessed by a desperate degree of urgency', recalling 'the trail of exhausted bodies' he left behind 'so sustained was the pace'.

Charlie and Bobby left the dam at Loch Treig, but as they climbed, two became one. With an injured knee, Bobby could not go on. It was around 3am. 'He decided to call it a day,' Charlie wrote matter-of-factly. 'I had a new pacer who kept encouraging me as we scrambled at a fast pace up Stob Coire Easain. Two summits within 20 minutes was good for morale, but Stob Bàn was a long distance away.

'Remembering a saying that you only think of one hill at a time, I reached the summit of Stob Bàn at 5.20am and got back on Tranter's route. From this point, we could see the next team waiting for us in the bealach between Stob Bàn and Stob Choire Claurigh. By 6.15am we were sitting by the cairn with less than six hours left. Unfortunately, the mist came down and reduced the visibility to a few yards. Thinking only of keeping west, I took the wrong turning at Stob Coire an Laoigh and after five minutes of downhill running realised I had wandered off the path. The amount of height you can lose by running downhill takes an awful lot of making up when you are tired. I was almost in a panic, but we managed to get back on the correct line, and the delay only made me move faster as I feared running out of time so much.'

Charlie had good reason to be anxious; increasingly, every second was going to count.

'I don't remember much about Sgùrr Choinnich Mòr,' he went on. 'My escort was beginning to feel the pace, but I would not stop or slow down. After contouring Sgùrr Choinnich Beag by a well-defined path, we faced the Aonachs, two great heart-breaking mountains. I had been told of a gully that was ideal for getting on to the summit ridge of Aonach Beag.' That agonisingly steep gully climb, rising to pass beneath a gigantic overhanging slab and typically corniced in winter, would enter the Ramsayist's lexicon as Charlie's Gully.

Once on Aonach Beag, the distance to the summit of Aonach Mòr is a little over one mile. I once timed myself between the summits, without putting in any additional effort. It was a 17-minute journey. Charlie took nearly an hour longer. 'I made my biggest navigational blunder,' he said. Charlie was relying on hand-drawn sketches of the route and despite knowing every hill 'inside out', the mountains befuddled even him. 'Obsessed by wanting to go west and quickly at that, I followed the compass without looking at the map, so losing an awful lot of height. I should have been going north to Aonach Mòr. Discovering my error, I almost cried. It is really desolating when you are tired. I had to sit down for a few minutes and work out the right route. This was easy but cost me about 40 minutes.'

The psychological blow would have been shattering and Charlie was convinced he had 'blown it'. From the top of Carn Mòr Dearg, he had one hour and ten minutes to cross the arête, summit the Ben and descend to Glen Nevis. Time was cruelly counting down.

'The Ben was getting nearer,' he remembered. 'I had

a perfect view, but my eyes were on the ground along the famous arête.' He had to pause several times on the final ascent to catch his breath. Friends handed him a lifeline of sweet, hot coffee on the summit, but there was scarcely time to drink it. Charlie's fate lay in the glen, three-and-a-half miles away – and he had 35 minutes to get there. Running three-and-a-half miles in 35 minutes for Charlie was a mere jog; he would scarcely break sweat. But three-and-a-half miles down a steep mountainside of rubble, falling 1,300 metres? Three-and-a-half miles of knowing that one slip, one twist, one fall, meant it was over? And three-and-a-half miles after 23 hours of running?

'I knew the way down very well and still felt I could beat 24 hours,' Charlie said. 'With ten minutes left I could see the youth hostel and the finishing line. Finally, I left the tourist route and linked up with the path that leads to the hostel. Once over the footbridge I had a mere 25 yards to go. With minutes on the clock I had cracked 24 hours.' Charlie had made it down in an astonishing 33 minutes. Scotland – and arguably Britain – had its classic mountain round. Unashamedly, Charlie called it 'Ramsay's Round'.

Charlie's legacy was also Philip Tranter's: a recalibration of possible and impossible. For nine years, Charlie's round remained unparalleled. Eddie Campbell – a Fort William taxi driver notorious for taking part in 44 consecutive races on Ben Nevis, a mountain he is reputed to have scaled some 1,200 times – was fittingly the first to attempt to emulate Charlie in 1980. Despite refusing to stop at any point on the round, prompting pacer Roger Boswell to pursue Campbell down the railway line on the Loch Treig shore for two miles carrying a carton of hot soup, he finished 40 minutes outside 24 hours.

Pete Simpson's solo effort in 1981 was plagued by wind and rain, but on reaching Mullach nan Coirean, he had time in hand and his attempt to run the first clockwise round seemed certain. On the lower reaches of the hill, Simpson plunged into a dense maze of trees. He confessed to losing concentration and then being a victim of obstinacy. 'Nothing would persuade me to retrace a single step uphill, so I took the worst option and ploughed on,' he said. By the time Simpson returned to the youth hostel, 24 hours had long since elapsed.

The Blackford Lounge in the University of Edinburgh's King's Building campus was full for the final event in a trio of Carnethy Hill Running Club winter talks. Northern Irishman Iain Whiteside – a former club captain who was preparing to emigrate to the US – was talking animatedly to the audience. From the rear of the room, I glanced over backs of heads. Unmistakable, a few rows forward, was the bald pate of Charlie Ramsay. Iain was explaining what he thought about when he was running. On one run that started like many others, passing through the streets of south Edinburgh, then climbing into the Braid Hills, he dwelt obsessively on Strava, a website that enables athletes to publicly share the intimate details of their training sessions – distance, speed, height gain, time taken to run specific segments, and so forth. If you look carefully at the GPS track of a Strava runner, you could probably even work out where they paused to relieve themselves. Nothing is sacred. 'I realised I had spent the previous thirty minutes thinking about what I was going to name this run,' Iain admitted. He then did something very unusual: he stopped running. Inspiration had come to him: 'At a standstill on Braid Hills,' he would later write on his Strava feed. Literally.

For Iain, the Braid Hills moment was the second part of an epiphany. The first came in a Keswick café after an attempt on a winter Bob Graham had quickly floundered in deep snow. A couple on a neighbouring table were consumed by their phones, immersed in the virtual world of a screen the size of a playing card. It was like the person before them – their lover, presumably – did not exist. The couple had been running, their clothes said that much. Who or what were they running for? Iain wondered.

After the 'standstill', Iain made a vow: he would divorce

Strava. It had become an inconvenience, a fixation, a poison. He went back to basics, asking himself the deepest philosophical question a runner can pose: why do I run? Or, for the hill runner: why do I run in the hills?

This was no diatribe against Strava, more what Strava represents, for the sharing platform is no more culpable than Facebook or Instagram or Twitter, outlets that answer our apparent craving for the approval of others – most of whom are strangers. Like a fizzy drink, the craving, of course, is a manmade affliction. But imagine a world without social media, a utopia in which humans did things for the sake of doing them, a place in which we lived for ourselves, not merely for online acceptance?

Following Iain was Martin Stone, an intense, quietly-spoken man originally from Exeter. Growing up in the 1970s, Martin was inspired by the adventurers of the time: the round-the-world yachtsman Robin Knox-Johnston, and the climbers Peter Habeler and Reinhold Messner. The latter's ascent of Everest – solo and without oxygen – bewitched Martin. Coupled with the influence of long walks on Dartmoor, Martin developed a 'fascination for minimalism'. He smiled, obviously recollecting. 'It must have left something in my psyche which came out in the following years.'

Martin's 'following years' were indeed extraordinary: he accomplished summer and winter Bob Grahams, as well as summer and winter completions of the Paddy Buckley Round, the 24-hour Welsh equivalent created in 1982, and was first to complete the three classic rounds within 24 hours. His prodigy extended to a traverse of the Scottish 4,000s: an 83-mile route linking the country's nine highest mountains, five in the Cairngorms and four in Lochaber, with a huge tract of wildness in the middle. His time of 21 hours and 39 minutes, set in 1986, would be untouched for 21 years. Almost everything Martin undertook in the 1980s – reconnaissance, failed attempts, successful attempts, and records – was solo and unsupported, and started with a commute from London or Preston. He was not a loner; he just liked to do things alone. Even in company, he sought solitude. When Martin was walking on Lochnagar with his twelve-year-old brother and had wandered ahead of his sibling, he passed a man in a kilt. It was Prince Charles, taking to the hills shortly after his marriage to Diana. When Charles came across Martin's brother several minutes later, he remarked: 'I see your beastly brother has left you behind.'

And what was it all for? 'These things were totally for my own satisfaction,' said Martin. No selfie on Robinson. No Instagram shot of a near-suicidal climb of Fairfield during his winter Bob Graham, as the light from a torch, held by a cord dangling from clenched teeth, played on the white floor. No course record Strava segments on Devil's Ridge. 'You didn't need people lauding you for something you wanted to do yourself,' he said.

Around 14 hours was Martin's tipping point. Then he would typically feel weak and tired. Motivation – without a buddy to chivvy him along or perhaps a tweet to lift his spirits – would ebb. But, as he explained in the context of his 'greatest achievement', his solo, unsupported midwinter Bob Graham: 'It would have been so easy to stop, but what kept me going was the confidence that it was going to be better further on.' Even if it was not.

Martin is emblematic of his generation, a representative of a golden era of mountain running in which men and women evoked the Edwardian spirit of Antarctic exploration. Ramsay's Round had been unrepeated for nearly a decade when Martin focused his attention on Lochaber. In the summer solstice week of 1987, the computer analyst set off alone up Ben Nevis, committed to a clockwise journey. Only his girlfriend knew his intentions. He distributed weight across his body in specially-designed, easily-accessible pockets. Along with spare clothes, two torches and a survival bag, Martin carried five pounds of food – the weight and baggage the consequence of travelling solo and without assistance. The hills were clear of cloud and the wind light as he progressed to Loch Treig and tackled the round's eastern outliers. He talked to himself, visualising what it would be like to succeed. Martin was not far from his 14-hour wall when he did the inconceivable. Leaving a card on the summit of Beinn na Lap stating, 'I'm going to add the extra two south of Ossian,' he left Charlie's original route in a deliberate ploy to sweep up two further Munros, Sgòr Gaibhre and Càrn Dearg. It was a carefully planned gamble by a man who knew his capabilities. On the train to Fort William the day before, he had calculated that he needed to run the equivalent of a traditional Ramsay's Round in 21 hours and 15 minutes to make the extension viable.

The scientific approach to scheduling was matched by an obsessive desire to be physically ready. At the start of 1987, Martin had only run four of the round's Munros, but when winter conditions began to relent in May, he overcame his inexperience in a frenetic burst of activity. As part of a three-day bothy trip with Jon Broxap, he reconnoitred the 'expensive' two-Munro extension, but the weather was so poor they only managed to gain Stob Bàn on the Grey Corries and the eastern portion of the Mamores on the other days. Martin returned later that month, a day after winning the Scottish Islands Peak Race with Mark McDermott. A 'mad week' began with a Monday mission over the Mamores the weather had previously forced him to miss. On Tuesday, he completed the Grey Corries. That night, Martin and Mark drove to Skye, and crossed the Cuillin ridge the following day, before celebrating with 'too much drink'. It did no long-term damage. On Saturday, they would both compete in the Isle of Jura Fell Race, with Martin finishing tenth in a field led home by Billy Bland.

'It never became totally dark,' he said. 'Although there was no moon, the yellow glow of the Northern Lights over hills to the north-east provided almost enough light to dispense with a torch.' Romance will only get the runner so far. Martin had already felt the pace 'beginning to come off' over the Ossian Munros when he was overcome by the need to sleep on the ascent of Sgùrr Eilde Mòr. Three times he drifted into slumber, knowing there was no-one to wake him. But the power naps were transformative: a heightened sense of alertness carried him across the backs of the Mamores to Mullach nan Coirean. Arriving at the hostel – having not seen another person since Carn Mòr Dearg – he had eclipsed everything that had gone before in these marvellous mountains, closing the ring in 23 hours and 24 minutes, and adding a further two Munros to make 26. The bar was raised again. Martin's run – still the most significant solo, unsupported 24-hour round ever undertaken – totalled 70 miles, climbing more than 9,000 metres.

'It's difficult to express simply what inspires me to attempt these runs alone and what motivates me while I'm out there,' Martin reflected later. 'I can't disguise the fact that it's partly to satisfy my ego. While I may never be a good fell racer, I seem to have found my strength in long-distance solo mountain running. The sense of achievement and satisfaction gained from adventures like this is unbeatable and for 24 hours I became totally detached from the reality of "normal" life.'

While Charlie Ramsay had demonstrated what was possible, those who followed – beginning with Martin – demonstrated just about anything was feasible. The theme would continue. A month after Martin's run, Jon Broxap blasted round clockwise – minus the two additional Munros – in 21 hours and 24 minutes. Martin had called Jon in the run-up to the solstice round, asking 'if he minded' Martin attempting to extend the route when the idea was a shared ambition. Jon said he was 'not ready' and gave Martin his blessing. Now the stamp of both runners was on Ramsay's Round.

The Ramsay-Stone-Broxap hegemony would not be broken in 1988, but the pause served only to heighten the dramatic tension of the denouement of the decade. The stage was set. The year was 1989, Helene Diamantides' *annus mirabilis*. Born in Yorkshire, Helene grew up in Ghana, then London – where she remembers her eight-year-old self putting closed shoes on her feet for the first time – and Greece, before returning to Britain aged 17. Leaving school with one A Level – a C in biology – she entered teacher training at college in Durham. Her upbringing seemed to imbue the spirit of the itinerant. After graduation, she wandered professionally from teaching to physiotherapy, and even a stint on a building site, and geographically from Coventry to Kendal. While life whirled and billowed, running was her constant. 'I never knew what I wanted to do. Running was what I loved and what kept me sane,' she said. Helene's yearning for long-distance mountain running inescapably led to a Bob Graham in 1987. She took the round more seriously in a second attempt a year later, and a lone, unassisted effort was verified by the Bob Graham 24-Hour Club as the fastest completion by a woman.

Helene dreamed large: she would run the 'big three', as they were now known, in one season. Gender should not be an issue in this story, but no man or woman had achieved such a feat. A Paddy Buckley in June and a Bob Graham in August bookended a 'secret' Ramsay's Round in July, sealing Helene her place in hill running history. Her handwritten account of the Scottish round is a self-deprecating parody that belies the fortitude required for such an undertaking. *Yet Another Yawn (Yarn?)* began: 'Oh, not another story to write.' The blasé prose continued: 'If there is one thing worse than doing a long run, it's the boring write-ups afterwards. Who reads these things anyway? And who cares at what stage you were in pain?'

Helene laughed off my 'golden era' description of the late 1980s. 'We didn't see it that way,' she insisted. 'I did these things to see if I could, and it really was enjoyable. Everybody was doing it. We were just feeding off each other. I look back and think, that was a different person in a different life. I think, how did I have the arrogance to set off with that certainty? I was young, naïve and thought I was invincible. Our attitude was, if you don't die, it's all right.'

Having read her account, I should have anticipated Helene's response. She never has taken life too seriously. 'A full moon hung in the dark sky,' she wrote. 'The dead hours were approaching. A veil of grey mist draped itself over the Scottish glen and silent animals moved beneath the sleeping firs, and, lo, there I spy one: Mark Rigby.'

Mark Rigby had form. He had created an eponymous mountain round in the Cairngorms the previous summer. Rigby visited all 17 – now 18 with the elevated status of Angel's Peak – Munros in the region, covering 75 miles with a cumulative ascent of 6,000 metres. Unlike the big three, the round is synonymous with solo, unsupported attempts, and reconnaissance is discouraged. The idea is simple: make the hard even harder. As he looped around the Cairngorms, beginning at Loch Morlich and heading first to Braeriach, the weather deteriorated. After battling the elements for some 20 hours, Mark retreated to the sanctuary of a bothy. Writing in *The Fellrunner*, the magazine of the Fell Runners Association, he noted: 'It was now pitch dark, and as I stumbled further along the non-existent path it began to rain heavily, so that I was glad of more shelter at the Fords of Avon refuge. Here I considered my position: it must be 2.30am or so, with 14 miles and 4,000 feet still to do, in a now raging storm and pitch dark, and running low on fruit jellies. I decided to gamble by sitting it out for an hour or so until first light.' When he finally decided to leave, he heaved open the bothy door and was 'immediately bowled sideways'. Undeterred, he began the ascent of Bynack More, the sixteenth and penultimate Munro. After that, there was just Cairn Gorm left. Noting at the end of his account that an Ambleside clubmate had that weekend completed a Bob Graham, he remarked: 'One is not alone in one's madness.'

Mark did not need to look far to find company for his next bout of 'madness'.

'We wuz gonna do that big round called the Charlie Ramsay,' Helene wrote. 'It's got 24 big hills and you gotta do 'em all in under 24 hours (or try to). Be sensible woman, you don't know who is going to have to read this. But it's so boring. Yet another long run – there's nothing to say really except it hurt a lot and I'm glad I don't have to do it again.'

Unlike Charlie, Helene and Mark climbed Ben Nevis first, with a pattern of preference for moving clockwise, thereby climbing the four biggest mountains first rather than contending with them in the punishing, fading hours of an attempt, already being established. Having never met, Martin Stone introduced the pair in Glen Nevis, with Martin telling Helene to ensure Mark took his turn in carrying the bag. Safely over the Aonachs, past Tranter's bed, Helene twisted an ankle on the loose rock of Sgùrr Choinnich Mòr, prompting 'a mixture of tears and words my mummy doesn't know I know'. Pausing at Loch Treig, the runners were well up on a 'survival' schedule and had also gained time on a 'hair-brained' 21-and-a-half-hour schedule dreamt up by Martin. 'Before I continue, I must explain,' Helene said. 'The previous weekend I had attempted to recce this section. Being ten to fifteen minutes behind the schedule by Carn Mòr Dearg, I had slunk off home, totally demoralised without even bothering to go over any others. The result was an ear-bending from Martin and the production of the "survival" schedule. This was a different story, however, and despite being crocked in both ankles, I was doing embarrassingly well.'

Helene does not even mention the hills east of Loch Treig. We can assume they happened. 'I don't remember it being a particularly nice bit,' she said when I questioned the omission. In stifling heat, the pain she foreshadowed in her opening paragraph – along with a swarm of horse flies – came on the 'runnable' glen section to the foot of Sgùrr Eilde Mòr. 'I arrived at the bothy by Loch Eilde Mòr barely able to be civil and unwilling to move a step further, let alone uphill to Sgùrr Eilde Mòr.'

Clouds descended on the Mamores; the wind, strong on the tops all day, began to 'bite'. Mark was 'bonking well' on the ridge to An Gearanach, while 'double vision, wobbly knees and lack of balance' characterised the journey to Stob Bàn, following 'nifty little trods' identified by Martin. 'As both

Mark and myself sat down and threatened to go to sleep, Martin fed us, watered us and moved us on after two minutes' break.' The last summit arrived and they found the way through the forest courtesy of a strategically-unfurled roll of bandage. 'As we crossed the imaginary line opposite the youth hostel, teenyboppers stared in amazement as two dishevelled individuals whooped and held hands down the road,' Helene recalled. The record had gone again, with Helene and Mark clocking 20 hours and 24 minutes. Still wearing their running kit, they reconvened in the Ben Nevis Inn. In keeping with the theme of self-deprecation, Helene attempted to source an 'I've climbed Ben Nevis' badge. 'There weren't any,' she told me, still disappointed.

'It was worth it,' she would note later. 'Without a doubt, the most serious of the rounds, it really is the king of them all.' After thanking the people who had helped, Helene reserved a final toast for the creator: 'To Charlie, for this brainchild we all feel compelled to attempt.'

The toast belonged to Charlie Ramsay, but the gesture was symbolic: it was to the infinite power of imagination.

5

A LONG-DISTANCE LOVE AFFAIR

As love drove Alec Keith to the mountains, love drove me from them. A year had elapsed when Fi called to say she was staying with family in Findhorn, 30 miles east of Inverness on the Moray coast. Did I want to come over? After supper, her aunt and uncle made their excuses and left us alone. 'I came to my senses,' I later wrote.

It is the closest my life has come to fiction. The author Ian McEwan is a purveyor of the literary turning point – the single instant on which providence hinges. That evening in Findhorn was my watershed. Looking back as I write now, every moment of the last eight years leads back to *that* moment. I would move to London to be with Fi. I would leave journalism and re-train as a teacher. Fi and I would get engaged in New York and married in London. I would teach in Croydon; Fi would teach in Tooting. Abstract conversations about children became a startling reality: we would have two. Finally, years later, we would call Scotland home. I would run in the hills again. I would write this book.

My wanderings among mountains remained unfettered. Nothing – even love – could interfere with that. Having committed to returning to London, the realisation that the hills would not always be there, that time in these places was not perpetual, elevated each encounter: the glimmer of low winter sun on a loch; the floating mist of thistle seeds in a glen; the beauty of simply turning back to glimpse an ever-shrinking world.

Perhaps the most wonderful day of all, that year and those that followed, was in the Cairngorms, on an autumn morning of passionate sunshine, fanned by the merest of breezes. The ascent of Braeriach from the Lairig Ghru was hot and slow, but as the plateau unravelled, the granite shimmered and twinkled. I felt as Nan Shepherd had: 'Up here, no movement, no voice. Man might be a thousand years away.' In mirroring brilliance, I came back to the plateau a fortnight later: peering into howffs by Loch A'an, passing the unruffled waters of Loch Etchachan, climbing tor-studded Beinn Mheadhoin. Once over Cairn Gorm, I paused to look across the bare tableland for a final time when I was stirred by the ricochet of dislodged stones. A reindeer herd processing upward split into two lines, passing either side of me as if I were a stone in a river.

As the days shortened, I made for the less glamorous side of the A9, gaining the innocuous Geal-charn Mòr and descending lumpy slopes of heather to eat curry and chips in Aviemore. There was time for one final expedition before winter swooped on the Highlands. I went again to the Fannichs, this time to run the two southernmost Munros in the range. From Meall Gorm, I could see the rubbly dome of Beinn Liath Mhòr Fannaich across a glen. It was real, after all.

If anything can be guaranteed in hill running it is that you will fall. I was on Craig Dunain – where else? – when the inevitable happened. As a foot caught a branch that had fallen across a path, I tumbled awkwardly, my weight crashing onto my right knee. Beneath the knee was snow; beneath the snow was mud; beneath the mud was concrete. Leaving a stain of red on white, I pressed on with the group, limping at first, then regaining relatively normal movement as the shock gradually dissipated. We summited in the lazy fall of portly snowflakes, as if in a film. On any other day, I would have appreciated the perfection of the moment. An hour later, as I cycled alongside the River Ness at high tide, my injured leg was too weak to drive the pedal. I dismounted and pushed, slipping in the still-falling snow. Once inside, I scraped away my trousers to reveal a swollen and bloodied knee. I placed a hand on the wound: it glowed red-hot against my white palm.

I hobbled into a new year. The Highlands were in the grip of a deep freeze. At its peak, I measured the depth of the glacier on the picnic table in my garden: 41 centimetres. With no car and unable to cycle on icy roads, I trudged three miles to and from work at an edge-of-city business park, my knee throbbing a little less as each day went by. As a temporary thaw began in mid-January, I was able to resume running and a month to the day after the fall, I stepped into that other world again on Craig Dunain. But I was destined for another world altogether: Fi and I were in the process of buying a flat in London. There was time for a last Craig Dunain hill race before I left. My hill running days in Inverness ended as they had started. 'Torture,' I wrote.

Driving south, the A9 rose to the Pass of Drumochter. I glanced at Geal-charn. The hill was grey and gloomy, decorated by strips of melting snow. The summit slunk away from the road. I did not stop this time. I tried to dismiss the place from my consciousness.

Home was a first-floor flat opposite an ambulance station in Streatham, once a hamlet on a street, now a seething mass of humanity. The view from our south-facing windows stretched across trees and rooftops to the three-mile Norwood Ridge of clay, adorned by two tall transmitters synonymous with this part of London. At night, even in the depths of winter, there were no stars. London dared out-glow the universe. The dazzle of aircraft lights, an orderly queue of languid shooting comets, took the stars' place. Streatham High Road, in places widening to a six-lane ogre once named Britain's 'worst street', was a half-mile walk away. I was horrified when I first saw High Road. This was London as I remembered in sporadic visits as a child from the Midlands: lines of seemingly identical and dilapidated shop fronts and takeaways oiled by traffic fumes.

I was in Streatham for a month. With a commission for a book that would become *Isles at the Edge of the Sea*, I embarked on a three-month journey among the west coast islands of Scotland. The trip became a glory lap of the Highlands and islands. I ran, climbed and walked up and over everything I could: Goatfell on Arran and the Paps of Jura in races; the Inaccessible Pinnacle on Skye; the ancient volcano of Askival on midge-addled Rum; the upturned boat of An Sgùrr on Eigg.

Having reached Conachair, the apex of the St Kilda archipelago that drops in sheer cliffs to the Atlantic, I began the longest journey home: descent to sea level, boat to Harris, bus to Tarbert, ferry to Skye, car-ride to Sligachan, lift to Inverness, bus to the airport, plane to Gatwick. A subsequent train drifted through Reigate and Croydon, and I disembarked at Clapham Junction, 'the world's busiest train station', before one further connection to Streatham Hill. I shouldered my rucksack on steps that I counted from one to 36, and plunged through ticket barriers, popping on to High Road. It was warm and busy, as it always seemed to be, even in winter. As I waited to cross, two thoughts collided: the woman I love is a half-mile away in a first-floor flat opposite an ambulance station overlooking trees and rooftops to the Norwood Ridge. But in the next moment: what have I done?

London would embroil me thereafter. I had a wedding to plan, children to teach, books to write. Life was happily chaotic. It was not until we had a daughter, Arielle, then a second, Aphra, 19 months later, that I realised how truly full a life can be. In parenting, we had found something more demanding than running up mountains. Scotland seemed to drift away, its high places becoming ethereal.

I remember once driving to Glen Feshie, a 40-minute outing from Inverness, with the intention of running the two Munros on the western haunch of the Cairngorms. As I climbed, the wind was up and my legs were unwilling. I was surprised to see pockets of snow on lower slopes in what was still early November. I just don't fancy this, I thought. Not today. I stopped and sat on a boulder, and decided to turn around, to go back to the car. And why not? There was nothing defeatist about that. The hills will still be here tomorrow, I reasoned. I also reckoned that I would never run out of tomorrows. I had not bargained on love, for there are not endless tomorrows in the Highlands for those who reside in London.

When I returned to Scotland as a tourist, my enterprises took on an air of desperation and irrational urgency. I was an impatient Sassenach, rushing and racing, and never truly being. I sought to dash up mountains in the way I hurried to top up my Oyster card before the train left Streatham Hill. It was in such a panic and on such an unstoppable treadmill that I scooped up twelve Munros in three foolhardy summer days.

Fi was eight weeks pregnant with Arielle when we spent a week on Skye. We were in that we-are-not-telling-anyone-yet stage, so when Fi swam from Skye to Scalpay across the 800-metre channel in an act of defiance to the independence she was about to cede, she could only be judged in retrospect. At the end of the week, I travelled to Knoydart, a west coast peninsula described so frequently as Britain's 'last wilderness' or the 'land of the giants' that the phrases have become clichés.

I woke early the next day, clammy in a sleeping bag, on the dirty floor of a bothy at Barisdale. My hands instinctively reached for my ankles, now dimpled with a rash of spots following the previous evening's encounter with an epidemic of midges on the six-mile walk from the cul-de-sac settlement of Kinloch Hourn. What elevates Knoydart is its splendid isolation. There is truth in the clichés. As I reached an immense, empty valley known as Coire Dhorrcail below Ladhar Bheinn, I was wracked with guilt. A throwaway comment to Fi that I 'might' go to Knoydart was an unhelpful starting point for mountain rescue. I gained a ridge, then the summit, seeing no-one. Touching the roof of Scotland's greatest tract of wild land was like being on the rim of a smoking volcano:

a proliferation of mist on one side; nothing on the other, offering an unobstructed outlook across an island-dotted sea.

That was the end of the poetry. The rest of the day was an unremitting struggle. Outside of racing or rounds, I have never subjected myself to such rash punishment. The arch of my right foot had ached from the first step out of my sleeping bag. I was happier – and in less pain – when climbing, even if that meant an unrelenting hike up the flank of Meall Buidhe. On the way to a third Munro, twice I turned an obviously weak and unstable ankle – the second time sparking a sharp surge of hurt – until I could no longer run. I felt like the 'first and last man' again as I finally clambered onto Luinne Bheinn to see an emerald Loch Hourn below. Pathetically, I shuffled, tried to jog, limped, hopped – doing anything required to get back to Barisdale.

Inexplicably, I could run again two days later, although *able to run* is a relative term. My ankle and foot merely seemed sufficiently healed to sustain another battering. From Kinloch Hourn, I had driven to Findhorn for a night's respite, then retraced my journey west the following afternoon, camping on a grassy plateau by the River Cluanie. Breakfast was a can of lukewarm macaroni cheese and without a fork or spoon I mounded the contents onto a Debenhams gift card. I ate facing what I could see of the South Glen Shiel ridge, a nine-mile line comprising seven Munros. I was after two more as well – Sgùrr na Sgine and The Saddle, that rise to the north-west of the main ridge. I could not see the tops. Cloud was taking care of them all. The forecast was for the theme to continue: mist and intermittent rain.

I do not know what compelled me to go to the hills that day. I had no need of them. They certainly had no need of me. I was committed, I suppose, as I had been in Knoydart. Once the conveyer belt of decision-making had been triggered, I could not alter its course. I had to go. There was no alternative.

I broke into a slow jog, soon passing my campsite of the previous night. The hours here had been dreadful. I was woken repeatedly by swirling wind, and then a nightmare. Sleeping on my front, I felt the weight of a man on my back, pressing down hard. As his mouth reached the back of my head, he began to lick my neck, immediately beneath the hair line. As hard as the pressing was, the licking was gentle – like a cat's tongue on a hand. I struggled frantically for breath. Three times I tried to cry out, but the shouts were strangled by terror. I woke on the third and lay petrified in my sleeping bag, such was the haunting lucidity of the dream. 'It's the spirits of the glen,' Moira, Fi's aunt, told me later with conviction. 'A Jacobite, no doubt, fleeing from the English to Skye after Culloden.'

Peter, her husband, is the pragmatist in this relationship. He was kneeling before a wood burner, pushing in fuel, shaking his head incredulously. 'Winter is coming,' he muttered. It was August.

The trouble with calling on nine Munros, particularly in mist, is that it is subsequently difficult to recall the charac- teristics of the individual mountains and summits, or even to remember their names. I have not been back since, but I am sure if I did, it would seem like I had never been there. As I moved west, the weather worsened, the mist now carrying a smirr. Amid the unpleasantness, there were the briefest moments of unexpected rapture: a bird's eye view to Loch Quoich and the twisting road to Kinloch Hourn as the cloud momentarily cleared; minutes later, some real birds: a dozen ptarmigan gallantly flapping in the wind.

Strangely, my motivation never waned, but motivation for what? I was compelled by the summits, by getting to the next one, then fixating on the one after. The mountains, in return, gave nothing. Why should they? I was the antithesis of Nan Shepherd. 'The mountain gives itself most completely when I have no destination, when I reach nowhere in particular, but have gone out merely to be with the mountain as one visits a friend with no intention but to be with him,' she wrote. Somewhere, somehow, I had forgotten how to do that. But deeper, unspoken emotions were also at play: Scotland and me, this long-distance love affair, it just was not working.

But you keep persisting, don't you? Keep hoping. Perhaps this relationship can be mended? I tried again. After a night at the bunkhouse at Tulloch, my intention was to run over Stob Coire Sgriodain and Chno Dearg, some form of demented warm-up for racing over two other Munros at Loch Lochy the next day. Even by the time I reached the end of the road at Fersit, from where a track continues to Loch Treig, I knew I was kidding myself. Feeling weak and dehydrated after two days of sickness, there was no way I was climbing mountains today. We needed a break, that was clear. I walked to the dam instead, finding a large rock to sunbathe on. They were innocent moments. There would be no time to pause to sunbathe by Loch Treig again.

I felt no better the next day, but I was here now, on the Loch Lochy start line – and I did not know when such an opportunity might arise again. To reach the first summit, it was classic Scottish hill racing: forestry track, open moorland, pathless bog, a formidable climb dotted with a queue of runners. London simply could not prepare me for the gradient and length of such ascents. The lack of any extended climbs within running distance of Streatham meant I was compelled to do hill repetitions – essentially, repeatedly running up and down the same hill. And so every Thursday night, I found myself on an angle of tarmac on the edge of Streatham Common. The climb started at about 50 metres above sea level, rising to 75, with each ascent taking around a minute to run. I would do eight – a height gain that would not get me a quarter of the way up the first Munro. I struggled on. Unlike on the South Glen Shiel ridge, I *really* had no choice: the fastest way to the end was to run the race. Back on the tarmac road to the finish, I glimpsed a runner ahead – the first I had encountered since the summit of the second Munro. Accelerating, I caught him quickly, glancing sideways at a man twenty years my senior. I finished and dropped to the ground. *Was it always this hard?*

Worse was to come. Arriving in Fort William by train, I walked the length of Glen Nevis and through the gorge to Steall. Dusk was upon me when I camped on waves of tussocks above the river. As the wind intensified, I crawled outside to reposition the pegs and add a circle of rocks. I was glad of my efforts: I would spend much of a sleepless night listening to a snarling, midsummer gale and torrential rain crashing on the roof. In the morning, I crossed the swollen river and marched up a zig-zagging path, trespassing on Ramsay's Round at An Gearanach. I proceeded over Stob Coire a' Chàirn in low-slung clag, before dropping off Am Bodach to the West Highland Way and Kinlochleven. From the village, it was a near 10-mile tramp to the Kings House Hotel in Glen Coe. Alone, I nursed a pint of something in the bar, then camped close by. Inevitably, as day gave way to night, midges descended, with rain – an unlikely blessing – later chasing them away. I awoke, stiff and uncomfortable, in the half-light of a Highland dawn, sensing an unusual weight on my legs. There was no Jacobite this time. The tent had buckled, snapping a pole. The flattened material now lay draped across my sleeping bag, transferring raindrops to down. With the bag saturated from toe to waist, my tent was no longer any sort of refuge. I wriggled free, emerging to rain falling from an ashen sky. My camp lay in a tangled pile at my feet.

Suddenly, I had no desire to be here anymore – a sensation and a decisiveness that filled me with shame. How could I reject this place? I walked as far as the road, rolled the pack on the verge to become a seat, and wrapped my hood over my head. I sat, waiting, checking my watch. I looked down the ribbon of road again. It was finally coming, a careering white oblong framed by moor and mountain. I flung an arm out and watched the bus brake to a halt, mists of water spraying from the wheels. The door hissed open, warm breath escaping. There was a flicker of doubt, then I climbed aboard, slunk into the first available seat, and almost wept with relief. Within minutes, as we hurtled south to Glasgow, those feelings of relief seemed absurdly shallow. An agonising guilt fell upon me. I was the cause of the split. I had abandoned the Highlands.

I lived in London for five years, a period characterised by a perpetual crisis of running identity. Where there was once Craig Dunain, there was now Tooting Bec Common. Choice was not the issue: South London was a hotbed of competitive cross-country and road running; there was a 400-metre track a mile from my front door; a short train journey would get me to the trails of the North and South Downs. But London is no place for the hill runner, with the Box Hill fell race the only concession to the sport in south-east England. In the end, I attempted everything and excelled at nothing. I ran cross-country in the winter, moving to the road in the spring, then track in the early-summer.

I traded in numbers, not summits. I can remember personal bests for every distance – from one mile to marathon – to the nearest second. Running was experienced through the digits on my watch, filling the vacuum hill running once offered. I spent one summer obsessing over my time for five kilometres, coinciding with a series of evening races held in Battersea Park. The events were run on the same flat course and the leading runners would comfortably break 16 minutes. My best time for the distance was 16 minutes and 30 seconds when I posted a time 22 seconds slower. I knew by the end of the second mile: my pace – by a mere five seconds per mile – had irretrievably fallen away. I was disconsolate on the jog home. My running identity seemed to have become even more complex in a matter of minutes. Disconsolate over 22 seconds? I struggled to realise then the extent of my obsession with time. I needed a distraction – the purpose mountains had served – but the memories of that morning at the Kings House Hotel had shattered any lingering romanticism. I needed something else, somewhere else.

It came soon, mercifully. As I left the track at Tooting one

night, I overhead a clubmate, Robin Sanderson, talking about
the Bob Graham. He was attempting the round with a group
of friends later that year and was planning a series of visits to
familiarise himself with the route. They were going to camp in
Borrowdale and track one of the later sections that connects
Wasdale and Honister Pass that weekend. Was I interested?
Rain was forecast, Robin announced cheerily. 'I'll come,' I
said, unaware what I had set in motion.

6

AN ENGLISH DISTRACTION

The hour was approaching midnight as the car swept west-
wards along the A66. Headlights momentarily illuminated a
road sign: THRELKELD. We had entered the realm of the Bob
Graham Round. Wiping condensation from the windows, we
looked out and up, peering into a heaving maelstrom. The
darkness was vast and perpetual; Blencathra was engaged in
battle with a furious monster. Someone was up there though.
Someone, somewhere. A fell runner. The woman had left the
traditional starting point of the Moot Hall in Keswick four
hours earlier. She would have paced nervously through the
alleyways of Keswick; she would have climbed the stony slopes
of Skiddaw, the fourth highest ground in England, where the
wind would have sought to whirl her away; she would have
paused at the summit, checking her watch, making a mental
note of the split; she would have dropped into a boggy trough
before rising again to Great Calva, reassured by a line of old
fence posts that lead the way to the cairn; she would have
forded the surging River Caldew and with water slopping in
her shoes started the long ascent of Blencathra. About now,
she should be descending that stupendous mountain. Threlkeld waited for her, as one day it would wait for me. We
looked again to where Blencathra should be, seeking the starry
glare of a head torch. The car bucked. The window wipers
thrummed from side to side in a frantic, thrashing action. We
looked again. Nothing.

There were four of us: Robin Sanderson and his wife Shayda,

Duncan Steen and me. What would Joss Naylor – whose valley we would steal into tomorrow – have made of us: an IT specialist, a tax consultant, an energy consultant and an English teacher, driving 300 miles in Friday night traffic from London, fuelled by a tray of Marks and Spencer sandwiches? Duncan and I would share a tent, pitched on liquid ground in a Borrowdale campsite in the early hours. A little over a year later, this then-stranger, who I first encountered on the forecourt of a Chiswick petrol station, would stand by my side on the summit of Robinson, the last hill on a clockwise Bob Graham, gesturing manically to the south and east, bellowing into the wind: 'Look at these hills; you own them.'

Joined by Adam Stirk, an IT project manager, and Andy Higgins, a mechanical engineer, in the watery light of morning, we went for a run, first over a mountain pass apparently haunted by a thirteenth century ghost named Bjorn, before sweeping downhill to the single-track road that punctures Wasdale. We came to a halt by a rickety wooden gate. 'This is it,' Andy said knowingly. 'It' was the start of a path to the top of Yewbarrow, rising some 500 metres above our heads. Yewbarrow is a middle-sized Lakeland fell, overshadowed by illustrious neighbours, Great Gable and Scafell Pike. Yet in the context of the Bob Graham, Yewbarrow is an appalling proposition. Put yourself in the shoes of an aspirant. You have run continuously for 12 hours, probably through part of the night, possibly in incessant rain, over 30 peaks, including the nine highest summits in England, covering 40 miles, when you are faced with Yewbarrow – the third longest and one of the steepest ascents of the round. Attempts founder here for good reason. The fell had claimed another victim that morning: the woman we had hoped to see descending Blencathra. Somehow, she had made it this far.

We went up, first to Yewbarrow, then to wonderfully-named places like Steeple and Pillar, with rain starting to fall as we reached the pinnacle of the latter. Weather in the Lake District has a knack of accelerating in seriousness with alarming alacrity. A fine day can evolve into an abominable one with merciless speed. And so it did. Light rain became heavy rain; heavy rain became hail. Visibility of miles was curtailed to a few yards. By the time I located a waterproof jacket and turned it from inside-out while it flapped madly in the wind, I was soaked. The spare kit – hat, gloves, thermal top – contained in my rucksack was also rapidly gaining moisture. Such was my fell running naivety, the notion of placing these in a waterproof bag had not occurred. Over Pillar and on the long descent to Black Sail Pass, I began to shiver in a way I knew would only worsen. I was a featherweight then as now and the cold seemed to tear at my core, making every step a small agony. We passed a walker going up, swaying in the wind. 'It's gone a little bit wrong, hasn't it?' he yelled.

I sensed panic in the group. We had stopped eating and drinking; hunch and hope had replaced rationality. In our haste, we overshot the summit of Kirk Fell. We looked back forlornly, instantly dismissing the prospect of returning, and blundered on towards Great Gable. We had very quickly become imposters. What use was a mechanical engineer or an IT consultant or an English teacher in the chaos of a Lakeland storm? It was, in hindsight, an unwitting examination – one that we would all just about pass.

There was no requirement to proceed to Kirk Fell or Great Gable that day. We could have changed course at Black Sail Pass, retreating to the safety of valley floors at Ennerdale or Wasdale. What would have made us descend? A broken leg? Hypothermia? Concussion? Being cold, tired or disorientated were unsatisfactory excuses. Choosing what appears to be the logical or sensible option is not the prerogative of a contender seeking to accomplish a Bob Graham or Ramsay's Round within 24 hours. Ironically, the psychologically easier solution is to continue the set course. That is when you know you are obsessed: when the chronic fear of failure overrules the urgency of common sense. So we stuck to the plan: running the entirety of the ten miles of the fourth leg, however horrible it was.

My teeth chattered as we ran in a line down Green Gable. My hands, bare and wet, were blue-white. I clapped them together, then made a cup, blowing hot air into the barrels of my curled fingers, creating momentary relief. Once over Grey Knotts, the final summit, the land fell sharply. Ahead, the air cleared for a moment, revealing a shiny coil of the Honister road pass, only for the mist to slam its door. Seconds later, we punched through the clag. The world had come back to us. Honister lay beneath our feet.

We traipsed into the shelter of the mine museum that occupies the pass. Someone unearthed a collection of coins, enough to pay for a mug of tomato soup between the five of us. Still shuddering, I found the gents and stood slumped by the hand dryer, repeatedly pressing the button to start the air, before Andy came to tell me we had to run a further four miles to the campsite.

Many years later, Fi and I would debate the purpose of *doing* anything: watching television, going to work, running in the hills. 'Because you enjoy it; there must be an element of fun,' was her argument.

'I don't enjoy everything I do,' was my retort. That exchange summarised my feelings on the Bob Graham. Having entered a circle of fascination, I could not extricate myself, even if I wanted to. Enjoyment – or lack of it – was not the point; the Bob Graham had quite unexpectedly become imprinted in my consciousness. Like Ramsay's Round would one day be, it was a calling that demanded an answer.

Convinced they were ready – ready to respond to the mountains' summons – Adam, Andy, Duncan and Robin, along with a single support runner, Konrad Rawlik, who had completed a solo round earlier in the year, made their attempt. At the same time, I was camping in Swanage on the south coast of England. When I went to bed that night, listening to sprinkling rain and the flapping of the canvas in the wind, I feared for them. I had seen the weather forecast.

For four hours, all was well. Then darkness dropped, and

night brought a nightmare: fierce headwind, driving rain, appalling visibility. 'We caught another group of runners at the summit of Clough Head: one guy on an attempt and at least a couple of support runners,' Adam said. The 'one guy' was Bingley Harriers' Andy Nicoll, and as the five contenders and their support descended, the pack fragmented. 'There was practically zero visibility with it being dark and claggy, and simply too many people with headlamps to work out who was who,' Adam remembered.

As the confusion unravelled, Adam, Andy and Duncan – who had stayed united – had no way of knowing if Robin and Konrad were in front or behind or even together, and, of course, vice-versa. Ordinarily, this would not be a problem, but the runners were not self-sufficient: Konrad was carrying all the food. 'Once we got onto the ridge itself, conditions were unpleasant – poor visibility, windy and wet – so Konrad stopped to put his waterproof on,' Robin said. 'I waited briefly beside him and checked the bearing. Once Konrad and I set off, we couldn't see the others ahead, so we trotted off briskly on the bearing I had taken to try to catch up. Konrad and I became more concerned and we pushed on faster. Our navigation turned out to be accurate, so although we didn't realise at the time, we overtook them. We were constantly scanning the ridge for signs of head torches but the visibility was so poor it was unlikely you'd see anyone more than thirty yards away unless their torch was pointing in your direction at the time.'

The others spent an agonising fifteen minutes squatting behind a cairn waiting for Konrad and Robin, not realising they had already passed. Conditions were getting worse. 'By now the wind was raging,' said Duncan.

'Stopping for that length of time in really grim conditions was the beginning of the end from a physical and mental point of view,' Adam added.

There was no contingency plan. 'We hadn't made any plans for what we'd do if we got separated,' Robin admitted. 'Konrad and I assumed the others were still ahead, so we continued to push on; the others assumed we were behind. Unfortunately, both groups were wrong so the error was compounded.' Robin saw sense and abandoned his attempt; Konrad went with him, descending to the road. At least they were well-fed.

The others pressed on, summiting the mountains they had to, in the teeth of a storm, arriving at Dunmail Raise in a wretched state. That they were demoralised and had haemorrhaged time was not enough to force them off the mountains – at least not yet for Andy and Duncan.

The pair walked up Steel Fell, accompanied, again, by just one pacer. Declan Phelan was a hardened Munro-bagger but unfamiliar with the Lakes and had never been on the route of the Bob Graham. 'The three of us made it through to the Langdale Pikes,' said Duncan, 'but morale was pretty low.' Andy was the first to bow to inevitability, ending his attempt at Rossett Pike. Duncan and Declan marched on to Bowfell. 'We went pretty much straight up,' Duncan said, 'and had to climb a dirty gully to the top. I think being on the go for more than twelve hours in bad weather and missing an entire night's sleep was taking its toll on my ability to navigate. At the top, we turned left and very quickly found a cairn which I assumed was the summit. Descending towards Esk Pike, the truth dawned on me: we hadn't actually topped Bowfell, but rather a subsidiary lump to the north.' They could not ignore the oversight like we had once on Kirk Fell; as rain continued to fall, they retraced their steps. For Duncan, it was the end: misery heaped on misery. Morale? It was gone. Duncan faced reality: he was not going to make it. 'I was fed up with being wet and miserable, and fed up with having to try so damn hard.'

That was that. The decision made, Duncan and Declan bypassed the next three summits, continued over Scafell Pike, then eased down to Mickledore, the defile between England's highest ground and Sca Fell, where they met Duncan's father. Ian Steen, who had attempted to fix a rope on Broad Stand, the rock climb that offers the swiftest passage to Sca Fell, had been embroiled in his own adventure: falling in a river; attempting to climb dripping wet rock using a complicated back-roping technique to protect himself from falling; becoming mildly hypothermic; bivvying behind a rock to try to get warm. Chastened and, on this occasion, beaten, the three descended. As for Andy Nicoll? He made it.

Some find it easy to dismiss the disappointment of a failed round, regardless of the conditions. Declan Phelan later described his hours on the Lakeland fells as the 'most grim' he had endured in the mountains.

Even so, Andy struggled to find closure: 'To say we were disappointed doesn't do it justice. I was consumed with a sense of failure and self-pity for weeks afterwards, feeling that Mother Nature and the Bob Graham had combined forces to humiliate four experienced and determined hill runners. In a sense, they had, but they did it for our benefit. The Bob Graham deserved more respect, especially in those conditions; it is so much more than a physical challenge.'

Robin was a little more circumspect: 'I just spent some quality time feeling grumpy.'

Robin and I made one last dash to the Lake District that year. Two days after the shortest day and two days before Christmas, it was the time of year when midwinter rounds are undertaken, with the paucity of daylight hours adding to the plethora of challenges that a late-December attempt poses. The round was attracting attention from elite ultrarunners and one of the best of them, thirty-seven-year-old Nick Clark, was in town. Kent-born Clark – who emigrated to the US in 2006 – had finished third among world-class fields in the Western States 100 and Hardrock 100, two of the planet's toughest ultramarathons, that summer. But coming to the Lake District, Clark admitted he was 'taking a stab in the dark'.

As he reached the summit of Skiddaw in the early hours before dawn 'all hell broke loose'. His thoughts echoed those of many a desperate mountain runner: in poor visibility and 'pummelling' sleet, with rocks covered in ice, Clark began 'to wonder what in hell's name had I been thinking in signing up for this gig'.

The headline act of the 'gig' was a thaw. The Caldew was flowing hard and deep, and it took Clark 30 minutes to find a safe passage. He persisted: up Blencathra, over the Helvellyn ridge, and into the hills beyond Dunmail Raise. Clark and Bill Williamson, his support runner, had reached Scafell Pike when the ultrarunner encountered the 'nastiest snow I've ever had the displeasure of moving over'. The metre-deep layer was melting on the top and bottom, leaving a freezing sandwich of slush in between. Every step held unknown peril. When Williamson screamed after sliding waist-deep into the mush, Clark thought he must have broken a leg. It was only cramp. 'This was not a cushy carpet of pow-pow that could be ripped down with careless abandon,' Clark said. 'It was a dangerous freaking minefield where one wrong step could spell disaster.'

In the pitch black, with Williamson navigating, they made it into a gully that leads to Sca Fell. 'The melt was in full effect,' remembered Clark, 'and we were climbing up rocky waterfalls, punching through snow up to our waists every fifth kick-in, before the final straw came for me as I dropped through a snow bridge into a snowmelt creek up to my shoulders. That was it. I was done. I wanted no more to do with this under-taking. After what seemed like an eternity, we finally gained the ridge. I tagged the summit block and then we got the hell out of Dodge.'

The attitude of the Lakes compared to Clark's stomping ground in Colorado made up for the lack of comparative altitude, he concluded. 'The British fells and the guys and gals who run on them are tough little buggers,' he added.

Enter two 'tough little buggers'.

Mike Park and Andrew Graham, both members of Cocker-mouth Mountain Rescue Team, set off a day later – at 8pm on the winter solstice – than Clark. At 7.35pm the next day, Graham returned. At 7.56pm – with four minutes to 24 hours – head torches were glimpsed down Keswick High Street. It was Park. He put his palm to the green door of the Moot Hall at 7.57pm.

With Robin a step behind, we marched up a gully on Steel Fell, where contours jostle like isobars in a hurricane above an ever-shrinking Dunmail Raise. Once on the undulating ground between Steel Fell and Calf Crag, we quickly learnt why two rounds so close together had experienced such mixed fortunes. The snow that blighted Clark for 40 miles had gone. The melt he had experienced had concluded. Had Clark waited 24 hours, like the mountain rescue duo, he might have succeeded.

We did an about-turn at Rossett Pike. I voiced a half-hearted suggestion to continue to Bowfell. The voice of common sense, Robin, dismissed the idea instantly. A prodigiously-white Bowfell was practically Himalayan to the eyes of runners unused to winter on the mountains. Hail chased us off Rossett Pike as we began our journey in reverse. We ate pork pies on Pike of Stickle and jogged all the way to Sergeant Man. The hills were ours. Cold and tired, we found the top of the gully on Steel Fell, paused for a moment in a still, pre-dusk chill, and plunged downhill. Ten minutes later we were driving home for Christmas.

A year to the day after I had pulled on a waterproof on Pillar, 30 seconds too late, I was in Yorkshire. The notion that if you complete a Fellsman Hike within 16 hours you can then run a 24-hour Bob Graham, had taken on the proportions of an eleventh Commandment. I had no interest in the credibility of the statement. If one led to the other, that was good enough for me. A 16-hour Fellsman is not easily won, however, and the 2012 edition of the race – a 61-mile horseshoe from Ingleton to Threshfield in the Yorkshire Dales – would be the most bruising encounter in its 50-year existence.

Conditions were not wintry and there was no snow on the hills, but a bitter wind blew persistently all day and as night crept over the Dales, the temperature nudged below freezing. A runner being airlifted off a mountain with a broken bone was always a possibility in such a long contest, but the misfortune was merely the starting point of a chain of near-cataclysmic events. At one checkpoint, 16 people were being sick; later in the day, a further 20 were hypothermic. The race was terminated for the first time in its history at 1.40am on Sunday, nearly 17 hours after it had begun. Runners were stopped at checkpoints and driven to the finish. At dawn, a competitor was plucked off a hillside suffering with wind-blindness, some five hours after the race had been halted. The organiser was in tears as she announced to those who had already finished that the rumours were true: the Fellsman had been abandoned.

At 1.40am, I was in my sleeping bag on the floor of a sports hall in Threshfield, having completed the Fellsman, while hundreds of people were still on the hills battling that crippling north-east wind and darkness. Jez Bragg, the race winner, had already tweeted that this Fellsman had been 'the hardest race of his life'.

In a mountain ultramarathon, a point will inevitably be reached when things only get worse. After 50-something miles and approaching eleven hours of continuous running, I decided everything ached: my legs, of course, but also my arms, back, stomach, chest. My ankles throbbed; my right knee was twingeing; my feet were desperately sore; my eyelids drooped. My thoughts, inevitably, meandered to the Bob Graham. Never, I decided. No way. I cannot feel like this again. Duncan Steen and I had been together for the last eight hours and had said little beyond confirming where we were and where we were going. We were running up Great Whernside, the last significant peak, in a blustery dusk, and had retreated into our own internal worlds. Resolving that I must eat, I stuffed a custard cream in my mouth. I bit once but the cold had locked my jaw, preventing chewing. I opened my lips and allowed the wind to blow away the crumbs like dust.

We lumbered on, besieged by a howling cold, but a conclusion did not seem a reality. Something forced us on, into the night. Even when Duncan fell awkwardly over a metal fence, he wordlessly got up and started running again. I understood then why he had got as far as he did on that ill-fated Bob Graham. Our pace was inexorably slowing, but there was no collapse, no capitulation. Suddenly, wonderfully, there was road beneath our feet. We were two miles from salvation. Enthralled by the alarming brightness of a village below, I surged into incongruous civilisation, sprinting downhill, flashing past pubs and an Indian restaurant, then tumbling through the doors of Upper Wharfedale School.

Sitting on a chair in the foyer, a forearm cradling my head, I could already feel a fuzziness shadowing the ghastliness. Had it really been so bad? A week later, the experience would seem positively romantic. As I lay awake listening to ripples of snores in the school gym, I mulled over the Bob Graham – not 'never', I decided, but when?

Failure is intrinsically more interesting than success. Three weeks after the Fellsman, Adam, Andy and Duncan got around. There is little to say on the matter. What could have gone wrong did not. Unwilling to repeat the mistakes of the previous summer, the trio set off together but with individual support runners. By Wasdale, Duncan was almost an hour ahead after gambolling across the central leg, with Adam and Andy running within minutes of each other further back. Nothing really happened – and that is just the way you want it. The weather was benign. Injuries sustained in the build-up did not worsen. They ate, they drank, they ran. They could have wished for no more. Duncan was in the pub, having completed in 19 hours and 32 minutes, when Adam and Andy finished some 40 minutes later. For Andy, demons had been slayed: 'I felt surprisingly calm and a strange sense of relief at completing, yet a reluctance to accept that this amazing day was over. For so long, completing the Bob Graham had been a dream. Now it was a surreal reality.'

My turn came in June. Duncan was by my side again as

we jogged towards Skiddaw, torch beams thrown back at us by the clag. The light of dawn arrived on Blencathra, but the glorious daybreak I had envisaged would never materialise. Above Threlkeld, the Helvellyn range was entombed in mist. I ran on quietly, becoming morose and frustrated. 'You're doing really well,' Duncan kept insisting. Inside, I was fighting an insatiable urge to escape, to stop. I simply could not fathom how tired I was. The further we ran, eventually onto the deserted plateau of Helvellyn, the deeper I became immersed in self-pity. Contemplating abandonment, I rehearsed conversations, considered the ignominy of failure.

But, like Scotland and its mountains, this was a love affair, and instinct told me to persist. Somewhere and somehow, after ten hours of running, I began to feel content. Weary, deprived of sleep, nauseous and weather-beaten – but content. As the clag began to dissolve, the Scafells rose into a blue sky. 'You're flying,' Robin said, and I truly believed I was. Back in the rubble of Bowfell or Esk Pike, I had passed an invisible line, a tipping point: the moment I realised the plausibility of what I sought.

What followed was a mesmeric, euphoric high that I wished would never end. I moved quickly and freely up Yewbarrow, then onto the hills of my Lakeland baptism: Pillar, Kirk Fell and Great Gable. I did not feel weary. Movement was joyous, almost effortless. I had no sense then that at the end of this I would be unable to run without pain in the balls of my feet for the next three months. As I came off Robinson, I could not recall the Lake District or mountains anywhere ever being so serene, and on the day that time meant everything it paradoxically seemed to be suspended. Duncan shouted those words, swinging his arm in an arc: 'You own them!' I was back in Keswick 19 hours and 33 minutes after last being there. It was not even dark. I felt many things in the immediate moments that followed, but disappointment seemed to swallow them all: I knew I might never feel like that again.

7

THE ROAD TO SWANSTON

I am running down a hill. I am running down a hill in Scotland. I am running down a hill while holding the hand of my squealing, skipping two-year-old daughter. I am running down a hill while wincing from a dull, groaning pain in my right ankle. I am running down a hill in jeans and a jumper. I am running down a hill nonetheless. From high on the Pentland Hills, Edinburgh is at my feet.

I live here. I live in Scotland.

And I can breathe.

The Pentlands today are a green and brown cluster of hills stretching twenty miles from Biggar to Edinburgh; some 430 million years earlier they were the mush of an ocean floor that separated continents. As the land masses shuffled nearer, the sludgy depths were propelled upward, eventually piercing sea level and moving to the sky. The Pentlands were showered with volcanic debris and hewn by ice. Aeons passed. It is an existence of unfathomable proportions. I try to always remind myself of that: even the humble Pentlands are greater than any monument humans could build.

From Edinburgh, the three northerly hills of the Pentlands dominate the skyline, concealing the wilder, rougher parts beyond. Above an artificial ski slope at the aptly-named Hillend, the trio of Caerketton, Allermuir and Capelaw rise from east to west, taking the form of an undulating ridge when viewed from central and southern Edinburgh.

While skiers are trapped on their brush ramps, the runner knows no fixed bounds. I look to Caerketton, Allermuir and Capelaw every day. They are a permanent part of my existence. Whether streaked in sunshine or silhouetted against a night sky, they remain constant, as they have done for millions of years, as they will forever. Sometimes they are concealed by cloud or hidden by haar. That does not matter; I still see them.

On my twelfth day in Edinburgh, I could stand it no longer: I went for a run in the Pentlands. Injured ankle, be damned. Where the hills succumb to Edinburgh's southerly margins and within earshot of the perpetual rumble of the city bypass is the dead-end village of Swanston. I parked, re-tied my laces and started my watch. From this departure point, a direct route to the summit of Allermuir climbs some 300 metres in a little over a mile. Ian Campbell, a runner with Edinburgh-based Hunters Bog Trotters – a club eponymously named after the area of marshy ground between Arthur's Seat and Salisbury Crags, and once considered too disrespectful a moniker to allow registration with the Scottish Amateur Athletics Association – ran up this way (and back to Swanston) 29 times over three days, clocking up an overall ascent to match Everest. I had more modest ambitions: a single climb. Barring a momentary downhill respite, the path rises continually at an average gradient of 14 per cent. If it was a road, it would come with a warning. I would *run* for as long as I could, I reasoned.

Up I went: immediately into woods, over a stream, along a lane framed by Swanston's thatched cottages, higher on a track of rising gravel, through a gate and forward on a rutted path before reaching open hillside. I looked at my watch: seven minutes. Ahead was a wedge of grass, angled like the steep, straight climb of a rollercoaster track. I yielded to Allermuir: I began walking. The liberation and relief of being able to move in the hills was replaced by the realisation of the pain the activity was causing. The entire right side of my body – back, hip and knee – had taken sympathy with the malfunctioning ankle, with each vying for attention. My ankle seemed connected by fraying strands of string, as if one clumsy manoeuvre might detach foot from leg. Back, hip, knee and ankle aside, I had forgotten how hard this was. I was heaving for breath, like swimming in cold, choppy water. I could breathe, of course, but the quality of the breath was insufficient, and as insufficiency mounted, a desperate fatigue emerged. When I could rouse the effort, I moved in a defiant shuffle. Ostensibly, I walked. It was dogged walking: hands-on-thighs walking, not-stopping-to-admire-the-view walking. But it was unmistakably walking. I was the epitome of irony: the walking hill runner.

There was a final slog up a wall of long grass etched with boot marks before I could go no higher on Allermuir. It had taken 18 minutes to travel a mile. I embraced the pillar perched on the summit and – rather than the earlier fleeting glances left and right that were quickly halted by the need to divert eyes to the ground – I concentrated on the land around me. There was something else I had forgotten: the extraordinary nature of this wild pursuit. Clouds were fidgety and low, the wind brisk. I would stand here countless times again: at sunrise and sunset, in mist and rain, in the cocoon of night, but this – the first time on Allermuir – could not be outdone. Transported back to the moment I stood on the apex of Geal-charn, I felt as I had then: as if in love, suspended in disbelief, incredulous that I had been all the way down there not very long ago and now I was all the way up here. Allermuir stood at the centre of the universe: a vision of hill, moor, sea, firth and city. The names of the places were incidental. I perhaps thought as Robert Louis Stevenson, the Edinburgh-born writer whose family leased a cottage in Swanston, had once done. Writing in Samoa, he conjured up a vision of his spiritual home: 'The tropics vanish: and meseems that I – from Halkerside, from topmost Allermuir, or steep Caerketton – dreaming – gaze again.' As I ran across the ridge to Caerketton, the setting sun was ablaze, blanching mountains in the faraway west in a red halo.

The essence of Nick Hornby's biographical *Fever Pitch* is that Arsenal Football Club is the author's constant in life. Amid the flux of education, work and relationships, happiness, sadness and indifference, Arsenal and football remain resilient to the vagaries of Hornby's being. Come what may, for Hornby, it is Arsenal yesterday, Arsenal today and Arsenal tomorrow. The affection is timeless and unconditional.

Running is my thread, my Arsenal. The sport links a scrawny, unknowing twelve-year-old boy on a cross-country course in Worcestershire to a husband and father on the run I will do tomorrow. Naturally, the business of life intervenes. Running has at times been pivotal; at other moments peripheral. But the thread – at times twisted and stretched, tense and ravelled – endures.

The snarliest knot in that thread coincided with children. Six weeks of two-hourly Thursday night sessions – with twitchy-eyed Christine from the National Childbirth Trust explaining mucus caps and episiotomy – had not prepared Fi and me for the birth of Arielle. During the first session, the couples were handed images of new-born babies, some still decorated in the blood of childbirth. 'What are you thinking?' Christine gently asked.

'I'm thinking …' Fi paused, framing a statement as a question. 'It looks disgusting?'

Our baby was not 'disgusting', but the rhythm of our individual and mutual lives, something we had moulded over many years, was destroyed in an early morning in a maternity ward overlooking Westminster Bridge. Our first week as parents was spent in a near-delirious trance. Looking back, we were undoubtedly in a state of shock. We were not sleeping, of course, and a cold that had lingered in the fortnight before Arielle's birth overwhelmed me, becoming glandular fever.

Something had to give. I stopped running.

Even at three months, Arielle preferred nocturnal living. One night – a night that was probably no worse than many others – was, on reflection, a psychological turning point. I wrote in a diary: 'I struggle for one all-defining adjective as every day the reality of being a parent is shaped differently. Compromise is the great battle. Where do my priorities lie? With my baby? She comes first, not some inconsequential trip to the track or a ten-mile run. But in giving Arielle life, has something in us died? No parent should feel guilty about maintaining a sense of independence, should they? Yet I feel ashamed for even intimating that my personal pursuits might – for some minutes or hours of a day – be more important than the upbringing of my daughter.'

Tentatively, I started running again. The knot loosened.

It is not always like this. Sam Hesling would be the runner-up in the Carnethy 5 hill race in the Pentlands a fortnight after becoming a father for the first time. Having had the 'race of his life', moving from fifth to first in the descent of the final hill, he was beaten by a second in a sprint finish. 'How are you finding it?' I had asked Sam, grimacing, offering the sympathetic face of a man who knows.

He seemed surprised by the question. 'Good,' he nodded. Better than 'good'; he was inspired. 'It's made me more deter-mined – determined for her to see me race at the highest level I can. I want her to remember her dad doing well. I don't want her to think her dad is a big idiot!' The words I had written years earlier jolted me again. Sam and I, we would run on.

Ramsay's Round was a blurry proposition in London. The quest was an exotic journey in a foreign, far-off, snow-capped land. The mountains surely belonged to fiction. I gazed meta-phorically at those high places through a rose-tinted prism, envisaging the day I might leap heroically from summit to summit under a brilliant sky. The statistics – the distance, the up, the down, the time – were too incomprehensible to be important. But then, in Edinburgh, the round possessed proximity and context. When the wind blew hard on the 164-metre summit of Blackford Hill, when I could scarcely stand against its ferocity and had to retreat to sheltered ground, I imagined what it was like at that moment on Ben Nevis or Beinn na Lap or Binnein Beag. Terrible, I knew.

But that did not stop me from taking the Road to Swanston.

I could reach Braidburn Valley Park, a neat, green valley split by a stream amid Edinburgh's prosperous southern fringe, within a half-mile of home. I entered via an alley called the Fly Walk and turned right onto the crest of a bank of grass, a century-and-a-half after Stevenson trod this way. Born into the family of lighthouse engineers in 1850, Stevenson found his light in words: he had written *Treasure Island*, *Kidnapped* and *The Strange Case of Dr Jekyll and Mr Hyde* by his mid-thirties. Aged forty-four, he was living in the Pacific and opening a wine bottle when he cried out: 'What's that?' He then asked his American wife Fanny if his face looked 'strange'. Hours later, having been overcome by a stroke, he was dead. Stevenson was buried on top of a hill above the ocean. The height of Mount Vaea is almost identical to that of Allermuir and Caerketton, the hills overlooking the Forth. Presumably, Stevenson – an atheist who did not want to 'live a life as one falsehood' – had no need to go higher.

Stevenson was no hill runner. His prodigious talents did not stretch that far. Not that such a pursuit would have crossed his mind. In Stevenson's lifetime, running up hills in Scotland was not a done thing, certainly not in the recreational sense. Queen Victoria had helped see to that. It was not until 1895 – a year after the novelist's death – that a man timed himself in a run from Fort William to the summit of Ben Nevis and back. On a day 'exceedingly hot and unsuitable for mountaineering', according to the *Inverness Courier*, William Swan, a hairdresser and tobacconist who would pause for a cup of Bovril at the top, completed his run in 2 hours and 41 minutes.

Paradoxically, the words of a non-runner writing in a world before hill running offer an impeccable summary of the sport.

Kidnapped is set in the aftermath of the Jacobite Risings in the mid-eighteenth century. Accused of being an accomplice in the murder of Colin Roy Campbell of Glenure and pursued by Redcoats, David Balfour, accompanied by Alan Breck Stewart, 'set off running along the side of the mountain towards Ballachulish'. David, narrating, breathlessly recounts his run: 'Now we ran among the birches; now stooping behind low humps upon the mountainside; now crawling on all fours among the heather. The pace was deadly; my heart seemed bursting against my ribs; and I had neither time to think nor breath to speak with.' The frantic episode concludes with a list of familiar sensations: 'My own sides so ached, my head so swam, my tongue so hung out of my mouth with heat and dryness, that I lay beside him like one dead.'

Having cut through the park, I would follow a path signposted 'Robert Louis Stevenson's Road to Swanston and the Pentlands'. I travelled the way Stevenson went on his journey from Auld Reekie to his holiday home, up a broad ramp of grass and along an ever-rising track that today borders back gardens and a school, past metre-high graffiti on the harling wall of a garage declaring BAN NUKES, and onward to Swanston. The description of his journey along what Stevenson knew as Cockmylane is immortalised on the wall of Swanston Brasserie, close to his family retreat: 'A bouquet of old trees stands round a white farmhouse and from a neighbouring dell, you can see smoke rising and leaves ruffling in the breeze. Straight above, the hills climb a thousand feet into the air. The neighbourhood, about the time of lambs, is clamorous with the bleating of flocks; and you will be awakened, in the grey of early summer mornings, by the barking of a dog or the voice of a shepherd shouting to the echoes. This, with the hamlet lying behind unseen, is Swanston.' Stevenson was home.

In a way, I was too. In a little over two miles, like Stevenson, I was in the Pentlands, moving upward. And this much I knew: if I wanted to run Ramsay's Round, I needed to take the Road to Swanston.

I did, again and again, and – as things do when you persevere
– the road became easier. Having followed Cockmylane one
Sunday, I reached the point at which I had resorted to walking
on my first ascent of Allermuir, and every subsequent visit
thereafter. Because I had stopped here once, it was instinctive to
break the pattern again. This time, I told myself, I will carry on
running for a little longer, even if it is just a dozen steps. Once
I reached the top of the rollercoaster track, the gradient eased
considerably and there was no longer an alternative: the going
was still up, but not enough to justify walking. I ran every step to
the summit. Pausing only to lay a hand on the cold metal of the
toposcope, I set off to Capelaw, running all the way. I turned at
the post on the highest point, noting how tempting Castlelaw,
a mile to the south-east and illuminated by god-rays, appeared,
and ran there too, the final climb a slimy, rain-eroded stripe
through heather. Then I ran all the way home: every step on the
bank of Allermuir, reversing the Road to Swanston, into the
twinkling embrace of a city. The Pentlands would, of course,
reduce me to a walk again – many, many times – but I was not
here to conquer hills; I was here to conquer myself.

A balmy September gave way to the realism of October.
Night, creeping inexorably forward, gobbled day. A long
winter was coming. But the hills still beckoned. It was dark
when I parked at Swanston and ran into the woods. For the first
time, I was conscious of the gushing roll of the invisible burn
and the rushing of leaves that clung hopelessly to branches
until the sounds became inseparable. My existence withered
to the dancing train of torch light. The rest was shadow. I
slipped through the empty village and up the gravel, with the
dim outline of Caerketton rising ahead. The bolt of the gate
snapped shut in an ugly clack – a noise I must have heard a
dozen times, but like the burn and the leaves, it seemed like
the first. Twice I looked back, shining the torch down the
track, expecting to see something following, dwelling on the
'fiendish noises' Stevenson said characterised 'lone places on
the hills' at night.

I climbed higher, stalked by the fear of I-do-not-know-what, glancing occasionally at a smudged moon. Night was still and poised. As I raised my head, propelling a beam of light across the rising ground, picking out long grass and tussock, the torch caught a slumped, rectangular shape, like a glacial boulder – an obstacle I had not encountered here before. There was a further stone to the right, another behind. A moment of trembling dread. Trepidation had found its physical manifestation.

But then: relief. Cows, I realised. Lying down cows. Just cows.

Such was the motivation of paranoia's tentacles, I seemed to float up Allermuir. As I stepped onto the last rise, placing my feet in the grooves of those who had been here before, I saw a clutch of bent-over figures, then – as I looked more closely – there were many more, perhaps twenty of them, all apparently men, silent and focused. They ignored me, as if I was some phantom or a figment of their imagination. The army, it seemed, had use for the hills at night as much as the runner.

I was going west, on the slushy plateau of Capelaw, when my attention was grabbed so violently it was as if one of the men had struck me in the ribs. My torch trapped the glare of what appeared to be numerous pairs of tiny lights, shining sharply, hovering a few inches above the ground. Soldiers, I decided. What else? Hundreds of them, crawling through the grass – and I have run headlong into a manoeuvre. I could see them in my mind's eye, wriggling forward, propelling themselves on elbows, only for a hill runner to appear in their midst. One of the nearest pairs lifted and shifted, and seemed to disappear. I heard the undergrowth rustle and I breathed easily again. Sheep.

Moving up and down Allermuir, and out and back to Capelaw, kept Edinburgh on a shoulder, a comforting presence of sprawling radiance. As I progressed to Castlelaw, the city vanished behind the hills, but gradually, a pulsating high emerged from the tangle of imagination. Being temporarily purged of fear was a delicate state. The baleful sound of the wind rattling the rope on the flagpole atop Castlelaw reignited a dread I could not extinguish and I ran furiously for Swanston.

Like swimming in the sea, I would never get used to the unknown depths that darkness presented, never quite get over the worry of what might be out there. As winter gripped Edinburgh, I stood on the icy rim of Caerketton, pointing a camera along the murky ridge to Allermuir. The flash momentarily revealed some apparently hideous shape. I descended immediately. Another time – in the search for altitude gain in as little time as possible – I was on a second consecutive climb of Allermuir when I spotted the prick of torch light rising to meet me. As our paths crossed, I greeted the runner. The hooded man, wordless and morose, stared quietly ahead, as if I had not existed, continuing his apparent journey to the summit. I abandoned a third climb.

The Pentland Skyline, a 17-mile horseshoe along the broad-backed ridges of the northerly range, begins like a hill race should. Starting from a slope adjacent to the ski area, runners are immediately sent trotting on their toes up a triangle of grass, the first steps of an unremitting climb to Caerketton. The qualities that make Scottish hill running especially hard – gradient, vegetation, rubble and risk – are of less significance here. In benign weather, the ridges of the Pentlands are safe and wide, and even in October, when the race is traditionally held, much of the terrain is perfectly runnable. Such runnability comes at a cost: the racing is fast and furious. I clock the fourth mile, albeit dropping from Castlelaw on a military road of loose stone, at five minutes and 59 seconds. At the time, Murray Strain held a course record that was 20 seconds per mile faster than any other finisher in the race's history. Strain had averaged eight-minute miles for a course that includes a cumulative ascent of Ben Nevis with Arthur's Seat perched on its rugged shoulders.

More than half of the route has been run when the racing line swings north across a rougher, less-frequented western ridge. This is where the Pentland Skyline infamously 'gets you'. Hare Hill comes first, with its descent on pathless moor, then

Black Hill, a sprawling bulge clothed in heather and dotted with peat hags. By now, racers are straggled across the hills, gaps growing to several minutes. You could easily assume you are alone. I run in unison with another. When I break into a walk, he walks. When I recommence running, he runs. It is a peculiar dynamic. I give the green light for submission. He willingly submits. We trundle up Black Hill, catching a glimpse of blue and yellow ahead. The runner, Oleg Chepelin, is a previous winner of the race. Head slumped and feet dragging, he mutters something indecipherable as we pass.

Runners in the Lake District speak reverently of the moment they glimpse Joss Naylor on the fells. To be acknowledged by Joss – a simple nod or a 'come on, lad' – is to be welcomed into the fell running fraternity. Joss is not waiting for us on the steepest section of Bell's Hill; Charlie Ramsay is. 'Charlie Ramsay!' I exclaim. He nods.

As we near the top, we catch another: Jon Gay, the first to run what had once seemed unattainable – a winter Ramsay's Round within 24 hours. First Chepelin, then Gay. I suppose they would be scalps in road running or cross-country. Not in the hills. Their suffering was a cause for humility, for it was the Pentlands doing the vanquishing, not us. Besides, it would soon be my turn. As we move onto Capelaw, my hour-long ally opens a small gap. He glances back, then seems to lift his knees a little higher in response to whatever he had seen in my eyes. In a moment, I am dropped.

As I descend Caerketton, I fleetingly take my eye from the furrow of the path and glimpse the curve of the ski slope. I know the finish is very close. I long to be there, to be able to cease movement, to be able to sit down. But I am checked by a memory, a recollection from my earliest days in Edinburgh.

I am running down a hill, a 430-million-year-old hill.

I am running down a hill and Edinburgh, Stevenson's precipitous city, is at my feet.

And I can breathe.

8

RUNNING FOREVER

Colin Donnelly cannot believe his eyes. The runner in front is inexorably slowing. His legs are faltering. Step by step, Colin is catching the leader. The gap narrows and slams shut. They run shoulder to shoulder. Colin glances sideways at his rival – and accelerates. He looks back. He is clear. There is no second wind from the man now in second. Colin leaves the road and careers into the finish area, surging around a grass track. The crowd clap and cheer – they have not seen a Scotsman win here for eleven years – but wonder, who is this – *boy?* He breaks the tape. Moments after, he is photographed. Staring ahead, Colin is dazed and bewildered, and in pain. His feet would later be treated for bad blistering. Two dignitaries appear to be holding him up, with Colin oblivious to their presence. The truth begins to sink in: scarcely a year out of school and still a teenager, he has won the greatest prize in British hill running. He joins the ranks of immortals. He is a champion of Ben Nevis.

To win Ben Nevis is to take a seat among hill running royalty: Eddie Campbell, who prevailed three times in the 1950s; five-time 1970s conqueror Dave Cannon; Bob Graham record holder Billy Bland; mountain running's greatest rivals, Kenny Stuart and John Wild; Pauline Stuart, the fastest woman; Rob Jebb who won four, Angela Mudge five, Ian Holmes six, Ros Evans seven; Finlay Wild, the monarch of the glen, the undisputed king of the Ben.

The race is the purest in Britain: a straight up, straight

down, no-nonsense affair, beginning from virtually sea level, climbing – as Charles Steel noted in his one shilling, 1956 short history *The Ben Nevis Race* – 'to the highest point in Her Majesty's British Islands.' This is Ben Nevis: the magnet to 200,000 visitors every year; the mountain every British school child can name; 'arguably the most dangerous mountain in Europe,' according to Hugh Dan MacLennan, the race's biographer.

Starting from the grass of Claggan Park, runners dash along a mile of road before joining the tourist track that skirts Meall an t-Suidhe as it rises above Glen Nevis. The race leaves the pony track at Red Burn, the watercourse that drains the western aspect of the Ben, to climb steep, bare slopes of rock. It is interminable. 'Strength of muscle and physical endurance are qualities which seldom fail to call forth admiration; but when these are employed in foolhardy and dangerous exploits, their possessor is surely acting in opposition to the laws of nature,' wrote William Kilgour after witnessing William Swan's timed run in 1895. Kilgour had a point. From Claggan Park to the summit, Finlay Wild will typically take around an hour to run four-and-a-half miles of continuous uphill. After passing Red Burn, the last mile-and-a-half to the summit climbs at an average gradient of almost 30 per cent. 'Foolhardy ... dangerous ... in opposition to the laws of nature.' You bet it is.

Only the summit plateau, yards from the cliffs of the sheer north face, offers a short respite from remorseless ascent. Relieved to have made it this far, you might relax for a moment – a time ripe for spraining an ankle in the litter of rocks. Ben Nevis never gets easier; it just gets a little less hard. Nor is there a moment to appreciate the view, even if there is one. Very soon, you are going down – and the real suffering begins. After I raced at Ben Nevis for the first time, Steven McIntyre, an Inverness Harriers clubmate, removed his shoes in Claggan Park to reveal the skin on both heels had blistered, then detached from his feet, like slices of cheese being removed from a block. He cut away the skin, enough to cover an apple, and dressed his feet. Later that day, he would begin a 13-hour shift in his job as an operating theatre technician. 'Just for a laugh,' he told me years later, 'I sent my brother in Glasgow the dead heel skin in the post. He said he was going to send it on to one of his friends, and they would keep it going. I don't know where my heels are now.'

It was late August in 1979 when Colin Donnelly came to Fort William. He was on the cusp of beginning his second year of study at Aberdeen University. He had climbed the Ben once before – as a walker aged twelve with his father. On the Thursday before the race, he asked Lochaber runner Ronnie 'Cammy' Campbell to show him the course. Campbell pointed out some 'short cuts', but the mountain remained a virtual stranger.

The precocious teenager led a field of 365 at the summit, but he knew what was to come. Not far behind the Scotsman were two Englishmen, Billy Bland and Brian Robinson. The former had won the previous year's race in what was then the second fastest time. Sure enough, Robinson first, then Bland, edged by on the descent. Although relegated to third, Colin was content: 'I didn't feel any pressure because I thought, Billy's here, Robinson's here, there's plenty of people who can beat me. I'm not going to win. If I get in the top four or five, that's fine, that's all I'm looking for.'

Having nipped in front of Robinson where the route momentarily climbs from a burn, Bland was racing down the tourist track when disaster struck: he slipped on an aluminium bridge, gashing an arm so severely it would require fourteen stitches at Belford Hospital in Fort William. Colin, inadvertently elevated to second, ran on, down the tourist track. Robinson had been a 'good way ahead' at Red Burn, but the chaser 'really started to shift', wrote Roger Boswell in *The Fellrunner*. Down the path, unbeknown to Colin, Robinson, like many others in the humid conditions, was wilting.

'A lot of people are going strong until they hit that road, and then their legs just go,' Colin says, 'and that's what happened to Brian. I thought, hang on a minute, what's going on here? I'm catching up. He's not going very fast. I overtook him.'

Boswell noted, creating a new word in the process: 'Robinson had no reply to Donnelly's pace on that tarmackiller mile, conceding over a minute.'

'It's like you are in a position of disbelief,' says Colin. 'I shouldn't be here. I'm not expecting to be at the front. The Ben Nevis Race.' His pitch rises with relived excitement. 'It's legendary. I'm in front. That was some feeling, one of the best feelings I've ever had in my life.'

Colin did not get the chance to defend his crown in 1980; the race was cancelled for the first and only time. The start had been delayed for thirty minutes – even though the runners had already been piped to the start – when referee Tom Mackenzie made an historic announcement: 'The police and medical authorities, taking note of conditions on the hill as reported by the mountain rescue, advise us that anyone getting into difficulties would be dead within twenty-five minutes. Gentlemen, we cannot take that chance with your lives. The 1980 Ben Nevis Race is cancelled.' In addressing the 'gentlemen', Mackenzie had overlooked the female runners – fourteen of them – who were among the field, two years before they were even allowed to be 'official' competitors.

'They were quite right to call it off,' Colin said in the aftermath. 'I am sure there would have been broken limbs.'

Not everyone agreed, notably Billy Bland: 'They should have advised us of the situation and left it to us.' In protest, Eddie Campbell and eight others ran the race route anyway, reaching the top and reporting conditions as 'flat calm' – effectively demonstrating how understatement in the face of adversity and reason is an essential quality of the hill runner.

Colin Donnelly grew up a 'typical Glasgow teenager' in the suburb of Newton Mearns, playing football at school and supporting Celtic, although his secondary education was spent away at a Dumfries boarding school. Having started running to keep fit, Colin realised he had found his calling. 'When I started to do it regularly – because people didn't in those days – I began to win things and do well. I remember winning a county cross-country and thinking, I am not super-duper, I am just one of those people who probably trains three or four times a week.' As a novice runner with 'lots of raw talent', he would later join Cambuslang Harriers, winning the Galloway and Renfrewshire Schools under-19 cross-country championship.

Even as a teenager, Colin did not like being told what to do. 'They were trying to push me onto the track when I was a youngster. I had heard about a race on Ben Lomond and I thought, if I tell them I'm doing that, I'll get out of this bloody track race. I don't like track races, never have.' For a moment, he sounds like Finlay Wild: 'What's the point in doing something you don't enjoy?'

Unwittingly, Colin made a life-changing decision. Others, at that age, would have bowed to the pressure of their coaches. Not Colin. He went to Ben Lomond. 'The heart wanted me to do it,' he says. Aged 17, he 'got in under-the-radar'; by the letter of the law he should not have been allowed to compete. He came 22nd, but position was incidental – it was Colin's epiphany. 'I loved the descent – out of control, and you're just holding it there,' he says.

When Colin finished school that summer, he began searching for a waiting job to fill the gap before the onslaught of university. The main criterion was easily established: the position must be in the mountains. 'It had to be a hotel near some three-thousanders, ideally at the foot of a three-thousander,' Colin remembers. 'I wrote away to about twenty or thirty hotels in the Highlands.' Only one – the Ledgowan Lodge Hotel at Achnasheen – responded with a firm job offer.

There is little to Achnasheen: a cluster of houses, some tourist shops, a railway station. Lying exposed in its valley, the village's Gaelic translation is 'field of storms'. Here, three

roads diverge at a roundabout: north to Kinlochewe, west to
Kyle of Lochalsh and Skye, and east to Inverness. The geography of the village meant Colin was driven to the mountains
by necessity. Achnasheen is not a place of pavements and
paths. 'I don't like running along car-filled roads,' he says.
Cross-country in its traditional sense was not possible either.
'You go off the road and you're into bog and heather and hill.'
Despite his performance at Ben Lomond, Colin still did not
identify himself as a hill runner. His 'regime' at that time was
to run cross-country and hillwalk on alternate days. 'I had
always thought, what if you could combine the two: forget
your hillwalking and do it as a run?'

Fionn Bheinn, a lone outlier of the Fannich range, is the
closest Munro to Achnasheen. 'I liked the idea of getting up
that one, but I had to work my way up,' Colin says. 'I went
up to about 700 metres. There was a wee flat bit and I would
have a rest, and eventually I thought, ah, I can tackle the whole
thing. I used to be puffing and panting, and I was getting my
ankles used to the rougher ground. Eventually, after maybe
a month, I was getting to the top, and I thought, right, that's
great, I've got the hang of this now. This hill running lark is
great fun.'

The following year, 1978, would be Colin's breakthrough,
starting with a third-place finish at Ben Lomond. 'There were
all these top blokes in Britain and they were going, "who's
this guy? We've never heard of this one." I was surprised as
well. I didn't expect to be up there. I thought, what am I doing
up near the front?'

It was no fluke. Colin went on to win the Manx Mountain
Marathon on the Isle of Man and came second in the Three
Peaks Race, but the summer was also spent 'exploring'. He was
in the Highlands again, running and walking in the Fannichs
and Torridon. His pursuits in those months of freedom, even
as an eighteen-year-old, defined how Colin would spend his
existence. He would work to live. He would race and win,
but nothing would be more important than simply being out

there, being in the hills – and so the mountains and wilderness of Scotland became his life-force.

That explains what happened to Colin in the early 1980s: quite literally his wilderness years. He focused on long, multi-summit expeditions. 'As much as I liked hill racing, I was more interested in exploring places, doing big rounds, big runs in the hills, bagging peaks, doing Wainwrights, Corbetts and Munros,' he says. The period is perhaps best characterised by a journey linking the 129 summits over 2,000 feet (610 metres) in the Southern Uplands. In the spring of 1981, Colin ran for eleven days, covering 380 miles, climbing 25,000 metres. After five days, he reached Talla Reservoir in the Tweedsmuir Hills in a state of physical and emotional capitulation. 'Mentally, I couldn't face going up Broad Law the next day. I went home to Glasgow, came back the following day, felt rejuvenated, and finished the other tops. It was just an adventure, really.' Adventures are what Colin does best. A year earlier, he ran the fastest known traverse of the Mamores, and might have broken the seven-hour mark had he not been 'held for several minutes on Na Gruagaichean, simply captivated by the view down Loch Leven'.

As he did on the hills, Colin drifted in life. After university, he spent two years unemployed, albeit doing seasonal and temporary work, including a stint as a stalking ghillie on the Attadale Estate in the north-west Highlands. 'Running around the hills all day? It was my dream job,' he laughs. He applied to be a radio operator with the RAF – and failed. He would eventually find a future with the RAF, however, working in the force's stores, distributing everything from clothes to fuel, and in 1984, Colin was posted to RAF Valley in Anglesey, becoming Senior Aircraftman Donnelly.

As he began to explore the running possibilities in North Wales, it was Colin's girlfriend and later first wife, Angela Carson, who encouraged him to race. 'She kept badgering me, telling me to do more races. I wasn't interested. "You go off and do your race, Angela," I'd say, "and while we're here, I'll go off and do this big round and bag some hills." She nagged and nagged, insisting I should go for the British championship.' Finally, Colin agreed, ran the designated races, and came second in 1986, just four points shy of Jack Maitland. Angela encouraged him. "You've done that and you were a wee bit half-hearted," she told me. "If you put your mind to it, you could win the British championship." So, I thought, I probably can.'

That year, Colin returned to Ben Nevis for the first time since 1980. Gone was the teenage naivety. He exuded swagger. 'I was very fit and I didn't have any trouble,' he says. 'It didn't daunt me at all.' Third at the summit, he won in 1 hour, 25 minutes and 48 seconds – still the third quickest time on record, 14 seconds slower than Kenny Stuart's record and 13 seconds adrift of John Wild's 1985 mark. 'I could have got that record. When I hit the road, it would've been nice if someone had said, "Colin, keep going at a bloody good pace and that record's yours." I think I was outside the stadium when somebody shouted, "you're quite close to the record." Well, it was too late by then. With 400 yards of track, you're not going to make it up.'

An injury sustained while cross-country skiing forced Colin to sit out the first two races of the 1987 championship, but he was third on his comeback at Ennerdale in the Lake District. The fourth championship race, Y Garn in North Wales, came a week later. 'I remember turning up and Angela saying, "Colin, if you don't beat this Malcolm Patterson, you won't win the championship." Oh, right, I hadn't thought about that. I suppose I should beat him. I ran my arse off and did beat him.'

Writing in *Athlete*, the journal of the RAF Athletics Association, Colin recounted his battle with Patterson. 'I was having trouble gaining the lead – as soon as it was mine, stubborn Malcolm Patterson would surge and claim it back. My legs felt so heavy after the descent. Malcolm's must have been heavier. His unsteady legs lost a tussle with a boulder and he

hit the ground in a welter of unprintables.' Colin then won
the Moffat Chase in July and Moel Hebog in August, both in
course record times. The final race revealed a canny side to the
Scot. Even though he had only to finish in the top five at Moel
Hebog to win the championship, he outmanoeuvred Rod
Pilbeam. The pair were at the head of the race when Colin
veered away from the path to follow a reconnoitred 'short
cut'. Pilbeam followed. 'Much of this involved clambering
up boulder fields on which I noticed Rod was unhappy. So I
forsook grassy ramps for as much rock and boulders as I could
find, adding in some wet, slimy slabs for good measure. Rod
didn't know the mountain. We were off the main route. His
hands were tied: no matter how much he disliked the ground,
he had to follow me. By the summit, my lead was sufficient to
allow me to relax on the descent.'

Angela deserves the credit for his success, Colin insists. 'She
was mentoring me in a way. Without realising it, she was
guiding me and got me into the idea of bagging titles. I'm not
really into titles, you know. A lot of people are into titles. For
me, it's no big deal.' The man uninterested in titles would
win three British championships, adding the 1988 and 1989
crowns to clinch three-in-a-row. 'By the time I got to the third
or fourth year, I was finding them quite addictive, and I was
thinking, I like this winning thing. It's quite an ego trip when
you're winning races. I was at my fittest in 1989, when I was
going to races and not bothered because I knew I would win
them. The only thing that bothered me was getting the record.
I did get quite a few records that year.'

Appropriately, Colin's most famous record came in a
long-distance challenge, not a race. There was no hanging
around to survey the aspect as he had on the Mamores when
he traversed the 15 Snowdonia summits over 3,000 feet in
1988. The clock, starting on Snowdon, and stopping at the
top of Foel-fras 24 miles later, read 4 hours and 19 minutes.
Innumerable adjectives have been attached to this unsurpassed
achievement – 'astonishing' seems apposite.

Some things cannot be removed: the 'typical Glasgow teenager' had three British championships. But it should have been four, he maintains. Despite starting nursing training in 1989, consequently 'catching everything under the sun', Colin was on course to win another title in 1990. The final race of the championship was Ben Nevis. What a story it would be: Colin would win a remarkable quartet on the Ben, the race in which he first triumphed as a teenager. 'I wrote away for a place and they said it was full, and you can't get in. This was May or something. I thought, it's a British championship race; if I don't do Ben Nevis, I won't count.' Colin was not alone. Some 60 others had also entered after the organiser's limit of 500 was reached. 'Emergency meetings were held,' reported *The Fellrunner*, 'but concluded nothing could be done.' The bitterness and frustration remains today, almost 30 years on: there was no place for the youngest winner, the two-time winner, the third fastest winner. 'What Lochaber should have done is put on an alternative Ben Nevis race, with a half-price entry fee. I think they would have elbowed that event out the way,' he says. 'I only needed to finish in the top 12 to win the championship.' Mark Rigby won the race. Gary Devine, in third, won the championship. Colin – who would later spend eight years living and working in Fort William, looking up at Ben Nevis every day – would never run the race again in defiant protest. Nor would he be British champion again.

I arrange to meet Colin at his home in Hawick, the knitwear and cashmere town of the Borders. The exterior walls of the building are piled high with chopped wood, seemingly enough to survive a nuclear winter. When he answers the door, Colin glances at me shyly, as if he had not expected this intrusion. A handshake is awkwardly executed. An ice-breaker is arranged: we are going for a run. The start is two miles away, and – to avoid even a moment of road running; he would later tell me that 'roads are for tyres' – we are to cycle there. We pedal along Wilton Glen, Colin leading the way. With a three-decades-old blue Reebok jacket that covers his shorts, he appears to be wearing a mini skirt pinched to his saddle. At one point, he swerves onto the pavement. Fastidiously, I ignore him, staying on the road. An oncoming motorist passes me, shouting out of the open window: 'This is a one-way street, you idiot.'

We stop by a farm and leave our bicycles in a layby of rusting machinery. The pace is easy as we follow a rising track, then cross a fence into a field of grazing cattle. The next hour is a joy. We wander through undulating fields of long grass, following faint paths. We stop at the highest point of a moor. The view, from scarcely 300 metres above sea level, is unbroken. He leads me around the 360 degrees, identifying every lump and mark on the horizon. 'You can see why the English and Scots fought over this,' he says. We continue, up a grassy incline to the summit of Wiltonburn Hill, sheep scattering left and right. Running side by side, as Colin had once been with Brian Robinson, he is fractionally ahead. And like he had done to Robinson, I knew that even at the age of fifty-six, if he wanted, he could drop me in an instant.

Back in Hawick, Colin hands me a mug of boiling water adorned with a chunk of bobbing ginger. He slides two slices of iced ginger cake on the living room table. We sit on a sofa, facing a large window overlooking the town. I glance around the room. He senses my thoughts: 'It's bothy-like, isn't it? I like it simple.' A set of shelves carries mementoes of his travels: a twisted piece of bark, a fir cone, river-smoothed wood. The walls are adorned with paintings, predominately of North Wales mountainscapes, although there is a picture of Ben Nevis above a fireplace. There are trophies and medals everywhere. Next door, a four-shelf cabinet is brimming with silver, and is simply not big enough to hold everything. On a table by the front door, there are piles of *The Scots Magazine* dating back to the 1980s.

Sitting next to Colin, he seems smaller than he had been when we were running, but I realise Colin Donnelly grows when he goes to the hills. I imagine him running up 129 mountains in eleven days; I imagine him charging down the scree of the Ben; I imagine him leading a perplexed Rod Pilbeam across the slabs of Moel Hebog. For a moment, I am awestruck.

Colin once said in an interview he sought to climb a cumulative 365,000 feet every year. The maths is staggering. That figure (or 110,000 metres) amounts to 9,200 metres every month or 300 metres per day. 'Is that true?' I ask.

He nodded. 'The whole idea is to get 1,000 feet (300 metres) a day. For the last few years, I haven't managed it because of injuries, but before that I was managing no problem. Maybe for twenty-odd years I did. I still keep logs of how much ascent I have done and there have been years when I have been well over 400,000 and getting towards 500,000.' Half a million feet. That is Claggan Park to the summit of Ben Nevis 114 times.

'It's good to have a background of doing big, long stamina runs ...' He trails off. Nicole, his girlfriend, has arrived. Her three dogs, mini long-haired dachshunds, all gasping on their leads, skitter into the room. 'I'm not a dog person,' Colin says, 'but I like these ones.'

'They wanted to see you,' Nicole says, backing out of the door, ushering the dogs away.

Colin's focus instantly snaps back to running. He goes on, as if the conversation has not been broken: 'You've got to spend time in the hills. All day out of the bothy after a big fry up, running over hills, covering a huge number of miles, back to the bothy, barely able to walk, stumbling, absolutely shattered after a day pushing myself over rough terrain for miles. After a week like that, I'd be whacked, but two weeks later I'd suddenly notice the benefit, and run fantastically well.'

It worked for Colin, but there were exceptions, he says. 'You know John Wild? One of the top guys ever in hill running. John never trained in the hills except if he was looking at a course. The likes of John Wild, Kenny Stuart, a lot of them who have done well, were speedy. Kenny was a top-notch marathon runner and John a fantastic cross-country runner.

He would have been under 50 minutes for ten miles, I'm sure; he did a lot of road running as well. These guys built their speed up, and if you've got speed, you can do hills. You've got to have a mixture of the two. It is advantageous to spend time in the hills, but I would do that anyway because I love them. Nicole lives in Lincolnshire. I could never live in Lincolnshire. I'd be driven demented. The highest point in the Wolds is 400 feet. I've been telling her, the bothies we've been staying at are 400 metres.'

We went back to the 1990s and I could hear the disenchantment in his voice again. 'I had proved myself, winning three times, and being deprived of four. I was a bit disillusioned with the Fell Runners Association about that and I thought, why should I support their championship? I'm going to do the races I like doing, and ever since then I've done that.'

There is symmetry in the Colin of the early 1980s to the Colin of the early 1990s: a decade older, but the same man. He turned his attention to the classic rounds. He did the Paddy Buckley first, travelling solo and unsupported in 1990, becoming the 18th person to complete. He did a Bob Graham on a whim. After working on cardiac arrest procedures on a Friday morning in 1991, then going for a five-mile lunchtime run, he decided to drive to the Lake District that night. Once again running alone, he ran down Skiddaw, the final hill in an anticlockwise direction, in 'shrieking winds and heavy rain'. The stringent rules of the Bob Graham 24-Hour Club, demanding that an applicant must have a witness at each of the 42 summits, means Colin is absent from the official list of completions. He does not care. The Bob Graham, once under his skin, was extricated, as satisfying as eliminating a skelf.

Colin saved 'the best' – Ramsay's Round – for last. On holiday in Orkney in 1995, he woke to one of those days when the hill runner will look to the sky and lament they are not somewhere else, for if there is a long day in the hills on their mind, they will only see a lost chance. Afraid of just that, Colin went to Fort William. It was not a vintage performance: his head torch conked out on the Mamores; he climbed Stob a' Choire Mheadhoin wearing a balaclava to protect his already-burnt scalp from the sun; once off the snow of Ben Nevis, he descended with the 'speed of a granny in high heels'. He ended a pithy report with words that could be the inscription on his grave: 'No fanfares, no fuss. Perhaps how these things should be done; just for the challenge.'

Colin could turn his back on championships and the Fell Runners Association, but never Scotland. An unashamed nationalist, he represented his country in 18 consecutive World Mountain Running Trophy races between 1985 and 2002, with a nineteenth appearance in 2004. The individual peak came almost inevitably in 1989, when he won an individual silver medal in the short race at Châtillon-en-Diois in south-eastern France. But the emotional summit was in Auld Reekie in 1995, when Colin was the third finisher in a four-man Scottish team that won team silver on Arthur's Seat. 'Running for the Scotland team on home territory in Edinburgh – it's the same feeling of wellbeing I got when I blundered into first place at Ben Nevis in 1979, when I didn't expect to be there, and the pipes were striking up, and I was running into the stadium,' he explains. 'We did our country proud that day. Scotland at football are always promising big and never delivering, but that day the Scottish hill running team produced the goods.'

In 1999, Colin turned 40. By the same age, Billy Bland had retired; Colin kept running and kept triumphing. In 2001, he won the over-40 category in the World Mountain Running Championship in Poland; he was third in the same race in 2002, this time in Austria, and then second in the over-45 group in 2005 when Keswick hosted the event. He continued to clean up in Scotland, winning everywhere he went: Ben Rinnes, Creag Dhubh, Two Breweries, Knockfarrel, Norman's Law. If he did not win, he was scarcely out of the top ten. A week before we met, he won the Oxton Border Games race; a fortnight later, he was first at Philiphaugh.

Mark Hartree remembers meeting Colin in 1985. Mark was a member of RAF Valley Mountain Rescue Service and Colin was sent to his group for a weekend trial. 'He was just a boy,' Mark said; even though Colin was the older of the pair, rank meant more than years. Staying at Llanbedr, they were spending the night in neighbouring beds. Rising before breakfast, Colin ran a fifteen-mile round-trip along the coast to Barmouth. Back at Llanbedr, he embarked on a full day in the mountains around Cadair Idris. Being on trial, he was handed a heavy bag containing a rope. 'After that, I'm pretty sure he went for a run in the evening,' Mark recalled. 'We just thought he was weird. A freak.'

'I went to see my cousin,' Colin tells me. 'Running was just a method of transport.'

'It's not very scientific, is it?' I pursue. 'No coach would recommend that as a day of training.'

Colin Youngson recounted a similar story upon meeting his namesake at university. 'Once or twice I kept him company on a training run. Apparently, he ran 60 miles per week, as hard as he could. When I suggested that a few slower recovery sessions might be a good idea, he ignored the suggestion completely.' Colin's tendency for excess extended to the bar: 'He turned up on a trip to the Isle of Man Easter Festival of Running. No doubt he ran well, but what I remember is his total innocence about the probable effects of beer drinking on an inexperienced young fellow!'

'I've always been quite a disorganised person,' Colin says, shrugging. 'I've bumbled around and not focused. I've never had a coach in my life, but a coach would be saying this and that – and I don't want to do this and that. I want to do things my way. I like my bothies. I like my big, long runs and exploring. I want my peace and quiet. It has given me a much more rounded life. These guys who have gone through their lives, doing all the championships, saying "I want to win it five times", or whatever, does that make them a rounded person? Do they really love the hills? Do they really love wild places? Okay, I haven't achieved everything I could've done, but I've got a lot of satisfaction from what I've chosen to do, and there's been nobody telling me you've got to do this and that.'

Is Colin Donnelly Scotland's greatest hill runner? He is unabashed at the suggestion. 'I suppose, yeah, but it depends what you're after: people who win loads of races? The guys who are going out winning the races, have they done the Bob Graham, the Ramsay? Have they had a crack at the Munros record?'

What perhaps lifts Colin above his counterparts is his role in creating a framework for hill running in Scotland that survives today. Like Charlie Ramsay, his achievements, particularly in the wilderness years of the 1980s, redefined the boundaries of long-distance hill running, but in that same period, he helped to re-shape the administration of the sport, giving hill running in Scotland identity and independence. Colin was part of the 'gang of four' that decided Scotland needed to break free of the shackles of the England-based Fell Runners Association. The idea of a Scottish equivalent – what would become known as the Scottish Hill Runners Association – was forged in the back of Robin Morris' Lancia after a road race in Glasgow early in 1984, and the first meeting was held after the Carnethy 5 a month later. Colin, along with Roger Boswell, Dick Wall and Robin Morris, would be the founding members, with Mel Edwards the inaugural chairman. The group's newsletter was called *Booze n Trouble*. And trouble the breakaway caused: it would be the great schism of hill running. The Fell Runners Association did not like it; the Scottish Amateur Athletics Association did not like it; many in the hill running community still do not like it.

Colin, of course, does not regret his role in the affair. 'It was very Anglocentric,' he says of the Fell Runners Association. 'Of particular annoyance to Colin was the use of the word 'fell'. 'I actually wrote to them at one point saying, this is ridiculous. Fell running is a regional term. It's the Lake District, it's Yorkshire. It's mountain running, if you want to have a view of a whole sport.'

Robin Morris felt strongly too, arguing that Scotland deserved the independence it already had in cricket, football and rugby, as well as the Commonwealth Games. 'Scottish independence from the Fell Runners Association was not only important, it was almost an imperative,' he insisted.

The doorbell sounded. It was the gardener. Colin came back in the room muttering. 'Fell Runners Association: that was just ridiculous. We weren't getting a voice. It was bringing back power to the people in a way. People need to feel they have a say in the sport in their own country.'

Ultimately, Colin is an amateur – an international-standard amateur – who for three decades before early retirement (from work; certainly not running) had to balance competitive racing and compulsive hill-going with the rest of his life. Unless you want to spend thirty years waiting on tables in an Achnasheen hotel, or you are prepared to dismiss the notions of marriage and children, a mortgage and a career, or your sport offers an avenue to professionalism, a complex, delicate juggling act is inevitable.

Colin's years in the RAF gave him time to train and weekend freedom to race. The mere existence of *Athlete* shows the RAF encouraged its runners. It was more difficult in nursing. 'Time off was a problem because I was working a lot of weekends,' Colin says. 'I resented that, as the job was coming between me and my great love of hill running. I ended up in nursing for twenty years not being able to do what I wanted to do, which was loads of races.'

At one point, he was taken to one side by the ward sister, puzzled at his numerous requests for weekend leave.

'Well, that's when all the races are,' Colin had said. 'I

don't request as many in the winter.' He was told others had complained. It was the same in Scotland. 'In Fort William, I negotiated – because we were doing twelve-hour shifts – that I would have a small break in the morning joined up with my lunch break, giving me forty-five minutes to go for a run.' Objections came again; others wanted to combine their breaks too. Colin was told he could not be an exception. 'I had to do a run in half an hour,' he says. 'You might say, you can get your run after work. But not after a twelve-hour shift when you're on your feet the whole time. This was eating into my ...' He struggles to find the right words and starts again: 'My whole being is running.'

He means it. 'Running has cost me relationships. I can remember one girlfriend saying, "Colin, you know I really like being with you, but the trouble is, you put your running first and me second." She was right. I did.' He laughs. 'There have been other relationships that have broken up for the same reason.'

'Is that obsession?' I ask. 'Is that healthy?'

'There's been a bit of obsession about it. It's taken injuries for me to try to put my life into perspective, to see that running isn't the be all and end all. Because it will come to a halt eventually through old age and injuries.'

'What is the obsession?'

'With that particular girlfriend? It was 1989 when I was top dog anyway, and I think the obsession was about wanting to win. It was wanting to prove myself. I had this dad that never showed us any love at all. He was a stern Victorian sort of dad, a bit of a disciplinarian, but he loved outdoor stuff and hillwalking. The only way I could please him was when I was doing well in running. He suddenly wanted to know all about it and I gained his favour. I think I was trying to prove myself through that. He took a big interest in my running career and he was always asking, "what's your next race?" and "I see you did well in that race". When I won Ben Nevis, he was delighted. He came up to watch. For the first time, I had a bit of love and attention from him. A lot of stuff comes back to childhood and us wanting to make something of ourselves.'

As I leave, two cards on a sideboard catch my attention. Handmade and faded, and obviously several years old, they are the work of Claire, the oldest of Colin's two daughters who live in Wales. The first has a podium in the foreground, on top of which is a man with a Saltire across his chest, holding aloft a cup. The background is framed by green hills. The second is a birthday card. There are mountains again, and this time a bothy with a bicycle outside. A yellow sun shines from a cloudless blue sky. A line wiggles up one of the peaks. Running up that line, running up that hill, is a runner: Colin. Like a photograph, the image is fixed and permanent, for Colin Donnelly will always be running up a hill.

9

THE INVINCIBLES

Adrian Belton no longer runs 120 miles a week. He 'potters' these days, jogging only when he feels the need, as his knees 'suffer a bit'. We are sitting in the beer garden of a pub in Wapping, a stone's throw from a swollen River Thames. Adrian is fifty-nine, but could pass for twenty years younger. Cleanly shaven, neatly bald and dressed in an open-necked, tucked-in shirt, he belongs in the company of the bankers, brokers and executives of this part of London. Adrian hands me a business card. The father-of-five is a chief executive working in the UK construction industry, splitting his time between London and Sheffield. In an interview with *Construction News* after his appointment to a £270 million-turnover company, Adrian said: 'What I am trying to do is encourage a culture of challenging the status-quo.' From any other mouth, such words would reek of corporate mumbo-jumbo. But not from Adrian's.

A man sitting opposite takes a drag of his cigarette, the smoke trailing across our faces. I wave a hand theatrically and want to shout: Do you know who this man is? Do you know what this man *did*?

'Invincible,' Adrian repeats. He is smiling, his mind pushing aside the detritus of 26 years to locate the memories, the feelings, the magic, of *those* 29 days. 'I was on a perpetual high,' he says. 'I felt invincible. That sense of invincibility is the weirdest of sensations. And then it goes – and you wonder how you ever did it.' An incredulous shake of the head.

The 'perpetual high' lasted for 29 astonishing summer days in 1989 when a man who was living in one of the flattest places in England redefined notions of human endurance. 'Status quo'? Adrian Belton obliterated it. Only eight people, six men and two women, have completed the three classic rounds in a calendar year. That is 12 months to plan, train, run, recover, and do it all again – and again. Even then, on average, only one runner manages the feat every four years.

Imagine being allocated 29 days to do the lot?

Some things do not need to be imagined.

What is more impressive? The stamina needed to accomplish each round? The extraordinary powers of recovery required to be ready for the next? The logistical nous to navigate across 190 wild, mountainous miles? And it was not just what Adrian did, it was the manner of his actions. In those 29 days, he extended the Paddy Buckley from 47 to 51 summits, and still finished in 22 hours – eclipsing all those that had come before, despite the additional peaks. In those 29 days, he ran Ramsay's Round faster than anyone else, a record that stood for 26 years, and precisely 28 days, 19 hours and 11 minutes after the countdown started on the Paddy Buckley, he completed a 'steady' Bob Graham with five hours to spare.

Adrian pushes a yellowing wad of paper across the table. 'It's all there,' he says. There are photographs too. One shows Adrian surrounded by support runners. He is at the centre of the picture wearing thigh-flashing Union flag shorts. On his head is a white sunhat, the type a child might wear on the beach. Apart from shoes and socks, he sports nothing else. He is topless. His right arm is bandaged. 'I'd spent several hours in hospital the day before with a suspected fractured elbow,' he explains. The snapshot captures a gait that looks bow-legged. In his right hand, he cradles a bottle. He looks like a cavorting, drunken Brit abroad; the men that flank him could easily be police officers or inebriated accomplices. Adrian *was* abroad: an Englishman in Scotland, in Glen Nevis, part-way through a 24-hour run in the mountains of Lochaber.

In the same way as runners today publish online blogs about a run or race, Adrian returned to Hertfordshire and penned six sides of A4 in neat black ink on his record-breaking Ramsay's Round. In the spirit of modesty, Adrian first listed seven reasons why the outcome should have been different: 'the weather was the worst of the week and getting worse; preparation was last minute; the schedule looked impossible, especially some legs towards the end, for the record to be broken; the pacers were beginning to get "paced out" from too much orienteering and helping on earlier attempts on the other rounds; we were going the "hard way" – i.e. Charlie's original route, finishing on the Ben as real men do; it was a mere 18 days since I set a new 22-hour record in Snowdonia for Paddy's round, extended to include all 3,000-foot mountains; I had been orienteering for three days, plus doing some Munro-bagging, immediately prior to the attempt.'

On 1 August, 1989, Adrian was embroiled in a two-hour orienteering course at Loch Etive, part of the third day of a week-long programme. The following day, 2 August, was scheduled for a rest. 'I had a calling,' Adrian says – a calling for an instinctive, improbable round. He pulled together a group of 'sceptical and grumpy' pacers at short notice, and drove to Glen Nevis.

He went the way Charlie travelled, through the forest, up Mullach nan Coirean, running against the clock. Adrian's schedule and splits for a 20-hour round were among the bundle of papers. Due to arrive on the first summit at 3.23am, he got there at 3.20am. Stob Bàn stole 12 minutes and Stob Coire a' Chàirn three, and it was not until he reached Na Gruagaichean shortly before 7am, that Adrian matched his hoped-for pace, a speed unprecedented on Ramsay's Round. But the early morning effort was taking its toll. Andrew Addis, Adrian's partner in a weather-bothered round of close to 26 hours a year earlier, had abandoned having 'already had enough'.

Minutes were gradually hewn from the schedule before a

moment of miscommunication took the round into the realm
of 19 hours. Adrian raced down the glen and skirted Loch
Treig, convinced he was losing time. It was not until he was
almost at the summit of Beinn na Lap that Kevin Harding, his
pacer, admitted he had earlier told Adrian the wrong split. The
contender was not haemorrhaging minutes; quite the opposite.

Be in no doubt: this is a mental game. And so? 'The effect
was incredible.'

Such was the pace, Adrian feared his support crew may not
be in place at the Loch Treig dam. He was right. 'We scoffed
food until we heard a screech of tyres, followed by four doors
simultaneously exploding open,' he wrote. 'Never before have
I seen pacers move so quickly into action.' Adrian paused
for only six minutes and began the climb of Stob a' Choire
Mheadhoin, forging relentlessly on, sculpting a legend with
every step. But there were many, many steps to go: 22 miles of
them, with ten Munros thrown in, separates Loch Treig and
Glen Nevis, a journey that took Charlie Ramsay on the only
other anticlockwise round 10-and-a-half hours. In drizzle and
clag, and fortified by rice pudding, it took Adrian – a man
who was 'recovering' from a Paddy Buckley – seven-and-a-
half. He would arrive at the hostel 18 hours and 23 minutes
after starting, a cavernous gap to indisputable class: three
hours faster than Jon Broxap; two hours ahead of Helene
Diamantides and Mark Rigby.

Years passed. The round became the stuff of mountain-
running folklore. The time was untouchable. Up until 2013 –
24 years on – no-one else could breach 20 hours, let alone 19.
The longer the record stood, the greater its invincibility. Did
runners no longer believe it could be usurped? Might it last
forever? Nicky Spinks, a Yorkshire sheep farmer, set about
unpicking the myth; in 2014, she became the first woman to
break the 20-hour barrier, completing in 19 hours and 39
minutes. 'I never would have guessed the record would stand
for so long,' Adrian says. 'I was waiting for it to be broken. I
was thinking, why haven't people done it faster?' By the end

of 2014, there had been 79 successful rounds. None of them had come within even an hour of Adrian's time.

And then along came Jez.

When news of the success of the expedition to climb Mount Everest was revealed to the world on 2 June, 1953, four days had elapsed since Edmund Hillary and Tenzing Norgay had stood on the summit. When Jez Bragg reached Glen Nevis youth hostel, surpassing Adrian's mark, the world knew in seconds.

Jez's round was symbolic of the technological age. For 18 hours and 12 minutes, his mountain toil was exposed to public scrutiny, as the matchbox-sized tracker that he carried updated his position every 90 seconds. It was as addictive as watching football scores on Ceefax. Nothing for 90 seconds, then the blue line would wiggle forward: a shuffle on an uphill, a great leap on a down. There were no such luxuries in 1989: Adrian noted splits with a chinagraph pencil; maps were guarded in sticky plastic and daubed with compass bearings.

Aphra is crying. I know she will not go back to sleep, but for once I do not mind. I scoop her from the cot, place her on a knee and rock forward and back for five minutes until she is silent. The glow of my phone momentarily illuminates her round, now-peaceful face, revealing the dry trail of a tear. I tap the Twitter icon, propelling me on a roughly northward journey of hundreds of miles, across the rooftops of London, through the fields of the Home Counties and the Midlands, touching the Pennines and the Lake District, flashing over Glasgow, and alighting in the Highlands. Jez Bragg had left Glen Nevis at precisely 3am. Gemma, his wife, had tweeted a picture of Jez and Cameron Burt, a support runner, with Charlie Ramsay to the far right of the shot, all waiting for the moment of release. Standing in darkness with head torches blazing, and Jez in short sleeves, there is no hint of what is to come.

Charlie leads a countdown: 'Four, three, two, one, go ...'

Then Gemma's voice: 'Good luck.'

'Gone. That's it,' says Charlie ominously.

At 5.26am, the blue line is poised on the cradle between Carn Mòr Dearg and Aonach Mòr. I am clasping a baby in a London bedroom. Boxes line the walls; we are moving in a week. I sniff Aphra's nappy and put my phone down.

When I check the tracker again at 7am, Jez is approaching Stob Coire an Laoigh. Soon after, Gemma confirms his location, noting that Jez is 'moving well' having ticked six summits in four hours. He reaches the dam at 9.57am, the tracker reveals. Gemma tweets again. In the photographs, the sky is blue and the day bright. Charlie sits nearby on a stool. There are other seats, but Jez is standing in all the photographs. I know what he is eating because Gemma tweeted a picture of Jez's 'fuel' a few minutes earlier: bananas, sandwiches, Coke and rice pudding. It is reassuringly low-tech.

It is 11am and I have taught two English lessons, although I cannot stop thinking about Jez and the blue line. We were reading *Macbeth*. I asked my pupils if they had been to Scotland. Three out of 22 had. I did not pursue the line of questioning further. Meanwhile, Jez was progressing up Stob Coire Sgriodain. After two further lessons, I check again at 1pm. He is coming off Beinn na Lap, nearing the railway line.

The emails begin. 'I was comparing his tracker to Nicky Spinks' schedule,' Duncan Steen writes. 'It looks like he's 30 minutes-to-one-hour up, so going very well indeed.'

Andy Higgins responds: 'I was doing the same. He was 30 minutes up at Loch Treig, but I'd say he is in the region of 50 minutes up on that schedule now. Mental. Isn't the record still over 18 hours?' It was, for now. Jez needed to finish before 9.23pm to outdo Adrian Belton.

I emerge from an hour-long exam invigilation at 3pm to see the blue line scaling Sgùrr Eilde Mòr. There were further pictures at Jez's pit stop by Loch Eilde Beag: more blue sky, Coke, Charlie. Jez is sitting this time, with a selection of food in grabbing distance on a bench.

Andy, at work in Newcastle, is getting excited: 'Looks like record pace to me. Come on Jez!'

Shortly before 4.30pm, Ramsayist Steve Birkinshaw tweets: 'He is going to be close to the record.'

Adrian Stott, the events coordinator at Run and Become in Edinburgh, resorts to Shakespearean inspiration for the modern generation: '#thegamesafoot.'

'There is no sense of solitude such as that we experience on the silent and vast elevations of mountains,' said Joseph Sheridan Le Fanu, the nineteenth century writer. But the Victorians had not heard of GPS tracking and social media, had they?

Still the tracker moves. Over the Binnein hills, onwards to Na Gruagaichean. With Arielle and Aphra sleeping, I run, a cautious, post-injury twenty-minute wander around the block. I think of Jez as I jog along Streatham High Road, dodging pedestrians. This street and Na Gruagaichean – could two places be more unlike? Gemma continues to tweet: Jez is 13 minutes up, then eight, then five.

Home again, I press refresh immediately. He is on Mullach nan Coirean. It is 8.26pm. A thunderstorm breaks over London. I shower, stretch, watch five minutes of *Don't Tell the Bride* and return to the computer. It is the 90th minute and I cannot take my eyes off Ceefax. Jez is descending Mullach nan Coirean rapidly, but his route kinks as he drops through the forest. I gasp as the twist unravels on the screen. Normality is soon resumed. He is on a marked path, heading north, dropping through the plantation towards the road, now running along the road, now seeing the hostel, now reaching the hostel. A line of red and white tape had been strung across the road. I know because it was on Twitter.

At 9.12pm, I make an announcement to Fi: 'He's finished.'

She starts to say, 'who's finished?' but stops herself, replacing the words with, 'did he break the record?'

I read Gemma's tweet aloud: '@jezbragg does it! 18hr12min – 11min record #RamsayRound a record that has been held since 1989, not anymore!'

There is a version of the story – a glossy, glorified, distorted telling through the narrow lens of social media. Now for what it is *really* like to take on Ramsay's Round.

Obsessively waiting and watching the who-knows-what-it-will-do Scottish weather is the prerogative of the would-be Ramsayist. Such had been the case for Jez. The weather preoccupied him for a fortnight and, as the assigned day approached, he scrutinised forecasts. It was bad news: mist, rain and a brisk breeze. If only he had chosen the day before, a Friday, when the weather was due to be dry and bright with light wind. But it was to be Saturday. The complex logistics of pacing and support were now in place. A carefully-constructed team had already devoted their weekends to a Dorset man living almost 600 miles from Fort William.

Jez took a chance. To break the record, to achieve his 'crazy dream', he had to be ruthlessly selfish. He sent out a message, bringing the attempt forward by a day, gambling that the advantage of favourable conditions would outweigh a potentially smaller support team. 'I just wanted to have a proper crack at this thing,' Jez reasoned, 'not least because these opportunities are typically few and far between. If I failed at this attempt, it would be another year at least before a re-attempt would be feasible. After spending so much time learning the lines and getting everything ready, I had to be bold and give the record a go.'

The new start time meant Cameron Burt – a runner who would complete the round later that summer, the third of five people to achieve the feat in 2015 – was the only capable person who could make it to Glen Nevis. Contender and supporter met for the first time at dinner in the hours preceding 3am. Together, they then went up the Ben.

'The next few hours turned out to be the most inspiring running I've ever had,' Cameron said. As the runners reached the snow line, the moon was setting and the sky burned with the rising sun. The astonishment of those moments on the Ben acted as a prelude for the innocence and purity that would characterise the early hours of the round. 'I pulled out the ice axes and we hurtled down the snow towards the Carn Mòr Dearg Arête like a couple of children released from school early,' Cameron remembered. Soon they were crossing Aonach Beag where the runners shadows were three times longer than their height in the morning sun. 'There was nowhere I would have rather been at that point,' Cameron said.

Chris Busby and Anna Hayes left the Steall Falls car park at 4am for an arranged rendezvous with Jez and Cameron – two men they had also never met – in the pass between Aonach Mòr and the start of the Grey Corries. They were not hard to recognise. Anna spotted the runners descending swiftly, a figure in a yellow T-shirt – Jez, they would soon find out – leading the way and 'whooping in response to the arms we raised in greeting'. The running – charged with adrenaline and excitement – felt easy at first. Reality began to bite: Cameron started to fall back; with his hamstrings cramping, Chris was hanging on through the heather; the cool of morning gave way to the heat of day.

Cameron arrived at the dam as Jez departed, following a pause no longer than the commercial break in a half-hour soap. 'He was still moving smoothly and looked strong,' Cameron said. 'I was in pieces.'

Olly Stephenson set off with Jez at a 'fair clip', with Loch Treig reflecting the surrounding peaks like a mirror. When the pair reached Beinn na Lap, even a Ramsayist like Olly was overwhelmed by what Jez still had to accomplish: 'Ben Nevis looked miles away to the west, with a multitude of peaks in between. It's perhaps a scale and perspective that would more normally be associated with a space station than a run.'

As the runners turned to home, Jez became increasingly silent. If he was struggling, he did not admit it, but the silence was a cover. More than most, Olly knew what Jez was going through.

'The change from feeling strong and confident, to weary and disheartened, had happened worryingly quickly,' Jez said. 'It was probably a direct result of the heat in the middle part of the day, and not allowing myself the time to cool off properly in the streams when the opportunity arose. It was an aggressive and probably quite risky approach I was taking. I feared letting my guard down to do anything other than move forward as quickly as possible.'

A slowdown wiped out a 20-minute buffer he once had. That Jez would get around within 20 hours was unquestionable, but he was eyeing something seminal. It is easier to chase, however, and he might have imagined Adrian Belton's time as a moving line on the ground. Jez just had to stay ahead of it, but victory would come at a price: suffering. 'My climbing legs felt trashed. The rough and steep pull up Sgùrr Eilde Mòr felt so hard, a hands-on-knees job to support my legs. I really wasn't sure I could even run again after summiting.' One Mamore down, nine to go in Jez's 'semi-tortuous' existence – an existence on the very edge. Jez 'hurled himself down the scree run' to Binnein Beag, Graham Nash, a fresh pacer, recalled. 'Rocks and stones were flying in all directions.'

Jon Gay, waiting for Jez close to Na Gruagaichean while incongruously clutching a carrier bag, knew what the hours ahead would hold: 'I had a fair idea that the pace would be relentless.'

Watches were scrutinised at Am Bodach: seven minutes had been gained since leaving the loch, a minute for every Munro. They ran on. Amid the chaotic pace to Sgùrr an Iubhair, Graham was running behind Jez. 'The downside of a day's diet of sugary snacks is backwind,' Graham said. 'Jez guffed one in my face and it caught in the back of my throat. I coughed and dry retched, thinking it would be bad form for the support runner to hurl. I kept encouraging Jez to make the most of the runnable bits. "Stay on Jon's heels," I'd say. The only reply was a loud fart. At the summit, we had lost two minutes. We needed to up the rate of progress.'

The temperature was dropping and clouds were building in the west. Three mountains remained. 'The last out and back was fast,' said Jon, and by Stob Bàn, he sensed that Jez was 'preparing for an all-out effort' to the end.

One last climb, one last endeavour: Mullach nan Coirean. Then down, down, down to the glen. 'Jez was giving it everything; the pace was getting quicker,' said Graham. 'He was asking for flat Coke, but it was long gone. At the summit, we'd lost three minutes. The time was tight.'

Leading the charge downhill, Jon screamed into the wind: 'Let's fucking do this!'

Graham was anxious nonetheless. 'I had previously timed the descent from the summit to the youth hostel and managed 53 minutes on fresh legs. Jez had 55 minutes on his schedule, but he'd been going for more than 17 hours.'

That evening, as I ran along Streatham High Road, watched *Don't Tell the Bride* and repeatedly refreshed the tracker, three men seemed to run for their lives down a Scottish mountain.

'How far?' asked Jez.

'A mile.'

Some 49 minutes after standing on the top of Mullach nan Coirean, Jez, fists clenched and grinning deliriously, ran through the tape.

There is a picture of Jez surrounded by his team outside the hostel. Sitting on his right is Charlie Ramsay. To his left is Graham Nash. Standing behind are Olly Stephenson and Chris Busby. Ramsay, Nash, Stephenson, Busby – a roll call of Edinburgh-based Carnethy Hill Running Club stalwarts beaming for the camera. 'I suspect his record will last a while,' said Olly.

He was wrong, and Gemma might have regretted the last two words – 'not anymore' – of her celebratory tweet. The new record lasted fewer days than Adrian Belton's had years.

Late on a Sunday night in July, three weekends after Jez's round, a news item was published on the Carnethy website.

The message was brief but shattering: a man named Jon Ascroft had set a new 'world record' for Ramsay's Round. The time was astonishing: 16 hours and 59 minutes. It seemed beyond belief. Jon was relatively unknown, certainly in comparison to the North Face-sponsored Jez, but then I saw the identity of the person who had posted the message. Written in red italics was the name Charlie Ramsay.

When Billy Bland ran the fastest time of 13 hours and 53 minutes for the Bob Graham in 1982, he had won the Ennerdale Horseshoe the previous weekend, finishing ahead of Joss Naylor and Jon Broxap. Three weeks after his round, Bland prevailed at the Wasdale Fell Race in a record time that was 20 minutes in front of second place.

As 2014 came to a close, Jon Ascroft had completed close to 100 Scottish hill races. He had won once, coming first at the Glen Rosa Horseshoe on Arran in a field of 25 runners. Even then he had to rely on Andy Symonds, the race favourite, getting lost, and Es Tresidder being injured. When his wife, Lorna, saw him with the winner's trophy, she asked if he was looking after it for Es. In the three months leading up to Jon's Ramsay he raced twice in the Scottish hills. He was 37th out of 239 athletes at Birnam in March, and 25th at Ben Lomond in a field of 166 runners, 11 minutes adrift of the winner, Tom Owens, in May. Sam Hesling, one of Jon's support runners on the latter part of his round, described him as a 'very solid runner'. No-one would describe Bland as 'solid'. Even by his own admission, Jon is a 'reasonable' runner.

So how did a forty-three-year-old architect and father-of two from Edinburgh become the fastest to run the jewel in the crown of the classic rounds? And how did a 'reasonable' athlete crush a time recorded by Jez Bragg – a former winner of the Ultra-Trail du Mont-Blanc, the world's most prestigious mountain race – by 73 minutes?

I was waiting for Jon in the Canny Man's pub in Edinburgh. Having locked his bicycle outside, he enters wearing a fluorescent yellow jacket. He places his lights on a table and orders a pint of Deuchars. Utterly normal. Just a bloke having a pint in a pub on a Sunday night. A bloke who a few days earlier had won the Fell Runners Association Long Distance Award. I push the picture of Jez and his support crew across the table. Jon's clubmates stare back. Born in Gloucestershire and university educated in Sheffield, Jon moved to Edinburgh in 2005 and immediately joined Carnethy. 'They didn't know I was planning a Ramsay,' he says. I repeat Olly's words. He shrugs.

I tell him about Bland's achievements before and after the Bob Graham. 'And you've won one race?' I say, adding a tone that suggests I am merely seeking clarification, in case a man whose company I had shared for only minutes took offence.

He laughs. 'Don't compare me to Billy Bland.'

Jon was *there* on the night Jez broke the record. Lorna had dropped him off at the foot of the Nevis Range ski station and he ran the last three Munros in what was his final outing on the route before he returned to attempt the entire loop. He arrived in Glen Nevis an hour after Jez. There was no commotion or evidence that anything exceptional had happened in the quiet glen. 'I was hitching up the valley and Pete Duggan, one of Jez's support crew, picked me up and dropped me in Fort William,' Jon says. Pete told him about the record. It did not change anything: Jon was convinced he could also run the round in 18 hours and for all of Jez's accomplishments and fame, he was 'not intimidated' by Jez 'as a runner on that terrain'.

Jon's rationale was entirely logical. He had completed a Tranter's Round a year earlier, running at a pace equivalent to an 18-hour Ramsay. Jon believed he could replicate that intensity on the longer round and began calculating summit-to-summit splits based on the assumption. After establishing a 19-and-a-half-hour schedule, he was persuaded to be more ambitious: he would aim for an 'aspirational' 18 hours. He remained tentative: 'I wasn't sure I was in the same form as the previous year.' But now, he felt, was the right moment. Leading up to July, his training was unspectacular, but 'solid' – that word again. His weekly focus was on height gain (and therefore also loss), not mileage. He aimed for 3,000 metres, but rarely attained that figure. His mantra was relevance – essentially, quality over quantity. He did long repetitions on the flat parkland of The Meadows in Edinburgh to maintain speed; he attended pilates classes to improve his core strength; from Swanston, he ran into the Pentlands, hoping to claim 800 metres of ascent and descent in an hour – more than would be required on the round. He was surprised by his clubmates who would typically run the established routes and well-worn paths of the Pentlands. Jon would look for rougher, more awkward ways up the same hills, actively seeking the heather. When he ran into the mountains above Blair Atholl that May, he deliberately selected routes that avoided popular trails. 'It just felt more rewarding,' he says. Those rewards would be cashed when he found himself on the pathless terrain in the far east of Ramsay's Round.

Family was a further complication. Jon's children were two and five when he ran the round. 'The training had to be of quality,' he says. Jon kept a record of his running on Attackpoint, an online log geared to orienteers, where athletes choose an effort rating for their session of between five and one, hard to easy. 'I never wanted to do training that was a three. I didn't have time for that.'

In meeting Jon, I hoped to discover a potion, a magic spark, a silver bullet. Just *how* had he done it? There was no discovery to be made. It was simple. The 'reasonable' runner had found Adrian Belton's invincibility; he ran the greatest race of his life. He was fit and injury-free. He controlled his enthusiasm at the start. He surrounded himself with a stellar support team. Apart from what he described as 'head fug' in the glen between Sgùrr Eilde Mòr and Beinn na Lap, he did not succumb to sickness. The weather was fine. Navigation was trouble-free. He was prepared for a long mental game in which he would be the victor. In completing a Bob Graham some twelve months earlier, he felt 'great' in the final miles. 'As I did the Ramsay,' Jon tells me, 'I kept thinking, that's how I'm going to feel again. I'm going to feel great at the end. I kept telling myself, I'm going to start to feel brilliant. I had the mental confidence that I wouldn't fade.' And he did not. He ran down Ben Nevis in 37 minutes – slower than Charlie Ramsay, admittedly, but these were two men inspired by differing objectives.

'I felt amazing,' Jon says, with an almost disbelieving grin. As the round entered its concluding minutes, his biggest fear was falling. He knew he was a twist or an awkward landing away from disaster. But it never materialised. Everything that could have gone wrong, that so easily will go wrong, that so often does go wrong, did not. Lucky, perhaps? That depends if you believe the adage of making your own luck.

As has become customary, Jon wrote an account of his round. It has none of the intensity of Jez's version. There is no flatulence, no flying scree, no swearing. There is little sense of the history Jon was making. He began to edge towards emotion as he reflected on crossing the Grey Corries, writing: 'the exhilaration was mounting.' Describing his feelings as he ran off Ben Nevis, he noted: 'The final descent I'll remember for a long time.' His closing words? 'It was a memorable day.' This string of sentences puzzled me at first. Any passion was buried under the weight of humility. After two hours in his company, I understood. To veer from modesty seemed tantamount to being boastful – and that is not the hill runner's way; it is certainly not Jon Ascroft's way.

Adrian Stott later told me that Jon had visited Run and Become on the Monday after his round and was served by his wife. 'He said that he had been running at the weekend. His hands had got cold, so he wanted some gloves,' Adrian said. 'He didn't mention what the run actually was.'

'I've had my fifteen minutes of fame,' Jon says. I point out that he had not courted publicity, that his fame did not amount

– by his own choosing – to even a metaphorical quarter-hour. Beyond the world of fell and hill running, he was anonymous. 'People have said, "you could get a sponsorship deal," but I don't really want to. I guess the only way my ego would be fed is if other people try to beat my record.'

That is exactly what he thought would happen. Names are bandied about. 'There are plenty of runners who beat me in races who could break my record,' he insists. 'The record was low hanging fruit.'

Now I laugh with disbelief. Was he being honest or resorting again to modesty?

'Not many people have made aggressive attempts,' he goes on.

I mention Adrian Belton. 'I don't think he considered it low hanging fruit.' Another shrug.

Jez disagreed too: 'I ran as hard as I could on that day.' After seeing his record erased so soon, Jez admitted he was 'gutted and somewhat shocked. The reason I was a little conservative with the schedule was simply awareness that Adrian's record had stood untouched for so long. I figured that was for good reason.'

Jon listed the numerous complications of the round: the difficulties of support, the committing territory, the uncertain weather, patches of snow that can linger into summer, the need to stay healthy and clear of injury, the tremendous height gain and loss – 'it's the 28,000 feet of descent that will get you first', he remarks – and the fortune, planning, and under-standing of the people around you, that goes into achieving long-term objectives.

'But isn't that the point?' I say. 'Even runners who are supposedly better than you on paper have to overcome these obstacles. But you are the person who did that.'

He nods.

Words on the round do not flow naturally for Jon: 'I wasn't lucid for much of the time,' he admits. I could not blame him for that. Yet eloquence flows when he speaks about the spirit of running and racing in the hills. 'Being wild,' he calls it. Jon is a climber and mountaineer first, discovering the hills for running in his late twenties, but the principles that define running as a sport had resonated since childhood. His family were road cyclists. 'I found all the gear distasteful,' he says. 'That aspect propelled me into running. Money doesn't help. Running in the mountains is an antidote to consumerism.' That explains why hill runners make up the bulk of Jon's friends – friends who, as he puts it, understand what it is like to 'feel the brush of heather on your legs'. He adds: 'The bond you have after a race comes from that shared experience.' At that moment, Jon reminded me of Adrian Belton: two men who had achieved sporting greatness; two men at peace; a pair of invincibles.

I shake Jon's hand outside the Canny Man's. He goes right; I turn left. A startlingly bright moon is high above the Pentlands. I move towards it. The pavement slopes down. I start to run – an instinctive, spontaneous movement. Like Holden Caulfield in *The Catcher in the Rye*, 'I don't even know what I was running for – I guess I just felt like it.'

10

MOUNTAIN MASOCHISM

I raised an index finger to wipe the line of moisture dripping from my nose, gathering in the cleft below. In a mechanical, rapid gesture I had done a thousand times, the digit slid easily from left to right, the nail brushing the stubble above my lip, grazing the skin that joins the nose. Instinctively, I inhaled. *Vomit.*

It was morning and Arielle was wailing. Lying in her cot, she was shouting 'mum-my, mum-my, mum-my.' As I pushed open the door, I was assailed by a vile smell. Something terrible had happened in there. Typically, when she knew the summoning had worked, when she knew someone was in her room, Arielle would throw herself onto her front, burying her face in a pillow, pretending she was invisible, giggling gamely. We would play along.

'Where's Arielle? I can't see her *anywhere.*'

'I 'iding,' she would gasp.

'Hide,' Fi would say, correcting the dropped 'h', Arielle's symbolic connection to London, her city of birth.

Not this morning. Arielle lay on her back surrounded by the half-digested contents of the food she had consumed the previous day. She was groaning, not giggling. Two-and-a-half years as a parent had prepared me for this moment – and every similar moment. I was emotionless. My programming was passivity: acceptance is always easier. 'I think that's scrambled egg,' I said aloud, 'and that's definitely a baked bean.' I lifted the duvet. 'A lot of baked beans.'

I plucked a now-gently weeping Arielle from the cot, carried her at arm's length to the bath and peeled off her clothes. Egg was matted into her hair and I combed the biggest chunks free with my fingers. The food did not even seem chewed. I turned the shower head on her and lathered soap through her hair. Arielle hated having her hair washed, but she accepted her fate meekly. Standing naked in the bath, head bowed, she looked pathetic and thin.

I laid her on the sofa. 'Milk,' she whimpered. She drank the milk in the manner she always did, gulping furiously and desperately. She reminded me of myself on Slioch all those years ago, hands urgently cupping water from a mountain stream. We are related, after all. Minutes later, after she had staggered drunkenly into the kitchen, the same milk flooded the floor.

It was 7.30am. 'Worst case scenario,' I had told Duncan Steen – how strange to think a meeting on the forecourt of a Chiswick petrol station could lead us here – the night before, 'we'll leave just after seven.'

We were entered as a team in the Original Mountain Marathon – the OMM, as it is commonly known – in the hour-distant Tweedsmuir Hills. Our packed bags lay in the corridor. Kit had been divided. Food had been cooked and bagged: cold pizza, tomato soup, couscous, custard powder, hot chocolate, jelly babies.

Aphra was crying now. 'Feed her, *please*,' I ordered Mum. Back on the sofa, Dad was trying to comfort Arielle. She squirmed on his lap, clothed now but still pathetic and thin. I had to decide: stay or go. With Fi away at a wedding, my parents were here to look after the girls; that had been the plan. But then came the profusion of vomit.

I hesitated, glancing at the bags, then Arielle. 'Let's go,' I said to Duncan. I hugged Arielle; she responded with a feeble embrace. We left. I do not know why. My two-year-old daughter was sick. But it is futile to defend decisions made years earlier. I suppose it was like that day on the South Glen

Shiel ridge: compulsion overruled what was the right course of action.

Vomit. Arielle's gift of scent, smeared invisibly into the creases of the 'Peter pointer' celebrated in our songs. *Remember me, Daddy.*

'Commit now,' Duncan had said as we jogged to the start. I understood the shorthand: you must now forget your daughter; you must now run for seven hours. I nodded affirmation, but thought of Arielle, naked and shivering in the bath.

Rain skittered across our hoods as we climbed the sodden ramparts of Hog Hill, an innocuous rise on the western edge of a wild tract of high Borders land wreathed in mist. As the gradient steepened, I realised Duncan was moving faster. There seemed an effortlessness in his gait while I was already breathing more deeply than I imagined I should be. I did not realise it then, but this was how it would be. A grim reality emerged from misplaced optimism: I was to be tortured; Duncan – aided by a brown and green enormity – would be my torturer.

Originating in the late 1960s as the Karrimor International Mountain Marathon (KIMM), the OMM is the Glastonbury of mountain marathons: both are filthy and teem with the unwashed, but unlike the festival that finds permanence in Somerset, the OMM's organisers annually seek new mountainous territory in England, Scotland or Wales, with the location kept deliberately vague until around two months before the event. Even then, you do not know exactly where you are being sent until you are handed a map sprinkled with obscure checkpoints on the start line. Glastonbury, I imagine, is also more fun.

Mountain marathons stretch the definition of fun. A two-person team must carry on their backs everything they need to survive for 36 hours on the hills. On top of camping and cooking equipment, and food – the burden of which can be shared – individually, runners must also transport a raft of other paraphernalia: waterproofs, hat and gloves, spare clothes, first aid, whistle and compass, head torch, survival bag, pen and paper, and emergency rations. On paper, the list seems onerous. It is better, nonetheless, than the alternative: hypothermia is even less fun.

There are plenty of mountain marathons in Britain, but none quite like the OMM. It is the most uncompromising of them all. The traditional late October date – typically timed to coincide with the culmination of British Summer Time and the subsequent gaining of an hour on the night of the year a cold, hungry, confined runner camped in a field in the middle of nowhere would least want an additional 60 minutes – lies at the root of the aggravation. Late October raises the likelihood of inclement weather: rain, high wind, low cloud and snow. Borrowdale in 2008 demonstrated just that: a month of rain in 24 hours, flash flooding, 100mph gusts, runners famously 'unaccounted for'. Late October means the mid-camp is inevitably cold and dark, with night arriving before 6pm. Late October tends to bring a ground saturated from autumn rain, frustrating the runner's ability to cross hills and valleys that have already been selected for their awkward, rough and pathless nature. Because of the inclemency and the darkness and the cold and the extra hour and the liquidity of the ground, competitors must commit to carrying more than they might in a spring or summer mountain marathon. There is no such thing as *just in case* at the OMM; *probably* is more accurate. Not that any of this puts people off. Some 1,500 runners and walkers – paying £150 per team for the dubious privilege – descended on the bleak, mist-smothered peaks of Tweedsmuir.

Quality mirrored quantity. The OMM had lured the year's doyens of British hill, fell and ultrarunning to the Borders. The male and female winners of the Dragon's Back, Jim Mann and Jasmin Paris, were racing with their respective partners, Nic Barber and Konrad Rawlik. Kim Collison, second Briton at the Ultra-Trail du Mont-Blanc, and Adam Perry, whose attempt to break the record for visiting the most Lakeland summits in 24 hours ended in clag and cramp on Yewbarrow, hilltop number 51, after 15 hours and more than 8,000 metres of ascent, had joined forces. Andy Fallas and Iain Whiteside were the strongest team Carnethy could muster, with Fallas a winner at Slioch and Whiteside a runner-up at the Pentland Skyline. Paired with Jean Brown, Nicky Spinks had not had a bad year either, having set a new women's record for the Bob Graham. In such exalted company, Duncan Archer and Shane Ohly, winners of the OMM the last time it came to Scotland, could almost have been overlooked.

Beneath Mann, Paris and Spinks, and the other 'elites', were the rest – the mortals, sprinkled among seven further categories. Five of the eight classes, including the elite, instructed runners to follow linear courses of varying lengths between checkpoints, at times labelled as obviously as 'trig pillar' but ordinarily as ambiguously as 'stream bend'. Nevertheless, the premise is simple: the fastest pair in a respective category to visit all the checkpoints is the winner. The remaining three groupings are known as the 'score'. Instead of a set linear route, the twosome are faced with a plethora of checkpoints – far more than even the most agile runner could hope to visit – of different numerical values, from 10 to 50, from easily accessible to infuriatingly awkward. The snag is time, not route: finish too late and you are penalised.

That is where Duncan and I found ourselves: racing the long score with a fixed completion time of seven hours on day one and six on day two. That is why we were here: the wind and rain-blasted malice of Hog Hill. *Seven hours*, I thought. *Seven.* Following a fence line, we descended by a broad ridge. The terrain was appalling: a confusion of slime and tussock. No two steps were the same; no rhythm could be gained. I flailed forward, chasing my teammate. Where the ridge plateaued, we crossed a fence and scarpered downhill to find our first checkpoint amid an avenue of trees in a plantation. Having gained 20 points, as if we had seen a bear in a cave, we did an abrupt about turn: through the forest, over the fence, across the bog, down a slide of grass, through a stream, and then rather than hiding under the duvet, we forged up the lower slopes of Broad Law, the highest point of the 400 square miles of the OMM.

I do not know what came first: mental submission or the physical equivalent. We were halfway up the dome of Broad Law when Duncan told me to hand over the stove, gas and tent to reduce the load in my bag. We had been running for less than an hour, but I was already slowing him down. It made no difference. If anything, the division seemed to make Duncan stronger. My body seemed overwhelmed by a brand of tiredness I had never experienced. I decided very quickly I wanted nothing more to do with the OMM. Except I could not say those words aloud. Duncan had to utter them – and then I might agree. But I knew Duncan too well; he would not say what he knew I must be thinking. Pride – if nothing else – kept me going. I trudged; Duncan ran. He was always 20 or 30 paces ahead. He would stop, check the map, scan the landscape like a mountain hare, examine the map again, seemingly satisfied, and off he would go.

We accumulated points steadily, with Duncan keeping a running commentary: 'That's 110 in two hours. There are 30 points ahead, then another 20.' I did not care. The notion of being competitive left me cold. If we were to do well, we must run quickly – and I did not want to go anywhere, let alone move through mountains with a sense of urgency. Duncan was momentarily out of sight when my foot sank into a hole. Dragging it out with a pop, I slumped to the ground. Just sitting, being stationary, was wonderful. I looked down to a river and across a glen to russet slopes, sighed, and for a few seconds gave up. And then I carried on.

'You okay?' asked Duncan.

'No.' He pushed three jelly babies into my palm and continued uphill. 'Greasy,' I said, 'and – meaty?'

'They were in the same bag,' Duncan said.

'As what?'

'The cocktail sausages.'

Seven hours. The rest would be unremittingly awful, I knew that. I swallowed two painkillers and hoped. Breaking my leg had never seemed such a pleasing proposition.

The OMM is unsatisfactorily billed as 'hard'. What counts as hard in running parlance these days? A parkrun? A marathon? A multi-day ultramarathon in the Antarctic winter? The blurb offers little clarity: 'The OMM is meant to be hard.' Getting out of bed can be hard; coping with grief can be hard; extricating the day-old remnants of scrambled egg from the scalp of a two-year-old who is irrationally obsessional about her father even touching her hair is hard. The word 'hard' is as graspingly and unimaginatively subjective as describing a fellow human as 'nice' or a book as 'good'. The OMM is undoubtedly one of the toughest undertakings in the British outdoors, but it offers difficulty and discomfort that goes far beyond the necessity of having to cover many miles, and ascend and descend thousands of metres.

Consider how humans like to move over hills and mountains. We follow defined paths; we cross rivers at bridges; we yearn for summits. Instinct (and logic) tells us not to step off the track, not to ignore the top, not to inexorably slide into the filth of a bog. Even in the mountains, humans are not as free as we would like to think. We still crave comfort. We remain constricted by the trappings of an easier life. As humans, we live in a profoundly oxymoronic world of wanting something hard to be easy. Whether we are walking in the Lake District or the Highlands, the Pennines or the Brecon Beacons, innumerable paths will be found connecting summits and valleys. Even runners in hill and fell races follow defined paths. Why wouldn't they? They are the fastest and easiest routes. That is why when Duncan found a trod – because it was never me who found a trod – he would gleefully shout 'trod!' And for a few moments I would be happy.

Trods – narrow, informal paths that punctuate

sparsely-visited terrain, and unmarked on maps – are unpredictable, however. Created by wandering sheep and deer or the occasional walker that followed in the footmarks of their predecessor, they offer the runner respite. Instead of hacking through gorse or heather, or crossing a welter of loose boulders, or an ankle-turning chaos of tussocks, they represent a clear route through the madness. But not for long. They will invariably and infuriatingly peter out, reappearing – if you are fortunate – as another sliver to the left or right, or, more commonly, vanishing into the hillside and disappointingly plunging the traveller back into calf-deep vegetation. Trods occur in places you would not choose to go – precisely where the checkpoints scattered across the OMM map demand attendance. They are deliberately placed to be problematic. Getting from A to B is meant to be a puzzle. They lie next to falling-down cairns at the end of long, nondescript ridges, by sheepfolds buried in bracken, and on peat hags that clutch and grasp.

Why would I want to go to these places? Where is the summit? Where is the path? Where is the bridge? There lies the intensity of the OMM: its insistent demand that you override decades of intuition, and for humans who fool themselves into assuming hills and mountains are in some way a total escape from the conventions of towns and cities, that is the problem. That is why the OMM is 'hard'.

Mike Stewart was told the location of the OMM before the mountain marathon public even knew the event would return to Scotland. He had a need to know: Mike – a fifty-seven-year-old engineer from Forfar and a veteran of more than 50 mountain marathons – had been appointed by the OMM to plot the routes. Armed with a clutch of Ordnance Survey maps, the course planner immersed himself in the hills, investigating glen, moor, summit and ridge, and recalling his memories of the OMM held here in 1994. Mike had changed much in the intervening period: he emigrated to New Zealand, doing 'anything conceivable outdoors' for three years, before returning to Scotland; he met his future wife; he spent a decade working in facilities management at the University of Edinburgh; he raced whenever and wherever he could. Amid the flux of a human life, the hills were unshakeably clamped.

An overnight camp by farm buildings at Manorhead was quickly established as the fulcrum; the checkpoints would necessarily form a lasso around the farm. With a confirmed start and finish, Mike began to draw the linear courses, with the locations of the checkpoints for the score categories emerging thereafter. The aim of the score courses, he explained when we met in Edinburgh two months later, was 'to reward people for going to difficult locations'. What started as rough etchings on a jumble of maps became a Harvey map re-printed 2,500 times.

Mike was an eighteen-year-old university student at St Andrews when he travelled south-west across Scotland to Galloway for the KIMM in 1976, an edition that would be won by a pair of world champion Norwegian orienteers. Amid the professionalism of Stig Berge and Sigurd Daehli, who were part of a European invasion of top-class orienteers racing for supremacy against the like of Joss Naylor in the 1970s, a story of farcical failure for a Forfar teenager unfolded in a watershed OMM. 'Half the controls weren't there,' Mike said. 'The Boy Scouts who were putting them out had given up and gone home. We went around on trust. There was no electronic timing like now.' Naturally, it was late October and the weather was 'atrocious'. Competitors were handed paper that was not waterproof and had to copy the course from a map provided by the organiser. 'You had to make it waterproof yourself.' I looked up from the page on which I was scrawling notes, seeking clarification. 'A plastic bag,' he muttered. 'You try marking up a map when it's pissing down with rain.' On his back, he carried a canvas satchel weighing around 25 pounds – three times the weight of mine. He ended day one 'soaked to the skin' and his partner's feet were blistered. 'We tried to bail out, but it was a remote camp on the side of Loch Dee and we couldn't. It was minimalistic in those days. By law, you must now have a clean water supply and toilet facilities at the mid-camp. We had burn water and a trench.'

The tale of catastrophe went on: lost tent pegs, no sleeping mat, a soaking sleeping bag, a tent with no groundsheet, a stove that would not light. 'We had the most miserable night and felt pretty sorry for ourselves. We bailed out in the morning. There was a film crew there and we were so pathetic, they took us back to a hotel.'

Less than 30 per cent of the field completed the Galloway KIMM. Asked by a BBC interviewer if the race was 'too tough', Gerry Charnley, the event organiser since 1968, dismissed the accusation. 'Everybody knows this is the KIMM, the toughest event on the calendar, and it's not a Sunday afternoon picnic.'

Mike would spend the next eighteen years hillwalking, Munro-bagging, orienteering, climbing and ski mountaineering, but the KIMM? Too 'hard'. He would not darken its door again until he found himself in the Tweedsmuir Hills in 1994. Now, with the event relabelled as the OMM in 2004, he was back again.

I wanted to know if Mike practised what he planned: whether he found fulfilment in immersing himself in typical OMM terrain, and whether such difficulties offer a heightened level of escapism from the emotional and physical confines of 'normal' life. 'No,' was the short answer. 'I'm not going to wander through a bog if I don't have to,' Mike conceded. 'I go to the hills for wilderness, and, yes, I do call our hills wilderness. There's wilderness in Norway, Finland, Sweden, Scotland and a bit of Iceland. The Alps and the Pyrenees? That's not wilderness. I like getting away from modern life. I won't take a GPS. I like to get away from machines, all those trappings of life.'

There is a series of photos of Duncan and me some thirty minutes before the expiry of our allotted seven hours. Duncan is captured first in graceful, alert flight over a burn, progressing to what would be our penultimate checkpoint. I come next: tongue out, chin down, white-faced. In the next photograph, Duncan stands alone by the checkpoint, scrutinising the time on his watch. There is a further picture of me. I seem bewildered. Duncan motioned uphill: 'We have time.' My gaze could not mask the two silent words in my head. Above was an ever-sharpening slide of long grass, decorated with a line of toiling runners. They seemed to move in slow motion, desperately clambering upward on all fours as if they faced some kind of awful persecution if they stayed below.

'Brave,' Mike said when I told him. The steepness of such ascents is characterised by the inability to change muscle groups. Runners are forced onto their toes for every stride, punishing the calves. I counted my steps to 100, then 200, then began to 300, until Duncan shouted and pointed to an orange and white swirl ahead. I ran. The first staggering movement, the transition from walking to running was dreadful, as if my legs were rooted in the mountain. I punched the control and turned to see Duncan already descending. 'Follow me!' he ordered.

As he had done for seven hours, Duncan carried me through the night. Our tent – pitched by Duncan, naturally – was one of hundreds on the sloping Manorhead field we had glimpsed from the final checkpoint atop that grass cliff. With eight minutes to lose 200 vertical metres, we had made it in five, running with a fluency and energy that had previously deserted me. Darkness came suddenly, prompting the return of the malaise. Duncan prepared dinner by the light of a head torch: soup from a packet, couscous from a packet, hot chocolate from a packet, custard from a packet. We ate from the cooking tin, taking turns with a spoon, the custard course tinged with everything that went before. 'Do you even know where we went today?' Duncan asked, before making me chart our route, checkpoint by checkpoint. When it was time to sleep, I wrapped my feet in gloves, then socks, placed them in the pockets of my jacket, swaddled a plastic bag over the lot, and then sunk them into my sleeping bag. Seconds later, I needed the toilet.

Morning. A skirl of pipes. A flutter of voices. Footsteps on wet grass. A flicker of hope. Perhaps it will be better today? In the darkness of pre-dawn, an outline of hills was silhouetted against the sky – a glimmer of stark beauty in this mountain masochism. We were called forward to the start. Pulling back a sleeve, I stared at the plastic dibber, gesticulating to my wrist. The tip – required for logging our arrival at checkpoints – was somewhere else: missing in action, trampled into a muddy field, buried in a sleeping bag. 'That's not right, is it?' I murmured. Duncan said nothing. Incredulity returned my stare.

I wondered many times what Duncan thought of me that weekend. We had run a Fellsman and a Bob Graham together, but he had never seen me worse. Pity, I decided, was the word. I had pitied him once. Some years earlier, Duncan, Robin Sanderson and I had caught trains to Guildford on a Friday night in January after work. The plan was to run home to London, some 35 miles away. We climbed onto the North Downs, negotiated a maze of paths on Box Hill and crossed the M25 at midnight, before emerging into the sprawl of London, from Epsom to Sutton to North Cheam to Morden to Mitcham to Streatham. The distance was much further than it had appeared on the map. On a long pavement stretch between Mitcham and Streatham, Duncan succumbed. The meltdown was spectacular. He was shuffling and stumbling, jabbering about jelly babies. I did what he did to me now: stayed a shouting distance ahead, looked back occasionally to check he was not dead, and never, on any account, offered a way out of the drudgery. 'What do you prefer, carrot or stick?' he had asked me several hours into day one. I shrugged. Only later would he admit his frustration: 'We would be together. I would run for what felt like twenty seconds, look back, and there would already be a huge gap.' I shrugged again.

I shrugged now. The marshal went away. A momentary

wave of relief – we might be forced to retire. He came back
and made me proffer my wrist. With a new dibber attached,
we were sent on our way. We did not mention it again. Duncan
would get his revenge: he set the pace.

The day took on a fuzzy reality. I was chasing again, being out-
thought again. The terrain for the first two hours was exhausting:
either saturated or coated in deep heather. We made our way
to a river, Megget Water, with the hills beyond it hiding three
checkpoints worth a combined 120 points. Duncan crossed first.
I followed, wallowing up to my thighs in brown water, facing
upstream. I was a step from the far bank when my supporting
foot slid on the green of a rock. Lunging at the mud bank, flailing
desperately at nothingness, I slapped into the water.

Duncan's sympathy was wafer thin. 'By the time you get
up there,' he pointed, 'you'll be warm.' Even at the top of the
climb, twenty minutes later, I was shivering. I put on every
item of clothing I carried. Duncan gave me his hat. My feet
were suffering the most. I seemed to be running on ice skates,
with the outer edges so numbed by cold the only remaining
feeling was down the centre of the foot. The consequence was
an alarming sense of disorientation, as if I was literally on ice
and that I could topple at any moment. Still shaking, I thought
of Arielle; now I was pathetic and thin.

We kept on moving, very steeply down, very steeply up,
down again, then up Broad Law for a second time. I walked,
lacking the coordination to run, fearing a stumble that would
cause horrible injuries. Duncan was a long way ahead – perhaps
two minutes by the time he reached the glen beneath Broad
Law. At that moment, I despised him. I imagined he returned
the hate. With the six-hour barrier rapidly approaching,
we relented to the inevitable: Duncan had to carry my bag.
I battled the notion for two minutes, then surrendered. My
emasculation was total.

As Duncan and I bagged pizza and counted cocktail sausages
on Friday night, Jim Mann and Nic Barber had travelled,

registered, then – having noted the tent of Shane Ohly and Duncan Archer, their elite category rivals, pitched in mud by the event centre – driven north to spend a more comfortable night at the home of Jasmin Paris and Konrad Rawlik. Nic was uneasy. Although it was his fifth OMM in seven years, this was his first outing in the elite group. Despite believing he was not as fast as his rivals, he was convinced of his capacity to suffer. He had come to the right place. Nic's nervousness stemmed from his partner's reputation. When his original teammate dropped out, the Sheffield-based runner 'put out a tweet as a bit of an experiment to see who would reply'. The 'who' came in the shape of Jim Mann, the Martin Stone of his generation. 'I was terrified,' Nic admitted. But it was only September. Nic embarked on seven weeks of 'serious' training, running between 65 and 80 miles a week. In two of those weeks, his total ascent reached 5,000 metres – equivalent to three-and-a-half ascents of Ben Nevis. Whether he was in the high Pyrenees or the moors of the Peak District, he was running.

Nic and Jim ended day one in second place, running for seven hours, covering 25 miles and climbing 3,300 metres. The pace was slow, around three-and-a-half miles per hour – akin to Jon Ascroft's 17-hour Ramsay's Round speed. Even the elite were overcome by the conditions and Mike would later admit the linear courses were 'overegged', with the weather and a wet summer diminishing the runnable nature of the terrain. Sounding like a modern-day Gerry Charnley, Mike was not about to apologise. 'This is the OMM. What do you expect?' he would write in his planner's report. 'Special thanks must be made to the Botanic Garden for the loan of heather and tussock, the assistance of the local keepers in digging bear pits and traps, my climbing buddies for advice on scrambling routes, and last but not least, Mikey (The Hurricane) Trout for meteorological assistance in providing typical OMM weather.'

At the third checkpoint on day two, four teams came

together, creating the intensity of traditional hill racing. Iain Whiteside and Andy Fallas were first to drop back, with Andy suffering from short-term blindness caused by a lack of food; Shane Ohly and Duncan Archer were next to cede to the furious pace. As Adam Perry began to struggle, Nic and Jim saw their opportunity to attack the overnight leaders. 'Adam was gapped by maybe 20 seconds, but Kim stayed on us – a tactic Jim had played earlier when I dropped a little,' Nic said. Adam recovered. The gap closed. The defenders would then become the attackers. On a short, steep climb from a clough, Adam and Kim 'eased away', with Nic and Jim's quest for OMM glory dissolving. 'They were only 30 seconds or so ahead, but that was the elastic gone,' admitted Nic.

Nic and I spoke on the phone a few days later. He was on crutches. How does a man who finished as a runner-up in the elite category of the OMM find himself in such a predicament? At the end of the second day, Nic removed a filthy, bloodied right sock, uncovering a blistered big toe and a fourth toe shorn of nail and skin. As the pain intensified on the journey home, Jim drove Nic to accident and emergency in Darlington. 'They were quite puzzled,' Nic said. 'They didn't know what to make of it. They asked me what was normal for this type of event, so I got my left foot out.'

As Duncan and I dropped off Hog Hill, we saw the event centre in the valley. I took my bag back: a minor victory – albeit for appearance's sake only. I mustered something resembling a sprint and crossed the finish line, running blindly beyond the last checkpoint. 'Jonny, dib!' Duncan yelled at my latest act of ignominy. There was still to be one more.

A kit check was obligatory, with missing items likely to lead to disqualification. An OMM official carefully looked us up and down, glanced at a clipboard, peered at us again, and said: 'Can I see your waterproof trousers, boys?' I laughed, probably for the first time in two days.

'I've lost them. They are up there – somewhere,' I said,

waving dismissively at the hills. I imagined them tangled and half-submerged in a bog.

They had vanished the previous afternoon. 'How long have you been running with your bag wide open?' Duncan had said at the time. It was the sort of question a parent would ask a child.

'What?'

'Your bag is wide open!'

'Oh … The stove?'

'*I've* got the stove.'

'Oh.'

Home still smelt vaguely of vomit. Arielle was in the corridor, playing with a doll, wheeling it round in a little pink buggy. She glanced at me and continued around a corner. 'She's been fine,' Dad said. 'She perked up a few minutes after you left.' Somehow her not being fine would have made things better; her not being fine would have given me an excuse.

'How did you get on?' Dad asked.

'We weren't disqualified,' I muttered. That might have made it better too. Like Colin Donnelly and Ben Nevis, I could have made a purportedly moral stand over a pair of waterproof trousers, vowing never to return to the hills of Tweedsmuir.

Gradually, the self-pity subsided. Only a flutter of disappointment remained – a disappointment that was nothing to do with the OMM. This was about the mountains of Lochaber, not the heathery hills of the Borders.

'When I get there, I will just get on with it.' What unrealistic nonsense those words seemed now. The equation was plain: if I cannot cope with the challenge of the OMM, how can I possibly do Ramsay's Round?

I wondered, idly at first, then obsessively: what exactly does it take to be a Ramsayist?

11

ANATOMY OF THE RAMSAYIST

You sense Alan Smith before you see him. I sensed him now: a near 13-stone man striding uphill, fingers characteristically knitted behind his back. Reindeer Man, they call him. With a bound, he moved in front. I hung on, transfixed by the thick woollen socks stretching up his ankles. We summited the pyramidal Eildon Hill together. I followed a path to the right. Alan continued directly over the nose and disappeared. He seemed to me to have run over the edge of a cliff. When I glimpsed him again, he was far below, galloping into the clasp of a pass, a rapidly shrinking form, then swerving left along a track, sweeping downhill to the finish line in the Borders town of Melrose.

'Straight down,' Alan says when I ask how he got from summit to pass. 'It was heather and rock, then scree – and on scree you can open up fast. Then there was a wee bit of rocky stuff, then back onto the path. I must have overtaken half a dozen people.'

On the flat, Alan 'plods like a carthorse'; going up, he is a diesel engine: robust but unspectacular; going down, with his size tens aligned to gravity, he is possessed with the agility of the willowiest reindeer. 'It's the strength in my legs, and it's up here,' he says, tapping a finger to his temple. 'If you fall, you fall, but I can probably count on one hand how many times I've fallen in races. If you hold yourself back, you jar your whole body. My knees are great – for a fifty-six-year-old.'

Alan has been at the races for three decades, running as many as 50 a year. His regime needs little discussion, he insists: Alan does not train. Raised in the Royal Deeside town of Ballater, he continues to run with the childish impudence that prompted his much younger self to race his father off the hills, rather than ride home on a tractor.

'I'm a farmer, you see,' he explains, 'so I chase reindeer around the Cairngorms – finding them and shifting them. We've got a farm at Tomintoul where we've got red deer and sheep. We've got a quad, so you've got to get out for your run as you've been sitting on your backside all day. You don't have to do much – just potter about, four, five miles a day. Every day though.' In winter, in preparation for the deluge of summer races, he will run further, always in the hills, perhaps up Ben Avon or Lochnagar – the mountains on his 'back door'. His one concession to 'training' is a Tuesday night session of intervals on forestry tracks with his Deeside clubmates. The tracks, he can just about bear. Roads are anathema. 'I can't get roads into my head,' he says. 'I'd rather go around a corner and see Ben Nevis.'

Alan stands a shade over six feet in his running studs and weighed 12 stone nine pounds that morning, he tells me, wincing a little, despite wielding a half-eaten meat pie in one hand. We sit side by side on a wooden bench in the sunshine, two meagre thighs, two substantial ones. 'That's three stone heavier than a lot of others,' he says, taking another bite of the pie. He looks sideways at me. 'We should have a handicap. You lot should have to carry a bag of bricks.'

Malcolm Gladwell's 1993 book, *Outliers*, argues that the route to excellence in a particular field is 10,000 hours of practice. Alan Smith's knees could not sustain 10,000 hours of descending. Even the longest continuous descent in British hill racing – Ben Nevis, free-falling some 1,300 vertical metres – only takes the average hill runner around 45 minutes to accomplish. Alan shrugs when I ask him how he descends so quickly. He did not know. Or if he knew, he could not explain.

Like any aptitude that has been embedded, when called upon, he acts instinctively.

Brothers Andrew and Iain Gilmore are watching runners dash along the finishing straight of the annual downhill-only race on Caerketton. In a little over one mile, the track drops 300 metres at an average gradient of around 20 per cent. Andrew had won the three previous races, becoming in 2014 the first person to breach the five-minute barrier. His split for the first mile was four minutes and 30 seconds. 'I just let go,' he remembers. 'It was very exhilarating.'

The brothers' brief but frantic races have been run. Iain showed me his time: 5 minutes and 14 seconds; Andrew had not worn a watch. With runners set off at short intervals, the fastest descender would not be revealed until the end. It would be a Gilmore one-two, but Iain – twice runner-up behind his older sibling – had come of age, finishing 21 seconds faster than Andrew. The prizes at the Caerketton Downhill are distributed by lottery and after his name was called, Iain returned to us clutching a two-litre bottle of Irn Bru.

'When I'm racing, the fears about tripping or injuring myself disappear, unlike training runs when you're taking it more easily,' Andrew says when I ask the brothers how they overcome fear. 'If you're properly going flat out, that takes over your mind. There's no room for anything else.'

Iain chips in: 'All your concentration is on running the right lines at full pace. You don't have time to think about the risks involved.'

The Scottish Hill Runner in the late 1980s was a satirical affair. 'The sport of hill running and particularly the attitude of its participants from organiser, marshal, champion, to the slowest boggie, is precious,' Pete Crane declared in his editorial in the January 1988 edition. 'So please let us all resolve not to take ourselves too seriously,' he added.

'Matey Jockland' was parodying – and knew his audience – when he penned *The Art of Descending* for the magazine.

Rule one is 'reduced sensory awareness, especially sight', he wrote. He advocated 'closing the eyes prior to descending', and failing that, 'consuming alcohol for longer lasting effects.' Rule two is 'mental instability'. Matey recommended the best way to 'reduce sensory input' was to undergo a frontal lobotomy. 'Rumour has it that certain of the more successful clubs operate a "lobotomy at birth" policy as a means of developing strong junior squads. A spokesman for Lochaber AC strenuously denied that his club operated such a policy, adding that the pre-natal method was much more effective.'

There is truth, of course, in satire. When Alan Smith was competing against his father's tractor, he was unwittingly skilling himself for a life in the mountains: where to place his feet, selecting the line of least resistance, thinking multiple steps ahead. Hundreds of descents, hundreds of thousands of footmarks. The Gilmore brothers are in their twenties, three decades behind Alan, but the same principle applies. Youth does not equate to inexperience. In seven years, since the brothers were old enough, they have run almost 400 hill races between them. Running his first Caerketton Downhill as an eighteen-year-old, Iain finished in 6 minutes and 48 seconds, a time that would have placed him mid-pack in today's race. As we speak – having also won Bishop Downhill, at 1,140 metres the shortest race in the Scottish hill racing calendar, and Nebit Downfall, the two races that bookended Caerketton in a late-summer downhill series – his descending speed was unmatched.

Malcolm Patterson knows how to get off a mountain. Coming to hill running via orienteering, he raced extensively in Scotland, notably winning at Ben Lomond and Dollar. He was ninth at Ben Nevis in 1984, in what was arguably the strongest field to ever contest the race, and won a Great Britain vest the same year, before making five further international appearances. He now works for Scottish Athletics, answering to the title of 'national coach mentor' for the country's best hill and mountain runners, as well as coaching at the hill running powerhouse of Shettleston Harriers. He reels off a list of the qualities that make a good downhill runner: strength, balance, coordination, agility, proprioception, anticipation, keeping the body in line, fast feet. I nod inwardly at the list. None of it surprises me. We come, inevitably, to the brain-off, brakes-off cliché. 'The classic quote is you have to have a screw loose,' Malcolm says. 'But running downhill is a calculated risk. Confidence comes from knowing you have done the right sort of training and that you have the strength and balance necessary for you to come downhill at speed without falling or breaking down.'

He acknowledges some runners are innately less scared, but believes instinctive dread can be overcome. 'It's about knowing you've fallen and survived; you've drawn blood and haven't died. A lot of this does come naturally, but you can overthink it too. That was one of my problems. I over-analysed rather than letting things flow. It's not about disengaging the brain and being reckless; it's about relaxing and calming yourself, and getting rid of tension. I used to think it was a macho thing about having the bottle – I don't buy that line.'

As Malcolm conceded, there is an argument too for simple genetics: those, in a sporting sense, born lucky. Stewart Whitlie is in his mid-fifties, but like Adrian Belton, he could pass for two decades younger. He is a self-confessed 'uphill specialist', switching to hill running after a decade of success in amateur cycle racing. 'There must be something in the way we are made. Right at the start of cycling, I could always cycle up hills fast,' he says. 'There's probably a genetic thing about strength to weight ratio, and some people may have this naturally.' The cadence and style of cycling uphill mimics the short, fast steps needed to climb. A slight figure, standing five feet and seven inches, and weighing around nine-and-a-half stone, Alan Smith would have Stewart carrying a bag of bricks. 'Compared to other runners going uphill – when you can hear them blowing – I don't feel like I'm breathing particularly hard,' Stewart admits. In a downhill-only race, Alan might be the better of the pair, but in conventional races, Alan will not be anywhere near Stewart. There is no shame in that. Few runners get anywhere near Stewart. He is a 14-time Scottish hill running champion: once as a senior, five times as an over-40, eight times as an over-50. Even in his sixth decade, Stewart strikes fear into the hearts of athletes half his age, racing prolifically and still winning outright. He is, it seems, ageless.

If Stewart has an equal, it is Bill Gauld, an athlete who notoriously won the 14-mile Seven Hills of Edinburgh as a fifty-seven-year-old. Two years later, a few months shy of sixty, he negotiated the immense tangle of scree at Jura, quite possibly the sternest race in the hill running year, in under four hours – a feat worthy of an engraved whisky tumbler. When I ran with Bill on Bruntsfield Links, on the sort of blue sky and breezy March afternoon that makes Edinburgh feel like the happiest place on Earth, the weather did not seem coincidental. He was trying to 'get fit', Bill told me. I looked down at a little snow-haired man in sunglasses, kitted out in tracksuit, fleece and running shoes, all the while clutching a stick in his right hand. He was eighty-three. We would run for a minute, then walk, before breaking into a jog again. He moved slowly but instinctively – as a three-time British over-50 hill running champion and world over-65 silver medallist would. There was no shuffle, no stoop. The stick scarcely touched the ground. We completed three laps of the Links, around a mile. He had already been up Blackford Hill that morning: 'I walked up the steps, then ran down to the road,' he said nonchalantly. That night, he was planning to meet a group of Carnethy women who run socially on alternate Mondays. I see him on the hills occasionally. On the evenings of the Carnethy handicaps in the Pentlands, if he is not running, Bill often walks partway along the course. He does not cheer or encourage; he just seems to look and think. We dash past him, every one of us offering a greeting: 'Hello, Bill.'

Alan Smith is non-conventional. He *would* claim not to train. What he means is he does not follow fads; he does not do anything flashy. You will not catch him uploading a run to Strava or wearing cushioned anklet socks. He lives offline, asking others to enter him for online-entry only races, but his ability to run competitively in the Scottish mountains is easily explained. He is as hill-hard as they come. And that is what links Alan Smith to the Gilmores to Stewart Whitlie to Bill Gauld. Unwittingly, they buy into the philosophy of Malcolm Patterson: that the best are made, not born. 'When I started hill running,' Malcolm said, 'I thought I would have to be the world's strongest man and eat rocks for breakfast.' He knows better now.

When the Gilmore siblings are jogging up Caerketton and careening downhill, refining their technique, Stewart is moving deeper into the range, running from Flotterstone, following the route of the Pentland Skyline. He will save surges for the climbs, pumping his legs and swinging his arms up Turnhouse, then Carnethy, then Scald Law. For almost twenty years, he ran short, fast repetitions on the grass at Edinburgh's Inverleith Park during his lunch break on Tuesdays. Such was his longevity, when his workplace changed – and he would no longer be able to make the session – a party was thrown in his honour. After completing yet another session of intervals, a four-person relay was staged, with Stewart running alone. For once, he finished last.

Stewart's other staple sees him in Holyrood Park for the so-called WASP, the anacronym for Wednesday Arthur's Seat pain. The clue is in the name: 30 minutes of self-induced torment. As well as the understatement characterised by Eddie Campbell, the other quality a hill runner must possess is a willingness to suffer – and suffering must be rehearsed.

Colin Donnelly has been suffering ever since he ran up Ben Lomond in 1977. 'Get a lap, say it's a half-mile, on the grass, don't do it on the road, set a plan of around ten laps,' he explained. 'Time your laps, and make sure that you get faster and faster, even if it's hurting.'

Bobby Shields expressed a similar sentiment in the 1980s:

'It's easier to chicken out because you don't know your limitations until you hit them. Although you're lying in the gutter, you might not be at your limit. People don't realise what the body can do until they're put in the position of having to do it.'

Aberdeen-born Jack Maitland, who won the British championship in his first serious year of competition in 1986, states the case even more concisely: 'It's what you're prepared to do yourself.'

Suffering, I get. That is a decision of will. But what about the 'genetic thing'?

Joe Symonds and Tom Owens are facing an audience at Kinlochleven Primary School on the eve of the Glen Coe Skyline. Joe had won the 2015 race; Tom would finish second in the 2016 version the following day. The question and answer session is arranged by Salomon, the race sponsor, and has a disjointed, awkward air. Joe runs 60 to 70 miles per week, he tells us, much of the volume accomplished by commuting from his family home to work as a doctor. Hill repeats, a threshold session and a long run in the hills are standard features of his week. When Tom speaks, he virtually parrots Joe; there is little to distinguish their training. I sense the audience searching for something: a collective yearning to know the answer to that crucial question: why are you *so* good at running? And perhaps more pertinently, why are you better than us? We ask about tapering and shoes – as if wearing the same studs as Joe and Tom will make an iota of difference. The questions continue: motivation, cross-training, race strategy. I cannot help but think of Stewart Whitlie's words about genetic inheritance. Perhaps they should use this platform to make a public apology? After all, it is not their fault.

Tom dismisses the notion when, several months later and days before he is due to fly out to Costa Rica to race in the six-day, 142-mile Coastal Challenge, I ask him to elaborate on the comments he made in Kinlochleven. 'One of the main things I like about running is that generally you get out what you put in,' he says. 'For me, that means a lot of hard work but also trying to be clever with training – focusing on key sessions, build-ups and of course proper recovery. I believe there are very gifted athletes, but without the commitment to hard work, they won't stick it out or will break down. I certainly don't think I have any particularly good running ability other than persistence, determination and a fairly positive mindset.'

In the world of Tom Owens, 'persistence' and 'determination' look like this: a solid base of winter mileage; two or three 'quality' sessions a week that could be hill work, a tempo run, flat intervals or a race, as well as twice-weekly visits to the mountains; a week or fortnight-long warm weather training camp in the peaks of the Canaries; a job as an ecologist that means many hours every day on his feet wearing heavy boots; miles of cycling because he does not own a car; a summer sabbatical in the Alps or Pyrenees running alongside some of the best athletes on the planet – in 2016, Tom ran the 100-mile route of the Ultra-Trail du Mont-Blanc in three days, then climbed Mont Blanc; racing regularly and racing hard – he has twice been a Scottish hill racing champion and a runner-up in the Extreme Skyrunning Series; at the end of a season, usually in November and December, running is temporarily replaced by cyclo-cross. And then it starts all over again.

I was still unsatisfied. Despite his obvious aptitude for hard work, how could Tom not accept that he was born lucky – that his heart, lungs and legs were better equipped for running than the overwhelming majority? He would dominate the Coastal Challenge, winning overall and each of the day stages. 'Would you accept you are blessed with natural ability?' I wrote in a message to Tom when he was home again. 'It is indisputable that not everyone can be a champion hill racer,' I explained. 'If two people undertake the same training and share similar discipline, talent will naturally separate them.'

Tom disagreed again, naming a handful of mountain and ultra-distance runners who he considered to be 'naturally gifted': Kilian Jornet, Jonathan Wyatt, Marco de Gasperi and Angela Mudge. Tom Owens, he insisted, was not on the list. 'Even then,' Tom said, 'they still have the desire to compete and train very hard. I certainly don't put myself in the same category as those guys. Without determination and training, and the ability to recover from training and racing, I would not have any success.'

In the end, I got an answer that satisfied my probing from Stephen Pyke, a runner who would know: he has run all the Munros in 39 days. 'Kilian – in terms of the physiology he has been blessed with – is that Usain Bolt freak of nature type athlete,' he said. 'Tom is probably blessed to be in the top five per cent of having a good physiology for running, and through hard work he has turned himself into a top athlete – but he has probably not been born with the physiology and talent that Kilian has. Ultimately, however hard he works, if Kilian works at the same level, Tom is not going to beat him.'

When utilised then, there is no substitute for raw genetically-conceived talent – but tenacity comes very close.

Kate Jenkins won three hill racing championships in seven years, as well as several Scotland vests, through sheer force of will. She is proudly alternative. 'I can't sit still,' she says. 'I never trained to race. I feel restless and I go for a run. That's the bottom line. It's my anti-depressant, my anger management, my frustration release; it's for when I'm feeling crap at work. And I love beautiful places. They make me feel at peace.'

Kate grew up on a Pentlands hill farm, walking the fields and moors barefoot. Burying sheep and cutting tracks kept her fit. She was 'feral,' she admits, and it was little wonder she was 'tomboyish' at school. At university, fellow students would ask, 'you're not running again?' Kate would nod – and go for her run.

'They would think I was a freak or weird,' she says. In later years, coaches wondered why she lacked focus, despite her obvious ability and endurance. She twice attempted to follow training schedules. The first – a six-month programme – had no effect, she insists. As for the second: 'I was injured after two weeks. I'd never been injured before, so I thought, stuff this training bollocks.'

Stuff convention too. When Kate won the first of her seven West Highland Way Race titles in 1999, finishing third overall, she was averaging a mere 30 miles a week in preparation. Her nutrition for the 95-mile route included 16 bags of crisps – effectively one packet every six miles. 'I eat what I want,' she declares. 'And I drink – lots.'

Perhaps it was Kate's carefree attitude that made her excel – an attitude characterised by eight extraordinary days in 2011. After winning her seventh West Highland Way, she raced in the Pentlands four days later, ahead of two long back-to-back weekend races, Arrochar Alps and the Lairig Ghru, taking her racing miles in that period to almost 150. A fortnight later, Kate was second Briton in the women's race in the Trail World Championships in Connemara, Ireland, but paid the price for her formidable effort: 'I ended up in the back of an ambulance.'

Kate's mantra for success is as credible as Alan Smith's: 'I am bloody-minded.' When we speak several months later, she tells me she has 'trashed her heel'. She was heading out to 'beast hill reps' nonetheless. Her rationale? 'I can't bear weight on it, so up on the toes work instead.'

It is the collision of talent and grit that prompts success in Ramsay's Round. It is why Adrian Belton held the record for 26 years. 'What the Ramsay requires is mental determination and focus – that and a bit of luck,' he says, before using the same adjective as Kate to describe himself. 'I just kept buggering on. I suppose I have a combination of doggedness and bloody-mindedness.' Those qualities propelled Adrian into the record books. But sometimes, in the rough world of Ramsay's Round, even that is not enough.

Bill Johnson was new to hill running in the late 1990s when he supported three fellow members of Macclesfield Harriers on successful rounds. 'I remember Craig Harwood sprinting down the road, eyeballs on stalks, to get in on time,' Bill said.

'I was amazed at those mountains: nature at its grandest.' He vowed to emulate his clubmates. Life intervened: family and work, and the alternative of a closer-to-home Bob Graham. A decade had slipped away when Bill's wife, Anne Stentiford, who then held the women's records for the Bob Graham and the Paddy Buckley, sought to complete the trio. They travelled north, with Anne convinced she was fitter than she had been on the previous rounds. As they neared Fort William, Bill and Anne, and a trio of leg one supporters, came to the scene of an accident. 'There was no-one else there,' said Bill. 'The driver had careered off the road into a field. He died.' Police interviews followed; the 4am start time slipped by. They lost the will. 'No-one's heart was in it,' Bill recalled. Anne never regained the same level of fitness and two years later had an operation on both knees. She will never run Ramsay's Round.

Pursuing the dream, Bill attempted for the first time in 2012, abandoning after 15 hours with crippling stomach cramps. He tried again three weeks later. Same problem, same outcome. After seeking advice on what he should eat – egg butties and boiled potatoes, he concluded – he returned to Lochaber in 2014. He would call Anne from the darkness of Beinn na Lap. There was a resigned sadness to Bill's tone: 'She tried to keep me going, but I knew I wasn't going to.'

The 'stubborn fool' went again. 'You're almost there,' a walker descending Ben Nevis encouraged as Bill began a clockwise attempt. He was as ready as he could be, having completed long back-to-back days in the hills and a Tranter a fortnight earlier.

And yet: 'I felt rubbish – no strength at all in my legs.' Bill decided on the Grey Corries to quit at Fersit, unaware that his crew had made a pact to dismiss such notions. He continued, carried forward on a wave of positivity and a reassuring sense that there was no way out, while explicitly aware that he was not going to crack 24 hours. It did not matter; that day, just getting around was enough. He made it back to the hostel, almost 26 hours after starting. Bill – one of the silent, unrecorded Ramsayists – went back to his rented lodge and lay down. 'I crashed out – sleeping the sleep of the just. Just finished. Just completely knackered. Just delighted.'

Mark Hartree is more Kate Jenkins than Tom Owens. He *could* run Ramsay's Round, but while the vagaries of terrain and weather, and a thousand other uncertainties, might have extended Jon Ascroft's round from 17 to 19 hours, such an occurrence on Mark's *would* tip him over 24. It was always going to be tight. Mark's strategy was constructed on unrelenting optimism, surrounding himself with hill running friends and filling his mind with verse. On Aonach Beag, he felt a twinge in his right knee – the return of an old injury. 'I hoped I would run it off,' he said. 'I put it firmly into the back of my mind, in a box, and shut the lid so I could not see or hear it scream.' The music – The Rolling Stones, Take That, The Killers – was not enough to drown out the insistence of a throbbing knee. As Mark trudged through the glen to Sgùrr Eilde Mòr, his pace inexorably slowed to a halt. Searching for a reason to carry on, he remembered why he was here: Molly Williams, a two-year-old from Sheffield suffering from spinal muscular atrophy, who had inspired Mark to run eight ultramarathons, ultimately raising more than £10,000 for her charity. 'I was blessed to be able to do this sort of thing when others can't,' he realised. It was enough to get him to his feet. He was going to finish no matter what, but within 24 hours? If you are moving and can keep moving, it is possible.

As Mark climbed Sgùrr Eilde Mòr, the vapour trail of a plane glowed crimson as it caught the dying rays of the sun. He was fed cashew curry and jelly babies, and sang *Wild Rover*. There was light, but then there was dark, and with the darkness came clag, adding a slick, slippery coating to the rocks of the Mamores. A dodgy knee, a bit of clag – it was enough. The balance tipped.

The day elapsed on Mullach nan Coirean. On the road, Mark broke into a trot. His knee had inexplicably stopped hurting. 'My left leg felt brilliantly strong and my right one was just numb.'

He heard the voice of Charlie Ramsay ahead: 'Get your arms up!'

'I wasn't a champion, so I put them out and ran through the finish line in 24 hours and 47 minutes,' Mark said. 'As we sat down on the wall to get a group picture, I looked up at the Ben. The top was clear with blue skies. The sun was out and it looked perfect conditions to do Ramsay's Round. I laughed. So much for planning.'

Great Borne rises in the Western Fells of the Lake District, casting a tumbling reflection into Ennerdale Water. Standing 616 metres, it is dwarfed by the summits of Lochaber. Bill Williamson had three times been unsuccessful on Ramsay's Round. When he tried again, he finally made it back to Glen Nevis: it was not enough; he was timed out. He would not be able to walk properly for three weeks afterwards. When he removed a sock, blood poured from a toe; closer inspection revealed the skin on his toes had been torn off. Infection followed. That summer, while his family played on the sand of a Cornish beach, Bill sat watching them, wearing a pair of wellies to cover his swollen feet. But, despite the pain, was he, like Bill Johnson, 'just delighted'? At the time, 'it felt like some sort of closure.' Who was he kidding? Bill Williamson would be back.

The weather had been characteristically cruel on his attempts – support runner Bob Wightman had to grab hold of Bill to stop him being blown off Na Gruagaichean as the wind gusted to 60mph, with Ian Charters, another water-carrier, cowering on all fours at the same moment, in one attempt – but it would be too easy to blame failure on the elements. Bill was repeatedly bothered by a recurring knee injury that could not cope with the extraordinary requirements of repeated ascent and descent. That physical affliction then ate into his belief that the round could be done.

Bill went back to his home in the western Lake District, wondering if Ramsay's Round was simply beyond him. He had accomplished the Bob Graham and Paddy Buckley, but the

Scottish equivalent seemed to reject his every advance. What was the difference? What did he have to do to be a Ramsayist? He looked up. The answer stared back at him: Great Borne.

He stood at the bottom of the fell and started running, climbing 500 metres to the bouldery summit. From there, he descended a grassy slope, reaching the falling water of Red Gill, then turned uphill again, rising a further 300 metres back to Great Borne's highest point via a rugged approach on Floutern Crag. Bill would run the route twice, three times if he was feeling sprightly, every fortnight.

That was only the beginning. There was the weekly tempo-style uphill session, either a 25-minute, mile-long climb up 450 metres of Great Borne, or another mile effort over 35 minutes on the north-west ridge of Grasmoor End. There was the monthly psychological slog on Crag Fell or Gale Fell, eschewing tourist tracks and finding deliberately steep lines buried in bracken and heather, the sort of place a person would wander only when lost. There were longer runs too, inevitably up Great Borne, then left into Mosedale and over Hen Comb, Mellbreak and Red Pike, or onto the heights of Grasmoor above Crummock Water. The purpose was fixed: controlled suffering. The preparation must match the objective. With a month to go before a fifth Ramsay attempt, he climbed 5,500 metres in a week; the following week he did 4,600. Around the same time, he ran a final seven-mile effort on forest tracks. The route – comprising around 500 metres of ascent – had once taken him 1 hour and 35 minutes. It was a session Bill had prioritised, knowing he needed to cover the theoretically runnable ground between Beinn na Lap and Meanach as fast as possible. This time the run took one hour and two minutes. Bill was ready.

Standing outside the hostel in Glen Nevis, three years after his last attempt, Bill was not apprehensive. He was excited. He was imbued with confidence. What did he have to worry about? 'I knew I could run much faster than just under 24 hours, but the main goal was to complete,' he says.

With confidence came a revelation: this thing now offered the potential for enjoyment. 'If you enjoy what you're doing,' Dr Lucy Rattrie, an Edinburgh-based sports mindset coach, told me, 'you're going to get so much more out of it.' So it would be for Bill. The hours spent hauling his body up Great Borne, Grasmoor End, Crag Fell and the rest had dislodged the abstract sense of the round. It was suddenly – and quite wonderfully – plausible. The doing would be easier than what had already been done. Heading clockwise, it took Bill a conservative eight-and-a-half-hours to reach Loch Treig, but he seemed remarkably fresh, as if he had been jogging.

Bill had found the difference – but it was not down to training alone. After reading Christopher McDougall's *Born to Run* and Tim Noakes' *Lore of Running* he was convinced the cause of the knee pain was poor running technique, not the far easier excuse of 40 years of walking and running in the fells. He transitioned to low-drop footwear and began drills in aqua shoes. 'Within a few months,' he says, 'I experienced for the first time since my teens the feeling of floating along as I ran, and the knee pain disappeared.' Bill was also 25 pounds lighter than he had been on his previous attempt, having adopted a near-paleo diet, massively reducing his consumption of refined carbohydrate. It was a logical step to becoming faster. Comparing times, his recovery pace was now the same as his tempo pace had been five years earlier.

I thought of Alan Smith and his meat pie, Kate Jenkins and her 16 bags of crisps – salt and vinegar before she could no longer stomach the flavour and resorted to ready salted. While sports nutritionist Renee McGregor would not specifically recommend a paleo diet, she makes a living by encouraging others to change the way they think about food and drink. When we speak, I attempt to dismiss diet as a 'marginal gain'. She gives the notion short shrift, insisting the balance of sporting performance hinges equally on the physical, the mental and nutrition. As a performance and clinical dietician, Renee's job is to optimise the ways in which nutrition can enhance an athlete's performance. Typically, that entails identifying a perceived weakness caused by ineffective nutrition and finding ways to reduce or overcome the issue. For ultrarunner Robbie Britton, that means periodising his nutrition over different blocks of training, whether he is returning from injury or conditioning at high-altitude in the Alps; for Paralympic fencer Piers Gulliver, that means maintaining blood sugar levels to maximise his ability to concentrate, particularly as fights become more aggressive and recovery time diminishes; for Holly Rush, another ultrarunner, that means careful planning of hydration and salt levels during races, factoring length, terrain and temperature. For Bill, it just happened to be a paleo diet.

The euphoria continued, not least on the prepared-for run to Meanach. 'It just seemed to flow effortlessly,' Bill recalls, 'as if I could run forever. I wish you could bottle that feeling.' At the bothy, he met Bob Wightman, Andy Kitchin and Jim Mann. 'I remember telling them I thought I was holding back, and I was told not to bother holding back any more. When I got to Binnein Mòr I found I had knocked an hour off my schedule. The rest of the final leg was surreal as I knew I would finish in under 24 hours.'

A low sun bathed the mountains in a cherry blush as Bill ran down Mullach nan Coirean. An easterly squall marched along the glen, the rain glinting in the fading remnants of day. The runner seemed to tread water, as if in a dream. Once on forestry tracks, he suddenly felt desperately tired. The merest incline reduced his movements to a walk. But still the reverie, like an 'outer-body experience', as Bill puts it, cradled him. He thought of how he had failed, over and over again – and then was catapulted to a hallucinogenic present. He is a Ramsayist.

12

PIZZA, PROSECCO AND ICE CREAM

The alarm sounds at 5am. Jasmin Paris opens her eyes. She knows what is to be done. She climbs out of bed, pulls on running gear and makes her way to the kitchen, where she scoops a handful of muesli into a palm and chews her breakfast as she ties her laces. She shuts the door behind her. As her breath condenses in the cold air, she adjusts the head torch and starts running, her studded shoes clacking along the road, the only sound in the darkness of a January morning. Within ten minutes, the road is a memory; she is among hills. The Moorfoot range, wild, high and illuminated by torch light, embrace the runner. They are well acquainted. An owl hoots. Deer skitter. Foxes gawp. She runs as she feels, across pathless hillside, through heather and bog. After an hour, with the hills still immersed in darkness, her smeared legs turn for home. The click-clack heralds her return. At the back door, she pulls off her muddied shoes, tosses them on a growing pile, and steps inside. She will be out there again tomorrow, and the day after, and next week, and next month. She will break trail in fresh-fallen snow; she will battle malevolent wind and frantic rain; she will watch apricot dawns. Sometimes, she will want to ignore the ringing of the alarm, to stay in bed for a little longer, to not step out the door. She goes nonetheless.

There is more than one way to make a champion. This is the Jasmin Paris way.

While she travelled along the faint tracks of the Moorfoots, Jasmin could have allowed herself to dream of what may be.

But this is a woman who understands cause and effect; a woman who dedicated six years to train as a vet, then another four to earn specialist European Diploma status; a woman whose parents, Jeff and Alena, are university academics renowned for their work on mathematical logic. While Jasmin's approach to running is 'uncalculated and spontaneous, and definitely not measured or considered', her efforts are underpinned by pragmatism. Once she had committed to being the best she could be, it was not enough to simply hope. The Jasmin Paris way is based on common sense: I will reap what I sow – and sowing is what Jasmin does best.

'The hardest thing is getting out the door,' Jasmin says. 'Once you're out there, it's okay. I like being outside and being in the hills, even on those bad days. I remember one time when I was running on the hills in a blizzard and thinking – in those white flakes at five in the morning – anyone would assume I was completely crazy.' She stops, turning her head to call into the kitchen. 'I don't sleep enough. Konrad would say that, wouldn't you?'

Konrad Rawlik is Jasmin's husband of three months. On the morning of their wedding on the Inner Hebridean island of Jura, the Paris-Rawlik Jura Whisky Chaser was inaugurated. Jasmin, dressed as a cow, and Konrad, wearing the attire of a milkmaid, along with a herd of mountain running friends, trotted up an island hill. The milkmaid had the edge, for the cow had been drinking Prosecco on the beach the night before, giving Konrad time to kneel and proffer a ring at the top. The happy couple took a dram with the group and raced downhill, the cow, even on her wedding day, leading the charge.

'Yeah,' Konrad shouts. He is making fishcakes for a dinner party.

The irony of the reversal of stereotypical gender roles – Konrad industrious in the kitchen, Jasmin seated, cradling a mug of tea – was not lost on me. This is Jasmin Paris: a runner defying stereotype. In the world of ultra-distance mountain running – the rougher the better – Jasmin is the equal of men.

'Gender isn't a big thing in my mind,' she says. 'I feel I'm level with men. I don't even think about gender inequality because we're the same, and if I know someone runs similarly to me, man or woman, I try to beat them.'

She points to the Dragon's Back, a five-day, 180-mile stage race across the mountainous interior of Wales. In 2015, Jasmin was second overall behind Jim Mann, while two other women came in the top six: Beth Pascall was fourth and Lizzie Wraith sixth. There were a further three women in the top fifteen. 'We can compete on an even playing field, especially in long-distance events,' Jasmin reiterates. She could easily have referenced the Fellsman: Jasmin finished fourth in the 2015 race, having never previously run further than 47 miles – and that was after getting lost in a 40-mile event – in a single outing. Such was her unease about the distance, she packed extra clothing with the expectation of walking to the finish. Or Jasmin could have mentioned the Glen Coe Skyline, also in 2015, when Swedish ultrarunner Emelie Forsberg finished only eight minutes behind Joe Symonds. Jasmin, having run with Forsberg for the first two hours, ended the day fifth, with a who's who of hill running – Tim Gomersall, Es Tresidder, Adam Harris, Jon Ascroft, Jim Mann and Jon Gay – finishing in her, and Forsberg's, wake.

It is late October when we meet at the newlywed's white-painted cottage on the edge of a Victorian reservoir that collects water from the Moorfoots. Jasmin's running year – a year characterised by an invincibility trademarked by Adrian Belton – was over, and frankly, the truth of it was hard to fathom. Adrian broke two records; Jasmin smashed the lot, becoming the fastest woman to run each of the classic rounds. But to fully appreciate the records, Jasmin's times should be addressed in their overall context, including men, and, by her concession, she does not mind such comparisons. Her Bob Graham was the fifth fastest of all time; a Paddy Buckley the fourth. Jasmin's Ramsay – sandwiched by the others – was the pinnacle: she was number one. When news of her record-breaking Bob Graham emerged, I thought immediately of her likely next intention, a Ramsay, and my conversation with Jon Ascroft about the athletes capable of a faster round than his. 'Jasmin,' he had said without hesitation. With the support of Jon on the Grey Corries, Jasmin did as he predicted, slicing 46 minutes from his time, finishing in 16 hours and 13 minutes. Cumulatively, her times for the three rounds were faster than any man. The next quickest, Chris Near, was six hours slower.

Actions speak louder than words: a woman could compete with men, could overcome men. But Jasmin Paris is not a symbol of some sort of female revolution. Humility – like her close friend Jon, she is imbued with the quality – prevents her admitting otherwise, but she is a one-off, unique, a freak even. 'I think it's notable how excited folk get whenever a woman ranks well against men,' says Helene Whitaker, the joint winner with Martin Stone of the first Dragon's Back in 1991 when she was still an unmarried Diamantides. 'Surely that says most about how unusual it is? Physiologically, the differences are impossible to overcome, but the longer endurance events always seem to level the field' – Helene chooses her last word carefully – 'somewhat.'

Helene is another one-off. Like Jasmin, she breathed the rarefied air of holding the outright record for Ramsay's Round. 'I had hoped to see more occurrences of outstanding female athletes, such as Jasmin and Angela Mudge, in the twenty-plus years since the original Dragon's Back, as technology and our understanding and knowledge of sports performance has escalated. But there are only one or two females doing so and – possibly I'm only one of a few able to say this and get away with it – the women who do are often more "masculine" in physique. We have smaller bums and boobs. We don't seem to have curves in any of the desirable places and quite frankly run in a very male way with aggression and an unashamed competitiveness that is frequently discouraged in girls but not boys. The fact that these women are exceptions rather than the norm by now suggests that endurance events simply come down to good genes, an awful lot of bloody hard work and an appropriate psychological temperament. Just the same as good male athletes.'

Wendy Dodds calls hill running a 'genderless activity' but recalls how female racers in the 1970s could only participate unofficially, typically starting some twenty minutes after the men and rewarded by items that might help in the home. The 'disadvantage' of being female did not hold Wendy back: she was the first person to complete the newly-devised Paddy Buckley in 1982 and ran an unmatched 53 Lakeland peaks in 22 hours at the age of 50 in 2002. She is an undisputed 'legend' of the hills, still running and racing in her mid-sixties, and unashamedly outspoken. Running as part of a team supporting two Canadians attempting the Ramsay for a television show, when Paul Trebilcock dodged one too many puddles on the track to the Abhainn Rath, she chastised the man nicknamed 'Turbocock': 'It's a waste of time because in half an hour we have to wade a stream.'

Women should be slower than men, Wendy, a retired consultant physician and rheumatologist, specialising in sports medicine, explains. Women have a higher proportion of body fat, reduced blood volume, smaller hearts and lungs, lower oxygen uptake and less muscle strength. The physiology is undeniable. There is, however, some logic to explain the success of women in ultra-distance events. 'Some studies have suggested that female skeletal muscle may have a greater capacity for converting fat to energy than male muscle,' Wendy says. 'It means that in ultra-endurance events, they have a larger store of potential energy on board because of their naturally greater proportion of fat.'

Dr Andrew Murray, a sports and exercise medicine doctor and director of the Scottish Running Clinic at the University of Edinburgh, concurs: 'The longer the distance, the narrower the gap in performance. Male runners are still at an advantage, but because running economy, fuelling and mental resilience take on increasing roles, the average gap is less.'

Jasmin Paris is one of the few to bridge the gap. 'Simple physiological differences mean that on average the fastest males are likely to be faster than the fastest females,' Andrew says, listing the reasons: higher testosterone values meaning more strength and aggression, along with greater lung capacities and blood circulating volumes, both of which lead to increased aerobic capacity.

'Jasmin's achievements are phenomenal,' Andrew adds, 'particularly when you consider she is smashing records for all-comers, despite the fact that for most distance records males are at a six to eight per cent advantage, and times normally reflect that. If you look at Paula Radcliffe's marathon world record, she is a country mile faster than any other female in history, but there were 100 men from one village of 4,000 people in Kenya who ran faster than her world record in 2016 alone.'

Whatever Jasmin is and represents, she remains a female. In the 2016 Rio Olympics, the Chinese swimmer Fu Yuanhui helped her team come fourth in the 4x100m medley relay. When asked about her performance, she broke a sporting taboo: she revealed she was menstruating. 'My period came yesterday,' she admitted, 'so I felt particularly tired.'

'I can recall a couple of times when I've gone to races and been emotional beforehand, but generally running makes it better,' Jasmin says. 'For me, it's more than a physical problem. It's a mental thing that means I might not quite have the right race head on, but normally running a race has snapped me out of it.' As for a record attempt on a 24-hour round: 'I would probably not want them to collide. The way it was arranged, it wasn't going to happen. To do the Paddy Buckley or the Ramsay, it would just be awkward. You want everything to be as easy as possible, so even if this isn't a huge thing for you, it's one extra thing.'

Jasmin speaks so openly about such a personal subject that

she could easily be a social media influencer or a feminist flag-bearer. That is not how she sees herself. But not wanting to be a feminist does not disqualify others from seeing you as one. Her example is enough. 'If I can challenge the idea that women can't do what men can, then that's great,' she says, 'but I don't have a hang-up about women being mistreated.' She recognises that increased female representation in running is not mirrored in the hills. I raise the subject as if I expect her to have an answer. 'I honestly don't know why,' Jasmin says. 'I guess women are just lacking confidence.'

Some months later, Jasmin agreed to be interviewed by the American Trail Running Association, specifically to give 'trail running tips for women' – a notion that could be interpreted as either helpful or deeply patronising. She spoke about having to carry a personal alarm when running in a strange city at night during a training year in Minnesota; she revealed she had bought her first 'dedicated' sports bra just a few months earlier; when asked what advice she would give to women who 'might not fit the stereotypical mould of a female runner', she unwittingly gave the answer of an indignant feminist: 'I'm not sure what the stereotypical mould of a female runner is.' Perhaps that is why women are 'lacking confidence'?

Shyness – like hill running – comes instinctively to Jasmin. Earlier that day, I had watched her talk to an audience at the annual Scottish Hill Runners end-of-season buffet, reliving her rounds, and noticed it took several minutes for the flushing of her cheeks to subside. After she had finished speaking, David Scott, one of the committee members, rose to thank Jasmin. 'Inspirational,' he said.

'I think it's weird,' Jasmin says. 'It's not that I'm uncomfortable with the attention; it just feels odd because I'm a normal person, like everybody else. I just go running.'

Born in Manchester in 1983 to a Czech mother and an English father, Jasmin was still in nappies when she was carried across the Andes on a four-day hike, with the toddler sleeping in a nook between her parents in a two-person sleeping bag. Her family were walkers not runners, and by the age of six, Jasmin, her parents and younger brother, Václav, were hiking and wild camping in the mountains of the freed Czech Republic in the final throes of the Cold War. 'My mum was very much of the attitude that if the sun was shining, you shouldn't be indoors,' Jasmin says. 'I still have this guilt complex when I'm inside and it's sunny outside. My mum made a real effort for us to be outside. She'd think of treasure hunts or we would play Swallows and Amazons or make a secret garden. We would go on trips to waterfalls and spend time playing in watercourses or by the sea.'

Jasmin was nearing the end of her junior school years when her teacher lined the class up at the bottom of a playing field and encouraged the children to race to the top. 'I was second in the year, to a boy, and I remember being slightly irked that he had beaten me.' While she did not race competitively at school, even in her secondary years, running was unwittingly imprinted in the fabric of her life. 'We would run with my dad as fast as we could, saying, "how fast do you think we are going?"' Her passion then was horse riding, a pursuit that would leave the teenager with no cruciate ligament in her left knee after she fell from her mount, but unexpectedly reminded Jasmin of her junior school running prowess. Taking part in a pony club triathlon of swimming, shooting and running, she was second fastest in the running element. 'I was surprised because I'd never done anything like that,' she says, 'so I guess that was an indication I could be a reasonably good runner.'

But not yet. After school, she went to Liverpool University to study veterinary science. She would jog for twenty minutes around Sefton Park to 'keep fit'. Following graduation in 2008, Jasmin started work at a small animal practice in Glossop, on the edge of the Pennines. One of her colleagues, Richard Patton, told her about a nearby four-mile race called Wormstones. 'You should try it,' he had said.

'Do I need anything?' Jasmin asked.

'No, you'll be fine,' he insisted.

She was 'fine', finishing the race in a state of 'exhausted delight'.

'I had only road trainers,' Jasmin remembers. 'I spent a lot of that run on my bottom, and I finished sixth lady and fairly low down the field, but I really enjoyed it. I thought, this is great: everybody racing around the hills.'

A year in Glossop was followed by a twelve-month internship at the University of Minnesota, where Jasmin's running was stymied by American geography: 'I wanted to run and do outdoor stuff, but there were not many trails and I didn't want to run on the road. Getting a bus out of the city was just impossible.' After a three-week post-internship break, Jasmin moved to Scotland, a country she had only twice visited as a child for hiking holidays with her family. She came to work at the University of Edinburgh veterinary school that had rejected her undergraduate application eight years earlier. 'I didn't even get an interview,' she says, shaking her head.

Jasmin was soon in the Pentlands, linking together the summits and paths of what would become her training ground. She was running a reverse Pentland Skyline when she met John Blair-Fish, who was stravaiging the same route in the opposite direction. Blair-Fish was an Englishman in Scotland, known for his long-standing antipathy to the Scottish breakaway from the Fell Runners Association. A forthright man and an undoubtedly accomplished hill runner, he told Suse Coon, who approached him for an interview for her 1987 book *Race You To The Top*, that the 'place for discussing races is the pub, not a book'. Jasmin asked Blair-Fish if he ran for a club. 'Carnethy,' he told her, before bluntly explaining she was running the 'wrong way'.

Ever prepared, Jasmin was readying herself for her first Scottish hill race. Blair-Fish had not put her off. Wearing the red and yellow of Carnethy, she would finish 56th at the Pentland Skyline that October. 'I wasn't very good at the start,' Jasmin admits. Her result was by no means unremark-able, but like her running at the end of 2010 and the start of 2011, the performance was tinged with an inexplicable lethargy. Her solution was to try harder, sometimes too hard. Having arranged to stay overnight at a friend's home in the Edinburgh suburb of Bonaly, she ran five miles over the Pentlands that evening from work, and intended to run back early the next day. Long before sunrise, Jasmin quietly let herself out, careful not to wake anyone. The door locked behind her, with the runner's shoes – left outside by Jasmin the night before, but subsequently moved inside by her friend – on the wrong side. Not wanting to cause a fuss, in case they thought her 'mad', she did something madder. She could do without shoes, she reasoned. She also had no head torch. 'The outcome of this venture was that I kicked a hefty rock at some point on the climb, and broke my big toe,' Jasmin recalls. 'On the plus side, my feet were so numb by then that I didn't realise there was anything amiss, and I made it to work in good time.'

The toe would mend but the tiredness remained. The reason would emerge at Stùc a' Chroin, a 13-mile race that climbs to the eponymous Munro above Loch Lubnaig. 'I remember it being really, really hard,' she says. 'One of these old fell running geezers said, "you've been overtraining, you're working too hard." I thought, I haven't been overtraining because I am right at the back of the field. I was second to last going up Stùc and was just hanging on. I made time up on the descent, but I had been rubbish on the climb. It was much more effort than it should have been.' Someone else was suffering that day: Konrad would finish 96th – 12 places behind Jasmin. If any good was to come of their mutual misfortune, it was the first meeting of a pair who would marry six years later.

Convinced she was anaemic, Jasmin asked her doctor to give her a blood test. Diagnosed with an iron deficiency, within a fortnight of starting a course of tablets, the change was staggering. 'It was like being given a magic bullet. I had a huge boost,' she says. Racing again, three weeks after Stùc a' Chroin, Jasmin won at Slioch.

Success followed in a tidal wave. In 2014, she became Scottish hill running champion and set the women's record for Tranter's Round, running every step with Jon Ascroft. In 2015, she reclaimed her Scottish crown and added British fell running champion to her résumé. That year she also won her fourth Scottish Long Classics series, excelling in longer races over rougher ground – a precursor of what was to come. She set women's records at two of those races, Jura and Two Inns, while a third victory came at Stùc a' Chroin, 43 minutes faster than her cursed first attempt in 2011.

At the end of 2015, the double hill running champion 'didn't do much at all'. She spent November and December running according to mood, rather than to order, as motivation waned. In her own words, she was a 'horse put out to pasture'. There was no need to forge on with training when the mind was reluctant. Crucially, having overcome anaemia and a succession of lower leg injuries – she listed the maladies: iliotibial band syndrome, tibialis posterior tendinitis, Achilles tendinitis in both ankles – she was in an injury-free cycle. At the end of November, writing in the quarterly *Carnethy Journal*, Jasmin made no secret of her intentions: 'I'm going to have a go at the three classic 24-hour rounds and hopefully test the records.'

When she was ready to resume training again, she set her alarm for 5am.

Quietly, with no fanfare, Jasmin and Konrad completed a winter Bob Graham in February, before returning a month later to re-run parts of the route, moving at 17 to 18-hour pace. That was the warm-up. A proposed mid-April effort at a fast round was postponed as Jasmin was recovering from the aftermath of food poisoning – the outcome of a dodgy salad eaten on the journey home from the Sierra Nevada mountains in southern Spain a few days earlier. The attempt was pushed back a week. Jasmin left Keswick with the splits of a 17-hour round in her head. In planning her schedule, she had either been cautious or modest. By Skiddaw, she was 10 minutes up, then 26 minutes at Threlkeld, growing to 51 minutes at Dunmail Raise. The support crew was an embarrassment of riches: Shane Ohly, Jon Ascroft, Jim Mann, Jon Gay, Iain Whiteside, Rhys Findlay-Robinson, Steve Birkinshaw. By the time she reached Wasdale, she was running splits that were akin to 15-hour pace. Unable to stomach food, she gorged on Haribo and Pepsi. As she was hurtling along the roads to Keswick, unbeknown to Jasmin, a 200-strong crowd had gathered by the Moot Hall. Although they were there for a charity event, not Jasmin, they formed an impromptu welcoming committee, creating a cheering funnel as she tore up the high street, pressed her hands to the doors, stopped her watch, and turned to embrace Konrad. The time was astonishing: 15 hours and 24 minutes.

The round had been a secret – and hill runners are good at keeping secrets. That is also the Jasmin Paris way. When she was planning her attempt on the Paddy Buckley later in the year, her chosen date clashed with the high-profile Hodgson Brothers Mountain Relay in the Lake District. Knowing that several of her would-be round supporters were committed to the race, she sent an email to the 425 members of Carnethy pleading for people to volunteer to replace the relay runners, thereby freeing up her support. She asked club members not to reveal her plans on social media. The subject of the email might have been labelled 'top secret'. In a sign of respect for the sport, and more for Jasmin, no-one uttered a word.

When Jasmin touched the green doors of the Moot Hall, the secret was out. For all the victories, records and championships, she had not transcended the sport. Outside the fell and hill running community, she was unknown. Even the average road runner would have shaken their head at the mention of the name Jasmin Paris. A simple combination piqued the interest of the public – the gender, of course, and the time on a hill running event that had singularly also transcended the sport. That the round had been kept quiet further imbued the achievement with a romantic spontaneity. Jasmin was flooded with messages of congratulation and adulation on social media. The same words were repeatedly tossed around: 'amazing', 'inspirational', 'phenomenal'.

She was propelled into public consciousness and would feature in spreads in running magazines, offering advice on training and racing. Interviewed in the *Guardian*, she was asked what was the 'best thing' about running. 'The feeling of being fit,' she said, 'the feeling that you could run forever.' Sports companies began to get in touch, offering sponsorship deals. She politely turned everything down, unwilling to 'muddy the waters' of a sport she calls 'pure'. Since 2015, Jasmin had been 'supported' – as opposed to the more committing term of 'sponsored' – by Inov-8, a sportswear company that makes the shoes that many hill and fell runners wear. Her fellow runners treated her with reverence. 'Was that Jasmin?' I heard a woman utter excitedly after spotting her marshalling on South Black Hill in a Pentland Skyline. 'Jasmin.' She joined the ranks of the greats. Like Billy, Joss and Finlay, a surname is superfluous.

Speculation comes with being public property. Could Jasmin go quicker? Could she have challenged Billy Bland's record had she set her mind to running faster at the start? She answered the questions conclusively in the aftermath: 'Some things are better left as they are, and I have a feeling this is one of them.' She met Bland for tea and bacon butties shortly after the round. '"This will give the men a kick up the arse," he told me. He thinks he has been placed on a pedestal that he perhaps should not have been.' Like Bland, Jasmin is uneasy with her heroine status. 'I just go running.' Those words again. 'For these long rounds, part of me just thinks, go out and try it, and you could do it as well.'

The pattern for Jasmin's season was set: race, recover, race, recover, and so on. There was little time for training. But, in the darkness of those Moorfoot mornings, the hard work had been done.

Jasmin came to Fort William in mid-June, a fortnight before the anniversary of the 17 hours in which Jon Ascroft recalibrated Ramsay's Round. Jasmin arrived with the same intention. Her basis was simple. She was Jon's equal in her fastest Tranter; she was his equal in hill racing in Scotland; she should, therefore, be his equal in the Lochaber mountains. But she hoped to be more than equal.

As she did in the lead-up to the Bob Graham, Jasmin delayed for a week, knowing that 'a record round was impossible without perfect conditions'. She checked the weather relentlessly, noting hopefully that conditions began to look increasingly favourable. 'Game on,' she wrote in a message to her support crew.

At 3am on a mild Saturday, under the light of a full moon with the midges biting, she set off. Jasmin summited Mullach nan Coirean, already three minutes up on Jon's split, moving at a pace that felt 'fairly comfortable'. Running towards Stob Bàn, the sky blazed pink, then orange, then purple. Clouds of fog cascaded over the Aonachs and Grey Corries like a vast waterfall. The mist jumped ridges, shrouding Binnein Beag, with Graham Nash leading a descent across loose rock, supplementing Jasmin with homemade carrot cake. Up and over Sgùrr Eilde Mòr, the runners headed directly to the glen and followed the Abhainn Rath in rising heat to Loch Treig. Every burn Jasmin came to, she lay down 'like a sheepdog in summer', submerging herself. As they climbed away from the loch to meet the West Highland Line, Charlie Ramsay and his wife Mary were waiting. More cake was distributed. Nearing the summit of Chno Dearg, a lone runner appeared in the distance. The athlete was Joe Williams, midway through what would be the then eleventh fastest completion of the round, albeit four hours slower than a woman in identical conditions. They embraced and continued in their respective directions.

At the dam, Jasmin was 49 minutes up on Jon's time. 'The

record was looking distinctly achievable,' she realised. 'That said, I had been with Jon on the last leg of his round, and I knew how fast he'd been going. I was expecting to lose some of the buffer I'd accumulated. The question was how much, if any, I'd have left at the end.' Under an unblemished blue sky, she proceeded up Stob a' Choire Mheadhoin with Jon Gay and Finlay Wild. Jon Ascroft would join the trio at the start of the Grey Corries, the first of which – Stob Bàn – was topped with a celebratory last Munro party. The runners swept over the shimmering quartz, climbed Aonach Beag, took the chicken run route beneath the ridge line of the Carn Mòr Dearg Arête, and began the ascent of Ben Nevis.

She paused for a photo on the summit of the Ben, throwing her arms delightedly in the air. Moments later, she was descending: swerving day-trippers, kicking up dust, sliding down scree. With Finlay leading the way, the sound of bagpipes rose from the valley to meet the runners. 'I was scarcely conscious of it at first, but as the sound started to sink in, so did the realisation of what I'd achieved. That final run-in along the bridge, getting sprayed with champagne, hugging Jon...'

Jon's presence was symbolic. 'Not many record-holders turn out to see their record broken,' Willie Gibson, Carnethy president and Ramsayist, would tell the club's AGM later that year. Not only had Jon seen his record taken away, he had willingly promoted its obliteration.

'It was all a bit surreal and simultaneously wonderful,' Jasmin remembers. 'I staggered around for a bit on unsteady legs. We drank bubbly, took some photos, and then headed to the pub to recount the day's adventures over burgers, beers and chips.'

Moss, the Paris-Rawlik's puppy sheepdog, was savaging a Salomon trainer in the front room. He had already destroyed a stuffed pheasant, depositing shredded white fluff about the cottage. Jasmin has shoes to spare. I counted fifteen pairs at her back door, while she had hurriedly closed another door that led to a room swamped with running paraphernalia. Half-Czech she may be, but she gave a typically British apology for the 'state' of the house as she showed me in.

'There is no "typical week",' Jasmin explains as she attempts to describe her training. As well as running rounds in 2016, she was continuing her work towards a PhD, with her research focused on the treatment of leukaemia. As Colin Donnelly found to his cost, the unending challenge for the non-professional is to fit running into the rhythm of a complicated life. 'It might be at nine at night or five in the morning; it might be a lunchtime at work,' she says. 'I couldn't tell you my weekly mileage or ascent, and I rarely know what I intend to do in training more than a day ahead.' She was running 'most days' in the build-up to the first of the rounds, before work on weekday mornings for at least an hour, plus longer runs at the weekend, typically up to four hours. 'Always in the hills,' she stresses. Once a week, she and Konrad went 'somewhere pretty steep' to attempt hill reps. A tempo run around the reservoir was another weekly fixture, with Jasmin running one way, Konrad the other. 'Where you cross is a sign of how you're doing,' she says. 'It makes it a bit more exciting. I guess that's my speed session.' She has no desire to be coached. 'I run how I feel. I don't go out thinking, I'm going to beast myself.'

Sacrifice is a word bandied about to describe the things a successful athlete must apparently forgo: family time, friends, a social life. Jasmin would not use the word. There is no sacrifice if you are living your life in the way you want. Pre-dawn hill runs in the Moorfoots, wild swims in the Gladhouse Reservoir, 20-mile bicycle commutes to work at Easter Bush. This is how she chooses to live her life. Success is merely a consequence. On top of running, she includes hiking. The trip to the Sierra Nevada was planned deliberately with the Bob Graham in mind. 'The aim was to not meet anyone for ten days, so we were carrying all our food in a big rucksack,' Jasmin says. There was a little running, she admits: 'I would run at higher altitude, maybe half the days, maybe 40 minutes.' Jasmin had earlier told the Scottish Hill Runners assembly that she did 'a lot of walking' in her three rounds. 'It's like a long hike in the hills,' she had joked. It may be, but Jasmin is still moving faster than most.

Perhaps the lack of a television – and the mind-numbing trap it can offer – is the secret? As for what they eat, the couple's diet is unremarkable. Instant mashed potato is a mountain marathon essential. To my right, I consciously count the number of Green and Black's chocolate bars stacked on the table: eight. There is a video clip of Jasmin at a checkpoint on the Glen Coe Skyline. With the traverse of the Aonach Eagach to come, she drinks a plastic cup of Coke from her right hand, then another held in the left, strokes Moss on the head, picks up two further cups, right, left, and she's running again. The episode took less than 15 seconds. She could be downing shots in an Edinburgh nightclub. Pragmatism again. After 22 miles of mountain running over five hours, with a 900-metre climb to the Aonach Eagach imminent, what do I need? A colossal injection of sugar. Asked at the end of the race about her prolific Coke-drinking, she said: 'I guess it was university days that taught me to do that.'

As with her training, common sense controls what she eats and drinks. 'I love fruit and vegetables. I would choose brown bread over white. We cook fresh meals every night, but there's no nutritional diary,' she says. 'I don't avoid anything, especially soup, cake and tea; they are part of the joy of fell running. Every time we go away,' Jasmin adds, 'when we come back on a Sunday evening and it's late and we don't want to cook, we buy pizza, Prosecco and ice cream.' Jasmin breaks off as Moss becomes over-familiar with his bed. 'Moss,' she berates while laughing. 'Konrad,' she screams. 'Have you seen what Moss is doing? And in company...'

The setting was a dark, empty car park in North Wales in the early hours of an October morning. Jasmin shook hands with two men she had never met. The first was Chris Near; the second Tim Higginbottom. The trio started running, following twisting quarry tracks to gain the foggy slopes of Elidir Fawr. Jasmin's Paddy Buckley had begun.

That the round would prove the hardest of the three was little wonder. After the Ramsay, she had raced four times in two summer months, winning the Tromsø Skyrace and the Glen Coe Skyline, finishing third in the Skyrunning World Championships in the Pyrenees, and running through a field of the best ultrarunners on the planet to place sixth in the women's rankings at the Ultra-Trail du Mont-Blanc.

The manicured trails of the Alps were a world away from the boggy trods of Snowdonia. Nor was there an easy rhythm like there had been in the previous two rounds and by the start of the third of the five sections, as Jasmin climbed Moel Siabod above Betws-y-Coed, she was struggling. The terrain was coarse and heathery, the ground waterlogged. At the next changeover point, at the sight of Konrad, Jasmin 'for a moment fell apart'.

'I don't think I ever contemplated stopping,' she says, 'although that doesn't mean I didn't want to.' Forcing herself up the next hill, Bryn Banog, Jasmin was conscious that she was now losing ground on Nicky Spinks' fastest time. Gradually, in the darkness, Jasmin – in unfamiliar territory of not having time in hand – started to claw back minutes. In a year of superlatives, perhaps it was this recovery, when character and desire were called into question, that was the greatest achievement of all? 'Things took on a surreal, dream-like quality,' she says. 'My world narrowed to the pool of light around my feet.' She fled off the final hill, Moel Eilio, delighting at last in a grassy slope, descending under a sky bursting with stars, surpassing Spinks' time. The overall record of Higginbottom, Jasmin's leg one supporter, was safe for now.

Martin Stone knows better than most how to re-write mountain running history. He has the final word on Jasmin: 'I have always felt that the very best records are not always the current records, but those that come out of the blue and represent a really significant improvement on what has gone before. Often they are achieved where there is no yardstick to measure them against and a great performance or achievement is something of its time. Just because folk come along years later and keep shaving a few minutes off the record, it doesn't lessen the original achievement. Jasmin is a force of nature with such an amazing gift for running long and fast in the mountains. Her resilience, consistency, determination and fearlessness have allowed her to complete a set of rounds in a way that is quite unlike anything that has ever gone before.'

The 'force of nature' had her own retort: 'For now, it's over to you, lads.'

ABOVE:

1. Charlie Ramsay, Pete Fettes (a support runner) and Bobby Shields in the minutes before leaving Glen Nevis youth hostel to run the first Ramsay's Round (Alex Gillespie)

LEFT:

2. Alec Keith racing on Ben Nevis (Alec Keith Collection)

3. Adrian Belton, flanked by Helene Diamantides, Andrew Addis and Mark Rigby, second, third and fourth from the left, at Loch Treig following his 28-Munro run (Charlie Ramsay)

4. Snow-capped Ben Wyvis rises imperiously above runners at Cioch Mhòr (Phil Hindell)

LEFT:

8. Murray Strain leads runners up
Salisbury Crags in the Hunters Bog
Trot (Matthew Curry)

BELOW LEFT:

9. A line of runners climb into
a snowstorm at the Carnethy 5
(Matthew Curry)

BELOW RIGHT:

10. Runners descending in whiteout
conditions at the Carnethy 5
(Matthew Curry)

11. Teams setting out on the OMM in the Tweedsmuir Hills (OMM)

12. Jez Bragg and his team pose outside the Glen Nevis youth hostel after his Ramsay's Round (Gemma Bragg)

Back row (left to right): Chris Busby, Cameron Burt, Olly Stephenson, Anna Hayes, Gemma Bragg

Front row: Murdo McEwan, Pete Duggan, Jez Bragg, Jon Gay, Graham Nash

13. Alan Smith at the Pentland Skyline (Harry Gilmore)

14. Bill Gauld on Caerketton Hill (Allan Gebbie)

TOP LEFT:

15. Stewart Whitlie descending Capelaw Hill in the Pentland Skyline (Harry Gilmore)

TOP RIGHT:

16. Alex Brett on Foinaven (Ross Bannerman)

LEFT:

17. Jasmin Paris and Konrad Rawlik climbing Beinn na Lap on Jasmin's Ramsay's Round (Jim Mann)

21. A runner in the Isle of Jura Fell Race (Iain Gilmore)

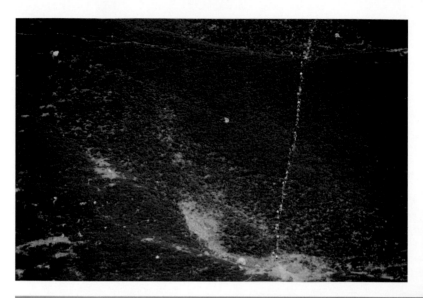

Top left:

22. The only way is up at Stùc a' Chroin (Matthew Curry)

Top Right:

23. Tom Phillips crossing the Abhainn Rath in his winter Ramsay's Round (John Carr)

Left:

24. Runners approach Sgùrr Choinnich Mòr on a Ramsay's Round reconnaissance (Anthony Hemmings)

TOP LEFT:

27. Rob Woodall on the summit of Stac an Armin, with Stac Lee in the background (Pete Ellis)

TOP RIGHT:

28. Angela Mudge in battle dress at the Carnethy 5 (Anne Nimmo)

LEFT:

29. The author and David Gallie, and Stob Bàn, reflected in the lochan of Coire Rath (Mark Hartree)

30. The author and David Gallie on the ascent of Stob Choire Claurigh on Ramsay's Round (Mark Hartree)

31. Runners in the Skyline Scotland series (Oriol Batista)

13

A WAY OF DEATH

Alex Brett was descending Beinn Alligin, the jewelled mountain of Torridon. Across a plunging glen stood the mountain-castle of Liathach. Atop this awesome wave of Torridonian sandstone was a quartzite froth: a splintered ridge of shards and pinnacles. Liathach was Alex Brett's destiny: he would soar with eagles; he would touch the sky.

Alex had been running for eight hours. Setting out from the magnificence of Glen Torridon, he had clambered into the dominion of the extraordinary: a theatre of nature. The most rugged of mountain loops was his objective, an extravagant oval linking seven forbidding summits. The majority had been accomplished: the twin peaks of Beinn Eighe, the zenith of Beinn Dearg, the Beinn Alligin crowns. Alex ran on, seeking more, compelled to close the coil. From the giddy heights of Beinn Alligin, the closest of Liathach's two mountaintops was Mullach an Rathain, five miles and at least two hours away. The going would be rough and steep, as it had been all day: a U-shaped chaos of rock and heather, first plunging some 800 metres, then rising another 900. How Alex's legs must have trembled.

In the glen at the nadir of the descent, he reached a footbridge, close to the tributary of two burns that drain into Upper Loch Torridon. It was a pivotal moment – Alex Brett's metaphorical fork in the road. Had he taken an easy path to the right, his feet would have touched tarmac within fifteen minutes. Jogging along a twisting coastal lane, he could have been perched on a bar stool, ordering a pint at the Torridon Inn shortly after. A fellow patron – having heard that Alex had been running for nine hours – would have expressed astonishment and offered the exhausted runner a lift to his car. On the way, the driver might have looked sideways at his grey-haired passenger and asked his age. 'I'm 65,' Alex would have said. Sensing the black wave above, Alex might have craned his neck to look at the seemingly impenetrable terraces of Liathach and felt a surge of regret. 'There's my car,' he would have said, gesturing to a lone parked vehicle in the dark of the glen. Limbs tired and cramping, he would have driven home to Dingwall. He would have lived to fight another day.

Alex crossed the footbridge, ignored the path and began the relentless climb of Liathach's far western shoulder. It was 6pm. The sun, now behind the runner's back, was beginning its descent to the horizon. By the time Alex reached Mullach an Rathain, it was dark. Peril lay ahead – and Alex knew it. Between Mullach an Rathain and Liathach's second Munro, Spidean a' Choire Lèith, is a precarious ridge line, climaxing in the Cuillin-esque Pinnacles of Am Fasarinen – or in its menacing anglicised parlance, The Teeth. A ribbon of a path ran beneath the ridge, but this path had become increasingly eroded and worn, and despite being safer than scrambling over the pinnacles, was agonisingly exposed. When the mountaineer and author Mike Cawthorne arrived on Spidean a' Choire Lèith as part of a continuous winter journey linking the 135 Scottish mountains over 1,000 metres, he was transfixed by the western vista facing Alex: 'From here the crest splinters into pinnacles, the notorious Am Fasarinen, and is flanked by plunging drops.' Ominously, he added: 'Certainly no place to be caught out in the dark.'

What was going through Alex Brett's mind in those two hours between Beinn Alligin and Mullach an Rathain? He would not be human if he had not considered stopping, not considered turning right at the footbridge. Weariness alone will trigger such action, but ruminating on something does not mean you will do it, even if the notion becomes a fixation. As he climbed Mullach an Rathain, Alex had multiple escape routes. Torridon was scarcely a straight-line mile from the summit. Something drove him on, drove him into inescapable night, drove him into the glare of danger. Was it a version of summit fever? A compulsion to complete a round of the Torridon mountains – having failed in a previous attempt – had needled him for years. It was now or never, he may have thought. He was a pensioner, after all. Right now, he was as close as he had ever been. Maybe he would not get another chance? It was the end of September. Alex was unlikely to get a further opening that year. Could he wait until he was sixty-six or sixty-seven? Would his body allow it? Or perhaps it was pride? The concept of abandoning, of running along a road, not a ridge, might have been too much to bear. He might also have thought about his family and friends, what they would advise, but perhaps not dwelling, for he must have believed what we all believe: *it will be okay; I will be okay*. Alex had good reason to have faith. As a member of a mountain rescue team, he had helped take bodies off mountains. He and risk were old sparring partners. Nor were The Pinnacles strangers. A decision was made: *I will be okay.*

From Mullach an Rathain, he moved east to Am Fasarinen. On tired, stumbling legs, having climbed close to 4,000 metres and now edging through darkness, the going must have been terribly slow. He reached The Pinnacles, nonetheless, and began to pick his way along the path beneath the southern lip of the ridge. In the shroud, he might just have been able to glimpse the outline of Spidean a' Choire Lèith, growing ever closer. At the summit, the ridge remains high, but danger reduces as exposure lessens. Alex just had to get there. Progressing carefully forward, toying with The Pinnacles' final offering, he was perhaps five minutes from salvation.

Death could have been looking elsewhere, or have been distracted, or have yawned. But Death's gaze was fixed on Scotland, on Liathach, on The Pinnacles.

Alex Brett stepped forward.

His foot reached for rock.

There was nothing.

Just air.

He fell.

Alex Brett would have reached Spidean a' Choire Lèith. He would have staggered downhill, back to his car in the glen. He would have slumped into the driver's seat, exhausted, relieved, exultant. He would have a story to tell for years. He would have finally finished the round. The memory of the risk he took would fade. A new objective would preoccupy him.

Alex was reported missing on Thursday. He had started running on Sunday. A passer-by noticed his car had not moved for several days and alerted the police. That Alex had not been in touch with family and friends was not unusual. His partner, Lynda Johnston, was on a business trip in South Africa at the time. She had been messaging Alex, but did not expect a response – he was not one for sending text messages. Nor had Alex called his daughter; he had missed a funeral; he had not got in touch with a friend for a regular run. But those who knew Alex would have thought what he too thought: *It is Alex. He will be okay.* But he was not. Appeals flooded the national news. His mountain rescue colleagues and clubmates from Highland Hill Runners took to the hills. They were joined by rescuers from the Torridon team and the RAF, along with search dogs and a coastguard helicopter. The police urged anyone who may have seen a runner 'wearing trainers and carrying either a small rucksack or bum bag' to contact them. On the third day of the search, a body was found. It was Alex. Above him were The Pinnacles of Liathach and the sky.

Russell McKechnie does not mention Alex as he gives his race organiser's briefing to the runners in the Cioch Mhòr hill race – except to call the event by its new title: the Alex Brett Cioch Mhòr hill race. Six months have elapsed since his death. Russell speaks about risk without saying the word:

the need to circle trig points to enable numbers to be taken; the safest place to cross a river; the barbed wire fences in the glen; the complications of Cioch Mhòr if mist descends. The runners are respectfully silent, giving the impression of intense concentration; they have heard it all before. *It will be okay; I will be okay.* Once the briefing is over, in single file they funnel through plastic tape, with some randomly selected for a kit check: map, compass, hat, gloves, waterproofs. Numbers are counted. It is a record turnout: 78 would start the senior race. In 2005, there had been just 12. Sam Hesling, Highland Hill Runners' club captain, moves to the front row of starters. Blond-haired Tim Gomersall, who had traversed the Cuillin ridge in winter conditions in record time and completed a ski mountaineering tour of Tranter's Round, both in partnership with Finlay Wild, in the preceding months, is close by. Is that Davy Duncan and Brian Brennan, the perennial racers of Scottish hill running? Of course it is. Where else would they be? Not far off, Alan Smith waits with his hands behind his back. 'No interfering with the sheep,' Russell warns as he calls the pack to attention, 'especially Inverness Harriers'.

I watch the runners disappear up a track, feeling momentarily hollow and useless. A lingering cold prevents me from going with them. Once a junior contest has departed and parents scamper after their offspring, the start line is abandoned. While the juniors run around a mile to a grassy summit and turn around, the senior racers continue down the other side, descending to a river. The ascent to Cioch Mhòr begins immediately after, shallow and boggy at first, then steep and heathery. There is a moment of brief respite on the little summit plateau, albeit spent cowering in the wind, before the runners plunge down the conical slope they have just climbed, dodging those coming up, as rising and falling runners try to find a way that avoids the deepest heather. The race had not been named after Alex Brett as a nicety. This was his race, his course, his legacy.

Following the route uphill, I wander through a field of

cropped grass, cross a stile, and find myself on a steeper rise in a field dotted with trees. As the gradient sharpens, a tightness in my chest and a quickening of pulse comes as a relief. I had been right not to run. I walk on, revelling in this opportunity to go slowly. As I gain height, I turn to see layers of low cloud on the Black Isle, the land slipping into the still, grey waters of the Cromarty Firth. Down the firth, the oil rigs parked off Invergordon belong in a post-apocalyptic world. I look back up the hill to see the first junior, wearing a Barcelona football strip, hurrying towards me. He hurtles by, a picture of flailing concentration.

I walk back into the field of trees. Iain Macdonald is marshalling at the top. Iain and Alex had been friends for more than thirty years, having met in the embryonic years of Highland Hill Runners in the early 1980s. 'I still expect to see him,' Iain says. 'I can't believe he's not here.' Together, Alex and Iain ran and raced, but ultimately shared a passion for high and wild places.

Alex had already completed the Munros when, in his thirties, running up hills replaced walking up them. Statistics are no measure of a life, but they do reveal an astonishing commitment and longevity. Alex ran the Ben Nevis Race on 32 occasions, the Highland Cross – a post on their website after Alex's death called him 'a true Highland gentleman and committed outdoorsman' – 28 times, and the Great Wilderness Challenge for twenty-seven years. As his legacy is symbolised by Cioch Mhòr, Alex's example lives on in the races that hosted his extraordinary dedication: members of Highland Hill Runners who raced at Ben Nevis in 2016 wore tartan ribbons in his memory; the Alex Brett Memorial Shield is now presented to the first over-60 in the long race at the Great Wilderness Challenge.

Running and walking took Alex around the world: to Argentina, Chile and Canada, to the Alps, and to the Himalayas to race the Everest Marathon. His other passion was following the Scotland rugby team. On one rugby-inspired trip to Italy, Alex's wallet was snatched from his sporran. In the melee that ensued, Alex was convinced he had identified the perpetrator, but had not seen the wallet being passed to an accomplice. Alex began furiously patting the pockets of the thief, demanding the return of his money. 'I'm going to get the carbonara on you,' Alex blurted out.

He slapped the perpetrator across the face. 'Why did you slap him?' Iain had asked incredulously.

'I didn't want to be arrested for assault,' Alex explained.

Iain demonstrates the slap in midair: a forceful back of the hand whack to the face. 'I reckon that's still assault!'

A runner is coming over the horizon, angling towards us. It is Sam. He seemed to be cantering, not quite at full tilt. Without a watch, he was unaware how close he was to Finlay Wild's course record until he was further down the slope. By then it was too late; the race was run.

There is a pause before the rest. 'About twenty years ago, Alex told me, "if I die in the hills, I will be a happy man,"' Iain says. 'I don't think he meant it to be the way it happened. He knew the risks. He was a very capable bloke.'

I jog downhill and cross back into the field where Ross Bannerman, a long-time running comrade of Alex, is standing. Ross knew a successful round of the Torridon peaks was high on Alex's running priorities. He had intended to attempt it with another runner, but when they had pulled out, clubmates thought Alex might change his plans and climb mountains south of Glen Torridon. The location of his car added to the ambiguity. He could have gone either way. Ross's hunch was the round – a determined solo effort. The police appeal garnered one witness. Alex was seen coming off Beinn Alligin at 5.30pm. He looked 'knackered' – or a word to that effect – according to the sighting. Ross was right. There was no doubt Alex was attempting the round. The search area could be significantly narrowed. It was a breakthrough, but one that must have been tinged with despair. The focus turned to Liathach; the rescue teams knew what that meant.

More than most, Ross recognised Alex had unfinished business in these mountains. The pair had set out on the round some years earlier, beginning where Alex had started his fateful run, but journeying clockwise, thereby crossing Liathach first when they were at their freshest. They continued over Beinn Alligin in searing heat, but faced with the awesome vision of Beinn Eighe, they relented, jogging down a glen to the start. Despite the sensitivities of the land and its owners – Beinn Eighe is a nature reserve; Beinn Alligin and Liathach are owned by the National Trust for Scotland – Ross was fixated on the idea of the route becoming a race. He reckoned the 22-mile course could be accomplished in around seven to eight hours by the fastest runners. The worst dangers were avoidable, Ross reckoned: the tricky Horns of Alligin could be bypassed and – crucially – Liathach would be crossed first in a clockwise fashion. Alex knew that. I had to ask the obvious question, knowing there was almost certainly no answer. Why did he leave Liathach until last? Ross shakes his head.

Tragically, Alex – who was due to carry out work on a stone dyke at the home of Ross's parents – had left a message on his friend's mobile phone in the days prior to him travelling to Torridon. 'I received Alex's voice message a few hours before I was told he was missing,' Ross says. 'For some reason, it didn't open for about a week until that day. I remember trying to call him back and thinking it was unusual for him not to answer. There's a good chance I would have gone along with him if I'd taken his call in the first instance.'

Given the opportunity, Ross would have also offered some important advice: do not get benighted. Alex's car had been caught on a roadside camera in Garve, around an hour from Glen Torridon, at 8am. It was safe to assume, therefore, that he had begun his ascent of Beinn Eighe at about 9.30am. Two daylight hours had been lost; there were just ten remaining. 'I still listen to that message from time to time, and for a moment it feels like he's here,' Ross says.

As we walk to the finish, the blur of a club vest occasionally sweeping by, Ross stops to demonstrate the vulnerability of a runner on The Pinnacles. 'You put your foot there,' he says, placing his right boot on the ground, 'and you're fine. You put it there,' he indicates, shifting his foot two or three inches to the right, 'and there is nothing. Imagine that in the dark. You only have to stumble on a rock.' Stumbling is what hill runners do; it is where you stumble that matters.

'He was a man of experience,' Ross says. 'I remember camping with him on a summer's night on the Forcan Ridge. I was taken aback by his knowledge. He seemed to know the name of every mountain. I was younger and looked up to him in that sense.' Ross, with his clubmate Dave Wilby, ventured across Liathach in the week after the discovery of Alex's body, 'trying to make some sense of it all.' From the glen, they climbed very steeply to Mullach an Rathain and proceeded east, the way Alex went. It was a picture postcard day: an indigo sky dotted with wisps of cloud. The view stretched forever, a bewildering procession of Highlands and islands. As they crossed The Pinnacles, Ross and Dave had their 'backs to the walls', quivering in the glare of their mortality. Knowing where Alex had been found, they could reasonably assume the point of his fall. 'From where he fell to where he would have been safe was about 100 yards,' Ross adds ruefully.

On the 600-metre contour, close to where Alex was located, Ross and Dave constructed a cairn memorial. Inside they placed a small deposit box containing photographs, a tartan Highland vest and whisky miniatures from the Ben Nevis Race. They said goodbye.

The Torridon round would be the race that never was. Any thoughts of sending people out to race in these mountains was abandoned. 'I was spooked,' Ross says. 'I lost the will.' The mountains no longer called. 'I seem to have abandoned the hills,' Ross told me a year later. 'I've only been to Ben Wyvis for a walk since I was up Liathach with Dave.'

Dundonnell Mountain Rescue Team cover an area stretching

the breadth of the north of Scotland, from east coast to west, some 2,600 square miles, from An Teallach to Ben Wyvis, Strathfarrar to Liathach. It is a daunting patch, with 35 members permanently on call. Although the team are not as busy as their counterparts further south, 'when we do get callouts, they can be prolonged because of the type of terrain,' Steve Worsley, one of the members explains – as three days in the Torridon mountains seeking one of their own would painfully highlight. 'It was pretty upsetting. We wanted to do our best for Alex, but unfortunately . . .' Silence. Words dissolve.

The irony of mountain rescue teams is their indelible connection to the people they serve. They are not doctors treating a toddler with a temperature. They are not paramedics wiping a drunk's vomit from their uniform. They are walkers, climbers and runners who – in the worst of times and conditions – go looking for other walkers, climbers and runners. That is what drives these unpaid volunteers, for, more often than not, they are searching for people who share their ethos. While it is hard to make sense of Alex's death, when his body was found, amid the grief and relief, their thoughts must have agonised with the notion: *I know why he did what he did. I understand.*

In high places, the thread between life and death is as delicate as gossamer. 'In climbing mountains,' Geoffrey Winthrop Young explained in his 1920 book *Mountain Craft*, 'danger is a constant element, not remote as in other sports: it is always behind the veil of pleasant circumstances, and it can be upon us before we are aware.' Terrain, latitude and remoteness make the mountains of Scotland hazardous even without the complications of weather, navigation and – if they conspire – hypothermia. Running is convoluted further by the requirement to travel light. If not, you may as well just walk.

'The risk is the fact that you're often running on your own and a long way from any help, and you tend to go lightweight, which goes against what I would recommend as a mountain rescue team member,' Steve says, trying to encapsulate an irreconcilable clash of identities. 'Since I've been in the team I'm certainly more aware of what could go wrong. I'm more careful than I used to be.' He elaborates on how he might 'hold back' when running. 'Possibly on a tricky descent where I'm more likely to go over on an ankle. Most accidents in the hills happen to competent people who just have a bit of bad luck or a simple fall. The question is, should the worst happen, can I get myself out of it? I always carry a phone. I always carry spare kit. But is that enough?'

It was not enough for Peter Brooks. A runner, climber, cyclist and sailor, Peter was at ease in the outdoors, especially among mountains: he notably devised the original running routes over the heights of Mull, Jura and Arran for the inaugural Scottish Islands Peaks Race in 1983. Peter was marking his 60th birthday by running the Scottish 4,000s over several day stages in January 1998, when, having covered some 80 miles, just Ben Nevis was left. The remaining distance was akin to a 400-metre lap of a running track at the end of a marathon. He sent a message to his wife, Miriam, in Edinburgh, saying he had only his 'old friend, the Ben' to climb.

The area above the now-eroded tourist path on the Ben is very different from that of the 1990s. For ascending walkers, once past Lochan Meall an t-Suidhe, it was common practice to follow a zig-zag path until it gave way to the rubbly, rough and pathless terrain of the mountain's western approach. Leaving the summit, Peter would have instinctively kept away from the Ben's corniced north-east rim, before pausing to take a bearing from an iron pole above Gardyloo Gully. He was aiming for the reassuring fold at the top of the winding path, close to the 950-metre contour and perilously near the cliffs of Five Finger Gully.

He descended safely on the bearing, not needing crampons, for the ground was free of snow. His grippy boots were made for this terrain: a straight descent on rock. The bend, however, was choked with drifting snow, best avoided by either passing on the inside or outside. Peter, presumably, opted for the latter, bringing him closer to the top of the gully. He would have known only too well from the previous 80 miles of running that the same ridged soles that carried him off the Ben tended to slide sideways when contouring or traversing. No-one, of course, knows what happened next, but somewhere on or near the turn, the runner's feet left the ground. Uncontrollably sliding towards, then into, Five Finger Gully, he simply could not stop.

The Fellrunner reported Peter's death, the words carefully crafted, a stoic defence of a sport emerging between the lines. 'There was no doubt that he was properly equipped and clothed, and his death was a tragic accident,' the editorial began. 'He was a highly experienced fell runner and had even taken the precautions of informing the police of his proposed route and ringing in on a regular basis on his mobile phone.' It was not surprising Peter went to what might seem excessive lengths. He was known affectionately as a 'faffer', a man who spent hours agonising about what to put in his rucksack before a day in the mountains. Peter simply wanted to be as prepared as possible.

'Because of the existence of areas of poor mobile phone reception and the fact that on Tuesday Peter had phoned from a call box,' the editorial continued, 'the police were not unduly perturbed when he did not call in on the Wednesday. However, when there was still no word by first light on Thursday, a search was launched involving Kinloss and Lochaber mountain rescue teams, a search and rescue helicopter from RAF Lossiemouth and nine tracker dogs. He was spotted from the helicopter lying at the foot of Five Finger Gully.'

Nor was it enough for Martin Hulme. Like Alex Brett and Peter Brooks, here was another man of the mountains: he had completed three rounds of Munros, as well as the Corbetts and Grahams; he was an active rock and winter climber, with at least 250 ascents recorded in his logbook, including the Matterhorn and the Old Man of Hoy; he had raced more than 100 times in the Scottish hills and was a national champion in his over-60 age category.

The sixty-seven-year-old was descending the mist-cloaked Crianlarich peak of Cruach Ardrain, dropping north on a steep path. Alan Renville, a long-time member of Edinburgh Mountaineering Club, was running ahead. The unpredictability of the hills, even as winter drew near, did not daunt them: they had spent their lives among them. Besides, they were thoroughly primed, carrying food, warm clothes, gloves and hats, and an emergency bivvy bag. Some things cannot be legislated. 'I didn't see what happened to cause him to initially slip,' Alan said. 'As he went past me, he was on his back and quickly gaining speed and was out of control. It was a mixture of grass and rock, and he disappeared from my view into the mist. I ran down the path shouting and trying to find him, and after a few minutes of frantically searching saw his body below me. When I reached him there was no sign of life.'

Alan alerted mountain rescue, knowing the devastating truth: there was nothing they or he could do for Martin now. His friend had fallen around 100 metres. 'Looking at the terrain above where I found him, my guess is he went over a crag, probably only a few metres high but the impact on landing at that speed would have been enough to cause fatal injuries.'

I am running a round of Borders hills above Glen Sax when Alan tells me this. It is the winter solstice; two months have gone by since Martin's death. The weather is dreich: windy, wet and claggy. After running on drove roads and following fence lines, the path disintegrates. Alan pauses to change his gloves. I jog on, then turn after two minutes, retracing my steps. *Where is he?* Alan remains where I left him, hunched over his bag, trying to pull a new pair of gloves over numb, unresponsive fingers. I silently curse him. I am cold. He, I think, is colder. We do not verbalise our fears. At least we are running again. Alan takes a bearing and we trudge across peat hags. I am moving faster. I look back, wait a few seconds, then run on, fearing if I go too far the mist will divide us. Finally, I see a pillar in the pall and know we are on the summit of Dun Rig. We pause. Alan tries to take a bearing to our next summit, Glenrath Heights, but his freezing hands cannot shift the housing. The gale blows furiously. We see only barren, wind-scoured moorland, ending abruptly in a grey wall. There is no path, no obvious way to go. Suddenly, I feel unfathomably cold. I cannot recall who said the words, but one of us thankfully spoke: 'We need to descend.' Alan points. We sweep downhill, cautiously at first, then gambolling with relief, before slicing through the mist. The wind, the rain, the clag – gone. We pause gratefully in the glen, looking up at swaddled hills. We are the lucky ones.

Tim Gomersall is sitting on a bench in the sports hall of Dingwall Leisure Centre. The soon-to-be qualified doctor is already changed, having finished second behind Sam Hesling. He is in good form. Six weeks earlier, on Valentine's Day, he and Finlay Wild had traversed the Cuillin ridge in 6 hours and 14 minutes, shattering the previous winter record by around three hours. The pair had only known each other for a month, having met at a ski mountaineering race that January. Tim and Finlay had not even climbed together when they stepped onto the path to Sgùrr nan Gillean – winter traverses are traditionally attempted north to south – to gain the start of the ridge. Fortune favoured them: the weather was ideal, others had cut trail, and snow conditions were as good as they could be for 'running'. Embracing cautious minimalism, they carried two ice axes each, a 38-metre rope and a 26-metre cord, along with slings and abseiling paraphernalia. Between them, they had two litres of water. They would survive on gels and jelly babies.

'I'm inherently more likely to take risk, but I do think I have a balanced approach,' he says. Words emerge from Tim's lips with methodical eloquence. I can see the sort of doctor he would become. 'There are certainly things I did during the Cuillin record – because we were trying to go quickly – that I wouldn't necessarily do on a training run. Sometimes the objective is worth the risk. There's a ceiling of risk you're prepared to accept before you start.'

'Had you and Finlay discussed that?' I ask.

'No.' He hesitates, deliberately again. 'But we did make a comment shortly after starting that we would push when it wasn't too technical, and when it became more technical or risky, we would go slower, consciously go slower.'

But everyone makes mistakes. Tim and Finlay were abseiling King's Chimney on Sgùrr Mhic Choinnich – a rock climb graded 'Difficult' – when they realised their lifeline was too short. 'We should have tied the rope and cord together, and abseiled on both, but we only used the rope because we didn't think the abseil would be that long. We ended up on a snowy ledge, having run out of rope. We down-climbed a corner, and if I went back, I wouldn't choose to take that risk again, but in the situation, that was what we did.'

'What were the consequences of you falling when you were down-climbing?' I want Tim to spell out the risk. 'You're going to fall a long way?'

'Absolutely fatal. We would have ended up in the bottom of Coire Làgan in a not very good state. But we accepted that in order to fulfil the day. I felt it was acceptable for me to take that risk. For other people, it would be very different. Breaking the record wasn't at the forefront of our minds; it was to go as quickly as possible and see what came out.' By the time Tim and Finlay had escaped King's Chimney, they were two-thirds of the way along the ridge, but faced a fresh threat. 'You get more tired and that limits the risks you're willing to take. The mistake is to rush into decisions late in the day. That's the riskiest thing.' Silently, I cannot help but make a parallel to Alex.

Would ambition have overruled common sense? 'I'm at a position in life where I don't have a partner or kids, so I'm obviously more likely to accept a higher level of risk.' I thought of Alex again. I wondered what Tim, today aged twenty-three, would be like when he was sixty-five, when he might be long-married with children older than he is now.

I expected Tim – or any person who accomplishes winter records for undertakings of the stature of the Cuillin ridge and Tranter's Round, notably within a fortnight – to be gung-ho, reckless even. Tim was not. He was perfectly rational, as rational as any hill runner or climber I have met – a young man who simply matched perceived risk to ability. Learned talent would get him out of trouble, not luck. 'I think it's the freedom that makes it worthwhile,' he adds. 'The pleasure comes from having the skillset to manage the risk. It becomes a confidence challenge.'

The race prize-giving begins with thirty seconds of celebratory applause for Alex, but it could not lift the sombre atmosphere. His family – Lynda, his sister, his brother-in-law – had come to watch the proceedings. The community was wedded in grief and for the first time I felt ashamed for intruding on the Highland gathering.

Like Steve Worsley, Ray Wilby, who is Dave's father and another member of Dundonnell Mountain Rescue Team, was looking for his 'best mate' in the Torridon mountains. It was Ray's stories of mountain rescue duty that had persuaded Alex to join. 'While the search was on, it wasn't too bad in a way because you were sort of focused on looking for him. I mean, you knew it wasn't good. Right from the word go, I was convinced he had come to grief. When he was found, the initial feeling was relief, then it just hit you – this sadness.

'One of my first feelings was anger. That's why it took me a long time to come to terms with it . . . well, I haven't really come to terms with it.' Ray looks into the distance. There were questions he wanted to ask his friend. 'Even now, you go out for a run and you just can't not think about him. It's there all the time. There's a Land Rover that goes around Dingwall that looks like his. Every time you see it, for a split second you think it's Alex. It's hit us all bad.'

Now in his seventies, Ray finished 56th. His best running

years are behind him – in his fifties he was five-times runner-up in the Scottish hill racing championship for his age group – but he will continue for as long as he can. Not even the death of his contemporary will stop him going to the hills. 'No,' he snaps back when I suggest Alex's death might have deterred him. 'It's one of those things, isn't it? We'll never know precisely what happened.' As for risk? 'You don't even think about it, not at all. In fact, you're probably less at risk than going for a drive in a car. We just take that for granted. You don't think about it. If you did, you wouldn't go.'

Geoffrey Winthrop Young regarded the countenance of true peril: the mountaineer lost a leg at Monte San Gabriele in the First World War but continued to climb on a metal peg leg. Even he added a proviso to his death-behind-a-veil warning in *Mountain Craft*: 'It can rarely be worthwhile to hazard life on the uncertain issue of a game. If the adventure is good enough, however, it may seem well worthwhile to take a good many chances.'

In remembering Martin Hulme, the Skye-based mountain guide Martin Moran echoed a similar sentiment: 'A trip, a slide, a tumble – how slender is our attachment to life, but how precious its gift when we are in the mountains.'

The adventure *was* 'good enough'; life in the mountains for Alex Brett was fantastically precious. He took his chance, as we all do.

The hall is emptying. Seats are being stacked, uneaten cakes and sandwiches stashed in boxes. Alex had been honoured in the best way they knew: by running and racing, and by living. Russell McKechnie would remark later: 'There was a wry smile from above, right enough.'

14

A WAY OF LIFE

At playtime, the children at Kinloch Rannoch primary were not allowed into the village. The school's playground rose with the contours of the lower slopes of Craig Varr. The pupils could go there instead, they were told. They could play on the hill.

Craig Varr rises abruptly above Dunalastair, staring down dimpling Loch Rannoch, with the mountains of Glen Coe in a dreamy far distance. The summit, a grassy bluff at the climax of a long ridge, stands some 300 metres above the slate roof of the old school. A cluster of stunted trees clings to the ridge line. The wind blows mainly from the west here – and it blows hard. To ascend, the way is steep and when it is not steep, it is rough and largely pathless. But it is not far from the village: some two miles there and back. The lunch break gave just enough time for an adventurous schoolboy to walk up and jog down, without being late for the first lesson after lunch.

Davy Duncan was a nine-year-old boy when he first made the journey to the bluff. It was sometimes the only place to escape the hillside bullies.

'How many times have you been up here?' We are following a path that threads around narrow trunks of woodland bedecking the lower reaches of Craig Varr. Some fifty years had intervened between those founding ascents of his childhood in the 1960s and today. Silence. We continue uphill. I had learnt

Davy was not good at giving answers that required numbers.

He sniffs. 'This will be covered in bracken in the summer. This high,' he says, pointing to his head.

'Maybe 100 or 200?' I venture.

'Maybe.'

I fancied it was many more.

Davy's distaste for figures is ironic; for this is a man whose dedication to running in the high places of Scotland is measured in unfathomable statistics. He has no equal. Davy has run more hill races than anyone, more than anyone probably ever will run. He reckons he might have done 800 – although the number is almost certainly higher – with 97 in a calendar year his record.

But this is not a story of numbers. This is a story of a way of life, a story that starts and ends on Craig Varr.

Hills and mountains are mere earth and rock. Humans named them, feared them, sought them, mastered them. In countless ways, setting physicality aside, they – be it Everest or Kilimanjaro, Denali or Craig Varr – are the same, for hills and mountains possess humans. As Everest possesses the summit-infatuated mountaineer, Craig Varr possesses Davy. The hill is part of him and one day he will be part of it. When he is gone, his ashes will flutter here. They will rise and fall, like the stride of the hill runner, before coming to rest on the ground, clinging to rock, grass, bracken and mud – and you can be sure of this: the mortal Davy will have been there first.

Davy was 45 when he finished his last shift for Scottish Power. It was a wet Friday morning. He went home to contemplate the rest of his life.

He rose early the next day, still suffering from the remnants of flu. He left his home in Clackmannan and drove to Inverness. He would finish mid-pack at Craig Dunain, before leaving hurriedly in case his route home via Drumochter became impassable by snow.

He went to Dumfries to compete at Screel the following

weekend, then Clachnaben, a British championship race, a week later. Retirement was never meant to be a rest. Davy had vowed to 'train hard and become superfit'. He wanted to win the Ochil Hill Runners club championship and record top-ten finishes. It was not that easy. 'When the lead runners were approaching the summit of Clachnaben, I was miles behind,' he says. It prompted Davy's epiphany. What did he want – or, more pertinently, *need* – from hill running? Quantity, he decided. He would run as many races as possible in the hill running calendar. The year was 2000 – a fitting time to start anything. He would eventually publish the story of the last day of April and the eight months that followed on the website of his club. Entitled *A Journal for all Hill Runners and Other Eccentrics*, the article sprawls to 6,000 words of prose, detailing race after race after race.

I counted a further 66 after Craig Dunain, touching every corner of Scotland. In those eight months, Davy seemed to have been everywhere, done everything. He completed a 460-mile round-trip to race three miles on Skye in the Highland Games at Portree. Twice he undertook 230-mile expeditions to the same place for a race that never happened. On the first occasion, he arrived in Fochabers a week early. When he went back a week later, hoping he had now got the correct date for Whiteash, he was told that there was no race this year – the would-be organiser was too busy. Davy was not a man to be put off: the next month he drove 330 miles to run for 25 minutes at the Achmony hill race at the Drumnadrochit Highland Games.

In those months of racing at least twice a week, he was injured only three times: a painful heel that he concluded was plantar fasciitis; a bruised toe, from which the nail would be sacrificed three months later; a foot that, in twisting, damaged tendons (but not enough to prevent him running). Davy did not have time to be injured; he stuck to the plan. When the heel was at the peak of its annoyance, he headed to Spittal of Glenshee to run Glas Tulaichean, supposing the absence of racing descent would limit any further damage. Peversely, the logic worked: the next day he could race at Yetholm, 135 miles away on the English border. The bruised toe was giving Davy a 'great deal of pain' later that season, yet amid the discomfort he embarked on his most frenetic schedule of the year, racing six times in eight days: Eildon 2 on the Saturday, Falkland on the Sunday, Cort-ma Law on Wednesday, White Tops on Friday, Dollar the following Saturday, Durisdeer the day after. Some years later, he would race five times in 48 hours. 'Your legs just get freer and freer,' he insists. When he damaged tendons at the Lomonds of Fife, he just carried on, albeit with a limp. After 'intensive massaging and stretching', he was racing again a week later at Oban Highland Games. Quantity remained the focus, the obsession. When the possibility of Jura loomed, Davy realised the journey to and from the island, and the race, would cost him three days. 'If I had gone there, I would have sacrificed three races for the sake of one,' he remarked in the *Journal*. He planned Aberfoyle Highland Games, Culter Fell and Scolty on consecutive dates instead. On the third day, Davy found what should have been the start of Scolty embroiled in a showjumping event. Half a dozen other runners arrived, as did the start time, but nothing resembling an organised race materialised. The others went for a run on Clachnaben; Davy did what he came to do: Scolty. 'At least I came first,' he wrote.

'Why do you race so much?'

It was not just numbers. He had a habit of swerving any inquiry, answering instead the question he perhaps might have preferred to be asked. 'I never enjoy the race. But will I be back next year? The answer is always yes.'

'Why do you keep coming back?

'I'm not sure . . . because it's hard, grinding, punishing.'

'Is it obsession?'

He neither agreed or disagreed.

Eventually, he spoke. 'I suppose,' he says slowly, his tone

almost questioning, rather than committing to the statement, 'it's a way of life.'

To my right sat Brian Brennan, a runner as infatuated with the sport as Davy; he just started a little later. In 2015, he became the first to finish every hill race in Scotland, a feat that not even Davy had accomplished. He leant forward, arms on the café table, confident and animated. 'You must meet Davy,' Brian had enthused after we were introduced at the Carnethy 5. Davy sat to my left. Despite the chill, misty air of a spring morning in Aberfeldy, he wore a pair of blue shorts. A Stùc a' Chroin race beanie was pulled over a whiskery head. Davy sat back from the table, arms folded, seemingly treating me with suspicion. He struck me then as a hard-to-please father-in-law, with me cast in the role of the would-be son-in-law. When I asked if he minded being recorded, he shook his head: 'I don't want to be recorded. I'm an introvert. That's why I'm a hill runner.' We made stuttering progress. Questions were half-answered. My notes were disjointed, a jumble of disconnected statements.

'I just love the hills and I always will.'

'It takes me to parts of Scotland I would otherwise not go.'

'I was never going to be a Finlay Wild.'

As the conversation meandered, I began to rue the two-hour journey from Edinburgh and the further two hours to come.

I stopped asking questions, and Davy and Brian quickly found their own subject matter: a hill called Craig Varr and a race to its summit. It was 1966 and Davy was twelve when he first competed. He had hoped one day to win outright; age and luck, and just not being as good as the best runner that turns up each year, means he almost certainly never will. The race, established by Major James de Sales La Terriere, owner of the Dunalastair Estate, in 1958, is an honest affair. Featuring as part of the Rannoch Highland Gathering, always on the third Saturday in August, racers circle the grass track of the games field, run a mile to the bluff by any route, which potentially includes wading or swimming the River Tummel at the outflow of Loch Rannoch, then come back, with getting wet again optional.

The 2014 race had turned into a celebration for Davy to mark his 60th birthday. Known for his yellow racing shorts – dubbed 'a pair of DDs' – fellow runners wore similar attire in tribute. Apart from Colin Donnelly and Steven Fallon, whose competitive spirit saw them drift ahead from the start, Davy was given the honour of leading the chasing pack around the games field and onto the road.

'I was thinking that I should burn a pair of shorts and put the ashes in an urn. It could be an annual prize, like the cricket,' Davy said. I laughed, thinking he was joking.

Brian nodded seriously. 'You could do.'

'How many pairs of yellow shorts have you got?' I asked.

'Five, six, seven . . .'

The conversation spluttered and died, and I was glad when the friends spoke across me again, answering in a roundabout way the question I had posed to Davy about his compulsive race-going. 'I can't imagine you not racing, not running,' Brian said. 'It's who you are. It's not a good answer, but it's true.' It was a pretty good answer, I thought. Davy nodded assent too. 'Bishop Hill in 2007,' Brian announced. 'I passed Davy on the line. Remember, Davy?' Another nod. 'I was first V50. I was so happy. On the Monday morning, I was travelling to London and got *The Herald* to read on the plane. I turned to the page of results. There was the top three and then first V50: D. Duncan.'

'I paid a lot of money for that,' Davy muttered, a faint grin on his lips. 'You know Brian once ran Clachnaben two weeks after a hernia operation,' Davy continued, turning to me. 'I was waiting for him at the end, I thought he had burst his wound and was bleeding to death on the hill.'

They continued, musing on a sport, juxtaposing beauty and disaster. 'Remember Nebit?' Brian said to Davy. 'I was the only guy in shorts. Everyone else had fourteen layers on. It

was a beautiful sight with head torches stretching up on a
moonlit night. Coming down a hill, there was Trevor Shaw,
me and Davy. My left foot slid, then it stuck hard, and we all
heard the crack. We were in a line and Trevor looked across
to ask if I was okay. I said, "no, I'm not okay, but on you go
guys, we're near the finish."'

'There was no way *I* was slowing down for anyone,' Davy
said.

'I could have sat down and said, "marshal, marshal."
That's a surefire way to get hypothermia,' Brian said. 'At the
end, there were guys swarming around this girl who had hurt
her knee. There was me, on my own, with a bag of ice on a
broken leg. It was the fibula. Six weeks in plaster. That was
December. I was back racing at the Carnethy 5 in February.
I had to run because it was my twenty-first race – you get an
engraved quaich if you do that many – and they kindly let me
start early. Never had a twinge since.'

Davy stood up abruptly. 'Back in a minute.' When he
returned, he was clutching a canvas picture, a joint gift from
his brother and sister. Davy was photographed at the Aberfeldy Highland Games, topless, arms aloft, yellow shorts.
He was smiling in the photo and smiling at me for the first
time. 'I tell you what,' he said, 'come and see me again,
and we'll go up Craig Varr, and then I'll tell you about hill
running.'

Davy greeted me at his front door with a handshake. Another
smile. He invited me inside. The father-in-law was mellowing;
I had won some acceptance. He wore a pair of blue shorts and
a Stùc a' Chroin beanie, and I wondered if he perpetually wore
a pair of blue shorts and a Stùc a' Chroin beanie. He led me
through the living room of his cottage, into a kitchen. 'Tea?'
he said, pointing to the table. The man sitting at the table
stood. Davy introduced us: 'Have you met Brian Marshall?'
I had, but I had not. That hot day on Slioch. We were in the
same race, but never quite in the same place.

Half an hour later, we were motoring along empty roads in Davy's Volkswagen Transporter towards Kinloch Rannoch. At the high point of the road beneath Schiehallion, the so-called Fairy Hill of the Caledonians, an astonishing view north became visible – it seemed like the whole of Scotland, and the whole of Scotland was mountains. As we drove, Davy pointed from side to side. That is where he runs – by the river, through the glen, over the ridge, up the hill. That is where he worked as a boy herding sheep. That is where he came off his motorcycle.

Davy's parents moved to Rannoch in 1951. His father was an engineer and had come to work for the hydro-electricity board. The family lived in a hydro house in Killichonan, a hamlet comprising a cluster of buildings on the northern shore of Loch Rannoch. The move was a shock for his mother who was used to the bustle of Aberdeen. 'There were no shops,' Davy said. 'A grocery and butcher's van came around once a week.' By the time Davy was at primary school, his family had moved east of Kinloch Rannoch, again occupying a hydro house, in Tummel Bridge. Twice daily, he travelled by bus on seven miles of twisting single-track to get to school. It was on this road that he ran for the first time. After being asked to stay behind to move desks, the bus left without him. Instinct told Davy he had better run home.

Davy would keep his promise. Close to the centre of Kinloch Rannoch, two signs claim to signal routes up Craig Varr. But they are walkers' ways, not runners', and we ignore them, continuing along the road that leads out of the village. The old school is one of the last buildings and, immediately beyond its driveway, Davy points us up a track that climbs a grass verge. At the top, we come to a metal fence with wooden stakes. 'Now, how are you going to cross this?' Davy quizzes. As I start to swing my leg over, he motions for me to stop, then uses a finger to lower one of the horizontal wires. 'Under,' he says. 'Tactics, you see. That'll save you a couple of seconds.' We follow the fence line steeply uphill until we reach a tree hanging low over the barrier. Richard Collins, a fish vet who raced Craig Varr many times, had once rigged a rope swing to one of the tree's branches. Hurtling down after summiting, Collins grabbed the swing and propelled himself across the fence, then ran on to win the race. 'That's the branch there,' Davy says jubilantly. I look at him incredulously. 'Ingenious. Seconds. Precious seconds.'

Reaching the edge of the tree line today, in April, the journey to the summit of Craig Varr has logic, despite the absence of an obvious path. There is too little overall distance to make route choice a complication, but this is a race run in late summer, not April, when the bracken can be dense and head-high. The hill then becomes a maze for the frustrated hill runner. Fortunately, knowing only too well the plight of the perplexed athlete, there is a man who helpfully cuts the bracken.

Colin Donnelly – who eclipsed Fallon to win the event that marked Davy's 60th – had gone up Craig Varr before the race to look at a route that was new to him. On the way up, he sensed mischief. 'I bumped into some other guys and was jogging with them, but they slowed down and I ended up detached. They did that deliberately. I went up the track and thought, right, where does it go now? It obviously goes up that hill, so how do I get there? That's interesting, I thought, someone has been in with a strimmer. I'll follow this path. This must be the route. You've heard this,' he said, as I started to laugh. 'Davy Duncan has cut a decoy path. I went down the decoy which ended up with the bracken up to here.' He sprang from the seat, gesticulating to his neck.

Davy hinted at the dubious methods embroiling Craig Varr in the *Journal*. 'Now it's not uncommon in the past for local knowledge (passed down generation to generation, father to son, from time immemorial) to play an important role here, and let's face it Richard Collins and I need everything going for us,' he wrote. 'But let me stress, and I'll swear on the Scottish Hill Racing calendar, absolutely none of this goes on nowadays: like the cutting of hidden paths through the bracken, or the cutting of decoy paths to lead the unsuspecting deep into the unknown, or shifting other competitors' markers just enough.'

We were looking to Brian who had moved ahead. 'Got it about right,' Davy says, remarking on Brian's choice of route across the hillside. A boy, dressed all in black, blond hair flapping across his forehead, then drifts by. Davy greets him. 'Hi, Harvey.' The boy murmurs a breathy response and continues upward, following Brian, moving slowly but always running.

His mother, Lisa Blackley, is close by, along with her partner, Jonathan Weir. If a league table of prolific hill runners was to be created, Davy Duncan would be the champion. Jonathan Weir would be third, Brian Brennan fourth. Not far behind is Brian Marshall. They share more than a mutual understanding – they share a way of life.

Compact and muscular, Jonathan's physique is not the typecast of a hill runner: he is built for power, not for running up mountains. He trained as a sprinter from the age of eight, going on to represent his club, Ayr Seaforth, and Scottish Universities. He had been in Inverness for an athletics meeting that was cancelled when he learnt there was a hill race, Knockfarrel, a short drive north, later that day. He raced, finishing towards the back of the field. 'I couldn't believe it,' he says, 'how all shapes and sizes of people just destroyed me, and I thought I was a fit, young guy then. That was the start.'

He has not stopped. Since Knockfarrel, he has raced more than 400 times in ten years. 'If there are a couple of races on, I will pick the hardest, whether it's the furthest away or nearest,' he says. 'I don't go to win, obviously, but when you turn up, pay your money, stand on the start line, you're training – but training on a different level to what you would do on your own or if you were on a bike or going to the gym. It's also a new place, a new hill, a new café to have a cup of tea in.'

Lisa is prolific too, having notched more than a century of races in six years. Not every way of life is a blessing, however. 'I hate it,' she insists. 'I wouldn't go if Jonathan didn't.'

Brian Marshall is everything Jonathan Weir is, and yet

everything he is not. Brian had been a promising cross-country runner at school and continued a lifelong love of hillwalking at university when a friend encouraged him to sign up for the Seven Hills of Edinburgh race in 1992. 'It was 14 miles with no training and no background,' Brian remembers. 'What I recall is the sheer hardness of it. Going up Arthur's Seat, I was in an absolute hell of a state, eating nuts, walking up, walking down.' Brian later watched Graham Ackland collect a prize as the race winner. How could anyone run so fast? Brian thought.

He would find out. Soon runners would look at Brian in the way he had gazed disbelievingly at Ackland. Brian would win everywhere; from Ben Lomond and Ben Rinnes, to Merrick and Goatfell, he developed a penchant for striking gold on Scotland's most iconic hills. To Brian's chagrin, Ben Nevis would elude him: he would finish no higher than ninth. He would look elsewhere to forge a legacy – on a hill that exuded fabled status long before Brian went over the sea to Skye.

The scree-cone of Glamaig rises forbiddingly above the finger of Glen Sligachan, daring to upstage the brilliance of the Cuillin across the glen. While pioneering English and Scottish mountaineers gave Skye mountains prominence in the late nineteenth century, it was a Nepalese Gurkha who brought acclaim to Glamaig. In 1899, Harkabir Thapa had reputedly gone up and down Glamaig from Sligachan in 1 hour and 15 minutes. The landowner, MacLeod of MacLeod, did not believe him. With the absence of a GPS trace to verify his achievement, Harkabir, apparently running in bare feet, did it again, this time in 55 minutes. 'The speed at which he climbed Glamaig was incredible,' Harkabir's timekeeper wrote afterwards, 'more like a spider than anything else.'

As the centenary of Harkabir's run approached, the owners of the Sligachan Hotel, and David Shepherd, a member of Carnethy, agreed to commemorate the Nepalese by turning his out-and-back route into a race. Shepherd died in an accident on his family's farm in Fochabers shortly before the event – consequently known as the David Shepherd Memorial – came into being in 1988, with 56 runners, led by Billy Rodgers of Lochaber, toeing the line for the first hill race to be staged on Skye.

Its faraway island location and exceptional brutishness ensures Glamaig will not be a race to attract large numbers, never more than 150 and dwindling to 24 in 1990 after its novelty value subsided. But therein lies the attraction. Glamaig is the epitome of hill racing in Scotland: £4 to enter, instructions that amount to run-up-there-and-run-back; assiduously low-key; fiercely competitive; a bowl of soup and a ceilidh at the end.

Pursued by the timeless pair of Alec Keith and Alan Smith in the 2003 race, Brian arrived at the summit of Glamaig 20 seconds behind Forres' Graeme Bartlett; by the end, Brian was two minutes ahead of anyone. Alluding to Harkabir's run of 1899, the Scottish Mountaineering Club's 1954 guide to Skye nonchalantly states that the mountain had been ascended from the Sligachan Hotel in 37 minutes and descended in 18, 'but this feat is not likely to be repeated.' Brian would be up and down in 50 minutes. Each year Brian returned to Skye; each year the same result: he won Glamaig. He would have won ten consecutive races had Finlay Wild not turned up in 2012 when Glamaig was nominated as a Scottish championship race. Brian was second, a cosmic six minutes adrift of a course record time of 44 minutes. As he watched Finlay collect his prize, Brian might have been reminded of standing on Calton Hill, the last of the Seven Hills, in 1992, contemplating Graham Ackland. How can anyone run so fast?

Not that Brian would admit that he was motivated by going fast. For Brian, a quietly-spoken arable farmer living on the edge of the Lammermuir Hills, just going is enough – and his going to races, like Jonathan Weir, also numbers more than 400. One time on Glamaig, Brian finished 69th; a modern day Harkabir, he was barefoot. 'What ranks equally with any achievement is the fun I've had,' he says. 'I still get a lot of pleasure out of racing, as much as I had when I was winning.'

As Jonathan and Lisa move ahead, following Brian to the summit, we catch Rab Anderson. To Rab, Highland Games were originally for throwing stones, not racing up hills. When he worked as a gardener on the Duke of Roxburghe's estate in Glen Esk, he and the other outdoor workers in the valley would train by lifting rocks and axles, and by abstaining from alcohol and cigarettes the night before. But what began as a 'jog around the field' to warm-up for throwing the hammer or shot became something that he just 'kept doing'. He weighed fifteen stone, but the more he ran, the more the 'weight came off', he says. 'The hammer and shot did not go so far.' A man with a need for physical activity found his fix in the hills. Now in his seventies and handicapped by a back injury sustained when he was hit by a falling tree, he aims to cycle the 22 miles around Loch Rannoch as 'a minimum'. The mountains still call, however. 'I get a vast amount of enjoyment from being in the hills,' he says. 'It's the solitude.' He repeats the word again, quietly: 'Solitude.' With that, he walks away from us, leaning on a stick, calling to his dog.

We are close to the bluff now. Harvey has beaten us all and is a silhouette moving higher on the ridge. Once across a pocket of swampy ground, we join a path that threads a way to the top. Walking, not running a step, we reach the turnaround point in the race. This is where, in Davy's words, a marshal will stamp your hand with 'the secret code for the day' before you can begin the return journey.

I circle the cairn and reach forward to touch the highest stone, before joining a line of recumbent bodies: Brian, Rab and Davy, and dogs. Jonathan and his family were already descending, black dots on a brown background. As hard as I try to locate the memories, I cannot recall what was said in the minutes that passed before the acknowledgement was made that we could not stay here forever. Davy would have pointed out the hills that surrounded us, I am sure. We sat on the damp grass, looking and watching. It was just about the most perfect place I had ever been. Unconsciously, we faced west, Schiehallion over our left shoulders, staring across the tan loins of Craig Varr that dropped to Loch Rannoch. In the far distance, a leaden sky merged hazily with the whitewashed mountains of Glen Coe. They seemed to belong to another, fantastical universe. Like a painting, Kinloch Rannoch lay still and fixed far below. Down there: that was where the school bullies dunked victims in the flow of the waterfall; that was where they would straddle the younger boys' torsos, beating chests like tom-toms; that is where they would roll helpless bodies downhill, through stinging fields of nettles. But not up here. Up here, we were untouchable.

On the third Saturday in August, I was leaning on a metal barrier at Welley Poley Park in Kinloch Rannoch, wearing shorts and a numbered running vest. A suited man, part of a wedding group, stood next to me, adopting a similar stance, watching runners in a four-lap race circling the grass track. They were being serenaded by pipes. The leader had pulled out a gap of around twenty yards over the rest of the field. The man took a drag from a cigarette. 'Who's going to win?' he asked.

'Him,' I said, pointing to the small, grey-haired man running in second. 'He's an international.'

The man laughed. 'Yeah, right.'

On the final bend, Colin Donnelly accelerated in front of the startled leader, winning the race to the finish line by a couple of seconds.

I turn to the man and raise my eyebrows. 'Told you.'

'But you're going to win the hill race, aren't you?'

'He,' I said, pointing to the winner of the four-lap race, 'is going to win the hill race.'

Colin was jogging warm-down laps when the hill runners began to gather on the grass. There were 25 of us. I had seen larger fields for track races in South London, but what the group lacked in numbers, it made up for in reputation. I looked across the assembly, mentally ticking them off: Colin

Donnelly, Brian Marshall, Jonathan Weir, Alan Smith, Davy Duncan. Hill running is like soap opera: the same protagonists, very often the same narrative, but always compelling. Since our run on Craig Varr, Davy had competed just twice: at Glamaig, a race he professed to hate, and Cairn Table in Ayrshire, finishing 42 seconds ahead of Brian Brennan, a result that pleased him no end. Plantar fasciitis had dogged Davy's spring and summer. Some things, though, are unmissable: Craig Varr on the third Saturday in August. 'Before the race started,' he had written in his *Journal* sixteen years earlier, 'I remember standing on the start line thinking, it seems such a short time ago when we were here last. The years are just not as long as when I was a laddie.' These games were unashamedly the 'pinnacle' of his year. 'I don't think it's any exaggeration to say this hill is in my blood,' he admitted.

As we waited to be despatched, I fancied Davy was looking to Craig Varr, re-imagining the day his schoolboy self had left his jersey halfway up the hill; fearing the punishment to come, he *had* to go back up, narrowly making it down in time for the bell. He was carried shoulder-high across the playground, a hero for the afternoon. After my first ascent of Craig Varr, Davy had beckoned me into an adjacent room to the village café housing an exhibition by a local artist. 'I like these pictures,' he had said. 'I'm thinking of asking the artist to do one for me of Craig Varr. There would be the hill and me, and chasing me up would be Brennan.'

But not today. Brian was in the middle of a two-month break from hill running to concentrate on writing a thesis. Even then, he was credited with a time at Ben Ledi in July. 'It was strange,' he said, 'as I didn't do it.' Perhaps that is the secret of his prolificity? Right now, Brian was working on his fifth chapter: the rise to power and prominence of Gilbert Kennedy, third Earl of Cassilis. We had other matters to attend to. On the command of the equally extravagantly-named Captain Ian de Sales La Terriere, we began running.

Colin and Brian did what came instinctively: they went

to the front. Running side by side through the village, they symbolised the contrast of hill runners. Brian was upright, lean and graceful. Now in his late forties, he had dabbled with chi running and racing barefoot. (The latter was the only way I could beat him.) Colin was moving like he was angry, taking almost two punchy strides to Brian's one. 'He's a ferocious competitor,' Brian would later tell me.

Onto the hill, up the fence line, under Richard Collins' tree, and through the woods we went. I watched Colin and Brian disappear into the bracken jungle. 'No decoy paths this year,' Rab Anderson had said when we met earlier in the games field. I looked at him curiously, wondering if the glint in his eye was the result of the undoubted 20-odd miles he had cycled around Loch Rannoch that morning or brazen dishonesty. I followed the leaders into the bracken, my feet flailing for a trod buried beneath the vegetation. With the undergrowth waist-high and already browning, Rab was vindicated: the cutting of false paths would have been futile.

As he moved ever further ahead, I watched Colin carefully, unable to decide if he was running or walking. He moved in an exaggerated stoop, his torso as horizontal as physically possible over the ground, his nose seemingly grazing the heather. It was effective: he was pulling away from Brian. I counted the gap between them, reaching twenty seconds and stopping, as to me, for such a short race, the lead already seemed unassailable. But Brian did not win nine consecutive Glamaig races without descending skills bordering on the maniacal, and it would be he who would make it back to the games field first. I owed the wedding guest an apology. What Brian did to Colin, Alan Smith – another way-of-lifer who ran his first hill race in 1983, when I was still in nappies – would do to me. Behind me all the way from start to summit, he thundered by on the descent. I fruitlessly gave chase. By the time I entered the woods, he was out of sight.

Davy was on his way back too: down the hill, through the bracken, into the woods, along the fence, over the fence, onto the road. He was clapped through the streets of Kinloch Rannoch. He crossed the bridge over the Tummel – no wet feet today – and turned into the games field. The pipes played on. The mist had cleared from a benevolent Schiehallion. As Davy, wearing a purple Ochil vest and a pair of DDs, approached the end, children drew up tape. He raised his arms aloft and smiled. The kilted captain, perched on his shooting stick, a monocle in his left eye, a microphone in his right hand, grinned with him. Behind Davy, framing it all, was Craig Varr, its crooked summit trees profiled on a navy sky. A way of life, I thought. This is no bad one.

15

FINDING MY WAY

I have stared many times into the darkness of a flawless winter night, contemplating the confetti of stars that flood a Scottish sky. I looked up now, counting. Seven. It was midsummer in the Highlands, where real night seems elusive. We ran into the gloom, edging deeper along the hushed glen. A shadow above demanded attention: Ben Nevis. As the road began to rise, I sensed Graham scrutinising the grass verge, looking for something: an x-marks-the-spot boulder.

'Here.' Graham motioned towards a metal fence beyond the rock, and once over we lurched through a web of forest, branches snagging shorts, dead wood snapping under shoes. Emerging onto a track, we contoured a hillside draped in trees, before entering the forest again, climbing more steeply this time to arrive onto a further road of gravel. Here the forest had been butchered into a chaos of decapitated trunks and stumps. Mist gathered in the glen, as if it now cradled a still, narrow loch. A series of stone steps took us higher still, and finally onto the boggy battlements of Mullach nan Coirean. Heads bowed, we marched silently uphill, as if half-sleeping in the growing light of a Lochaber morning. We turned off our torches. I glanced at the time: 3.35am. There would be no glorious sunrise; slowly and simply, night moved into day, as if some higher force was poised over a dimmer switch.

From the summit of Mullach nan Coirean, Graham pointed eastwards to the quartzite-capped peak of Stob Bàn, two miles away via a high, pitching ridge of grass and rock. Even from here, the mountain seemed colossal. Mullach nan Coirean and Stob Bàn: the first two of 23. Imagine doing them all. I could not. I dismissed the idea. One day, maybe. Today was a day for reconnaissance – or 'recce', the hill runners' colloquial term for such ventures. To recce in the context of the classic rounds is to rehearse the journey you might take from summit to summit (and on at least four occasions on the Ramsay, these are undertakings of more than an hour), to familiarise yourself with the terrain, to engrain the fastest or least complicated course to make the movements instinctive, rendering map and compass redundant. So when you come here again – when the mist prevents you from seeing beyond a grey veil, when the wind courses so cold the last thing you want is to grapple with a flapping map – you know you must fill your water bottle at that lochan, you know you must avoid that gully, you know you must find a way around that carpet of ice. Ultimately, this was a rehearsal – one of many – for the day that might be that *one day*.

High pressure had dominated the Lochaber weather for a fortnight. The rocks were dry; the bogs were turning to dust; the streams were reduced to trickles. Significantly, the snowfields that can some years linger long into June had melted. The mountains were bare. As such, Ramsay's Round had, in theory, rarely been more achievable. Theory became reality: runners were getting around. Over the course of 13 days straddling the end of May and beginning of June, five runners, all going clockwise and none faster than 22 hours, took the list of completions to 90. I saw only missed opportunity. It could have been me.

But I was here now, moving anticlockwise if only for the romantic reason of ending, like Charlie, on the Ben. I would run as far as possible. When my ankle started troubling, which I knew it would, I would descend to the glen and run back. I heard late from Graham that he could join me. He was obviously feeling confident. 'We could do a Tranter if you fancy it,' he wrote.

Graham Nash, a forty-six-year-old finance director and accountant from Edinburgh, would think nothing of *just* doing Tranter's Round. At the time, he was one of three people to have done Ramsay's Round twice; incredibly, he would become the first to do a third and a fourth round. The first, a midsummer round, left him a 'physical wreck'. Finishing in 23 hours and 19 minutes, he kissed the youth hostel sign, then his wife, before bursting into disbelieving tears. The second was the realisation of a dream – to undertake a solo, unsupported Ramsay in winter conditions. Shortly after midnight in the shade of an April morning, Graham ate a tub of rice pudding and a banana, before setting off towards Mullach nan Coirean, where he found snow lingering on the ridge. Graham ran through dawn, across the Mamores, and beyond the psychological midway point on Chno Dearg, when a group of puzzled walkers on Stob Coire Sgriodain called after him: 'How many are you doing today?'

'Twenty-three,' he bellowed back.

At Loch Treig, he hunted for a stash of food he had hidden the previous night. His heart sank. The store was peppered with mice holes. If the food was ruined, Graham could not carry on. He carefully examined the stockpile. Rodents had gnawed through plastic bags, but boxes containing the food were untouched. He went for the rice pudding first. Relief was tinged with a stinging realisation: he had to carry on now.

Once on the Grey Corries, Graham's feet plunged into soft snow. He longed for the sun to set to refreeze the surface into a hard shell. The nub of the round was ahead – the ascent of Aonach Beag. There were three options; two were immediately rejected. A steep ridge of rock to the right was corniced. Charlie's Gully was choked with snow. Graham was forced into a third option, a channel on the far left, a choice that would typically be the last option for a runner on a summer round because of the extra descent and re-ascent required. Even the final choice was a perilous prospect. 'The lower slope was fine,' Graham said, 'but, as it steepened, the snow covered more of the grass until I was climbing the rocky outcrops to the side. Eventually, I reached a point where it was just possible to up-climb, but would be very difficult to down-climb. The snow was corniced and I couldn't see what was to the right, behind the rocks. I committed, climbing fluidly until I was faced with a four-metre wall of snow – but no overhang. Axe back out, I pumped my legs and wasted no time kicking steps and flinging my axe and free hand into the soft snow. I hauled myself over the edge onto the flat top and lay in the snow, legs burning with lactic acid and heart racing.'

There lies the reason for most contenders choosing to move clockwise on Ramsay's Round, tackling the highest hills first – to avoid such obstacles so late in an attempt. There was one more to come: the Carn Mòr Dearg Arête. As Graham tiptoed along a ridge of snow as narrow as a dinner plate, he watched dislodged blocks of ice rush into the night.

A little over an hour later, his body lay crumpled on the grass outside the hostel. 'Are you okay?' a voice asked. 'We were watching your light descending from the top. Have you just run up Ben Nevis and back?'

'Something like that,' Graham said.

As the high places had belonged to Graham, so they were ours today. From Sgùrr a' Mhaim to Am Bodach to An Gearanach, there was no-one but us. Beyond our ridge, we were surrounded by mountains, girdled by rank upon rank, braid upon braid. Reality would puncture the wonder. I had expected pain, and so it came. Every step was a trial, my gait cumbersome and dawdling. A cloudless heat had overtaken the chill of night. I was chain-eating fruit pastilles. I could feel the veins in my calf, stretching down to the Achilles, beating hard, as if the blood was on fire.

From Binnein Mòr, we could see the Ramsay mountains to the east, the five Munros that cummerbund Loch Treig. They seemed squashed in the grandeur that immersed them. The group were not so reticent when I encountered them earlier that month. It had only been three weeks after Graham's 'wintry' round, but the mountains were transformed: the temperature had soared; the snow had gone. From Fersit, I had ventured up Stob a' Choire Mheadhoin and Stob Coire Easain, the summits' rocks glinting in the sunshine. I descended, faithfully following a compass bearing, strangely surprised by the enormity of these mountains, as if I could have forgotten. Ben Nevis seemed hopelessly distant, standing at the end of a long line of gargantuan mountain offerings that form an eight-Munro route known as the Lochaber Traverse. What should have been inspiring was demoralising. Twice I tripped in the heather, each time cautiously getting back to my feet, on the long drop to Lairig Leacach, a glen that felt lonelier than the wildest reaches of Knoydart. I forded a river, then followed a boggy, intermittent path to find Creaguaineach Lodge, an abandoned building standing on a spit of land where the Abhainn Rath and the Allt na Lairige flow into Loch Treig. The serenity here is unsurpassable, but, as the sight of Ben Nevis over the rooftops of the Grey Corries had triggered a disquiet, so did the brilliance of the mountain-encased loch. It was fear – fear of what I sought: Ramsay's Round. I felt like an imposter, as if I was trespassing in a place I had no right to be.

With mental frailty came physical fragility. My ankle began to ache on the hard track above Loch Treig and up towards Loch Ossian, turning my stride to a hobble. The climb of Beinn na Lap was slow; the descent steep and rough – just about the worst place for an ankle that now twinged with every step. As for the subsequent ascent of Chno Dearg, I simply remember blistering heat. I should have been more grateful; I did not know the terrible truth of Chno Dearg in those days.

Climbing Chno Dearg then felt like following Graham up Sgùrr Eilde Mòr did now: excruciating. Any lingering doubts on the prospect of continuing for another eight hours on the route of Tranter's Round were expunged. The idea was laughable. From the summit, the other Stob Bàn seemed to belong to another universe – an impression that sparked Olly

Stephenson's space station metaphor. As we wallowed swollen ankles and feet in a burn that drains into the Abhainn Rath, Graham pointed out where we would have started the next ascent. Another prickle of missed opportunity. I tried to muster pragmatism instead. The right to run Ramsay's Round, let alone complete, must be earned. The originator – with his 1,600 miles and 80,000 metres in six months – had set the precedent for others to follow. I had not earned that right. Only 90 people in 38 years had. It was impudent to suggest I could be among them. Not yet.

During my first winter in Edinburgh, snow was a marvellous novelty. I remember cycling home from school one night, turning off the main road, and pedalling along a deserted residential street amid tufts of falling stars that glowed orange in the lamplight. I was the protagonist of my own Christmas movie. Such things did not happen in London. 'It's snowing,' I would tell Arielle, with increasing regularity as winter suffused the city, frogmarching her to a window. 'Look at the snow,' I would point. 'Look at it!' She would shrug and walk off.

In the Lochaber mountains, snow comes and stays, languishing in north-facing nooks long into spring. The Pentlands are more promiscuous. The hills can be clad in white one day, only to be stripped bare under the cover of darkness. When night fell on the Pentlands, on the eve of the Carnethy 5, they were brazenly green and brown. By Saturday morning they were clothed in modest white.

To this white world hill runners went, dumped by coaches in a field next to the main road to Biggar. Cocooned in layers, we trudged in a sullen column to the start, pathetically trying to avoid premature wet feet by hurdling the saturated ground. We arrived at an Armageddon: amid a sodden, snowy waste-land stood a cluster of tents containing half-starved shivering people, clasping hot liquid and looking across to a hazy white chaos encasing the hills, all wondering the same thing: what the hell are we doing here?

The field also happens to be the site of the Battle of Roslin. In brief: Scotland versus England; the year, 1303; Scotland won; William Wallace, inevitably, had a tenuous involvement. A hill race should commemorate the battle, Jimmy Jardine decided, and the Carnethy 5 was first held in 1971. The event has been described in cinematic terms, as 'something to behold: 500 runners like extras from *Braveheart* lined up for battle'. There was *some* similarity between us and a fourteenth century Scottish army. Separated by more than 700 years, we were presumably thinking the same: what the hell are we doing here? And: will someone stop those bagpipes so we can get this over with?

The Carnethy 5 – run over five hills of the Pentlands and covering a little over five miles – has become a traditional season-opener for not only Scotland's leading runners, but also the class of the Lake District clubs, with Ambleside, Borrowdale and Helm Hill bringing large contingents across the border. Finlay Wild, Tom Owens and Joe Symonds would lead the charge for the Scottish clubs, but it would be Prasad Prasad, a forty-year-old London-born waiter living in the Trossachs, who would prevail. The time on the clock was 54 minutes. Jimmy Jardine would be on the hill for another 1 hour and 16 minutes, eventually descending Carnethy Hill, the final summit, to finish in a position ninth from last. If anyone epitomises the cliché that the taking part is what counts, it is Jardine: this was his 44th consecutive Carnethy 5.

I had listened to a podcast that morning extolling the merits of mindfulness. As I clambered up a slope of ice to Scald Law, grimacing against a wind whipping snow in my face, I mused on the concept. Mindfulness – I looked it up to confirm – is 'a mental state achieved by focusing one's awareness on the present moment, while calmly acknowledging feelings, thoughts, and bodily sensations'. I 'calmly' addressed the list, deciding very quickly that my 'feelings, thoughts and bodily sensations' were deeply unsatisfactory.

As for the 'present moment', it was something like this.

Heaving and quite frankly in a state of near-shock, I eventually found my way to the summit. I had been here before, of course. Not that I recognised anything in the furore. It could have been the moon. I ran after the dark bodies that accelerated into the whiteout, arrowing towards South Black Hill, the second of the race summits. From the top, a path traverses to a col known as Cross Sward. The cambering track was slathered in powdery snow, flipping runners onto their backs and sides. Further along the racing line, on West Kip, desperate marshals were huddling beneath the ridge trying to escape the ferocity of the wind. I knew exactly what they were thinking: what the hell are we doing here?

The route spilled downhill again, dropping to the glen that splits the east and west ridges of the northern Pentlands. I tried to summon effort. As gravity did its thing and the reduced altitude meant a mellowing of the weather, I was tricked into thinking everything was going to be just fine. I will not let anyone overtake, I told myself, and started to count the number of people I passed. I had reached seven when a hole hidden by snow grabbed a foot. There was a momentary tug-of-war and for a split second I was looking at low, heavy clouds, then an instant later, all too closely, white, cold ground.

I was soon marching upward, an aching hike to Carnethy Hill. Be mindful. Focus on the moment, the glorious, precious soon-to-be-gone moment. Easier thought than practised when slogging up a snow-filled gully, fighting a freezing hairdryer, while poised inches from the rear end of a Lochaber AC veteran. I was midway up the gully – the Lochaber backside replaced by a Hunters Bog Trotter one – when I looked at my watch. I had run a little over four miles in 47 minutes. By this time, Gavin Bland, in breaking the course record in 1999, would have been back at Armageddon. (There was £250 for the runner who could challenge the record; Prasad would not even get within seven minutes of it, such was the severity of the conditions.) I still had to get to the top of this dreadful climb, stumble up and over Carnethy Hill, flounder down a zig-zagging slope of snow-immersed scree and heather, and cross the battlefield to reach the end. It was a humbling thought.

I was humbled too when I saw the results. I was 91st, one second behind a man in his seventh decade. But that (after a great deal of internal head-shaking and sighing), I decided was the essence of it all: to be chastened by the elements, by the landscape, by our own insufficiencies. Besides, I was just another in a long line of Englishmen to be humbled in the hills, glens and fields of the Pentlands.

The last thing I wanted to do the next day was run, let alone run in the Pentlands. But then I had cause to go to IKEA. Situated beyond the Edinburgh bypass in the former coal mining town of Loanhead, the store and car park occupy a position perpendicular to the Pentlands, offering an undisturbed view of the range. Sir Walter Scott could have been standing here in a quest for Swedish flat-pack furniture 200 years earlier when he noted: 'I never saw anything more beautiful than the ridge of Carnethy against a clear frosty sky.'

The mountains were not calling. They were bellowing as if they were ablaze: 'Get over here!' I obeyed, stepping onto a rising floor of sparkling crystal. That the wind had been hysterical, that snow had whirled, that the sky had roared, seemed hardly believable. Now: silent, motionless, flashing sunlight, long shadows, the sky an ocean-blue infinity. The philosopher would have called the white-attired Pentlands sublime: infinitely noble, splendid and terrifying. I descended Carnethy Hill by the way I had toiled 24 hours earlier, then re-climbed the peak by the line we had ricocheted down. It all seemed so easy. Away to the left was Scald Law, its flank smeared in a streak of dark graffiti where 499 head-bowed runners had disappeared into a maelstrom. As utopia emerged from the horror, only poetry could describe the new world. I was reminded of the words of Stevenson: 'Black are my steps on silver sod.'

As for the hills? What else can offer such magnificent

juxtaposition? Here is so much despair and ugliness yet limitless beauty and hope.

I raced sporadically after the Carnethy 5 – an evening dash in the green hills above Peebles; a scrappy Scottish championship counter on the trio of Eildons that rise above Melrose; a Saturday afternoon contest around Arthur's Seat: through Hunter's Bog, over Salisbury Crags, up the Radical Road. I excelled in mediocrity, with any hope of unbroken training scuppered by perpetual soreness in my ankle. For a long time, I thought it was psychological, that this pain, the same pain I had felt when I had jogged downhill holding Arielle's hand, was somehow imagined. There was, however, *actually* something wrong with me: a scan would identify a fingernail-sized tear in the webbing of the tendon that stretches from Achilles to heel.

Somehow, over the weeks that followed, the tear just seemed to get better. I rested, I stretched, I half-heartedly attempted yoga. Above all, I hoped. Gradually, I returned to the hills, taking the Road to Swanston but not *to* Swanston, before I was eventually able to run through the village again, and up thereafter – up to the hills. I seemed to re-discover the Pentlands. I saw a brocken spectre on Allermuir; another time, I climbed into an inversion above a haar. Wind blew, sun shone, rain came down, mist loitered, stillness fell – each a different kind of perfection. I watched the seasons change: the snow vanishing for good; the yellow glow of flowering spring gorse; the muirburn tingeing the air with stale smoke; the green unfurling of bracken stalks like aliens' palms; the popping of gorse pods; the unfurled rugs of purple heather.

Summer quickly subsides into an exaggerated autumn in Scotland. The bracken swamping the hillsides bronzed and like the winter snow simply dissolved. I raced again, staying close to the familiarity of the Pentlands. The first was Caerketton, a two-mile out-and-back sprint from the bottom of the ski road at Hillend. After dropping off the summit ridge, we descended a slope of ankle-deep vegetation, made slick by a soaking pall of mist. Out of the corner of my eye, I saw a woman, contouring on my left, draw level. In a moment, she was down, flailing headfirst into heather. She seemed to bounce, as if the stunt was contrived, then wordlessly continued her foot-borne motion. I followed, wondering how she had not broken her neck. I would visit Caerketton again, twice in three hours, in another Pentland Skyline. In still and dry conditions, Kris Jones would snip 31 seconds from Murray Strain's course record. I suffered: first from raging thirst over Carnethy Hill and Scald Law, then by simple fatigue on the journey home.

It was October, a fortnight after the Pentland Skyline, when I went back to Lochaber. Since I had last been in Charlie's mountains a further five runners had made it around, most notably Jasmin Paris. She is among the immortals, but there had been mortals too. Among them was John Parkin, a primary school headteacher from West Yorkshire who came to Fort William having completed Bob Graham and Paddy Buckley rounds with just 23 minutes to spare across both successes. A round within 24 hours in the hardest of the three in an unpredictable August seemed fanciful. But as the end neared, he voiced an epiphany to Ben Rowley, a support runner on this occasion but one of the class of 2016 Ramsayists: 'I'm going to do it, aren't I?' The question was rhetorical; the tone defiant.

Descending Mullach nan Coirean, tears came and did not stop. He was to become the 44th person to complete the big three (and, cumulatively, probably one of the slowest), and the 94th to finish the Ramsay. 'I look at the names on those short lists and see race winners and fell champions,' he said. 'Giants of mountain running. I have raised myself to be among exalted company.'

To a chorus of hoarse stags, I would run for six hours, crossing the Grey Corries from east to west and going as far as Aonach Mòr before looping back to my start above Spean Bridge. After the year that had been – a year of an abandoned

Tranter's Round, a year of injury interference, a year of indifferent racing – I expected nothing. 'If I have to walk the whole way,' I had told Fi the night before, 'I'll walk.' But I ran. And as I ran, I felt less awed, less hurried, less frustrated by the long descents or going the wrong way, less shocked by the scale of the mountains, less irritated when my body did not quite do what I would have liked. I was not envious of Graham Nash or Jasmin Paris or John Parkin. I no longer saw the victory of others as symbolic of my failure. Their right was undeniable. I was here to win mine. John Parkin was not in exalted company. He *was* exalted company.

Something was different. The mountains held a significance that was no longer intangible. They were not merely anonymous, arbitrary monoliths of mud and rock that could be ticked off and forgotten. They were the theatre for stories of endurance, fortitude and joy, layer upon layer of decades of narrative. I imagined the popping champagne corks of the last Munro party passed by Jasmin Paris. I remembered Jon Ascroft smiling across a table at the Canny Man's as he told me about the blocks of rock that line the Grey Corries ridge like a high-level pavement. I thought of Jez Bragg exhausting his pacemakers. I imagined the gently-falling flakes that sprinkled on Glyn Jones some forty hours into the first successful winter round. I thought of Adrian Belton eating rice pudding and tinned fruit, and picking up the pace again. I contemplated Charlie Ramsay, driven by unstoppable will, unaware of what he was creating.

Cloud engulfed the ridge, with the glistening snake of the Abhainn Rath the only hint of anything beyond the shroud. As I descended the final peak of the Grey Corries, like a tsunami in the sky, the wind wrenched the mist away, revealing the immensity of Aonach Beag. I shuddered, a movement sparking a memory. Geal-charn.

Directly ahead, across a high col, was the crux of Graham's do-or-die dilemma: Spinks Ridge – a rocky line named after Nicky Spinks who descended this way on her 2008 round when snow blocked all other routes – on the right; Charlie's Gully at the centre; a third gulch, the scene of Graham's high adrenaline, on the far left. I headed directly up the grassy ramp of Charlie's Gully, ducking beneath the dripping overhang, before an abrupt, anxious, exciting scramble – a slip here would result in a potentially catastrophic fall – across slick grass and rock that brought me onto the shoulder of Aonach Beag.

I belonged, I realised. That was it; that was all. I was finally at peace in the hills that, physically and emotionally, had troubled me most. They had possessed me, becoming stained in my psyche – a colossal Craig Varr. While I had sought to conquer them, it was they that were conquering me. They were part of me like a physical attachment, as they had necessarily been part of those who had come before.

Touching the cairn on Aonach Beag, I wondered where Philip Tranter had made his bed. The summit occupies a featureless plateau, but a stone's throw from the highest point, the east ridge falls in a series of frightening crags and buttresses. I peered over the edge, into nothingness, for cloud had returned. The mountain was riddled with snow patches and ice had already formed a cornice on the rim of the east face. The spectre of winter loomed. The hills would soon begin a hibernation, cocooned in a blanket of snow. They would reappear when they were ready.

I tried to imagine being here in the vehemence of winter, the Aonachs transformed into frosty cathedrals, when daylight shrinks to fewer than seven hours, when the air shrieks and snow billows. I thought of Glyn Jones again, looking upward at snowflakes dancing in a shadowy sky, and closed my eyes, attempting to convey myself to this hoary realm. I opened them. I could not imagine. The truth was unfathomable.

16

AMBUSHED BY CHNO DEARG

A voice splits the darkness, echoing across a silvery plateau, then swallowed by the mountain. Glyn Jones tries again. 'Pete!' The call is hoarse; the breathing ragged. 'Pete!' He waits. An immense silence roars in his ears.

The new day's light is scrubbing the snow to chaste white, bringing a morning of nectarine-tinted peaks as a reward for those who tread the hills through a winter's night. As the radiance intensifies, the glare strains Glyn's eyes – eyes that are frantically scanning the arctic enormity of the col between Chno Dearg and Stob Coire Sgriodain. He longs to see a dark speck, a flicker of movement – Pete. But stillness reigns. The world dare not move. The soft susurration of rolling snow grains accentuates the purity of the dreadful hush. Guilt rips the maddening beauty of the morning apart.

This was Glyn's second dawn. The first came on Mullach nan Coirean, as he and Pete climbed into the Mamores, two pioneers with a fantastic plan: to be the first to complete Ramsay's Round in winter. The hills were double wrapped: snow and then mist. They had been travelling for 16 hours when they reached the valley floor by the Abhainn Rath. Below the snow line, they tramped through wringing heather and bog. As Pete crossed the river, he slipped, drenching gloves and sleeves. A coldness penetrated deep inside. The pace slowed from a jog to an amble. At Loch Treig, they halted, burying themselves in bivvy bags, desperately seeking sleep. After an hour, they re-packed and continued, up the protracted whaleback of Beinn na Lap. Glyn remembers the tedium. How he would long for tedium again.

Encased in ice, Chno Dearg rose to the north. The mountain had been toughening her thin shell into a frozen carapace during the long hours of darkness. The ground was white-tiles-and-steel hard under the runners' feet. Sleep-deprived and emotionally exhausted, they stumbled into her lair. The gradient sharpened before they realised the danger, before they could add crampons to their shoes. Glyn looked across the sloping ice rink, searching for a sign of weakness: a line of rocks or protruding tips of grass that might be surrounded by safe, soft snow. Finding what he sought, he moved towards it, first in a diagonal downwards slant, but then, as he attempted to step horizontally, plunged straight down, sliding some ten yards in the flicker of a heavy eyelid. Pete, wearing lightweight studded shoes to Glyn's trainers that were customised with bolts, seemed to be faring better. Glyn gathered himself, and together, in the blackness of a November night, with ice axes rasping, breathing heavy and the rumble of crashing water rising to meet them, the friends traversed the pearly bone of Chno Dearg's forehead. The mountain beyond the beam of their torches held unknown dangers; it was as well to be blindfolded from them.

Making his way to an outcrop of crags, Glyn looked to Pete, ready to beckon him across, but his partner was stuck, pegged to the ice by his axe. The torch light glared bluish from the unmoving, hunched body. The fragility of human endeavour was suddenly and grotesquely explicit. Fear exploded in Glyn's heart.

Slowly, with triceps straining, his body pressed to the ice, Glyn hacked steps – eight hissing bites to a rung – to reach Pete. How he wished he had sharpened the adze blade. Down Glyn worked until shards of ice leapt around Pete's head, then his shoulders, then his knees.

The ladder was complete: the staircase to safety.

Pete reached out a foot, ready to place it on the first rung. In an instant, he was gone: crashing downhill, thrashing his axe at the ground until it bit deep enough.

A gradual lightening gave hope. Dawn was nudging night. There had to be a way out of this. How close they were to the edge of a steep lip that receded to less treacherous ground, Glyn realised in the growing brightness. How long had this mountain been playing with them? One hour? Two? He began to climb, to examine the ground ahead. As the realisation of impending escape began to take hold, he noticed a numbness in his toes, a soreness in a shoulder. He looked down the mountain again, back to Pete. Nothing. This time he had disappeared.

Glyn Jones ekes out an existence of semi-reclusion as a crofter on a smallholding in Wigtownshire, Scotland's remote south-west extremity. When he gets off a bus in Edinburgh to meet me, he confesses to being overwhelmed by the city. 'The noise is incredible,' he says. He is not here by choice. An accident to his 'running gear' – a broken foot – means he must attend a hospital appointment in Glasgow. A brief trip thereafter to Edinburgh, to get a fossil identified, seems logical, and so his misfortune is my fortune: I can meet the man who completed *that* fantastic plan.

'Old, white hair, grey holdall, black specs,' Glyn wrote in a text message to identify himself. A mobile phone was his concession to the twenty-first century. He was entirely accurate: ten minutes later, standing before me was a 'white-haired one' in his mid-sixties.

Like many of his contemporaries, Glyn had a background in mountain marathons and orienteering, and what he lacked in talent, he made up for in determination and endurance. He ran Tranter's Round twice, in summer initially, before becoming the first to succeed in winter, finishing in a mammoth 29 hours and 49 minutes – close to one hour for every mile. As arthritis took hold of his knees, a winter Ramsay's Round became his 'final frontier'. He had run a summer version in the 1990s, albeit outside 24 hours, and had twice attempted in winter early in 2002, both times on his own, abandoning on each occasion. Glyn was the unlikeliest first – a fact double-failure epitomised. There was no shortage of hill runners and mountaineers capable of a fast winter round, notably the Ramsay pioneers of the late 1980s, but the practice was not fashionable. 'There was a thought at the time that it would be setting a bad example because it was promoting something that's very dangerous,' Glyn says. 'Me? Whether I succeeded or failed was unlikely to encourage the inexperienced or deter the talented. I had nothing to lose. I wasn't well known. I was fifty-two. I was quite content to stop being a hill runner. I thought that after a winter Ramsay's Round, I would have done all the things I wanted to do.'

Glyn is half-right. There was a notion that undertaking the classic rounds in winter contained unacceptable risks. Joss Naylor had criticised Selwyn Wright's decision to run a solo midwinter Bob Graham in 1985, for instance. There were, however, others tackling Ramsay's Round in winter – they just did not share Glyn's motivation. While he aimed to join the circle irrespective of time, others believed that for an attempt to be classified as a true round it must be accomplished within 24 hours. That was Al Powell's philosophy when he twice sought to beat the day in the 1990s.

On the first occasion, starting on Christmas Eve, he stopped after eight hours at Fersit, with conditions 'not right'. He tried again eight weeks later with near-disastrous results. 'In the middle of the night, in the middle of nowhere, in the middle of winter,' Al puts it, as if writing the narrative of a children's story, he dropped his map in soft snow on Beinn na Lap. Lost and becoming hypothermic, he feared the very worst: 'one slip in lots of places and you've had it; you're very vulnerable on your own if something goes wrong.' Knowing he was around five miles from the closest bothy in Lairig Leacach, he wandered in blind hope, stumbling on Creaguaineach Lodge first. 'There was some discarded food inside and I slept upstairs in a rusty old bed under some mouldy blankets,' Al recalled. 'Next morning, I found my compass outside – I'd lost that too the night before when I got cold – and headed west for four hours, finding some chocolate in a bothy en route. I then dropped down into the head of Glen Nevis and finally hitched a lift back to the youth hostel.' Enough was enough. Al, a climber who was then pushing big routes in the Alps and Himalayas, would not try again.

The criteria of a winter round is the subject of conjecture. Charlie Ramsay defines winter as the first day of December to the last day of February. The Bob Graham 24-Hour Club similarly views the period as falling between 1 December and 1 March, but also identifies a 'midwinter' round as 'the weekend before the shortest day through to the first period of decent weather after the shortest day, but to be completed no later than 10 January'. What 'decent' entails is another debate. Glyn focused on 21 December too, but viewed it as the middle date of a twelve-week 'season' straddling late autumn and early winter. That period, he reasoned, offered the prospect of four 'good moons' and the likelihood of genuine winter conditions. Charlie has considered amending his definition to distinguish between the wildly varying conditions a runner might experience in his three-month 'winter' window. He came to a shrewd conclusion: 'Difficult to define and manage.' It was a sensible decision. Who would want to be the arbiter of such debate?

It is, of course, entirely feasible that circumstances in December, January or February may not be wintry and snow cover intermittent. When climbers Martin Moran and Paul Potter attempted late in 1989, the hills were naked. The enemy was the lack of light – moon and day – not snow. Moran was suffering from the effects of a stomach bug and ended his attempt at Stob Coire an Laoigh. Potter, who would be killed in an avalanche in Glen Coe in 1996, gave up at Loch Eilde Mòr, despite being just 40 minutes outside a 24-hour schedule. 'Had I been able to continue with Paul he might have had a better chance,' Moran reckoned.

The opposite, of course, is true in summer. Snow could theoretically fall or cover the high summits of Lochaber any day of the year, making the environment, by definition, wintry. Hill runners generally agree, however, that there are various prerequisites for winter conditions: snow cover to around 800 metres, below-zero temperatures, short days, and the need to use the mountaineering hardware of crampons and ice axe. The paradox is that the winter runner will then wait for the best of the worst conditions: little or no wind, high pressure, good visibility and low avalanche risk.

Paradoxes were not of interest to Glyn. His successful winter Tranter was undertaken in 'immense solitude'. His experience was existentialist, giving tangible meaning to Byron: 'Are not the mountains, waves and skies, a part / Of me and of my soul, as I of them?'

As Glyn gazed at the Grey Corries in the dawn of a second morning immersed in mountains, he found 'my God, my Truth'. His thoughts began to run wild: 'I feel apprehensive, awed, wanting to become part of such eternal energy, yet not quite willing to sacrifice myself on this altar tonight. Dangerous! Very dangerous trains of thought, conveying me to that land where the lark rises higher and higher on her bursting song of victory.'

Several months later, Glyn discovered that a couple, also set on Tranter's Round, had left Glen Nevis two hours after him. He was not overtaken, but one of the pair, Nick Carter, finished the course 26 minutes faster, meaning Glyn's record had stood for around an hour-and-a-half. He was not bothered; records were inconsequential. That was not his reason for being in the hills. Glyn had travelled solo and unsupported, a standard, as on the Cuillin ridge traverse, that would permeate the ethos of future attempts in winter. Even the purist has the sense to make the harder easier, but by choosing to travel alone and resist assistance, he or she ensures the ordeal is harder again. For Glyn, the challenge was defined by three words: 'Winter, solo, unsupported. That was the ultimate in adventure in the hills.' Indeed, on his Tranter, Glyn imagined the words 'solo and unsupported pointing like a signpost to Ben Nevis'.

But he was a realist too. After two solo failures and haunted by the insatiable calling of the mountains, he recognised the need for companionship on Ramsay's Round. He turned to his old mate and Ramsayist, Pete Simpson – the man who was the first to conclude a winter Bob Graham in 1979 in 'classic snow conditions', the man who would vanish.

From the heights of Chno Dearg, Glyn scours the mountain-side. As dreadful possibilities run through his befuddled brain, one thought crystallises in his mind: I need to get off this hill. Only then can he raise mountain rescue. As for his 'final frontier', it is over. Reaching a col, hope is renewed: he sees the unmistakable grooves of fresh stud marks in the snow. But as he progresses to Stob Coire Sgriodain, the marks, like Pete, disappear. Then, as quickly as they went, they reappear: a clear right Walsh print, seemingly lacking a crampon; a smudged left one. A preposterous notion struck Glyn. Maybe it was not over? 'If it is Pete ahead, then he's going fast, so we've dealt with the crisis and feel strong again, don't we? Nothing further – as bad as last night – can happen, surely?'

The deliberations seem absurd at best, reckless and suicidal at worst. But, for Glyn, this – carrying on in the face of terrible adversity – was not principally about the completion of a subjective round of mountains. 'Inwardly, I'm slipping into another country where the true grail is to be found – that kingdom of the soul where vision and imagination are the masters, making an inner reality very different from the concrete one outside. In this country, I am privileged to be an occasional pilgrim, finding that joy which transcends pain, that clarity of perception which increases as the physical body recedes. In this country, where the silence is music, an old man's spirit can dance unfettered. The glory is in the doing, not in the having done. And wanting to hear music and to dance to it, is what keeps luring me back to the hills ...'

I cried when I first read those words.

Glyn sees a figure ahead. It is Pete. He staggers after him. Reunited, they are overwhelmed with relief – relief they made it through, relief they did not let each other down, relief they are not dead.

Reaching Fersit after 27 hours, Pete's struggle is over. Glyn crosses the dam and begins to climb Stob a' Choire Mheadhoin, driven by a desire to regain a 'lost faith' in his identity. 'My need to do this challenge, to reaffirm belief in who I am, is absolute. I do not want to re-invent myself – just find that person I used to be and the inner strengths I thought he had.' The afternoon slips by and as Glyn stands on the summit of Stob Bàn, it is night-time again – a night of introspection, a scarcely imaginable night of subsistence and persistence among the Grey Corries. Progress is desperately slow. Walkers' boot holes gleam like lanterns under the glow of the torch. Cornices loom startlingly close. The heavens open – 'large, soft, gently falling flakes'. Glyn has no means of communication – he deemed a phone to be 'support'; 'self-reliance came long before mobile telephoning was born,' he would tell me – to either raise or dismiss an alarm. He slips on Sgùrr Choinnich Mòr and an eye narrowly avoids being impaled on the axe point. When the clouds finally part, it is to reveal a stupendous glimpse of Aonach Beag. On the way there, he rests, brushing away snow, sitting in his survival bag. 'I am so desperately tired I cannot worry about hypothermia. I just have to believe that I will wake when knee pains get fierce, or when cold seeps far enough in to make me shiver, but before it gnaws too deep.'

From Aonach Mòr, it will take three-and-a-half hours to travel less than two miles to Carn Mòr Dearg. Glyn knows that Pete will have put mountain rescue on standby: 'My mind is prey to hearing voices, seeing lights and twice the muted beat of helicopter blades.' His speed in comparison to the faster progress he and Pete had made across the Mamores was bound to raise concern. On his Tranter, despite the 'perfect weather', Glyn had decided not to divert onto the Ramsay route because he believed the longer undertaking would last 36 hours. As he climbs Carn Mòr Dearg, the runner moves into a forty-ninth hour, a third day. He ties himself to the axe, jams the tool between boulders, and breaks again. If sleep overwhelms, the axe will be his hook to the mountain.

Pete is waiting for Glyn on the Ben Nevis path. Together again, they walk downhill to the glen, arriving unnoticed and unheralded: 'I'd returned from the realm of my soul; I was once again a white-haired one.' It was over – a feat transcending physical endurance; a profoundly symbolic act. 'That bureaucracy has not yet made it impossible for us to go on the hills alone in winter,' he proclaimed, 'we should be glad. That we can still find adventure when we want it, in this soft underbelly of the rich world, is a right that we should not give up without a fight.'

They did not – and so Glyn would celebrate that his milestone lasted less than five months. Gary Tompsett was an experienced mountain marathoner, orienteer and mountain biker, and from 1999 a multi-sport adventure racer, often competing over several days and coping for up to 36 hours without sleep. Knowing Glyn's time and being familiar with the two major ridge lines, Gary decided that a winter round would be more fulfilling than a quick-but-not-record-breakingly-quick summer effort. 'Within weeks, I had established what equipment and philosophy would work and just did it,' he said. 'No training. No more prepping. Just a lifetime aggregate of aptitude and commitment. I didn't push too hard. I wanted to enjoy it. I was solo and not as fast as a mountain runner, but I had staying power and belief in the fluency of my approach to the challenge.'

After getting around in 32 hours and 48 minutes, Gary claimed 'it was all pretty straightforward'. The word 'straightforward' must be qualified. Visibility on steep, convex snowfields was poor – Chno Dearg, again; a 30-minute sleep was 'accidentally' taken in the heather at 3.30am; the wind in the later hours was 'howling'. That sort of 'straightforward'. Like Glyn, Gary sought to make the hard harder by borrowing the former's three-word philosophy. When friends met him at Fersit, it was to check his safety only; he took no shelter or food, nor did he jettison anything. When Gary met another contemporary at Lairig Leacach bothy, he did not go inside the building. He carried a 22-pound pack for every step. There were no pre-arranged water or food stops.

There was logic to travelling alone. 'I felt that with support, there were more conduits to bailing,' Gary explained. 'Cold, hunger, minor injury, low morale: these could prevail and it would then be easy to take help from others, and to perhaps bail out with them. It's a very remote route, so when solo you have little choice but to continue. Going solo and unsupported (and in winter) immediately sets the bar at its highest for other future aspirants, and creates better conversations!'

Success in winter was won by a willingness, even a desire, to suffer. The innovators showed it could be done, but humans inevitably seek more. How fast could it be accomplished? Twenty-four hours – was that enough time? Shane Ohly, a professional climber specialising in free climbing before turning his focus to running, thought so. In 2007 – the year before his assault on the Ramsay – he dominated the mountain marathon scene. His ability to navigate over rough terrain, his endurance over many hours, along with his obvious climbing ability, marked him out: he would surely go faster than those who had gone before, but could he outrun a day?

Climbing Ben Nevis first, Shane embraced the fast-and-light mantra of the elite mountain marathoner, his strategy depending on being able to move swiftly. 'If the weather deteriorated, especially if it rained, I'd be in big trouble,' he admitted at the time. Treading a delicate balance, Shane made rapid progress over the first four mountains, but was descending Aonach Beag when the insistence for speed over-whelmed him. He was losing height by kicking steps in the snow, making frustratingly slow progress. Noticing a rock buttress to his right, he traversed and began leaping from ledge to ledge, moving at a pace that felt quick again. 'I jumped to another ledge and the second my foot touched the snow, I knew I was in big trouble,' Shane remembered. 'The snow on the ledge cascaded down the buttress as I landed, and I started to fall with it. As I slid over the edge, still a long, long way above the col, I smashed my ice axe into the remaining snow on the ledge and came to a stop, half my body dangling over the void.'

It was dark when Shane found himself on Chno Dearg. Reaching the top, he raced gleefully off the summit, reminding himself that success and survival depended on constant forward motion. An ambush lay ahead. 'The ground started to fall away, with my torch lighting up a smaller and smaller area as the void of blackness in front of me grew,' he said. 'I stopped and double checked the map. A few seconds' pause, and I could already feel the sweat on my body turning icy cold.' He resumed running, taking long strides, zig-zagging down the steep mountainside, the snow crunching under his feet. Suddenly, he was on the ground, skidding on hard névé. 'I was sliding, accelerating into the blackness. For a second, I was pleased that I was covering the ground even quicker than when running. My brain was starting to be numbed by the hours of hard effort and it took another half-second to realise the danger. Ice crystals sparked into the night sky, illuminated by the beam of my head torch as I braked with my ice axe. I came to a stop, heart racing. I had slid a long way, maybe 50, 60, 70 metres – I couldn't be sure in the dark.'

To be ambushed on Chno Dearg was becoming synonymous with the round in winter. Before Shane, John Fleetwood – who at the time also held the record for the fastest winter Tranter, set two days before a December solstice – had become the third to make it round in the toughest of seasons, finishing in a gruelling 47 hours and 55 minutes in 2006. As he bridged the gap between Beinn na Lap and Chno Dearg, an arctic gale

sucked the warmth from his battered body. After a relative
respite on the ascent, he entered a tempestuous darkness on
the plateau of Chno Dearg: 'The wind reasserts itself and the
cloud descends, leaving me plodding rather aimlessly upward,
buffeted by the wind, lost in my own murky world of dark
and driving spindrift.'

Despite living on the edge of the Lake District, John was
drawn to Scotland, particularly in winter when the hills took
on 'a very different proposition to those in England and Wales',
with long rounds becoming a test of mountaineering skill and
indomitable endurance. The rounds – typically 40 to 80 miles
in length and climbing thousands of metres – were his niche
and he knocked them off with alacrity, undertaking efforts in
Fisherfield, Glen Coe, Glen Etive, Glen Shiel and Knoydart.
The time and season was of minor importance; like Glyn Jones,
the doing was John's barometer of success. His memories of
the Ramsay, written in the present tense as if they are relived
for the first time on every reading, are infused with a special
kind of Chno Dearg-conceived horror: 'On a compass bearing
in the dark with blinding spindrift, it's almost impossible to
choose the best line through the snow, which leads to much
floundering, cursing and staccato lunges forward. Perhaps
because of attempts to avoid the drifts, I suddenly find myself
going in completely the wrong direction, recognising that I've
ascended too far and am heading up Meall Garbh. I rue my
mistake since it requires me to descend the very deeply drifted
slopes that I've just painstakingly staggered up, but there's
nothing for it but to do just that and seek the next top in the
confusing undulating ground.

'In negligible visibility, I am really struggling to stay on
course, especially as the compass seems to be wobbling all
over the place before settling down to indicate the way ahead.
The gale is blowing just as hard, the snow is deep, the spindrift
is zipping right into my unguarded face, my hand can barely
hold the compass, I can see nothing but the immediate slope
in front of me (or I could, only I dare not raise my head to

be stung by the driving snow), and it's 4am. This is about survival, nothing else: no-one can get me out of here but me, and I guess therein lies the attraction – me against the mountain; no get out clauses, no options, no turning back. It is an elegantly simple challenge.

'The time wears slowly on as I painstakingly traverse the tops to Sgriodain, concentrating fiercely on the navigation, trying to hold in my mind the aspect of the slopes and the distances. The terrain is most confusing in the conditions, but I make no more mistakes and eventually slump on to the summit cairn. It is 5am. I have taken two hours from Chno Dearg, an unbelievably slow time which crushes my spirit, but there's little to do except face the wind once more and stagger down the ridge to the dam.'

As Shane continued, heading in the opposite direction of travel to John, the mountains seemed imbued by dreadful spirits: 'The blackness of the wilderness night slowly changed as wisps of cloud reached out for me.' By the time he reached the Abhainn Rath, Shane knew he was in trouble. He simply could not move at a pace sufficient to generate heat to keep warm. A numbness in his toes could be ignored no longer. With his shoes frozen, he realised he would have to urinate on his laces. He stood in the glen, desperately trying to answer a call of nature. Nothing. He was too dehydrated to 'even get a dribble'. He spat on his hands instead and began to rub the moisture into the icy laces. He repeated the process, before he could eventually wrench the shoes open and change his saturated socks. After running for a further 20 minutes, the cold forced him to stop again. He had not thought to warm his toes to recover the circulation. Shane put off the need to pause again, slogging uphill, hoping the exertion would fire life into his feet. By the time he bowed to the inevitable, his shoes had refrozen. Spit, rub, spit, rub. Any chance of a 24-hour round disappeared in the dreadful cold of Sgùrr Eilde Mòr. He carried on nonetheless. 'I wasn't going to fail,' he had decided.

The rest, frankly, is hard to fathom. Climbing Binnein Mòr at 5am, he buried his head against the rocks, gasping for breath, fighting exhaustion. He fell heavily again, this time on Na Gruagaichean, sustaining only bruising. Anything more serious, anything that would cause immobility, might well have killed him. Then the hallucinations came: a dragon among the rocks of Sgùrr a' Mhaim, whispers of classical music on Stob Bàn, a herd of unicorns on Mullach nan Coirean. Even as he descended the final mountain, he took a wrong line. 'I was beyond caring now. I really didn't care about anything,' he said. 'Every step my legs were wracked with pulsating pain.' He walked to the finish, ending his exceptional struggle 29 hours and 59 minutes after setting out. Gary Tompsett had left a note under a window wiper on Shane's car: 'Champagne waiting for you in the youth hostel.'

Triumphing in the white hills of Lochaber is a lottery. Shane's record had stood for four years when runners lined up to buy a ticket. Brothers Dan and Jon Gay, running clockwise, and Andy Kitchin, moving anticlockwise, would be defeated. Shane would also try again, seeking to better his own record. He had slipped outside 24-hour pace but was convinced he could regain time on the Mamores when acute pain in his right ankle, caused by a crampon strap rubbing on ligaments, ended his attempt at Meanach. 'It was very painful,' Shane said, 'but a fraction of the pain and discomfort I went through in 2008.' Ultimately, the dramatically worsening weather – a windchill of -27 Celsius was recorded at Nevis Range – was the deciding factor. The injury would have slowed his pace to a shuffling crawl in a wind-lashed environment colder than a kitchen freezer. He had survived one frightful night in the Mamores. To do it again was to push his luck.

A fortnight before Christmas in 2012, Tom Phillips, a 49-year-old Cumbrian, threw the dice. A visitor to Scotland since his father walked him into the Lost Valley of Glen Coe as a five-year-old, Ramsay's Round was the natural progression from a lifetime of climbing Munros in winter. By Stob

Choire Claurigh, he was 35 minutes outside a clockwise schedule of 23 hours and 50 minutes. 'I knew that I couldn't go any faster and had to reserve energy to complete another potential 20 hours-plus on the mountains,' Tom said. 'I just had to keep moving efficiently and carefully, and see what happened.' He had watched an impressionists' dawn as the Mamores glowed pink, and skated the frozen Abhainn Rath, when, while climbing Sgùrr Eilde Mòr, he acknowledged he would not breach 24 hours. A man attuned to endurance from an early age – at fourteen he cycled 200 miles non-stop from Oban to Inverness via Skye – he pressed on, changing his shoes to trainers on the Glen Nevis road and finishing in four minutes under 27 hours.

The words of one of Tom's support runners, John Carr, who had previously never ventured further north than Loch Lomond, eloquently summarise the astounding test that Ramsay's Round in winter poses. Bivvying by the dam, John remembered shooting stars and meteor showers, and a silence that was 'deadly'. At 3.51am, Tom and John stepped across the dam. 'Every foot you climb,' John said, 'it gradually gets a little whiter until *crunch*. Just like breaking a meringue, the hard exterior gives way to soft snow underneath. It's not running, it's speed mountaineering at best. It can be quite demoralising if you let it. Normally, when you're climbing you can look up and focus on a point to help keep tunnel vision, but in the dark you see just snow, endless snow, like you're in this bubble floating in an eternal abyss. It's silent in the outside world, like a vacuum; the only noise is from your lungs and feet, and by contrast they are deafening.

'I had one focus in my mind. Do everything I can to pace Tom to the last section on the track where it should be easy running. Tom was down on the schedule, so the magic number kept in my head was three miles per hour or 20 minutes per mile. When there is no finish line it takes a different mindset to keep the momentum going. The first mile took 27 minutes, then 39, 25, 23. You try to tap out a rhythm and just when it's

going well – *crunch*. Snow past your knees. Then again and
again. Every step your shin hammers against the crust.'

As an English teacher, I occasionally find myself having to
define bathos, the literary device of anti-climax. I cannot
think of a clearer definition than the denouement to come: Jon
Gay's winter Ramsay, the first success under the sought-after
24-hour barrier.

After the five heroic acts of Jones, Tompsett, Fleetwood,
Ohly and Phillips, there is rightly an expectation of the next.
But hearing the story of Jon's 2013 round reminded me of
Adrian Belton in 1989, Jon Ascroft in 2015 and Jasmin Paris
in 2016. What can the runners do but acknowledge they may
never be so fortunate again?

Jon Gay had succeeded in a summer round in 2010, and
because he lived in Fort William, the summits were quite
literally his backyard. After running several Tranter's rounds
– including a new fastest winter time of 18 hours and 59
minutes in 2009, accompanied by his brother Dan and Paul
Manson – and helping numerous Ramsay attempts, he arguably knew the hills better than anyone.

Jon had raced cross-country the previous weekend and
was training for April's Lochaber Marathon when a weather
window opened in late February. High pressure was to dominate. The expectation was for mountains frozen to sea level,
a snow line at 600 metres, and a -20 Celsius windchill. The
moon was full. For Jon, there was 'zero cause for concern'.
Opting to run solo but arranging for food support at Fersit, he
set off, knowing he would not know the true conditions – and
the likelihood of success – until he was up high. Like those
who had gone before (and failed), Jon was convinced that
breaking 24 hours was possible.

Although he and Dan had aborted their attempt the previous
winter, with Andy Kitchin suffering the same fate, by moving
in different directions and unknowingly passing in the mist
between Chno Dearg and Beinn na Lap, the trio had effectively

completed a relay round. Jon aggregated the times, with the maths revealing that the round could, theoretically, be done in a day. Dan was not so sure. 'My brother said at the time he thought the winter round was doable in under 24 hours, something which I doubted very much. I suppose that's one of the differences between us: those who believe something is possible generally end up doing it.'

History also suggested otherwise. Prior to Jon's round, only 69 runners had completed the Ramsay within 24 hours. The earliest was 5 May, the latest 13 September. Not only had a true winter round never been accomplished, there had been no successful rounds between late summer and the end of April. Perhaps even more remarkably, when Jon stepped onto the hills in February 2013, the last completion was nineteen months earlier, dating back to July 2011.

The cloud was thick on Ben Nevis. Here we go again, Jon thought, but as he emerged onto the rim of the Carn Mòr Dearg Arête, he entered 'an alpine wonderland'. Looking east, across a line of snow-covered peaks, he could not believe his eyes. 'I have traversed the Grey Corries many times but never had the running track been this amenable,' he said. 'The hard snow covered nearly all the rubble.' Traversing faster than he could in summer, Jon had to call Tark Gunn, his support at Fersit, to warn him that he expected to arrive ahead of schedule.

There is almost an apologetic tone to Jon's account of travelling over the north ridge and then all the way to Beinn na Lap. 'Not once did my foot go through crust; the surface was reliable. There was no ploughing through heavy snow. In some popular areas preserved footprints enabled crampons to be avoided, saving time. There was water ice in the valley, meaning I had dry feet. Much of the heather was covered. My split of about nine hours at Chno Dearg illustrates the strength of the conditions. I witnessed stunning orange alpenglow as the sun set when I was descending the hill – at twice the speed of heather bashing.'

Even Chno Dearg had relinquished its curse for Jon Gay.

The 'dream' could not go on. Not in winter, not in these mountains. Climbing Sgùrr Eilde Mòr – a mountain that possesses its own curse – Jon felt 'sick, weak and dizzy'. Several times he stopped, lying down in the snow, before the cold forced him to his feet. 'It was a thorough effort of will to move,' he said. He *had* to move; the other option was more chilling: hypothermia. 'If there had been any weather threat or higher wind chill, I would have force-marched myself immediately down.' The Mamores hold less snow than their marginally more northern counterparts, meaning rocks and rubble protruded where they had been buried on the Grey Corries. He battled on, resisting the tantalising lights of Kinlochleven. 'I have done the Mamores too many times and can be forgiven for not feeling an appropriate sense of adventure at points,' he admitted. 'Sgùrr a' Mhaim's ascent was soul-destroying, especially against the clock. I had haemorrhaged two hours in the Mamores, no doubt from my earlier over-exuberance.'

Seeing Mullach nan Coirean under moonlight raised his morale, but he fell twice as he refused to stop to pull on crampons. Like Shane Ohly, he was too tired to care. Soon it would be over, 23 hours and 18 minutes after it had started. Too soon. 'It was almost disappointing to stop running, such was my exhilaration at the end,' Jon recalled.

Fortune is fickle. Jon knows that better than most. 'Paradoxically, I believe that the snow surface made significant parts of the run easier than summer,' he said. 'I have been extremely lucky. I was obviously delighted to complete, but felt humbled to have got a decent time in winter when many runners could have gone faster in such wonderful conditions.' Jon understated his achievement, but he would: he is the personification of humility. When I first met him in a Fort William chip shop, he approached me shyly and was so softly spoken I had stop eating and make a conscious effort to pick up his words.

To accomplish Ramsay's Round is to join an exclusive club,

but the club within the club – comprising those six winter adventurers – are at the top table. They know more than the rest: they have found that kingdom of the soul where vision and imagination are the masters; they have found that joy which transcends pain; they have heard music in the titanic silence. More than anything, they have found glory – but it is a glory not in the having done, but in their doing.

I would like to end there. It seems fitting. But I cannot. The story goes on, and it is an acrimonious tale. The record would be lowered twice more, first by Donnie Campbell, then by Jim Mann a month later. The fortitude to run Ramsay's Round within 24 hours in winter, whatever the weather, is indisputable. But the weather – or the lack of it – was, ironically, the problem.

When Donnie, a Skye-born ultrarunner notable for a continuous 184-mile run between Glasgow and Portree, climbed onto the Mamores on the second day of Charlie's 'winter' window, he found the ridge clear. When snow began falling, it dropped for around 30 minutes, accumulating to an inch or two, a depth too insignificant to suit even microspikes. Conditions were similar on the Grey Corries, albeit with the snow freezing to become ice. With the usual bridge under repair, Donnie had to wade the knee-deep River Nevis to reach the road in the glen. Moments later, he was flashing by the youth hostel, then lying creased in the back of his van. He had sliced 12 minutes off Jon's record. This was no tale of Glyn Jones derring-do: he did not need to be lowered into snowy corries like Tom Phillips; there was no necessity to urinate on his shoes; he wore shorts throughout; an ice axe was never required.

So what? By definition, he had run the fastest winter round, and because of his association with Salomon, the feat was reported widely. His run would feature heavily on the BBC, notably on the Scotland-focused *The Adventure Show*. It was not Donnie's fault that the media's interest hinged on speed, and that the conditions, style or assistance were secondary. After all, most people cannot relate to ultrarunning over mountains in December. But there are some who can: amid the acclaim, there were voices of dissent, and they came from hill running ranks, notably from those who understood best – Ramsayists.

On the day of Donnie's completion, Pete Duggan, who completed what he called 'Charlie Ramsay's monster' in 2010, was in the Mamores, running a lap of Am Bodach and Stob Coire a' Chàirn from his home in Kinlochleven. 'Brown earth paths, no ice, no frost, but some patches of older snow with the lightest dusting of fresh stuff on the summits,' he reported. His meaning was clear: Donnie's round may well have fallen in 'winter', but conditions were hardly wintry.

Shane Ohly was more forceful: 'When records are at stake, it is crucial that the nature of the round is fairly described and having read the coverage of Donnie Campbell's round, many experienced mountain runners felt that the reporting was inaccurate. Let's be clear, Donnie's round was the fastest round completed in winter months and that alone should be cause for celebration. However, this round was not completed in winter conditions, and attempting to claim otherwise is disingenuous.'

Shane's words were swiftly followed by a four-page article in the *Scottish Hill Runners Journal*, hurriedly penned by Dan Gay – the older brother of Jon, then living in New York – two days before the publication went to press. 'If you're to claim winter records,' he wrote, 'you need to be clear that circumstances qualify as such: no grey areas – or big brown and green ones.'

When I contacted Dan, he conceded that the controversy was to the detriment of the 'ethos of prior endeavours' – but it was for those endeavours he sought to defend the notion of a winter round. Moreover, he felt he was speaking for the 'number of hill runners and climbers expressing their reservations' about Donnie's round. 'Genuine winter makes for a qualitatively different experience,' he said. 'It's mountain-eering as much as running. I think the need for the frequent use of crampons and axe might be one verifiable indicator of the difference between summer and winter.' Charlie's dates are 'wrong', he insisted. 'It should be from solstice to vernal equinox. Deciding whose round is the "wintriest" is a futile exercise and there's no need, but winter has certain basic characteristics.'

Donnie kept his counsel. 'No-one bothered to contact me to find out what the conditions were like,' he told me six months later. 'I didn't bother trying to correct them as I didn't want to get into an argument online or in person. No-one asked me why I didn't go up Charlie's Gully. If they had, they would have found out that I had recced the gully a few days before, finding it corniced, and with the mild temperature, it looked like it could collapse at any time.'

When I met Donnie, less than a week after his round, I found him humble and straightforward. He did not give the impression of someone chasing publicity – and if he did, it was because his livelihood partly depended on it – or of claiming something that was not his to claim. Conditions were not those of a 'classic' Scottish winter, he admitted, but that is why he had made the attempt. It takes a special kind of madness to deliberately seek out appalling conditions. Give him his due: he ran without company over the first 13 Munros; when he did have an ally in the form of Tom Owens, the pair had only one functioning head torch between them; he did something that only 93 other people had done.

Soon another could be added to the list. Wondering how to celebrate his 40th birthday, Jim Mann considered the Paddy Buckley. He contacted Jasmin Paris and Konrad Rawlik, asking if they were available. They were committed to racing in Scotland on the Saturday, but they could be in Glen Nevis on Sunday.

After Donnie's round, there was only one question Ramsay-watchers wanted to ask: what was it *really* like up there? 'It was not full-on classic Scottish winter conditions,' Jim said, 'but we certainly knew it was winter.' Finding Charlie's Gully 'full of snow', he had to divert, while the Aonachs and Carn Mòr Dearg proved to be the most difficult part of the round, with 'lots of consolidated snow, sections of ice and a fresh, albeit thin, fall of snow hiding the condition of the ground beneath'. Even then, Jim only needed to use crampons twice. Having watched the aftermath of Donnie's round, Jim distanced himself from provoking the controversy further. 'There's still no doubt,' he maintained diplomatically, 'that the benchmark and best winter round remains Jon Gay's phenomenal solo round in classic winter conditions.'

Perhaps Jim is right. But the words Martin Stone used to describe the nature of Jasmin Paris' record-breaking spree again come to mind: 'Often they are achieved where there is no yardstick to measure them against and a great performance or achievement is something of its time.'

There is one winter Ramsayist, therefore, who is elevated above them all: a man quietly getting on with a life on the periphery, oblivious to the fuss over Donnie and Jim; a man, who when he shuts his eyes, glimpses again the frozen, lethal face of Chno Dearg, propelling him to the kingdom of his soul.

17

ANSWERING THE CALL

David Brown faced the urinal and sighed. 'Best-thing-worst-thing I've ever done,' he announced. I nodded sagely. There is only so much emotion a man can display at a urinal. It was 2 January, a bank holiday in Scotland, and the day of David's fourth Greenmantle Dash. The race is a mere two miles, but to get back to the Borders village of Broughton, runners must scramble over a stone wall, wade a river, wallow through a turnip field, then climb a steep funnel of grass to gain a spur of Trahenna Hill. From there, on jelly legs, they slide down the cone and charge along a road to the finish. The race is pitiless enough, but if Hogmanay was celebrated to excess, the Green-mantle Dash becomes a unique kind of punishment. David had got progressively slower in each of his four attempts, and today finished 85th in a field of 90, his time eleven minutes slower than his first race. But that was not the point.

'You have to be mad,' was the fifty-two-year-old's retort when I asked him, after we had escaped the gents, why he runs in the hills, why anyone runs in the hills. 'The other thing is the camaraderie.' My shorthand training as part of a jour-nalism diploma did not stretch to Borders' colloquialisms, but as I scrawled indiscernible shapes across a pad, I got the gist. There was a woman called Kirsty who overtook David on the ascent. He caught her on the tarmac, geed her on when she said her hips hurt, and – with a competitive streak overcoming chivalry – snuck in front of her at the end. Kirsty did not mind. 'She gave me a cuddle,' David said. 'What a laugh!'

Standing close by in Broughton Village Hall was Andrew Douglas. Brought up in Caithness, the Inverclyde AC runner had loftier ambitions – to represent Scotland in upcoming European and world championships of hill running. He was clutching something that would be of very little assistance in that regard: a crate of Broughton Ale, presented to him as the race winner. There is irony, I thought – like giving haggis to a vegetarian.

'Do you drink?' I asked.

'Yes,' he replied, 'although it'll take me a while to get through this.' I pointed across the room to David, now cradling a bowl of soup, explaining why he was here. What about Andrew? 'The attraction of hill running is going to different places and having fantastic scenery, but in terms of racing and the guys you race against, there's a community spirit that you don't really get with track running,' Andrew explained. 'Track running is quite intense; people are focused and don't socialise much with each other. In hill running, you feel like you're all in it together. You can race seriously, but afterwards or beforehand you can have good chat and banter with the other guys.'

'Do you enjoy the view?' I ventured, immediately regretting the inane question. During the climb to the spur, a flash of brightness had drawn my gaze from the ground to the sky. A shaft of sunlight was bursting through grey clouds. It was beautiful, but in an instant, my eyes snapped back to mud.

'In racing, I guess I don't,' he said, 'but when you're training, you can look – and then it feels like you've left your normal life behind and you can just be at one with nature.'

It is dusk when we climb onto the white slopes of Mount Maw. We had left the Borders village of West Linton twenty minutes earlier, running single file on a twisting track in the woods above Baddinsgill Burn, before following a road and then farm tracks that were beginning to refreeze as night beckoned. Ross Christie leads, breaking trail, puncturing a pristine carpet with every lift of a knee. We run sporadically, until the movement is impossible. In drifting snow, we wade, thigh-deep, to a wind-hounded summit. Ross and John Ryan are running to Hillend, a further fifteen miles away. I am running home, some seventeen miles distant. The idea suddenly strikes me as preposterous: it has just taken twenty minutes to cover a single mile. The next summit, The Mount, is a further mile away, across a broad ridge laden with snow. We flail forwards into darkness and chaotic spindrift.

Spilling over the top of The Mount, the others follow me. I have no idea where I am going. I have been here once before – on a fine, clear summer's morning when The Mount was a benign place. Right now, I could be anywhere, in any mountain range on Earth. We drop into a void, John shouting at last when he recognises the dull outline of a reservoir. It is our salvation. From the dam, we can follow a track to the main road, pause for a drink at the Allan Ramsay Hotel in Carlops, laugh about our futile attempt to run across the night-time Pentlands in a snowstorm, then jog back to West Linton. The idea must have occurred to the others. In my mind, I am already perched on a bar stool.

We say nothing. Instead, we cross the dam and rise again, onto a second ridge, a place that seems darker and more confusing than the first, dwelling on the realisation that we are now committed to the course. We proceed north, onto West Kip, three beams of light piercing the abyss of a February night. The rest is a muddle: the wind gathers in ferocity; my hands are bitterly cold in soaking gloves; I fall awkwardly, triggering shuddering cramp in both thighs. Climbing Castlelaw, I glance back at the stooped figure of John a little below me, like a spider clinging to a white wall. Once over the shoulder of Allermuir, Edinburgh appears, a smudge of yellow and black seen through watering eyes. At the top of the ski slope, we split: Ross and John descend to Hillend; I scarper downhill to Swanston, along Stevenson's Road, then onto the pavements of Morningside, stopping outside the

luminous glare of a shop window. Pulling a damp £5 note
from a back pocket, I smile at Nan Shepherd, and hand her
over. Her words, etched on the note, had rarely seemed more
appropriate: 'It's a great thing to get leave to live.' Five hours
after running away from West Linton, I walk up Morningside Drive, scooping haggis pie – the last remaining item on
the frying racks – and chips into my mouth, feeling like the
luckiest man in the world.

When Jim Savege arrives in work on a Monday morning, he
cannot help but hear the conversations about other people's
weekends: trips to the beach, visits to relatives, shopping in
Aberdeen. Invariably, Jim has been out in the hills. 'I think I'm
a fat little office worker,' he says, 'and I still manage to do the
Glen Coe Skyline in 12 hours. I get a satisfaction knowing that
I'm still pushing it, getting out there, and having adventures.'
   Jim then heads to his office and gets on with the job of over-
seeing the running of Aberdeenshire Council's £700 million
business.
   We speak in March, with Jim, sitting in front of a fire,
preparing for the Dragon's Back in two months' time. I ask
about his training. He does not seem to hear the question. 'It's
just the most audacious line on a map,' he announces.
   The words quickly establish his approach to high places:
like Byron or Wordsworth, he sees mountains as aesthetic
pleasures that can only be experienced by physical immersion.
'I love moving smoothly and fluidly through the hills, and
time and experience in the mountains is profoundly enhanced
by running,' he says. 'Mountains are innately inspiring and
as runners we're able to move and journey through them in a
unique way, creating our own line.'
   Born and brought up in Hertfordshire, Jim trained as a field
studies and outdoor education teacher in Liverpool, with hill
running in the Peak District and North Wales becoming part
of the 'week-by-week fabric of life'. It was what he seemed
destined to do: 'As a bairn at school I was short-sighted, but I

didn't know at the time, and I couldn't catch a ball for toffee. What I could do was run.'

Now Jim lives among the hills, a stream at the bottom of his garden the only barrier to a forest. If he crosses the road in front of his home, another forest awaits. Scolty Hill, topped by a twenty-metre brick tower that throws views across Deeside and the Cairngorms, is less than four miles from his front door.

For the chief executive, it is the hills that provide a happy juxtaposition. 'It's a contrast with the job,' he says. 'You're doing something on your tod, in the back of beyond, standing in a pair of shorts, and you just have to get yourself together. I like that feeling of having to keep yourself competent and look after yourself to do these things with confidence and comfort. I spend most of my days with people in meetings, in an office, wearing a shirt and tie, and talking council business. To have space for myself and to be able to push myself in an amazing environment, that's the contrast I need. That's why I go.'

Richie Collins has been racing uphill for 40 minutes, from the bottom car park of the Nevis Range to the café on the scarred northern slopes of Aonach Mòr that straddles the 650-metre contour. He is 31st; there are still twenty-three others to finish, including a stream of his Lochaber AC clubmates. There is nothing exceptional in that. Except Richie has cerebral palsy, a condition affecting three of his limbs. 'Imagine,' his father Alan explains, 'you're running with your hands in your pockets and a stone in your left shoe. That's what it's like for Richie.'

Aonach Mòr could be the spiritual home of Richie's hill-going. It was his second racing appearance on the mountain that year, the first on New Year's Day – a contest he had finished seven times in eight years – and the latest in April. 'There is sometimes ice on the boardwalk on the New Year's Day run,' Alan says. 'Because of Richie's balance, it can be a bit dangerous. Other runners will help him, but as soon as he is off the boardwalk, he will leave them. The others don't pander to him. He won't give way either and doesn't get frustrated.'

I cannot speak to Richie. Or, more accurately, he cannot speak to me. He can communicate verbally, but only in a way that his father and sister can really understand.

If Richie Collins had been born a generation later, he might have been a flag-bearer at the London Paralympics, a symbol of the obstacles a disabled athlete can overcome. Richie, who also has learning difficulties, was eighteen when he was nominated by his adult training centre to run a mile in the Queen's Baton Relay ahead of the Commonwealth Games in Edinburgh in 1986. When another athlete dropped out, Richie, escorted by two runners from Lochaber AC, had to cover two miles in fourteen minutes. 'That boy can run,' Roger Boswell, one of the escorts, told Alan. 'Get him down to the athletics club,' Roger implored. 'We'll look after him.'

In 1990, Richie competed at the Glasgow-hosted European Summer Special Olympics for athletes with learning difficulties, winning silver in the 1,500 metres. It was not until 1993 at the equivalent Scottish championships that Richie was told he was in the wrong place – he should be pitting himself against runners with physical disabilities instead.

'That's how bad the publicity was then. I had no idea,' Alan says. The realisation brought opportunities Alan and Richie could never have thought possible. Richie was invited to join the Scottish squad coached by Janice Eaglesham of Red Star AC, a club for athletes with physical difficulties. Seeing the potential noted by Roger Boswell, Janice increased Richie's training from three to ten sessions a week. The hard work soon paid off: Richie, representing Great Britain for the first time, won a silver medal in the 400 metres at the Para World Athletics Championships in Berlin in 1994. Unable to race his preferred event – the 800 metres – at the 1996 Atlanta Paralympics, he was fourth in the 100 and 200 metres, but two days later won individual bronze in the 400 metres and then team bronze as part of the 100-metre relay quartet. On his return to Scotland, he was piped through the streets of Fort William.

Richie was a full-time athlete funded by lottery money in the run-up to Sydney in 2000, continuing to train six days a week, splitting his time between Edinburgh and Glasgow, when he would live in his father's caravan, and Lochaber. Alan had already sold his guesthouse to fund Richie's ambitions. Despite making the finals of the 400 and 800 metres, Richie finished outside the medals. Aged 32, like every athlete at some point, Richie had to accept his fate: he had peaked. 'He started too late,' Alan insists.

But Richie was not finished. He stills runs five to six times a week. 'He can't do a job, so running gives Rich a life,' Alan says. The racing continues too – up Aonach Mòr; along General Wade's military road and through mud and gorse to Cruim Leacainn; into the forest of Druim Fada above Loch Eil. 'It's his freedom, doing something that other people can, and doing just as well,' Alan continues. 'Doing it in the hills magnifies that freedom.'

Moments after three Tennent's-swilling men are seen laughing in an Edinburgh pub in *that* advert, their image becomes a photograph in the hands of a woman on the London Underground. She stares dismally ahead, her desires obviously faraway. The train door slides to the left, symbolically trapping her in the carriage.

The woman could be Amy Capper. Brought up in the Borders hamlet of Westruther and then a student at St Andrews, Amy 'stuck with small', before her career in cancer drug development took her to London. Now in her early thirties, she lives in Fulham, part of a six-square-mile borough thronging with 180,000 people. It is a far cry from the rural idyll of Westruther, but she makes the best of it: footpaths stretch along the River Thames; Richmond Park and Wimbledon Common offer relative wildness; the North Downs Way is a train journey away. As the women's captain of Fulham Running Club, she has rejuvenated cross-country, the sport that is perhaps the closest relation to hill running. 'Running has always been a constant,' she says. 'I have just had to adapt it to where I am.'

Once a month she comes to Edinburgh, staying with her boyfriend a mile from Hillend. 'It feels like I'm coming home. It's nice to breathe a little bit. When you are down here' – I can hear the groan of traffic on the phone line – 'it's nothing like the freedom of the hills.'

I had been running in the Pentlands earlier that day, climbing Caerketton on a breezy May afternoon on paths bordered by the buttery aroma of decadent gorse. The Highland cattle turned their heads and stared – but they were not wolf-whistling builders; the rocks were cracked – but they were not pavements.

Absence makes the heart beat stronger. When Amy watched runners compete at Stùc a' Chroin, she was mesmerised: 'The line of tiny ants slowly moving up the mountain in the distance was a fabulous sight and I couldn't help thinking that one day one of those moving ants might be me.' She might have been describing runners on the slopes of Ben Lomond, Goatfell or the Paps of Jura, those other quintessential duels of May that form the spine of the hill racing calendar in Scotland. It just happened to be Stùc a' Chroin.

There is no sequel to the Tennent's advert. If there was, the woman on the Underground would surely do the same as the man, abandoning London for an Edinburgh hostelry. Or perhaps the Pentlands? Maybe Amy Capper *can* play the heroine? The plan is to 'come home', she assures me, and to one day be among that train of 'moving ants' inching up a Scottish mountainside.

Cock Rig revels in obscurity. Protected by bog, heather and tussock, there is little reason to come here. Adrift in the pathless heart of the Pentlands, I doubt anyone else has visited today, probably not all week. Why would they?

I am close to leaving. I have waited twenty minutes, gazing

south at the line of descent from East Cairn Hill, desperate to catch a glimpse of runners, becoming increasingly convinced that I have somehow missed them. I look again and see movement, a red streak giving them up. I run down to meet the group. Mick James seems lopsided, one shoulder lower than the other; Jamie Thin moves as if his legs are made of wood. I let them off: Mick and Jamie have been running for 17 hours. To celebrate their 50th birthdays, they are going for a run – a very long run.

What remains for two men who inhale the rarefied air of those who have completed the three classic rounds? They invent their own round, that's what. Cock Rig is summit 45 on a 50-hill, 60-mile circuit of peaks south of Edinburgh in what would become the James-Thin Round.

We press on, down the heathery slopes of Cock Rig before meeting a drove road, where we join the western margin of the Pentland Skyline. It is 11pm when we climb Bell's Hill. The schedule has been ripped up; they should have finished nearly two hours ago. Even the long light of mid-June will not save them from darkness. Jamie is walking behind, head bowed, holding a torch in his hand, while I am level with Mick on his 'least favourite climb'. He started running after his children were born, he tells me. He still wanted to go to the hills – running was the most efficient way. 'That's how I got into it,' Mick says, 'but then you find you're liking it, and then you find it gets easier, and then you find you get addicted, particularly to the rush you get, the way it makes you feel, and you hook up with people who have got plans, and their plans are often pushing the envelope. You start off, you run 10k; somebody says, "let's go and run 20." Then you do. "Let's do 40" – and on it goes. And you just fall in with a bad crowd: those bad boys. There's always someone badder than you. The extraordinary becomes, not achievable; it becomes aspirational. Or maybe not aspirational, it just changes in your head. When people say they run for 24 hours, you start out thinking, that's nuts. But if you've got friends who are doing that, you think: they have done it, why can't I?'

For Mick, the 'extraordinary' was the big three. 'You get to a point where you know you have got it in you to finish,' he says, 'but your body's broken and your mind is just pushing you on. A big part of the experience for me is working out where my body breaks. I have broken myself twice in my ultrarunning career and that's an interesting experience.' It was not 'interesting' at the time – firstly, on the 180-mile La Petite Trotte à Léon in the Alps when overwhelmed by food poisoning; secondly, on Snowdon during a doomed Paddy Buckley. 'It's not normal or very good for you,' he continues. 'But I have been intrigued by this for a long time – you know when you see refugees who have walked hundreds of miles just in the clothes they are wearing, nothing else. The reason they can do that is because humans *can*. Of course, you must be so far out of your comfort zone to have that experience. This is like a first-world version of that. You have just got to push yourself as far as you can, and see what that feels like. It's a bizarre experience.'

My mother-in-law hands me a pile of books and pamphlets that belonged to Fi's grandfather. Tom Lea was an Englishman in love with Scotland – or, more accurately (if such a word existed) – a Skyeophile. He visited the island twice annually for four decades, almost always staying at the Sligachan Hotel, his base for climbing and walking in the Black Cuillin, mountains that held him transfixed.

The bundle reeks of age: stale, dusty, a hint of cigarette smoke. There is a scramblers' guide to the Cuillin, a programme from the 1961 Glenfinnan Gathering, cuttings from a Scottish Mountaineering Club guidebook, headed notepaper from the Sligachan, a 1970 Scottish Youth Hostel Association handbook, a MacBraynes timetable from 1960, and, at the very back, a 20-page booklet, *The Cuillins of Skye*, written by Herbert T. Coles, a Kirkcudbright-born man of God. Reverend Coles' 'hills of infancy' were the Galloway peaks, his 'hills of boyhood' the Pentlands and the Nilgiri of southern India. Then it was the Selkirk Range in the US and India's Western Ghats. 'Yet their magnificence pales before the older and homely Pentland Hills,' he wrote. 'No hills in the world can hold deeper associations for me, and yet, here in middle life, I have come across a new order in the build-up of mountains and a new spell has cast itself upon me. I refer to the Cuillins of Skye.'

The Cuillins of Skye is a sermon and a metaphor: nowhere did Coles feel closer to God than the 'vast temple' of the Cuillin. Coles lambasts those who do not 'really see the hills' – those, for instance, who step off a boat at Loch Coruisk and remark: 'There I have seen them. Oh yes, lovely.'

To find God and to find mountains, we must climb into them, he asserted. 'Some use binoculars,' Coles continued. 'This is merely an indication of getting something on the cheap (however expensive the glasses). It may be akin to rudeness, and can be an indication of spiritual blindness. It may be an unlawful attempt at intimacy.'

I am reading these words in Wales. It is early July. Finlay Wild has won the Triple Hirple, a trio of races over two days in Lochaber; John Hammond is second at Dollar, his local race; in-form Jill Stephen finishes 23 minutes ahead of the second woman in dreadful weather at Arrochar Alps. From the garden of a hotel on the coastline of the Llŷn Peninsula, the peaks of Snowdonia ring the sweep of Cardigan Bay. I take a photograph. The result is horrifying: trampled and washed out mountains. To understand them, I must go there, step on them. 'Some try to paint the scene on canvas,' Coles wrote. 'This is better, but even a painting by a genius can give only one phase of the scene. For the Cuillins never appear still, even as seen against a cloudless sky. They are never the same for they appear to be moving in a countless pageantry of colour, design, mood and rhythm.'

Perhaps fittingly, Coles concluded with poetry: 'Here is the turmoil of a craggy waste, / Men find their souls and cast off

haste, / In patience do they now possess The Word, / And find
themselves the prophets of the Lord.'

I had not been to the Pentlands for almost a month. After
ten days in Galicia, we had embarked on a lengthy road
trip north from Gatwick to Edinburgh. Spain had been hot;
England – riding on an August heatwave – was hotter. The
'hills of home', at last, offered refuge. I was among a group
of four Carnethy runners, at first climbing the broad back of
Blackford Hill, then turning south to our objective. Once over
the bypass, the view of the Pentlands was unbroken, with the
evening light sharpening every dimple and crack, and clouds
raced over the tops. We gained Capelaw, the final half-mile
across long grass and tussocks, and turned to face Allermuir.
From there, the ridge to Caerketton inevitably summoned.
Pausing by the pile of stones on the summit, we gazed down at
Edinburgh, struck silent at the marvellousness of the summer
evening – an evening we wished could last forever, the type of
evening we knew would soon evaporate.

Manuel Zeller, an engineer from the Black Forest region
of south-western Germany, stood on my right. His first taste
of life as a Carnethy athlete was a Thursday hill session on
Arthur's Seat, a weekly fixture known fondly as Wintervals.
It was raining and dark when he arrived at Holyrood Park.
After a short warm-up, the runners climbed onto the inky
slopes of the Seat.

'I didn't have hill running shoes, only my road running
shoes,' Manuel said. 'I was slipping. I hated the downhill.
It was still fun and friendly though. "You should get proper
running shoes and come back next week," they said.' 'They'
were Iain Whiteside, the then club captain who was leading
the group, Liam Braby and Konrad Rawlik. There was a
woman too. 'I saw her and thought, at least there's a girl, I
won't be last. And then she kicked my ass on the first rep. I
thought, even the girls are super-fast here.' Manuel had made
the acquaintance of Jasmin Paris.

Manuel was not daunted. He raced in Scotland for the first time at Glamaig, having hitch-hiked from the mainland when his car broke down. 'At the top, I noticed the scree was super-dangerous. I saw two guys with open knees. I said, "are you okay?" and they were like, "yeah, yeah, just go for it!"'

I shout the question over the skirl of pipes. Steph Provan nods. She has just won the hill race at the Braemar Gathering. 'I run because I love it,' she explains. 'I just absolutely love it, but also because I need exercise. When I don't get enough exercise, I feel miserable and depressed, and exercise makes me feel great.'

Steph's words carry the evangelical zeal of the converted. Hers is not the story of a lifelong runner. She describes what is, unfortunately, a clichéd upbringing: active as a child with endless family walks and permanently trying to keep up with two older brothers; late teenage years characterised by dwindling participation; university life when she did 'nothing'. Steph was unhappy but did not know why – she could not then make the link between exercise and mental wellbeing. 'After university, I really got into cycling,' she says, 'finally realising that consistent exercise is a great anti-depressant.'

Running seemed a step too far, requiring a level of fitness Steph did not possess, she recalls. But when children came along, mountain biking was not compatible with this new way of living. 'Trying to fit in long rides when you have kids isn't easy,' she says. But nor was doing 'nothing'.

'I soon felt depressed if I didn't get my exercise fix. I remember cycling when I was heavily pregnant with my daughter while I had my two-year-old son in the child seat at the back. I'm sure people thought I was mad, but I just needed some exercise.'

Her daughter was one when Steph went for the first run in her adult life. 'I started to run on my own in the dark around Aboyne when nobody could see me. I found I got a buzz from a short run that I couldn't get from a short cycle. I adored my children when they were babies, but when they are little, it's

24/7, and it's hard trying to find time for yourself. Running was a lifeline.'

As Steph gradually worked out a balance between being a mother and a runner, she found the sport came instinctively. 'I realised I was halfway decent and it spiralled from there.' Being 'halfway decent' mushroomed to Steph being a Scottish hill running champion. 'I'm not very good on the flat – and I don't find the flat much fun – but a few hours of running in the hills I just love.'

Steph will always be a mother, but running is her expression of independence. The two are inter-dependent. 'I'm no good as a mum if I'm not happy – and I know that I'll be depressed if I don't exercise, and for me there is no better exercise than running in the hills.'

Dumyat stands at the western edge of the Ochil Hills. Languishing in the great plain to the south is the Forth valley, a bold flatness seemingly elevating the Ochils to greater heights than the range's literal altitude. Beyond the estuary lies an arc of mountains: the Pentlands, the dome of Broad Law and – on a very clear day – the heights of Galloway. There are few finer views from one of Scotland's little hills.

There is an easy way to get up there – and a hard way. The hill runner chooses the latter, a contouring climb across rubble on the southern slopes, then an ascent of a grassy gully, emerging on Castle Law, the remnants of an ancient hill fort, built some 500 metres south-west of the true summit. Today there are no Pentland summits, no Broad Law, and certainly no Merrick. Even the thrusting tower of the Wallace Monument, rearing from a Stirling hillside to the west, is blurred in mist. I stop on Castle Law, confused by the pall, then see a runner descending below and instinctively follow.

'Hill running is a challenge of navigation and survival,' Ewan Paterson would tell me an hour later. We meet on the street in Menstrie, the Clackmannanshire village that squats beneath Dumyat. He has not raced today, but is here to pick up the accolade for the men's over-60 champion at the Scottish Hill Runners end of season prize-giving, traditionally held in October. It has become *his* prize; Ewan has won it for five consecutive years, every year since he entered a seventh decade. It is an age category that could easily be dismissed as non-competitive. After all, who runs up hills in their sixties? Plenty of people, men and women, it seems. Thirteen of the 89 finishers at the Dumyat Dash are aged sixty or over; the first two, David Scott and Les Turnbull, place narrowly outside the top-third. A further nineteen are in their fifties.

Longevity is often attributed to runners who find the sport later in life, a notion that buys into the terrifying inevitability that the lifespan of an athlete's 'running gear' – to use Glyn Jones' term – is finite.

'I've run all my life,' Ewan says reassuringly. 'I did 800 and 1,500 metres as a kid, and a lot of road racing as I got older.' Ewan was running ten kilometres in 31 minutes in the 1980s, but discovered hill running in the same decade. 'I was third in a Pentland Skyline in the mid-1980s and I thought, hey, maybe this is something that suits me. Being lightweight meant that on the uphill sections I felt pretty good. I always saw myself as a runner, rather than a racer, and as I've aged, I just enjoy getting out into the hills and doing long distances.'

Running on athletics tracks and roads was a consequence of being able; running in the mountains was a choice. 'A run in the hills can be life-affirming: enjoying the experience of quiet mountain glens, ridges that are so windswept you're almost blown off your feet. It gives me meaning, bringing something to my life that nothing else does – very much a sense of satisfaction in the atmosphere of mountains. People worship cathedrals and there are a bunch of us who look at mountains as cathedrals. We have some sort of connection with Mother Earth, not that it's a religious experience, but it certainly brings something of that to mind.'

Living in Aviemore, the Cairngorms, as if painted in a blue and white saltire, are the hills that call Ewan. 'I can be running through glens considering the Highland clearances or going over mountaintops where you know there were battles fought. I'm a Scot and I see myself as belonging to the country, and that is affirmed through my connection with the mountains. Running on the roads is about racing, putting yourself through the mill in terms of pain and hurt. It's not that the mountains don't do that; it just feels different. Mountains bring the challenge of navigation and survival, and that is a more satisfying experience.'

It was one of those dreary weekends in November between the bangs of fireworks and the lights of Christmas when time and motivation drifts. Racing seems to grind to a near-halt, with only Knockfarrel and Tinto interrupting the month. The latter offers a one-mile race for eight to twelve-year-olds, the Tinto Tiptoe, with entry costing a princely ten pence.

Having taken three weeks off after racing at Dumyat, I took the Road to Swanston on day 22. The Pentlands were sheathed in mist, coating the ground in a white froth. As I jogged upward, an outline of a runner emerged through the murk. She moved slowly but steadily, tapping out a fluent rhythm on the wet ground. Gradually, I caught her and passed with a nod, continuing to Allermuir. I waited for her there, watching her ghostly form emerge from the greyness as it had first appeared on the lower bank.

The runner was Joanne Anderson, a champion in her own right, having won the over-40 category in the Scottish Long Classics series in 2012, eight years after she was a member of the Carnethy group that did the double, winning the British and Scottish team championships. Tinto had been Joanne's last race, where she finished eighth woman irrespective of age.

I ask her why she is here and, having put her on the spot, sense a runner who has raced across the Paps of Jura, up and down the jewels of Glamaig and Slioch, over the summits on the Glen Rosa Horseshoe and the Scottish Islands Peaks Race, and battled repeated Carnethy 5 races, in a running career spanning two decades, clawing for words. 'You're free, I suppose,' she finally says. 'Running is a different way to explore the hills, moving at a faster pace. It's doing something different to the masses. I could run around a park, but I would always choose this option.' Joanne is merely passing time. She is meeting a friend in an hour for a hill walk. Until then, she might as well go for a run.

As Joanne slips through the gate on the summit of Allermuir, she pauses to look back at me. 'You asked me why I run. Well, why wouldn't I?'

'You caught me by surprise,' she would later tell me. 'What I meant is that I couldn't imagine not getting to the hills.'

She closes the gate behind her and begins to descend. In a moment, she is gone, swallowed by the haar.

'There are a lot of great runners in Scotland, but I'm still brushed off as just a hill runner. Running a road marathon will show them that I'm actually an athlete, not just a guy who can run up and down hills where there's no competition.' Robbie Simpson was talking to Emmie Collinge and Phil Gale for an article published by *Tracksmith*, shortly before clocking a time a shade over 2 hours and 15 minutes at the London Marathon in 2016. It was not good enough. Three Scots would run the Olympic marathon in Rio. Robbie would not be among them. He is 'just a hill runner', after all.

It is 23 December when we speak. I read the quote he gave to Collinge and Gale back to him. 'It's not so much about recognition,' he says. 'You get a lot of people saying hill runners have no speed or it's an easy event and they do it for the vest, to make the team. I turned up to a 10k a few weeks ago and there was a guy I know who does a lot of track running who said, "you'd be fine if there was Ben Nevis in the middle of this race or it was uphill for a thousand metres." I was thinking, no, we'll see. In the end, he was quite a bit behind me. He didn't expect that. I want to show that it's possible to do a bit of everything.'

Scottish hill running is what it is, but for Robbie that was not enough. It is not that he finds hill racing in Scotland 'easy'; it is just that he is prodigiously good at it. 'Some people want to win races, which is fine, but I want to be as good as I can possibly be, pushing myself to the max. I find it difficult to do that some of the time (in Scotland). I'd much prefer to race somewhere and come 15th than win a race by several minutes.'

Winning races by almost embarrassing margins was precisely what he was doing. When he won Stùc a' Chroin aged eighteen in 2010, he was seven minutes ahead of Brian Marshall, effectively eclipsing the runner-up by around 30 seconds per mile. When he broke the course record at Ben Rinnes in 2012, he was almost ten minutes ahead of Jethro Lennox – a Shettleston runner who had won his fourth Scottish championship the previous year – in second. The presence of Finlay Wild meant Robbie would not become the youngest winner of the Ben Nevis Race, but he was one of the few who could take on the monarch of the glen in his own backyard, beating him at Aonach Mòr on New Year's Day in 2014.

Robbie and Finlay were already destined for different things. By then, Robbie was a full-time athlete, training in Austria, running more than 100 miles a week, and testing himself against elite trail and mountain runners in Europe.

For ten days over Christmas he is home in the Deeside village of Finzean. His family used to live in Banchory, but now he can see the granite tor of Clachnaben and neighbouring Mount Shade from his bedroom window. When he first visited his parents' new home, he headed straight for the hills behind the glass. 'I found a way up, a direct way, through the trees, over the river and straight up, through the bogs.' He laughs, seemingly talking to himself. 'Yeah, it was good.'

I ask him what training he will do over Christmas. He has been ill, he says, but a 20-mile tempo run is slated on his schedule for the next day, Christmas Eve. If he is not up to it, he will delay for 24 hours to Christmas Day.

'If you are well and you could run anywhere tomorrow,' I ask, 'where would you go?'

'The Cairngorms,' he says immediately. 'I would like to go and run the 4,000s, starting in Aviemore or Braemar, and run really hard, as fast as I could around all the tops. It's good up there, really wild. In the Cairngorms, you're far from the nearest road. In the Alps, you're always close to a road or a ski resort.'

Seeking an alternative to track running, Robbie ran his first hill race as a thirteen-year-old at Banchory, realising quickly he could descend 'quite fast'. Aged fifteen, he won the selection race for the Scottish junior squad on Scolty Hill for a race in Italy. 'With track running, I got to go to Aberdeen and Grangemouth. From fifteen, I thought, this is what I want to do. Hill running is what I always come back to. It's what interested me in running and training hard. I race in Europe and everything is about sponsorship and advertising and selling things, expensive entries, wearing expensive gear. Hill running in Scotland is just simple. You turn up, get a number and run: up the hill, get to the checkpoints, back. It is the ultimate experience.'

Four months later, I am watching the end of the 2017 London Marathon. The first Briton, Josh Griffiths, has crossed the line, but there, close behind, is Robbie. 'Come on, Robbie!' I shout at the television, suddenly overwhelmed by emotion.

I remember him telling me about 'hard work'. 'If it was easy,' Robbie had said, 'everybody would do it – if it was sunny every day, nice dry hills, soft grass paths. Sometimes it's miserable weather, pouring with rain, snowing, and I'm running up a mountain, and I can't see a thing and the wind is blowing me over; sometimes it's running on the roads doing horrible double sessions. But that's what I like – pushing myself to the limit.' I had checked his festive training after we had spoken. The tempo run had been delayed until Christmas Day – a bewildering 19 miles, running each mile at an average pace of five minutes and 20 seconds.

He crosses the line in The Mall, running only marginally quicker – 34 seconds – than a year earlier, but at this level fine differences open chasms of opportunity. He would be selected for the world marathon championships; he had met the qualifying standard to wear a Scotland vest in the Commonwealth Games in 2018. Not bad for 'just a hill runner' – but, right now, that is how I see him: a hill runner again, tramping through bog and heather, the wind ruffling his hair on Clachnaben, laughing.

CLIMB EVERY MOUNTAIN

Rush hour on Glasgow Road. The Edinburgh-bound bus judders to a halt, trapped in a jam of glinting metal. The driver glances in the rear-view mirror. Rows of heads. It is mid-August: festival season. He looks to the right, immediately finding the Pentlands. As ever, Black Hill broods, bedecked in purple heather; the peaks of East and West Kip stand hopefully, straight-backed to their slouching neighbours. The hills seem to call. He sighs – and dreams.

He is 1,100 metres high, climbing in mist and rain. The summit of Braeriach is out there somewhere. He checks the map again, scrutinising contours. Then, in a moment, the clag is gone, removed like a magician pulling a cloth from a laden table. He has risen through the clouds and as if in a rock-strewn heaven, he stands lordly above them. He is spellbound. There is the top. He has been here before, but today the mountain seems reborn, as if Braeriach is his discovery. Euphoric, he runs on.

The driver's eyes flick back to the road. He reaches for the gear stick. The bus creeps forward, shakes and stops again, now buried in the bowels of the Gogarburn underpass. He looks to his right: a bald, concrete wall.

He is twenty-one, a university graduate. He has a forty-cigarette a day habit and drinks too much. He and his mate decide to enter a half-marathon. From their flat, they plot a one-mile route, a road loop around a golf course. He feels terrible. But he perseveres. He thinks, if I can run one mile, how much harder can it be to run two? There was a transfer of addictions. The mate gave up. He runs on.

John Hammond likes lists; he likes running too. For him, it is logical to combine the two, and he noted down his top five Scottish hills: Cairn Toul, Schiehallion, Ben Cruachan, King's Seat, Arthur's Seat. A running journey linking the peaks was not as attractive as the individual constituents. One thought led to another. What about the five highest mountains in Scotland? Or the Scottish 4,000s? Where there is no ceiling to aspiration, you are free to act with extraordinary ambition. A bold new idea fermented. John *would* attempt the 4,000s, but with a twist: he would also visit Ben Lawers, the country's tenth highest mountain, on the same journey, and he would run the lot. He made a rough calculation of distance and height gain: 220 miles and 12,000 metres. It was a colossal undertaking: a six-day ultramarathon averaging nearly 40 miles a day, a fusion of road, trail and mountain. He was unperturbed. John had come a long way since relying on 40 fags to see him through the day.

With little fuss and no fanfare, he started, first climbing Ben Nevis, then picking off three more of the mountains. Braeriach, the fifth, lay 70 miles away. He ended the day on the south-western corner of Loch Laggan, covering 36 miles in nine hours. The heat had been stifling. He sat in his father's campervan beside the A86 and wondered how he could run the same distance a further five times. His last race had been the 53-mile Highland Fling when thigh cramps had hampered him from mile 24. One ultramarathon had been punishment enough. Now he was asking his body to do six in a row.

John had run every day since 11 October, his thirtieth birthday. Waking up the next morning, seven-and-a-half months into his fourth decade, he was not about to quit the streak or overthink what was to come. He pushed headphones into his ears and prepared himself for 39 miles of running, along the banks of Loch Laggan, through valleys beneath mountains that must wait for another day, to Glen Feshie, on the cusp of the Cairngorm plateau. When he was sick of Bruce Springsteen, he moved onto electro; when he was tired of electro, he turned to drum and bass. The rhythm of the music seemed to merge with the rhythm of his feet.

Braeriach arrived on day three, along with the four other Cairngorm 4,000s: Sgòr an Lochain Uaine, Cairn Toul, Ben Macdui and Cairn Gorm itself. Context is everything. If John had started the morning in brilliant sunshine, the plateau might have seemed less wondrous. But for two hours, there was clag, painstaking mapwork and frustration. My luck has run out, John thought. It had not. When he pierced the cloud, his joy was elevated by what had come before.

What followed seems the epitome of futility: running for the sake of running. After summiting all but one of the mountains, John was committed to getting back to the start in Glen Nevis – via the very considerable deviation of Ben Lawers, amounting to 121 miles over three days. In the context of John Hammond, however, it was standard behaviour. This is a man who runs back-to-back Pentland Skylines; this is a man who completed the eight south-of-Forth Carnethy-organised races – totalling 48 miles of running, 5,000 metres of ascent and 150 miles of driving – in a 15-hour period; this is a man who undertook the Seven Hills of Edinburgh by returning to Calton Hill after each of the six other summits, adding 21 miles to the usual distance. Ideas – 'mini-challenges', he calls them, without appreciating the irony – burst out of him. He wants to see how many times he can run up Arthur's Seat in a day. Two ascents per hour, with a total climb of almost 10,000 metres, we quickly establish. He then seems literally fidgety when I tell him there is no official record for the number of Munros climbed in a week. He is immediately planning: 'If you knock off the Ramsay mountains in two chunks, that's already 23.' He often thinks about what it would be like to run Edinburgh's bus routes. He has done his – the 100 – of course. John is also one of the very few hill runners in possession of the required durability and willingness to undertake a fast, continuous round of the Munros – 'the holy grail of big runs in Scotland,' he says. Getting six weeks off work would be the problem. The day after he completed what he named the 'Highest Ten Round' – modesty prevented him from calling it after himself – he went for a run, climbing 346-metre Bank Hill above his home town of Dollar. 'I didn't think it was anything that strange or different,' he insists. 'It's just what I do.'

John was quite correct, for he was acting in the way Scots drawn to mountains always have.

In 1879, Willie Naismith, then aged twenty-three, walked 56 miles from his home in Hamilton to the crest of Tinto Hill and back. When he was sixty, he undertook another out-and-back journey between Glasgow and Ben Lomond, this time walking for 20 hours and clocking 62 miles, reputedly sustained by a bag of raisins.

In 1889, Sir Hugh Munro, wearing cape and kilt, and reliant on the hospitality of Highlanders for shelter, set off on a cross-Scotland journey, climbing mountains and passes in short February days, from Knoydart to Loch Ness then west again – via Mam Sodhail and the Five Sisters of Kintail – to Mam Ratagan, from where he climbed a final mountain, Beinn Sgritheall. Munro's Tables would appear two years later, documenting for the first time the Scottish mountains of more than 3,000 feet.

In 1895, William Brown and William Tough sought to be the first to ascend North East Buttress on Ben Nevis. The pair had walked and cycled from Kingussie to Fort William, sharing a single bicycle as the other had punctured, and hiked to the foot of the climb. After a deluge, they proceeded upward, only to be overcome by a 'man-trap'. Avoiding the seemingly impassable slabs, they summited the Ben shortly after 10pm. A telegraph that captured the apposition of mountains was immediately sent off to the editor of the *Scottish Mountaineering Club Journal*. 'Extremely difficult and sensational,' it read. The pair slept for an hour, then descended, eventually reaching Edinburgh after 45 hours of non-stop travel.

Had he been born a Victorian, John Hammond would have been a pioneer too. Moreover, had the pioneers been asked to explain their motivation, they would not have veered far from John's script: 'It's just what I do.'

But like Naismith, Munro, Brown and Tough, for John the doing does not necessarily come easy. On the fourth day, as he ran through Glen Tilt towards Blair Atholl, he was enraptured, revelling in a when-everything-comes-together moment. By the afternoon, his energy levels had plummeted. The last two miles to reach Loch Tay were tortuous. The tumult continued. After another emotional high, this time in summiting Ben Lawers on the fifth morning, frustration and tiredness began to grow. He glanced at his watch. Right now, he thought, he would normally be getting ready for work – a 5am to 1pm back shift driving an Airlink bus between Edinburgh Airport and the city centre. Perspective returned – at least until the midges descended on Bridge of Orchy that evening.

After a night of disrupted sleep and sickness, some 40 miles of the West Highland Way remained. What drove him on? 'It's addiction; it's obsession,' he admits. 'I suppose it's the satisfaction of having achieved what you set out to do. I can't say I felt any better about managing the highest peaks run than my first half-marathon, because they were both within the expectations of what I thought I could achieve at the time. I like being good at things – good is a relative term though; it is what I perceive as good. I am not the best runner in the world, or the best guitarist, or the best songwriter, but I like doing these things because I feel like I'm quite good at them – and I push myself to be better. I don't do anything by half measures. What I set out to do, I do properly.'

He had certainly done it properly. When Donnie Campbell and Andrew Murray climbed the same ten mountains as John, they did it in 13 hours. They also drove between the three mountain areas, spending four of the 13 hours in a car. John ran every step. As he neared Glen Nevis, he was racing, his only rival and judge himself, until he was back where it all began. As he sat in front of me, joyfully reliving the journey, he seemed as consumed in the retelling as he had been in the running. When he finished, we were startled into silence, as if waking from a slumber we did not want to end.

After Martin Stone had extended Ramsay's Round to 26 Munros, the two other male protagonists of the golden generation – Jon Broxap and Adrian Belton – began to believe in the viability of 30 Munros in a day. It is a figure implausible to a hillwalker of any era, but also unthinkable for all but the very fastest, hardiest and luckiest mountain runners. To achieve such a deed, the athlete would have to cover around 80 miles and climb some 10,000 metres. Without carefully coordinated support, the attempt would be beyond the reach of anyone, but those supporters must also be capable of pacing a runner at the very peak of their physical powers. Even then, where can the aspirant find 30 Munros clustered closely enough to be accomplished in one day, and then hope that on that chosen day they are not overwhelmed by the terrain and the vagaries of Scottish weather? The variables are limitless.

A further extension of Martin Stone's round of 26 was theoretically possible, for a clutch of Munros, stretching to the Ben Alder plateau, rise to the east. In 1988, Jon Broxap, then a youth hostel warden from Keswick, looked further north, however, centring his planning on the concentration of summits that inspired Blyth Wright in the 1970s. The Glen Shiel mountains could be linked to the peaks of Glen Affric, Jon reckoned, enabling him to summit at least 28 Munros, and perhaps as many as 32. In preparation, he reconnoitred the lines, climbing 42 Munros in 10 days, before finishing third at Jura a few days later. With imminent plans to emigrate to Australia, Jon set an attempt date for the end of June. There could be no Jasmin Paris-style delaying: a one-way ticket was booked for the following day.

The story of those almost-24 hours has a split narrative, for while Jon simply kept running, his team of supporters had the near-impossible task of keeping up with him. John Blair-Fish had succumbed to the pace by the third Munro on the South Glen Shiel ridge; Graham Hudson would admit he too was suffering and would meet Jon on the col beneath The Saddle, the ninth Munro. Les Stephenson was despatched early from the Glen Shiel road, with Jon giving chase and soon catching him, climbing close to 1,000 metres in a 'directissimo, hand on knees' mile-and-a-half. Like the others, Les began to struggle, finally losing touch on Ciste Dhubh, Munro number 15. Jon then arrived at a support point in Glen Affric almost two hours ahead of schedule, startling John Gibbison and Mark Rigby and spurring them into frantic bag-packing.

Later, descending Mullach na Dheiragain in the dead of night, John tumbled and screamed, turning a double somer-sault in mid-air. Some 10 miles from the nearest phone box and isolated on the edge of a remote Highland mountain, the runners wondered what was to become of them. Bruised but not broken, John retrieved his torch and carried on. With the pace 'still hot', Mark was the next to tire, opting to sit out the dog-leg climb of Carn Ghluasaid, the 26th summit. It was nearly over. Soon Jon was plunging off the last mountain, Mullach Fraoch-choire. A finish line had been chalked on the road at Cluanie. Having climbed 28 Munros in 23 hours and 40 minutes, a 'celebratory Guinness' was consumed on a muggy, midgy morning. 'A day later,' Martin Moran would write, 'like the will o'the wisp, Broxap was gone, but the legend of his run lives on.' Jon's subsequent report in *The Fellrunner* never once suggests he was in pain or suffering; those feelings seemed reserved for others. He might have noted the magnitude of those 24 hours had he a looking glass into the future, for his achievement would become a benchmark of human endurance.

Adrian Belton was sitting in Belford Hospital awaiting the consultant surgeon's verdict. He had been coming off Beinn

Bheòil, scrutinising a potential eastern extension to Ramsay's Round, when he fell. If these mountains could be linked to Charlie's 24, as the number was in the early 1990s, a 32-Munro round within 24 hours was feasible. Feasible, that is, for Adrian Belton in his prime. Now he was sure his elbow was fractured. He had seen the bones moving through the gash. Alone on the mountain, he was fortunate not to faint. He gathered snow into ice balls to numb the pain. In his mind, he wrote the post-mortem of his running and mountaineering career. It was over.

He waited.

A diagnosis came: stitches were required, but the damage was bruising only. The post-mortem was ripped up, the pieces tossed in the air.

Three days later, Adrian was standing by the dam at Loch Treig, looking up at a cloudless sky. He moved anticlockwise, beginning with the long ascent of Stob a' Choire Mheadhoin, his only top-half protection from the late-morning sun a bandage extending over his injured elbow. Some nine hours later, having sailed by 'the whole world who seemed to be on the Ben Nevis plateau that afternoon', Adrian was in lonelier territory: crawling up the heathery slope of Mullach nan Coirean, pursued by Roger Boswell and his dogs, and the ubiquitous John Blair-Fish. Once over Sgùrr Eilde Mòr, 21 Munros had been seen off in 13 hours. Had he continued on the route of Ramsay's Round, he might have smashed his own record – but something greater was afoot.

The run through the glen to Corrour should have been easy, but in the darkness progress slowed and Adrian jarred his elbow crossing the Abhainn Rath. Approaching Càrn Dearg, he was 'lacking willpower' and felt compelled to succumb to sleep. He entertained abandoning. He knew what that felt like. Twice the previous year he had set out to extend the Munro record; twice he had been thwarted. On the first occasion, he halted after 16 hours, knowing he was not moving fast enough. On the second, the weather did its worst: wind, rain, clag. Ironically, the attempt ended on Ben Nevis in 'perfect conditions', but by then it was too late.

On that long journey to Càrn Dearg, Adrian was at a similar crossroads. What he needed was some of his own invincibility. *What can I do in the remaining six hours?* Adrian had wondered after his 18-hour Ramsay's Round. He was about to find out how much he would suffer in pursuit of an answer. Even then, the decision was effectively made by others. 'If I had been on my own I would have given up there and then,' he said.

Adrian fittingly describes the dropping of clag as 'clamping'. The clamping on Sgòr Gaibhre forced Adrian to acknowledge that he would have to omit the far eastern Munros of the Ben Alder range, most notably (and confusingly) a second Càrn Dearg, his designated number 29. There had been no need to visit Beinn Bheòil after all. On top of his weakening physical state, he had to overcome the emotional blow that he could now only accomplish a maximum of 28 Munros in 24 hours, the same as Jon Broxap.

As it turned out, he would be lucky to even achieve that. Conditions rapidly deteriorated, with summer cascading into winter. Driving snow accompanied Adrian across the Munros of Geal-Chàrn, Aonach Beag and Beinn Eibhinn in the early hours. At around the same time, Charlie Ramsay was driving north to meet Adrian at Fersit. He looked to the mountains in amazement: snow was falling on the second day of June. Adrian – ice forming on his beard – communicated in snatched words with his pacemakers, Helene Diamantides and Mark Rigby. They agreed to a 'freefall' descent off Stob Coire Sgriodain to reach the railway line; from there, it was a two-mile run to the dam. With 16 minutes remaining before 24 hours elapsed, the runners came to the track. It was 'eyeballs-out' thereafter. With three minutes to spare, Adrian collapsed by the dam wall, too exhausted to cry.

Jon Broxap and Adrian were effectively equals: both had achieved rounds of 28 Munros, set three years apart. What elevated Jon – albeit by a smidgen – was time: he was 17 minutes faster. Neither, however, could have predicted what came next. In 1997, the Scottish Mountaineering Club took a long look at Sgùrr an Iubhair in the Mamores – a mountain that had previously been elevated to Munro status in 1981 – and decided it was no longer worthy of the title. It was demoted to a subsidiary top of Sgùrr a' Mhaim. At the same time, Sgùrr na Carnach – one of the Five Sisters of Kintail above Glen Shiel – was elevated. As luck would have it, on his way to Sgùrr Fhuaran, Jon had passed over the stony summit of Sgùrr na Carnach. His Munro count rose to 29; Adrian's dropped to 27.

That was virtually that. Colin Donnelly, almost inevitably, had a go, making it to the top of 27 Munros in the Broxap hills in 1997. It was not until 2008, when Stephen Pyke drew up a 31-Munro schedule, that someone else dared have another go. The weather won again: the runner ended his attempt after 16 hours and 21 Munros. 'Whether the 31-Munro route is possible is still to be determined,' Chris Upson, one of Pyke's supporters, wrote in the aftermath, 'but everyone seemed keen to give it another bash once the dust has settled.'

That sounded familiar. After his 28-Munro run, Charlie Ramsay wrote to Adrian Belton: 'I am convinced that 30 Munros will go, and given the right weather conditions, it will go in style, as the headbanger brigade now have the taste of the challenge on a bigger scale than before.'

Writing in his 1996 book, *The Munro Phenomenon*, Andrew Dempster was confident too. 'The 30-Munro barrier will be a difficult one to break but with the young, eager, super-fit fell runners around today it shouldn't take long before this magic figure is reached.'

For a very long time, they were all wrong.

As for Stephen Pyke, or Spyke as he is known, he went home to the Peak District and had another idea. A year later, he was made redundant from his job in renewable energy technology. There was no cause for panic. He would take a break, he decided. Spyke – a 'keen, amateurish pub footballer' turned runner – had excelled on the road, lowering his time for 10 kilometres to a fast 30 minutes. Having only climbed his first Munro in 1999 aged thirty-three, he was a late arrival to mountains and running up them. He became the 41st Ramsayist in 2006, then broke Martin Stone's record for the Scottish 4,000s the following year. It was the latter that made Spyke realise he had an aptitude for running long distances in the mountains. In April 2010, having summited Sgùrr nan Gillean at the end of a traverse of the Cuillin ridge, Spyke had completed the then 284 Munros. It had taken him 12 years.

A fortnight later, he was on Mull, beginning a second round. This one should be quicker, he decided. Spyke would run, walk, cycle or kayak between the mountains, never resorting to transport that was not self-propelled. If the Munros were climbed in continuous fashion, from Ben More in the far south-west to Ben Hope in the far north, it would be a journey of around 1,600 miles. He set himself a target: 40 days.

An uninterrupted round of the Munros was nothing new. Hamish Brown started it all, completing as a walker in 112 days in 1974. Ben Hope, his final summit, memorably resembled 'a dead sheep: bare ribs sticking out through a tatty fleece of cloud'. Hugh Symonds was the first hill runner to link the Munros as part of a never-repeated journey between the 3,000-foot mountains of Scotland, England, Wales and Ireland in 1990. Moving south, Symonds reached his concluding Munro, Ben Lomond, on day 67. 'There was no real sense of victory,' he wrote in *Running High*, 'just a hint of sadness that there was no more wilderness to the south.' Two years later, Rory Gibson and Andrew Johnston, former pupils of Glenalmond College in Perthshire, lowered the record to 51 days, bringing it tantalisingly close to the 50-day barrier.

Charlie Campbell, who swam across the sounds of Mull and Sleat, eclipsed them all in 2000, arriving on Ben Hope 48 days and 12 hours after leaving Ben More, having climbed seven more Munros than Gibson and Johnston following revisions to the list. Campbell would undoubtedly have been faster had he not been hampered by bad weather and injury, the latter forcing him to take a rest as early as the fifth day due to tendonitis. There was an improvement on both fronts until he reached Torridon on day 44, with a muscle strain above a knee making descending painful. His left knee was 'certainly not fine', but what did he expect? As he sensed a conclusion, Campbell's final two days were effectively merged into one: after climbing eight Munros, he cycled through the night, slept for an hour, then summited Ben Klibreck and Ben Hope the next morning. By then, the sun had come out.

What possesses a runner to undertake such exploits, to continue running over mountains day after day? Unlike the Munros, a non-stop assault on the Corbetts was a fresh concept. Manny Gorman, a runner since his days as a schoolboy in Kirkintilloch, stepped up to the plate. On the day Charlie Campbell stood atop Ben Hope, it was Manny who chased the Munroist around the summit spraying champagne. The Highland Council maintenance officer also had previous: he had run 450 miles in 21 days from Ben Hope to Ben Lomond, climbing 112 Munros on the way; he had also crossed Scotland from west to east, adding the Munro outliers of Ladhar Bheinn and Mount Keen, plus the Scottish 4,000s, in a 200-mile solo run. Even with that history of endurance, joining the scattered dots of the Corbetts was an awesome undertaking.

'The drive is being in the hills,' he explains. 'It's total escapism. Work, phone, family, life logistics – gone. As soon as you start something like this, that becomes your project. It's the only thing you're thinking about all day long.' But what about when you are cold, wet, hungry, tired, fed-up or injured, possibly all at the same time, knowing tomorrow will be like today? 'You have to recognise that those feelings are temporary. It's not often you're down and stay down. If you're not enjoying it, that's the time to stop.' These words need to be read in the context of Manny Gorman: a man imbued with a hill endurance that very few possess. He was *the* man for this job: starting on Clisham in Harris, sailing between islands to avoid motorised travel, and finishing on Ben Loyal in Sutherland, he climbed them all, 219 Corbetts as there were then, running and cycling 2,400 miles in 70 days.

Here is another infused with fierce resolve: Stephen Pyke. Poised on Ben More on a wet, windy morning, the weather lashing Spyke imitated the dreich conditions faced by Hamish Brown on Ben Hope some 36 years earlier. Perhaps it was a good omen? The clock had already started. Spyke ran down to the road, before clambering on a bicycle and pedalling to Fishnish. Across the Sound of Mull lay the village of Lochaline, the gateway to the Morvern peninsula. Eschewing the CalMac ferry, Spyke breached the gap by kayak, paused in Lochaline for a bowl of porridge, then remounted his bicycle for a 56-mile ride to Glenfinnan, from where he climbed two further Munros: Sgùrr nan Coireachan and Sgùrr Thuilm. He returned to his base camp – the campervan of John Clemens, a drinking buddy and retired fell runner – shortly after 8pm, ending a 14-hour day. The rhythm of the next 38 days of his life was established.

The following morning he cycled from Glenfinnan to Fort William, then ran 10 snow-covered Munros: Ben Nevis, Carn Mòr Dearg, the Aonachs, the Grey Corries, Stob a' Choire Mheadhoin and Stob Coire Easain. On day three, he ticked off seven Munros in the Loch Ossian area. The day after, he completed the seven Munros north of Ben Alder, taking his Munro count to 27 in four days. And so, bewilderingly, it continued.

'It was good fun,' he insists. 'I'm glad I did it. It was hard work, obviously, but never a slog. There was just an intense purpose about what I was doing.' What motivated him? He paused for a moment, clearly dwelling on the question. When the answer came, it was as straightforward as it could be: 'Once underway, you're committed and doing it.' It was a simplicity that underpinned the entire adventure. Even in the planning stage, Spyke's logistics had involved 'staring at a map, then putting various mountain groups on an Excel spreadsheet, and thinking that's day one, that's day two, and so on'.

Spyke climbed his hundredth Munro on day 13. Statistically, he made it to halfway by the end of the twentieth day. On day 23, Spyke was on the Mamores, tagging summits in the diminishing light of day. The glow of sunset was drenching the west, illuminating Ardgour across Loch Linnhe. 'Despite increasing fatigue as I climbed Sgùrr a' Mhaim and onwards to Stob Bàn,' Spyke remembers, 'I felt that in conditions like this, there was nowhere else I'd rather be.'

The Skye Munros were completed on day 29, one of 11 days on which Spyke claimed more than 10 mountains. In Glen Shiel the next morning, a man with a grey beard approached the gathering of Spyke's supporters as they waited for him to arrive. 'Which one of you is Spyke?' he asked.

'None of us,' someone replied. 'He's cycling here from Skye.'

'That's a shame,' the man said. He introduced himself: 'I'm Hamish Brown.'

Moments later, Spyke arrived to save his friends' embarrassment. They shook hands, posed for a picture, then went their separate ways. For Spyke, that was five further Munros, taking his tally to 213. After criss-crossing Scotland, he was now in the far north. Superlatives remained: the mountains of Mullardoch and Monar; the peaks of Torridon, Fisherfield and An Teallach; Assynt and the two northerly outliers, Ben Klibreck and Ben Hope. 'The hill running bit almost looked after itself,' Spyke says. 'On day one, you set off up the first hill, and you think, bloody hell: the enormity of it hits you. It's a cliché, but you have to take one hill at a time. But after a day or two I was in a routine and the run was almost incidental. It was an excuse. If I wasn't doing this, I wouldn't be out on a mountain at 11pm watching the sunset. The run was the reason I was having beautiful days out.'

Spyke touched the summit cairn of his final Munro, Ben Hope, 39 days, 9 hours and 6 minutes after starting his journey. A parcel from Charlie Campbell, buried in the cairn and containing a bottle of Singleton malt, was passed to Spyke. There was a note. 'Savour the moment,' Charlie had written, 'as the Munro memories will last forever. It takes a singular determination and character to see an enterprise like this through to a successful ending, and you have done that.'

Imagine standing on the summit of Ben Nevis on a day of exceptional clarity, a spring morning perhaps, before the haze of summer arrives. There are too many hills and mountains to count or name, circling the Ben like an immobilised ocean of landskein. 'He towers high and majestic, amidst a thousand hills,' the nineteenth century poet Mary MacKellar wrote of Ben Nevis. The waves of those 'thousand hills' stretch as far as the islands of Jura, Rum and Skye to the west, the Affric summits of the north, the rolling humps of the Cairngorms to the east, the peaks of Argyll and Stirlingshire to the south. Imagine, just imagine, climbing them all.

Rob Woodall was fourteen when he claimed his first hill – Carnedd Llewelyn in Snowdonia. He was a comparative slow starter. The youngest person to climb the Wainwrights is Coel Lavery, who completed his last summit, St Sunday Crag, aged four years and ten months. John Fleetwood's son, Ben, had been the youngest to finish the Munros at ten, until nine-year-old Daniel Smith – a hillwalker from the age of three – gained his final mountain. Daniel was six when he tagged his first Munro; Rob was twenty. Aided by an 80-pence booklet, *Scotland for Hillwalking*, the Englishman started where many Scots, young and old, typically begin – Ben Lomond, the closest Munro to Glasgow, followed by another cliché: Ben Nevis.

'It began in Scotland,' Rob tells me. 'It' – despite the late outset – is the most remarkable record of peak-bagging in Britain and quite possibly the world. Rob does not just bag hills, he bags lists of them: 214 Wainwrights, 220 Grahams, 222 Corbetts, 282 Munros, 446 Nuttalls, 526 Hewitts. Obsession bred obsession. At 15 rounds, Steven Fallon holds the record for the most circuits of the Munros, but Rob is not a man to merely repeat. His compulsion is fed by finishing lists and as the ticks pile up, his pursuits inevitably move into the realms of eccentric obscurity.

Rob lives in Peterborough, a unitary authority in northwest Cambridgeshire with a high point of 81 metres where the boundary line meets Northamptonshire. Not far away, across the other side of the cathedral city, is Holme Fen; here the land falls to almost three metres below sea level, the lowest place in Britain. And ironically, Rob's work is based underground: he makes computer models of urban drainage systems, mostly sewers. We speak on a Wednesday night. He had spent the previous weekend in East Devon walking so-called TUMPs – an ever-increasing list of hills, approaching 17,000 in number, that qualify by having an all-round drop of 30 metres. He is nearing a full set of the mainland English and Welsh TUMPs, but completing the Scottish summits seems unlikely: 'There are too many sea stacks and even the mainland has a few things pretty well unclimbable, like the Old Man of Storr and the Quiraing Needle, as well as lots of obscure, remote hills,' he says. That coming weekend he planned to chalk off island summits on the Significant Islands of Britain list. Suffolk's RSPB-managed island, Havergate, was among his proposed destinations. He would not have far to walk – the highest point is two metres above sea level.

Perhaps there is little else for a man who was the first to visit all of Britain's 6,190 triangulation pillars – Ordnance Survey presented him with a commemorative flush bracket as a keepsake – to do? Several months after we speak, I see Rob has been busy: bagging surveying control points on Guernsey; summiting the islands of Loch Lomond; visiting highest points in Cyprus and Morocco. Rob's criteria for his efforts is uncomplicated. It does not matter whether he is high or low, it is the highest that counts. Be it Aconcagua – his literal peak at 6,962 metres – or the mud flats of Havergate, a tick is a tick.

By 2008, Rob was a 'hillwalker that sped up', and became the 46th person to fulfil Ramsay's Round. He had been due to support Nicky Spinks in her attempt, with Nicky returning the favour a fortnight later, but in fine weather both completed, Rob finishing six minutes behind Nicky. With an unexpected free weekend in Scotland soon after, Rob ran a solo Rigby Round. He would also run the Bob Graham and Paddy Buckley within 24 hours, but his legacy in round-running came in the form of his own creation: the Cuillin Round on Skye. The route, starting and finishing at either Glen Sligachan or the southern shore of Loch Coruisk, crosses 59 tops, includes the main Black Cuillin ridge, Bla Bheinn, the Red Cuillin and Glamaig, and climbs some 7,000 metres in a mere 34 miles.

Characteristically, after completing the circuit, Rob devised a radical alternative that he called the Transcuillin: a west to east traverse taking in every Cuillin top between Gars-bheinn and Beinn na Caillich, including everything with at least a 15-metre drop all round, within 24 hours. The number of summits rose to 70, the mileage to 38, the ascent – most notably – to 9,000 metres. Rob had made it to 19 hours and 64 summits when he succumbed to the weather. After descending An Coileach of Glamaig – a hill scouted through binoculars from the A87 – he came to the main road and his waiting support crew. The wind suddenly seized Rob, convincing the pair he was continuing without even pausing. He stopped eventually. There was no other choice. 'Instead of hypothermia and broken ankles, I choose life,' he said at the time.

Rob is fifty-six. He has no partner or children. He has no time for such things, for his weekends and holidays are dedicated to list-ticking. He typically claims more than 1,000 'bags' per year. Do the people who know him – beyond a circle of like-minded peak-baggers – think he is unusual? He seems surprised at the question. 'I just like getting out, really,' he says, 'and going to different places. I think people generally get that I'm not the sort of person who likes to spend the weekend hitting the shops.'

Among the lists targeted by Rob are the Marilyns – a 1,555-strong group of British peaks that have clout because, although the hills can be of any height, they qualify by having a significant drop of at least 150 metres on all sides. It means that while 251-metre Arthur's Seat makes the cut, 1,221-metre Aonach Mòr does not. By 2003, Rob had climbed all but six of the Marilyns. Four more came in 2009 when he reached the Marilyns on Boreray, Dùn, Hirta and Soay, the main islands of the St Kilda archipelago. There was a reason that two remained, the reason that the list had never been completed – a pair of inaccessible pinnacles. Stac an Armin and Stac Lee are a brace of sea stacks, teeth-like protuberances that emerge from the boiling waters off Boreray, both rising higher even than the very top of the Forth Road Bridge. From the sea, they seem to swell almost vertically, black and forbidding. Their heads, daubed guano-white, could be imagined on the crests of Himalayan peaks. When the Victorian yachtsman R.A. Smith sailed in these waters he derided the stacks as a haunt for terrible beings: 'Had it been a land of demons, it could not have appeared more dreadful, and had we not heard of it before, we should have said that, if inhabited, it must be by monsters.'

Despite their appearance, once on the stacks, the task of climbing is relatively straightforward. Generations of bird-hunting St Kildans scaled the islands until the archipelago was abandoned by its remaining permanent population in 1930, as well as ornithologists and Hirta-based military personnel more recently. Simply getting to this starting point – mainly by overcoming the tremendous Atlantic sea swells in the worst six months of the year, October to March, when access is permitted – is the problem. Rob had been on M-2 status, or The Wall as it is known, for four years, when he ventured west, spurred on by a hopeful mid-October forecast, mindful that an attempt the previous autumn had foundered. As there are no places to land a boat, a vessel must be manoeuvred as close to the rock as a skipper dares, near enough for the occupants to hurl themselves over the side and desperately cling to the island. It was 'easy' on Stac an Armin, Rob insists, and he would be among a party of eleven that would summit the stack.

Advancing across a bobbing sea to the titanic frame of Stac Lee, Seumas Morrison, the boatman, was more pessimistic, but agreed to attempt an approach. Rob and a smaller party jumped again, using crampons and spikes to grip sea-washed rock. He looked around, noting no monsters, but spotting the gannets the stack is notorious for, as well as groups of rock pipits and turnstones, and got down to the matter at hand. The main pitch to reach the sloping shelf to the summit had a 'couple of hard moves', undertaken in a two-inch layer of guano. 'Initially I ran out of holds, then searched around, found a couple of little in-cut holds and got up okay,' Rob says. The difficulties were not over. The long upper ledge leading to a little cairn on the highest point was slippery with more guano and fearfully exposed. Is exposure more beguiling when the end is ocean not corrie?

A few more careful steps and Rob was there, atop – 39 years after his first – his last Marilyn, number 1,555. He looked back to the dreaded incisor of Stac an Armin, across to the freefalling cliffs of Boreray, then over the waves to Hirta, and beyond to the enormity of the Atlantic. He shook his head in triumphant disbelief. He had climbed every mountain.

19

THE GREATEST

Buffeted by diagonal December rain, I prise open a wooden gate and tap on the door of a white cottage. The knock triggers a furious barking chorus. The door opens a crack. Three Jack Russell puppies squirm out, pursued by two adult dogs, and then a cat. 'Tegan!' a woman shouts from the doorway, then urgently to me: 'Have you shut the gate?' I nod furiously. 'I've spent all morning looking for a dog because *someone* didn't shut the gate.' I nod again, as if to confirm my innocence. The woman – glasses, short hair, mid 40s, supported by crutches – orders the menagerie indoors. We follow them in, and with a thump, the chaos of early winter in the Trossachs is shut out.

'Tea?' she asks. Lurching past a sofa and wood burning stove, towards a kitchen, taking large, swinging jumps, she is chased by the mob of dogs. Leaning by the sink, she begins to swill out an unwashed mug. She looks down at her crutches and the swirling pack. 'You might have to make it yourself,' she decides.

She is recovering from surgery. Unable to recite the precise medical terms, she hands me a letter from the doctor who recommended a dual-purpose operation: to repair a ruptured spring ligament and to 'extend the posterior tibial tendon', the part of the ankle that stabilises the foot when it strikes the ground. If you happen to be a hill runner, functioning posterior tibial tendons are expedient. The patient would spend six weeks in plaster, then undergo several months of rehabilitation. To what end was uncertain; recovery was not assured.

Lowering herself into an armchair, she puts her sticks to one side. She does not suit crutches. She motions for me to sit on a neighbouring sofa. A puppy claws its way up my leg and onto my lap. It is followed by another, jolting my hand, sending tea splashing across the floor. As wind and rain rattle the window panes, I skim my eyes around the room. There is an image of Suilven behind the invalid's chair. On another wall is a picture of an Inverpolly landscape. A bookcase is lined with at least 100 worn Ordnance Survey maps. I read the letter again. The patient was a 'fell runner of international renown', the doctor noted.

Angela Mudge was born into adversity: her feet had been bent in the womb. 'I had a small mother,' she remarks, 'and a twin.' Her sister, Janice, had one foot 'slightly twisted'. I grasp for an image of Angela's feet. I had read in different accounts that 'both her feet were pointing backwards' or that they 'faced the wrong way'. She handed me another piece of paper: 'congenital talipes equinovarus,' it said. Club foot, in layman's terms.

Place both hands in front of you, palms down, pointing ahead, imagining they are feet. Turn both hands inwards, the right to 10 o'clock, the left to 2 o'clock, then lift the fingers two centimetres. These were Angela's feet at birth: the feet of a 'fell runner of international renown'.

That was 1970. Two-and-half years of hospital visits followed to straighten her feet. They were plastered and re-plastered, gradually pushing bones and tendons to where they should be, until her toes pointed the same way as her nose. Angela remembers nothing of it: 'I was too young.' The need to always wear orthotics would be the hangover. The memories of the beginning of her running life are clearer: 'I played hockey and netball badly. I happened to be good at cross-country.' Aged sixteen, she would run at school lunch times, clocking 30 miles a week, but her training hit a brick wall. In her desire for a top ten place in the English Schools cross-country – her best position was 15th – she sustained a stress fracture of the fibia. She persevered, despite her parents' indifference. 'Dad would sit in the car and listen to the footie while I was racing,' Angela remembers, 'but I think they would have been disappointed if I had given up and didn't try to achieve what I was capable of.'

She achieved just that. Angela Mudge would become the greatest female mountain runner on the planet.

In the spring of 1996, Angela sent her training log to Martin Hyman, a Second World War refugee from Jersey who placed ninth in the 10,000 metres at the 1960 Rome Olympics. In his role as Scottish Athletics' national coach for hill running, he replied to Angela: 'Thank you for letting me see your log. It reflects the annals of someone with exceptional stamina, and with an overwhelming affinity for long runs in the hills. I have no doubt that if you continue to train as at present, you will achieve lots of success and fulfilment in long, tough races.' Martin was scripting his words carefully, for a well-intentioned *but* was coming. 'I happen to believe, however, that you also have the capacity to do well in any sort of hill or cross-country race, if you were prepared to train for it. Only you can judge whether that is worthwhile.'

What is of note is that Martin considered the effort very much 'worthwhile', for Angela was far from the finished article, physically and emotionally. In 1995, she had come second in the British fell running championships, but only 46th in the women's race at the sport's flagship international event, the World Mountain Running Trophy. 'When you write off a result as not good enough because "the course was too flat",' Martin continued, 'you are in effect saying, "I know that I can do well if the course is long and tough, but not if it is short and fast." This may be true and certainly tends to be self-fulfilling. But you could turn it around if you wanted, by a process called training. By training I mean not just going for runs, but following a strategy which is planned to bring about a desired adaptive response.'

Angela describes a *Wuthering Heights*-esque upbringing on Dartmoor: playing, running, exploring. 'I was brought up on the moor, and being in the hills is what I have always done, what I have always loved,' she says. 'I'm one of three and my big sister absolutely hated going to Dartmoor and was dragged, whereas if mum said we were going to the moors, me and my twin would be the first to get in the car. In the environment I was brought up, I was exposed to little hills. In my late teens, I went to the Lake District on a school holiday and didn't appreciate how hills could be that steep or that long. I loved it. I have always liked going uphill. They go on and on forever, don't they?' There is not even a hint of sarcasm in Angela's voice.

Hers was a childhood that would heavily influence later life. After growing up in the west Devonian town of Tavistock, Angela gradually emigrated north: first to Leicester to study chemistry, then to Stirling for a MSc in environmental management. She joined Ochil Hill Runners soon after moving from England and raced in her first Scottish event, Dumyat, in 1992. 'I was the first university student; apart from that, I wasn't very good,' she declares. Theoretically, her talent should have been harnessed at Leicester. Her time in the East Midlands coincided with the emergence of a crop of young cross-country runners who trained with Angela at Leicester Coritanian and would go on to represent Great Britain in the sport. 'I was at the back,' says Angela. 'Compared to them, I was rubbish.' What could have been an opportunity, propelling Angela onto the treadmill of top-level athletics, was lost. She blames the coaches: 'They did not see potential in me.'

Once in Scotland, her penchant became long, hard days in the hills, exploring high and wild places – a yearning forged in those early, innocent wanderings on Dartmoor. Her fix was gained from simply being there. Gently, initially, then increasingly with more force, Martin pointed out this was not enough to maximise what Angela could potentially accomplish. He recommended she organise her training to include flat repetitions of between 800 and 1,500 metres, short hill repeats, and a weekly 'thrash' of 8 to 15 minutes on more technical, hilly terrain.

I visited Martin, aged eighty-three when we met, at his home in Livingston with a principal question: Did he think then – in 1996 – that Angela Mudge could be a world champion? 'I didn't know she would be the best in the world,' he said deliberately, 'but people are often limited by their own view of themselves. I encourage people to think in a different way.'

Angela does not know herself. 'He is a scientist and very analytical,' she says of Martin. 'He must have seen something.'

Martin would never formally coach Angela; his role was to mentor from afar, to involve himself as much or as little as the athlete desired. He proposed she 'build in a reasonable proportion of high intensity training, but with the minimum intrusion in your need for spontaneity, and enjoyment of running in the hills'. His message lay between the lines: you have great potential; it is up to you whether you want to fulfil it; if you do, I will help.

'Did she take your advice?' I asked.

He nodded. 'She quietly got on with it.'

At the start of 1997, Martin wrote to Angela again, offering to review her latest training log. 'Your future is as bright as you are prepared to make it,' he noted. After scrutinising the diaries, he wrote back: 'I approve without reservation what you did when injured and what you have done since! I expect that you will even come around to thinking that tough disciplines like interval training and hill reps are enjoyable. Not in a ha-ha sort of way, but in the satisfaction you get from feeling that you are using your fitness to produce a quality session.' By July, Angela had secured her first British and Scottish championships, and finished fourth in the European Mountain Running Trophy in the Austrian Alps. After winning the women's race at the final British championship counter at Donard-Commedagh in the Mourne mountains of

Northern Ireland, Angela told *Athletics Weekly*'s fell reporter Gareth Webb, 'I haven't really thought about what it means to be British champion. You do the races and then see what happens, basically. Having said that, it's obviously very pleasing because it's there in the history books for all time, isn't it?'

She had only just begun. At the end of the season, Martin wrote a rallying cry: 'From your rate of progress over the last two years, it must be very obvious to you that you have a very good chance of progressing further still. But you can never be sure, and there is only one way to find out!'

At the time, Martin spelled it out more explicitly. 'Martin Hyman told me I would win a medal at a championship event "in the next few years",' Angela says. A medallist on the international stage? She thought he was joking.

His tone changed, however, a few months later. Writing on a postcard early in 1998, Martin questioned Angela's 'decision to race all over the place this year because you won't have time next. Sounds like trying to eat everything on the menu, cos it's your last free meal. Or use a scattergun to shoot at everything in target, rather than taking careful aim at a selected target.' In a final plea, he called on Angela to 'structure your life thoughtfully'.

What had he meant? 'She was doing long races all over the world,' Martin said. 'I believe you should plan races that include optimal preparation and recovery.'

As she began to know Martin better, Angela could guess at his responses to her logs and racing plans. 'I was quivering in fear about what I was going to read,' she says, 'but he hit the nail on the head. He got me doing quality, not more miles.' Regardless of Martin's warning, over the next two years, Angela's racing – and winning – would span continents. Once again, in 1998, she committed to racing in the British and Scottish championships, and won both. Then, in 1999, she did the hat-trick, clinching a third consecutive British crown, as well as winning the senior women's race at the Inter-Counties cross-country championships in Nottingham.

She was victorious too at the Mount Kinabalu International Climbathon in Malaysia, a race that ascends 2,200 metres on a six-mile course of rainforest and naked granite. On the same mountain, she would finish seventh in the World Mountain Running Trophy. She had come a long way since 1995. Coming seventh was now seen as a poor return, a disappointment only offset by success in the European equivalent, with Angela finishing runner-up. Martin was right: Angela was an international medallist.

A new century dawned. The little girl born with club feet, the overtraining teenager who induced a stress fracture, the fledgling athlete whose early progress was hampered by anaemia, the runner who was overlooked by her university coaches, the woman whose future was as 'bright' as she was prepared to make it, stood on a precipice. That year, she would complete a PhD on mass spectrometry, win a fourth British title, and finish fifth best in Europe.

Although she went to Bergen in the Bavarian Alps for the World Mountain Running Trophy hoping for a medal, the prospect of gold seemed fantastical. A German runner, Birgit Sonntag, had been unassailable all season, notably finishing ahead of Angela in the European championships in Poland earlier in the year. 'She had come from nowhere and was beating all of us in the grand prix races,' Angela remembers. She did not even think to pack a recording of *Flower of Scotland* in case the unimaginable happened.

Turning up to the race just minutes ahead of the start, Angela started cautiously, running in around 20th place, before beginning to move through the field. The uphill-only course rose through woodland and emerged onto open hillside, with the track featuring numerous steps. Unevenly spaced, the steps broke the natural rhythm of the runner. It was Angela's 'kind of climb'. She could have been on Jura or Stùc a' Chroin or Ben Wyvis, such were its hallmarks as a classic 'grind': a little piece of Scotland in the Alps. Those who went off too fast inevitably fell off the pace, as the route climbed almost 1,100 metres in five miles. With around a mile to go, Angela pulled clear of the rest. 'I was surprised to be there,' she says. 'It's the fear that somebody is going to go past that keeps you going.' The race culminated on the uphill slope of a downhill piste. 'It would be a bit embarrassing to win a world championship walking. I can't remember if I was running or walking, but I can't remember running fast.' It is not Angela's style to look back, but had she glanced over a shoulder, she would have seen Sonntag, some 20 seconds behind, grimacing on the final climb, overwhelmed by the pressure of trying to win on her home soil. Victory, Angela says, 'took a long time to sink in.'

The Scottish Hill Runners calendar dropped through my letterbox in February. The racing year started and finished in Lochaber: Aonach Mòr on 1 January, Cruim Leacainn on 26 December. The bottom line of each race entry revealed the incumbent male and female course record holder. I looked for 'Angela Mudge', imagining the editor of the calendar furiously cutting and pasting, for the name was everywhere: Carnethy 5, Chapelgill, Criffel, Deuchary, Stùc a' Chroin, Dumyat, Scottish Islands Peaks Race, Goatfell, Kilpatricks, Cort-ma Law, Glas Tulaichean, Durisdeer, Traprain Law, Seven Hills of Edinburgh ... It went on. I had not even reached July. Eventually, I counted 29.

Her prolificity extends far beyond the confines of Scotland, however. In 2001, she finished fifth in her defence of her world crown in Italy. 'Because I won in 2000, many people assumed I would win a medal in 2001, not taking into account the course profile. The race in 2000 was uphill-only, not up and down – a completely different race, and I had over-raced by mid-September,' she later said. Her aim in 2001 had instead been to win the 19-mile Sierre-Zinal in the Swiss Alps, starting in Sierre at 585 metres, topping out at 2,425 metres, and finishing in Zinal at 1,680 metres. With significantly more up than down, the race – like the Bergen course – suited Angela's style. She delivered. 'I ran through a corridor of people. It had an atmosphere like a world championship and I was the first woman to break three hours. I was proud of that.'

She seemed unconquerable, able to turn her legs to anything. She even contemplated attempting to represent Scotland in the marathon at the Commonwealth Games in 2002. 'I thought it would go on for years,' she says. 'I didn't see an injury around the corner. When you're young and feeling well, you don't think things will go wrong.' The cause of a sore knee in 2004 was identified. It was very bad news, a potentially career-wrecking revelation: the cartilage in her femur had worn away. But like Angela had done before, and would again, she recovered, first from surgery, then through rehabilitation. She spent a year away from running and returned triumphantly, celebrating her veteran status as a thirty-five-year-old by winning the World Masters Mountain Running Championship in 2005. She spent the next three years dominating the Buff Skyrunner series, winning races in Japan, Spain, Italy, Switzerland, Andorra and – in the 2008 series – Scotland, at Ben Nevis. Excellence continued into her late thirties and early forties: she won the Everest Marathon (finishing eighth overall and breaking the course record) in 2007, and was runner-up in the women's race at the Commonwealth Ultra Trail Running Championships in North Wales in 2011. Even as a forty-four-year-old in 2013, she was breaking records, at Meall nan Tarmachan (where she was fourth overall), and winning, notably at Carnethy 5 and Ben Nevis. It was imperious form that would see Angela win her fourth senior Scottish championship, despite her age, 16 years after her first.

While Angela has no memory of the adversity that dogged her first years of life, the unwitting consequence of overcoming that misfortune had set a pattern for life: to fight, fight, fight. 'You either have it or you don't,' she says. 'I'm very competitive. You have to want something to be driven to get it. It's built into my nature. I'm a born pessimist, but when it comes to running, I don't look at the negative side. I don't think about what can go wrong.'

Angela's talent, even if it went unnoticed at Leicester, is undoubted. But breaking records and winning races is merely a consequence – a consequence of an instinctive craving for the mountains of Scotland, the country she adopted despite being born an Englishwoman. Her living room is significant for the absence of running memorabilia. A medal for Sierre-Zinal hangs discreetly and a sculpted prize for finishing first woman at the Highland Cross duathlon stands on the mantelpiece, merely because she 'liked that one'. There is little else. What dominates are the pictures: Inverpolly, Suilven, Quinag, a now-gone Jack Russell on the Brothers of Kintail. It is clear what matters.

After becoming world champion, Angela was nominated among five British sportspeople for the Laureus World Sports Award. The other nominees were global superstars: David Beckham, Jonathan Edwards, Lennox Lewis and Steve Redgrave. She did not attend; she had already booked a holiday to New Zealand. 'I'm not one for posh dos and the thought of wearing a frock frightened me away,' she says. 'It's not my kind of thing.' While black tie events may not be her 'thing', the recognition alongside symbols of sporting greatness showed that Angela too could rise above her sport – a feat achieved by very few hill or fell runners. Joss Naylor has done it in England. Angela Mudge did it in Scotland.

'Do you think you transcended the sport at that point?' I asked Angela several months later, knowing the answer she would give.

'No,' she said emphatically. I could have scripted her response: 'The only people who know about hill running are hill runners. We all know about Kilian Jornet, but that's a marketing thing.'

The Scottish Sports Hall of Fame, conceived in 2002, 'celebrates and pays tribute to Scotland's iconic sportsmen and women from the past 100 years, and inspires future generations.' The aims are noble and – as it is led by sportscotland, the national agency for sport – it has credibility. In total, 28 sports are represented, from the more obvious pursuits of football, golf and rugby, to the minority sports of shooting, table tennis and water polo. The list also recognises the sports that define what it is to be Scottish and to live in Scotland: curling, Highland Games, mountaineering and hillwalking, and shinty. Hill running, however, is a puzzling anomaly. For a pursuit that has existed in Scotland since the eleventh century and is practised across the country, from the Highlands and islands, to the city centre of Edinburgh and the Borders, this is a sport, like the 100-metre sprint in athletics, that very many people can empathise with. I would pity the child who has not run up or down a hill, feeling the burning breathlessness of an ascent and the joyful freedom of a descent. Such exertion is a rite of passage. Arguably, hill running *is* the nation's minority sport.

When I contacted sportscotland for an explanation, a response was immediate and emphatic. Hill runners had not been nominated, and since the process of adding names to the Hall of Fame is done by nomination, there were no hill runners on the list.

Angela is not prone to outbursts of raw emotion. As I prepare to leave, I ask if we might have missed anything. 'You'll have to ask me directly,' she admits. 'I'm not very good at volunteering information.' She has a reputation for disliking interviews. Reputations tend to be inaccurate. Angela is straightforward, that is all. She does not suffer fools; she rises above nonsense. Despite her transcendence, however much she rails against it, she is cultured in a time-honoured hill and fell running tradition, crafted in the Lake District, of diversion and understatement, where self-promotion borders on the grotesque. That, presumably, explains the absence of hill runners from the Hall of Fame.

Ultimately, standing shoulder to shoulder with Scotland's greatest sportspeople is of little interest to Angela. We talk again about what matters most – the mountains – and she seems to glow. As she speaks, staring in the direction of the wood burner, a smile touching her lips, she is somewhere else, somewhere elevated and remote and windswept. I look down at her crutches, momentarily overcome by the disaster that was upon her.

'When I'm in the hills, it's about being there, and seeing and experiencing what the elements are doing to you – if you're fighting the wind or getting soaking wet. You can start off in fine weather, but you climb halfway up and it closes in. You're now going to have completely different experiences in the ascent and descent. You're eventually going to go back to calm again. If you run around the streets, you don't get that, do you? It's just the same – the weather pattern is going to be the same for the whole run. I love Sutherland the best. The terrain is rough. Bog and heather make me happy. I would stay there at Christmas and go for a long, steady run over rubbish terrain.'

Lacking that fix, she admits, is the personal tragedy of injury. 'As I've always loved running in the hills and being out and about, this has definitely brought it home. When I've gone back to the hills after injury, I'm only walking, not running, but I realise what I've really missed is just being there. If it was a choice between, you can't go to the hills, but you can run, I think I'd go to the hills and not run. For me, to run is to be able to run in the hills. If I could only run on a confined athletics track, I'd probably say, "no thanks, I'd rather walk in the hills." It's the same if it's a gorgeous day in the summer. I think, I could go for a two-hour hill run or I could spend all day walking – and I would spend all day walking.'

Angela completed a first round of the Munros in 2002, with Slioch on a January morning the final summit. Like many others, she went on to complete the list of Corbetts. Surprisingly, for a hill runner, the peaks were predominately hiked not run, for Angela frequently went to the mountains with Janice, whose long-term injury prevented movement faster than walking pace. Slowing down did Angela good; it is part of the reason for her prolonged distinction and stamina. 'Walking is great for endurance. I don't think people appreciate that,' she says. 'I was once hillwalking in the Glenfinnan hills when

I met Roger Boswell who was running. It was me, Janice, and a friend, Adam, and we walked up a hill, met Roger, walked down, walked up the next hill, and beat Roger to the top. He said, "how did you do that?" I said, "us walking uphill is a lot quicker than you running uphill, Roger!"'

I had been talking to Angela for nearly two hours. The rain continued to thrash the windows. 'The dogs need to pee,' she says, instructing everyone outside. We pause on an oblong of grass at the front of the cottage, arms folded against the cold. Standing next to a world champion, a woman who was once one of the greatest athletes on the planet, I watch three puppies squat on the lawn.

I ruminated on that word in the months that followed: greatest, Scotland's greatest. I would not ask Angela outright. That would be a futile exercise. Greatness is subjective, of course, but it can be measured by success, by records, by longevity, by the esteem of your contemporaries. 'It has to be Angela,' Malcolm Patterson would tell me. 'World champion, British champion, all the records she's got. It would have to be her. Colin Donnelly would come quite close. Jack Maitland would come close. But it's Angela.'

Yet greatness can also be gauged by what people hand back to their sport. A single anecdote will suffice. In the spring of 2001, Angela was still the reigning world champion when she offered to help set up Glas Tulaichean, an uphill race to the crest of the 1,051-metre Munro above Spittal of Glenshee. In pouring rain, she taped the final 400 metres, from where the race route left the safety of the path. Angela was back the next day, on the start line. She was, inevitably, first woman to the top, and tenth overall, setting a course record that remained untouched 16 races later. Back at the start, Angela accepted a lift over the Cairnwell Pass and was dropped off in Braemar. From there, with a tent and sleeping bag on her back, alone and in drizzle, she ran into the hills. She would not be seen again for days.

Nominating her for an athletics award in 2004, Martin Hyman captured the essence of a world champion who just wanted to be on her own in the mountains. 'I have no doubt that, had she chosen to compete in a higher profile televised sport, she would be a publicly recognised sports celebrity,' he wrote. 'Angela's exploits are so well recognised within our sport that a new word has come into our vocabulary: to be "Mudged" describes the situation when a male star finishes behind Angela in a race.

'Having followed Angela's career closely over the past ten years, I am bound to be in awe of her prowess. Nevertheless, I find her personal qualities to be uniquely admirable. In fifty years of close involvement with international athletes, I have never met anyone with less interest in personal publicity or in financial gain. Other athletes, many of whom have achieved less than Angela, aspire to earn large sums in grants, in sponsorship and in prize money. For warm weather training and for competition they stay in expensive hotels, attended by a supporting entourage, sometimes separate from their teammates. Angela runs in the mountains because she loves the mountain environment and is fulfilled when she challenges the physical limits of her prowess. She has sometimes received modest funding from Sports Aid or Lottery support and has used it to travel to the Alps, where she lives frugally for weeks on end, with only a tiny tent and a little gear, which is limited by what she can carry on her bicycle.'

The relationship between coach and athlete is complex; the relationship between Martin Hyman and Angela Mudge is even more intricate. Even now, more than twenty years after reviewing her diaries for the first time, to Martin, Angela remains an enigma. 'It was easy to discern that she loved being in wild places and lacked any trace of materialism,' he said, 'but I found it almost impossible to penetrate her inner thoughts.'

After a winter of discontent, the crutches were finally put to one side. Angela would go to the hills again. Ben Ledi, in the company of Prasad Prasad, would be her first outing some five months after we spoke.

'Did you go to the top?'

Sitting at home with the phone pressed to her ear, I imagine Angela wrinkling her nose at my question. 'I wouldn't go if I couldn't get to the top,' she says, as if the suggestion was ludicrous. 'I couldn't run downhill because I'd lost the proprioception on rough ground, but it was just good to be out in the hills. That's what I had missed the most.'

Her racing comeback arrived in the autumn, running a leg of the British relay championships at Luss. 'It wasn't great for a dodgy ankle in deep mud,' she admits. Angela then tweaked a hamstring at the Devil's Burdens relays in Fife in January, an injury that indicated she would be forced to miss the Carnethy 5 three weeks later. The forecast was atrocious, with fierce winds and whiteout conditions predicted, worse even than the circumstances in the year I had repeatedly wondered *what the hell are we doing here?* What was anathema to others – 120 paid-up, pre-registered entrants failed to show – was a source of revelry to Angela. What a way for her to run her seventeenth Carnethy 5. 'I can't miss this, I thought. You'll never get this set of conditions again,' she says. With the wind gusting to 45mph, causing a windchill of -15 Celsius on the summits, in a field led home by Finlay Wild, Angela finished 119th, some 16 minutes slower than her course record. Nine other women beat a world champion that day.

'Do you think you'll recover – fully recover?' I ask tentatively.

'I should hope so,' Angela replies immediately, 'once my left leg realises it needs to be the same size as my right.' She ends on a question masquerading as a statement, an epitaph even: 'You don't think I'd give up, do you?'

20

GLORY

I had never forgotten the uncomplicated words of Alec Keith. 'When I get there,' he had said. 'I will just get on with it.' When I needed them most, the sentence appeared as bold, capital letters in my mind. The next three words were the abstract, the metaphorical mountain: 'And I did.'

I got 'there' – a layby opposite the youth hostel in Glen Nevis – in the late afternoon of a Friday after school.

'Javi?' I shouted from the car door.

A man sitting on a bench outside the hostel looked up, smiled and waved. Originally from Navalcarnero, a town south-west of Madrid occupying the plain between the Alberche and Guadarrama rivers, Javi was a mountain runner before he came to Scotland, exploring the peaks of the close-to-home Sierra de Gredos and Sierra de Guadarrama. The Spanish financial crisis brought Javi and his girlfriend to Inverness, where he was working as a primary school teaching assistant. Like me, his first taste of hill racing in Scotland was on Craig Dunain, but it was Cioch Mhòr that acted as a christening. 'It was the first time I had run a race without the route being marked,' he explained. 'There were fences, snow and rain, a burn, a bog. I loved it.'

With a handshake and a nod, at precisely 5pm, Javi and I faced up glen and started running. The last time I had been here was with Graham Nash, creeping through the halcyon hours of a Lochaber morning. Today, the valley temperature was 28 Celsius, the wind like the midsummer sigh of the

Mediterranean. 'Warmer than Ibiza,' the *Daily Record* would boast. The initial steps seemed like the first of my life: stiff, slow and tentative. Just then it was incomprehensible I could accomplish what had only been done 99 times.

As we moved through the forest, I told Javi about Alec Keith, about the bananas and the powder sachets, about getting around with ten minutes to spare, about falling out of his car at Tyndrum. 'I know about him,' Javi said. They had met at races, but only long enough for a snatched greeting.

Under a cerulean sky, we continued up Mullach nan Coirean, running when the gradient eased, walking the rest, carving seven minutes off a 22-and-a-half-hour schedule. 'One hour and thirteen minutes,' I said.

'Thirteen or thirty?' Javi asked.

'Thirteen,' I repeated.

He asked the question a second time, seemingly in disbelief, then shook his head. 'Too fast.'

It was fast – only four minutes slower than Jasmin Paris' record-breaking pace – but conditions, for now, were flawless: light, clear, warm, the wind placid, the ground parched. The moment was ripe for the runners' equivalent of making hay.

For Javi and me, this was a blind date. The meeting outside the hostel two hours earlier was our first. Our profiles matched, but that was no guarantee of a union in Glen Nevis in 24 hours' time. A week before, we had not even known of each other's existence. I suppose I should have done: Francisco Javier Cabrera Valdes is not a forgettable name. Highland Hill Runners had posted an account of one of its members running Tranter's Round in the snowmelt month of April. I had skim-read the article, my curiosity for the conditions, not the runner. But when that long Spanish name appeared in my inbox, it triggered a memory: *was that the bloke who did a Tranter?* It was – and Javi's ambitions had since multiplied: he wanted to run Ramsay's Round. Specialising in long, solo and unsupported mountain runs, Javi had already attempted to fulfil his aspiration. Leaving at midnight, he traversed the

Mamores, aggravated a knee injury on the descent of Sgùrr Eilde Mòr, twisted an ankle on the descent of Stob Coire Sgriodain, and limped down to Loch Treig, accepting – after 14 hours – he would go no further. To accomplish the Ramsay was, as others before him had described it, a 'dream'; he wanted to run with me, 'as far as his legs' would take him.

Before replying, I searched for his report of what had been a completion – Tranter's Round. Wearing a mountain bike windstopper, Spain football shorts and box-fresh fell shoes, Javi had set out alone in drizzle at first light, not knowing then how to unlock the puzzle of the plantation on the slopes of Mullach nan Coirean, and like a latter-day Pete Simpson found himself blundering 'among felled trees with no hint of a path'.

With the Mamores enclosed by cold fog, he made three navi-gational blunders, always on descents. Having only committed to the run the day before, he had not tested what he cryptically described as 'custom-made bag arrangements to carry food and water'. They did not work. 'Having a couple of pouches clinging and hitting my stomach wasn't comfortable at all,' Javi said. The fastener on the waist strap then snapped, forcing him to contrive a tangle of knots to secure the bag to his back. Martin Stone, he was not. With the travails at least offering a mental distraction, Javi crossed the Abhainn Rath and began the long haul to Stob Bàn, not knowing if his efforts would be thwarted by snow on Aonach Beag. In the Grey Corries, he asked every walker he saw if they knew of conditions ahead – no one did; they had come from different directions.

From Sgùrr Choinnich Mòr, Javi could see the approaches to Aonach Beag were painted white. With no winter gear, he dismissed the notion of Spinks Ridge, proceeding to Charlie's Gully instead. 'The snow was soft enough to let me nail down my hands and feet, but hard enough to hold my weight while climbing up, preventing me from sliding to the bottom of the gully,' he said. As he neared the top, he escaped the steep snow, finding a band of rock, mud and grass to wriggle up.

If you get this far, you will probably get to the end, especially on Tranter's Round when the demands of time are less insistent. Escaping the shadow of fog on Ben Nevis, he could see a line of lights in the glen, but an aching knee and tight iliotibial band plagued the descent to the hostel. Back on the road, Javi got in his car, changed his clothes, drove to Fort Augustus, slept for 25 minutes, then continued his journey home to Inverness.

What made me nervous about Javi also endeared him to me. He was a glorious amateur, possessing a naivety matched by a compulsion to keep going, revelling in the company of mountains. He reminded me of Alec Keith.

There is a lucidity that comes in the hills. Life in the Mamores was boiled down to its simplest constituents: the need to move, to eat and drink, to be. The task had not seemed so empirical some 48 hours earlier. I had assigned the last weekend in May as the date of my prospective attempt, with the long-range weather forecast suggesting it would fall at the end of a period of high pressure bringing clear skies, offsetting the absence of any moon. The weekend clashed with the fell race on Jura, precisely the sort of outing anyone capable of supporting a Ramsay's Round would undertake. I persisted, clinging to the belief that benign conditions with little support was better than the reverse.

As time cascaded to the weekend, I realised I was in danger of the worst combination: scant support and rotten weather. The high pressure was to collapse sooner than initial forecasts had predicted. 'Buffeting will become widespread, with particularly sudden, possibly ferocious gusts, even on lower slopes, passes and cols,' read the latest bulletin. My window of opportunity was narrowing: if I set out at the scheduled 1am on Saturday, I would run into thunderstorms by early afternoon, around the time I would be on the Grey Corries. Only once had I been caught on mountains in a lightning storm. I had run a round of the five White Mount Munros that encircle Glen Muick and was standing on Meikle Pap, admiring the cliffs of Lochnagar, when thunder reverberated from a swirl of low-hanging black cloud. The mountainside seemed to literally shake. As corpulent raindrops fell, the leaden sky was lit up by sheets of lightning, making the hills froth and fizz. The world was wicked for a moment – and I fled from it.

Faced with little alternative, I brought the attempt forward by eight hours to 5pm on Friday. The consequence would be not sleeping before the attempt, meaning by the end – if there was to be a true 'end' – I would have been awake for almost 36 hours. But that prospect was eminently more enticing than running along the Carn Mòr Dearg Arête in a hail of lightning bolts.

Later that evening, I asked Graham Nash about the prospect of starting with Javi. Pedigree was not the issue. Javi's best time for the Ben Nevis Race was ten minutes faster than mine; familiarity and understanding was the quandary. The response was decisive: 'You need to be selfish and single-minded to complete these things,' Graham said. 'You will have highs and lows, and they rarely coincide with the person you're running with. Personally, I wouldn't run with someone I haven't run with before, but then I'm a selfish old git.'

Soon after, Ross Bannerman, knowing of my plans, sent a message: 'Take a day off. Torrential rain will spoil it.'

I hammered out a frustrated reply: 'I can't take a day off.'

The next message was from Javi. The maths on my schedule was wrong. Not only had I calculated the splits incorrectly, I had come to a total without including the descent of the Ben. Perhaps he should have been the one doing the doubting?

We were climbing Binnein Mòr when I asked Javi how he felt. He shook his head. 'Not good. It's too early to feel like this.' I let the doubts fly into the wind, unanswered. I understood. In the same instant, I remembered Graham's words and knew that at some point, sooner than I had expected, I would have to be 'selfish'. Yet I was also puzzled. Javi was not struggling with the speed; he was climbing well, even gapping me on Binnein Beag. From the top of the first Munro to the summit of the tenth, Sgùrr Eilde Mòr, took us a little over five hours, akin to 21-hour pace. There seemed little reason to doubt we could comfortably run the round within 24 hours.

At midnight, we were easing down Sgùrr Eilde Mòr, closing in on two distant beams of light: one belonging to Mark Hartree who was camped near the ruin of Luibeilt to meet us; the other on the head, I assumed, of John Busby, a Carnethy clubmate, running from Lairig Leacach. Food was lined up along the central reservation of the track, with Mark reading us a menu as we arrived. I had been here two months earlier, stumbling into the mountains from Kinlochleven on another Friday night that would spill into Saturday, when the route had been buried in melting snow and I had to cross a high, freezing Abhainn Rath, before the beam of my torch picked out the sanctuary of Meanach. The next day, four of us ran over the Grey Corries and the Aonachs on snow-banked ridges, picking out islands in the west. From Aonach Mòr, we descended into Coire Giubhsachan, the lonely saddle to the east of Carn Mòr Dearg, patiently kicking steps with crampons, not moving until the ice axe had grabbed. After bumping downhill to Steall, we tramped through the glen, hungry, weary and dumbfounded by mountains.

Mark washed my socks in a burn, then handed me a spoon and a pouch of lukewarm rice. Javi was sitting to my left, hardly moving, bathed in darkness apart from the downward glow of his torch. I realised that while I had been running to reach a moment in a different place, some 15 hours from now, Javi had been running to get here. This was his end. At the time, I imagined him suffering. That was not the case, he would insist later. Javi was guided by pragmatism: 'I was fine, but I wasn't going to do it, not at that moment at least. You could call it the end of our journey together; that reflects the way I felt.'

Mark went through the menu again, with Javi dismissing it all. 'Just eat some food,' I heard Mark mutter. He tried again: 'Come on. Eat some food. You'll feel better.' Javi relented, swallowing some granola with water. 'Whatever you do, you can't stay here,' Mark said finally, 'you're going to have to get moving.'

Our 'journey together' was not quite over. Javi got to his feet and followed John and me across the boggy ground that runs down to the river, aiming for a fence line that is obvious by day, invisible by night. Mark shouted after us: 'Come back. I forgot to take a photo.' We forded the Abhainn Rath too far west, with the water lapping our waists, and proceeded into a mild early morning. I led, running and occasionally walking when overwhelmed with waves of ominous nausea, to the bridge by Creaguaineach Lodge. Javi, always a few steps behind, announced he would make for Fersit along the five miles of train track on the eastern shoulder of Loch Treig. He slipped back and when I turned to check on him, the light of his torch was gone.

'When did you know?' I asked Javi a week later.

'Before I even started,' he admitted. 'I was sure I wasn't ready.'

The difference between us was wafer-thin, a divergence in belief, not a physical distinction, I told him. He agreed: 'It didn't matter too much to me; to you, I knew it was everything.'

John and I said little, despite it being the first time we had seen each other for 18 months. When we were last together, after running legs of the Devil's Burdens relays, he had been on the cusp of spending a year studying in the Netherlands. We had spoken then about the ground we were now treading. 'If you go to the Highlands,' he had said, 'the landscape is different, but you don't appreciate how different it is until you feel it with your feet. You can look at mountains from a distance, but running allows you to not just see them, but feel them.' John would not race again in Scotland that year. 'I have an idea of what the Dutch landscape may be like.' A pause. 'It's going to be flat,' he said solemnly.

Beinn na Lap is the antithesis of Amsterdam. While there is little to note about a mountain considered one of the easiest Munros due to its modest altitude and an elevation of 400 metres from typical starting points at Corrour or Loch Ossian, Beinn na Lap is to the summer Ramsayist what Chno Dearg is to the winter contender, and perhaps what Yewbarrow represents to those undertaking the Bob Graham. The slope of long grass rises interminably, a frustrating march from a bridge that carries the West Highland Line. I had tried to prepare myself for this moment: this is where Jasmin Paris had felt unwell; this is where Charlie Ramsay had struggled; this is where a deflated Bill Johnson had phoned Anne Stentiford.

The reality was worse than I could have imagined. In the darkness, the silhouette of the summit plateau seemed to rise in perpetuity and for the first time in nine hours I was stopping, taking micro-pauses, trying to suppress the realisation that I had not even reached the eastern limit of the round. The calorific content of my midnight meal had long expired. I was not hungry, but dizziness told me I needed food. When I tried to eat – pizza or tortilla – I chewed and chewed, driven mad by mastication, the food becoming an insipid paste that I could not swallow. Single jelly babies, carried off with a gulp of water, became my limit. I carried on, motivated only by the conviction that climbing Beinn na Lap now was better than ever having to ascend it again.

The relief in finding the top was tempered by what I knew was ahead: a grim nosedive through rampant gorse to gain the quietest of dells, then the infamous climb of the concave approach to Chno Dearg. As we gained the crooked line of the summit ridge, hearing the faintest murmur of birdsong, I knew at least the worst of the night was over. Those hours, even on reflection, had been dreadful. But, as if I needed reminding of this sport's juxtaposition, they were also exceptional – to run through a Scottish night, to be befuddled by the sun's movements: way out west five hours earlier, now adrift in the east. 'How glorious a greeting the sun gives the mountains!' John

Muir wrote in *The Mountains of California*. How glorious a greeting the sun also gives the mountain runner, for as I watched the illuminations drip deeper, like the wax on a melting candle, I was happy. Perhaps this is what John Busby had meant? Such happiness is hard-won, but it can only be gained by profound immersion in mountains. To only look cannot be enough.

The Ramsay has a habit of snatching such moments from you, for the need to concentrate, to fixate on heather and rock, to not fall over, quickly overwhelms romantic notions. The descent of Stob Coire Sgriodain is such a place, tendering an abrupt, pathless plunge to Loch Treig. The discomfort is countered by the final third of a mile: a high step through a broken fence that only the Ramsayist would know about; a passage through a ribbon of crowded forest branches to reach the train line; a run between the tracks to a flight of steps down to the dam; from there, a jog across the wall as someone bellows encouragement from the far side. It feels like a finish line – for some, all too soon, it is.

This is no story of heroism. I was not a pioneer. I was not chasing records. I was not the first; I was not the last. This is no account of particular boldness. Nor is this the narrative of a by-the-seat-of-your-pants contender on the edge of being tipped into a second day. This is the story of someone trying to remember the words of another: 'When I get there, I will just get on with it.' There is little allure in just getting on with things, in putting one foot in front of the other, but I persisted in doing just that. Besides, I had no excuse not to. That I was fatigued, struggling to eat, light-headed, convinced I was going to vomit, and sleep-deprived, was inevitable. In the normal world, I would have phoned work and made my apologies, or been sent home sick. Today was not normal: when I started running 13 hours earlier, I knew my fate was to suffer. That really is the only way it can be done.

But it is in the doing that 'clarity of perception' is found.

From Loch Treig, the Ramsayist must re-ascend close to 900 metres to gain Stob a' Choire Mheadhoin, yet the peak might have been Craig Dunain, for it seemed I was back where *this* had all started. With me were three contemporaries from Inverness; two of them, David Gallie and Gordie Taylor, were the pair who had contrived to mock my Englishness above Loch Ness.

'If you finish this,' David said, 'I'll never call you a soft lad again.'

He pulled out a cylinder of blue plastic, no more than an inch long, from his bag and held it towards me, a thumb and index finger on each end. It was a peg from Frustration, the board game his brother played constantly. When David went to see Iain at his nursing home in Nairn, he would hear the ping of the game's perspex dome before he even reached his room. Iain insisted on playing with the blue pieces. Since his death the previous year, David had carried a blue barrel with him every time he stepped onto the hills. He has hidden pieces on Ben Wyvis, Craig Dunain – the hill the brothers last ran together before Iain's accident – and the highest point of the Great Glen Way.

David gestured ahead to Karen Lyons, the fourth member of our early morning quartet, and Gordie. 'They are carrying them too. I don't believe in an afterlife, but my mother does. When she's on the bus on Bridge Street in Inverness, she looks up at Ben Wyvis, knowing a blue Frustration piece is up there, and smiles. She no longer thinks of Iain stuck in a room in a nursing home.' David was running a step ahead of me. He might have mistaken my heave for a grunt of effort, but as I looked across a mountainside wearing a beret of mist, tears were gathering.

Joy – a strange, miraculous joy – erupted from the hollowness of sorrow. Mountains had rarely seemed so marvellous. To be here was to be on the crest of existence, rising on a great travelator to the sky. We might have brushed the fingertips of Iain Gallie. As we descended to the high pass beneath

Stob Coire Easain, our brocken spectres, haloed in the cloud, waved back at us.

I knew too much to not know what would happen next. As David and I trudged up the grassy wing of Stob Bàn, Gordie and Karen were already circling back to Fersit. Gone was the cooling sheen of mist; gone were the brocken spectres. We climbed in the glare of sunshine, my head fuggy, unsure we were on the right line until the cone of Stob Bàn emerged from behind a shoulder, still a long way off. I was fixated on locating a track I had found here previously. That I could not gain it was maddening, as if this somehow counted as failure. What was of far greater concern was my inability to eat. Like on Beinn na Lap: minutes of chewing, a revolting gunge forming in my mouth. David encouraged, cajoled and eventually insisted – until I just wanted him to leave me alone. Why does the body reject food when the need is greatest?

The length of my pauses grew longer – a second or two before David tapped my back, urging progress – and more frequent. Seconds might seem insignificant, but they were symbolic of a mounting malaise, a deepening slump. For the first time, I found no pleasure or relief in reaching a summit, and cagily descended the loose scree of the north-west ridge, scarcely faster than a walking pace that I knew was too slow to succeed. Arriving at the lochan in Coire Rath, my face was the colour of dust.

'Sit down,' a voice instructed. I had not expected to see Mark Hartree, who had walked here in the dawn when sleep eluded him. I lowered myself to the grass with a grimace. Just then I looked like Javi had at midnight: a runner in agonising conflict, physically browbeaten, mentally denuded. The finish – at least six hours away – seemed as distant as ever, too distant to be real. To dress this up in colourful prose is difficult. The words I expressed at the time are the most effective synthesis: 'I feel like crap.'

The statement was indisputably true, but then I dared utter poisonous half-truths, words that had been teetering on the edge of my consciousness since I had stepped onto the ramp of Beinn na Lap, even with that moment of enchantment on Stob a' Choire Mheadhoin: 'I can't do this.'

I was flooded with regret; I did not mean what I uttered, but the act of speaking aloud my thoughts was cathartic.

Mark turned on me. 'You feel bloody awful? I should hope you do.' He handed me rice again, then a watery porridge. The words seemed to have cleared the blockage in my throat. I could swallow. 'You're going to eat this, then we're going to run up that big hill,' Mark explained, gesticulating to Stob Choire Claurigh over his shoulder.

And we did – or at least walked, but a walk without pauses, a walk of conviction, a walk of rediscovered belief.

On the summit, as I looked up to see a meandering line of shimmering quartzite, I was imbued with absolute certainty: there was no way I could *not* do this. I ran downhill, my legs moving with the freedom they had on the descent of Mullach nan Coirean. The phoney mental war was over. For hours, I had been debating a choice. Now there was no choice. There could only be one outcome: getting back to Glen Nevis within 24 hours.

At the time, it felt like a verdict was made there – as my hand felt for a loose rock on yet another highest point. The reality was far more complex than I could appreciate at that moment. The choice had been made long ago, in the days and weeks and years before, even as far back as the moment a twelve-year-old boy told a hockey teacher he wanted to do cross-country instead. I had been unwittingly readying myself for these precious hours my whole life, but even then, inadvertent preparation did not mean I was capable of running Ramsay's Round. I could not have contemplated the idea without the six months of obsession that had led to today, but then nor was it conceivable without the years that had preceded those six months.

Having taken a three-week break from running, I had started again the previous November, returning gradually at first, compulsively strengthening back and hips to ease the burden on my right ankle. When I was staying on the horizontal Fylde coast at Christmas, I concocted a 30-rep session of 20 minutes up and down the mound of a sand dune. On the stretch of beach between St Annes-on-the-Sea and Blackpool, I overruled instinct, seeking out the line of greatest resistance – the dry sand, the loose rocks, the rolling dunes.

Gradually, in the new year, I increased distance until I was averaging 50 to 60 miles a week and climbing at least 10,000 metres a month. I ran variations of the Pentland Skyline on five occasions in eight weeks, creating extensions to raise the time to five hours and adding pathless routes to lose and then regain the eastern ridge. On an anticlockwise trip, the moon was haloed by millions of ice crystals; going the other direction, eating cheese sandwiches on Black Hill, I toiled as John Ryan moved at a pace that seemed pre-determined to drop me. I ran repetitions on the Craiglockhart hills; I went to Arthur's Seat after work for Martin Hyman-style thrashes or to climb the Lion's Haunch by its steep western flank; I took the Road to Swanston. Every Tuesday, I ran intervals alone in The Meadows – watching the seasons change even there: sleet and snow in January, frenzied wind in March, blossom in April – immersed in a bubble of hurt. As I had in London, I lived by the numbers on my watch, but when I looked up to Arthur's Seat there was always a human shape breaking the silhouette of the hill. I was down here so I could be up there. After, I would jog to school, passing dozens of students unsure how to respond to the sight of their teacher lacking a suit and tie, and climb the stairs to my classroom, counting the forty-five steps, calculating the height gain, however insignificant. The same two or three girls would glance up, then look straight back down, as I pushed open the door, breathless and sweating, wearing shorts on a cold February morning. In the gents, I would splash my face, pat myself dry with paper towels, change hurriedly in a cubicle, spray myself with aftershave, then walk back up those 45 steps, pretending nothing had happened.

I raced sparingly, seeing such efforts as the path to injury. I was right. I tweaked a calf at Feel the Burns, a half-marathon on mist-smothered, snow-streaked moorland above Selkirk, in January, and badly blistered a heel at a 42-mile race in the Lake District in April that took three weeks to recover. In between came that brilliant three-day reconnaissance in the Ramsay hills: a scary, dark, bitterly cold run to Meanach, the light of my torch catching the fiendish glances of deer; a 10-hour expedition the next day; an ascent of the steepest side of Sgùrr Eilde Mòr – a 700-metre climb of a triangle of grass, heather and rock from the eponymous loch – to simply 'have a look' at a descent I would never take, as I ran out to Kinlochleven.

When I ran – whether it was on The Meadows, the Pentlands or the Grey Corries – I thought of what was to come: the small pile of stones that marks the start of the east ridge descent of the Mamores' Stob Bàn; the target island in the Allt Feith na h-Ealaidh when leaving Beinn na Lap; the trod that traverses Sgùrr Choinnich Beag, avoiding the unnecessary addition of 50 metres of climbing. I imagined myself there: steadily progressing over Devil's Ridge, then back again; lunging between boulders on the Carn Mòr Dearg Arête; touching the youth hostel signpost at the end.

A fortnight before my attempt, I parked at Swanston and ran directly to Caerketton, a climb of 300 metres, and down to Hillend. I returned by the same route, then repeated the entire course again, summiting Caerketton four times in two hours, earning the equivalent height of Aonach Beag from sea level. It was on the final descent, as I gazed down on the village, that I committed to an imminent assault on Ramsay's Round. Looking back, my assurance astounds me. What made me think I was ready? Why now? Why not wait until the longer days of the spring, or the summer, or even the following year? But then, why wait? I might be faster, fitter and stronger at another time, but I might not. This seemed to be my moment – and if there was one thing worse than failing, it was not trying in the first place.

When I showed Jasmin Paris a draft of *Pizza, Prosecco and Ice Cream*, she queried a reference to her morning training. 'She makes a mental tick,' I had written.

'It's what I want to do,' Jasmin had explained in an email. 'Running is to a large extent just a by-product of the many happy hours spent outdoors.' I deleted the sentence, realising I was transferring my motivation to another, for it was me who found reassuring logic in training and knowing precisely how I had prepared, not Jasmin. It is what lent me surety when I made my ruling on Caerketton. Every run, every repetition, every rung on the stone staircase at school, was a literal step towards achieving Ramsay's Round. It was these thousands of choices across three decades that enabled me to make this choice right now: I will persevere; I will finish this.

I would not be the hundredth though.

Andy Fallas and Helen Bonsor, who we met on Stob Choire Claurigh, had encountered a patched-up Pete Duggan earlier that morning at Corriechoille. With Tim Ripper, he had helped pace Alicia Hudelson, an American ultrarunner and climber who purchased a map of Ramsay's Round the day after she completed a Bob Graham, from Lairig Leacach to Glen Nevis, in a successful round at the second attempt. It had taken 38 years and 10 months, but at last a century of rounds had been accomplished.

Alicia had started at 5am – 12 hours before me – running through the balmy heat of day. Where we were now, Alicia had been in the minutes around midnight. It was the light of her head torch Javi and I had seen from Sgùrr Eilde Mòr, not John Busby's. Reassuring her as they left the summit of the Ben that 1 hour and 15 minutes was ample time to descend, Pete fell while trying to bypass the only remaining snow patch on the tourist path, with his head striking a rock. 'Alicia stopped running,' Pete said, 'but Tim called for her to carry on. After checking I wasn't dead – we both agreed that, not being dizzy or queasy, the quickest way off the hill was just to keep running – I set off after her.' Later, at Belford

Hospital, Pete's head wound was glued and an x-ray revealed a fractured metacarpal on his four-fingered left hand. Because he broke the third metacarpal – a finger naturally splinted to the fourth – the doctors could do little else to secure it.

'I think 101 sounds better, the first of the second hundred,' Helen said, as we went our separate ways: David and I faithful to the way of the Ramsay; Andy and Helen to Corriechoille. Helen had seen what she needed. Not long after, she would forge her own glory, setting a new women's record for Tranter's Round.

The rest seemed to belong in a slow-moving dream: meeting a waiting Chris Busby in the pass beneath Aonach Beag, as he had once paused for Jez Bragg; forging up Spinks Ridge; sinking to the ground as the world seemed to sway on Aonach Mòr; taking a biscuit from Chris, a smear of hummus from David; climbing the kinking ringlet of ridge to Carn Mòr Dearg, reaching out for the cairn; advancing along the arête; crawling through the Ben's waterfall of boulders. There was no stopping now. Alicia had found a similar fluidity. 'I would love to be specific about how I managed to go from a semi-zombie state to making fairly good time,' she said. 'Sadly, I've got no idea. It certainly wasn't more food, and I didn't have any caffeine. I suppose the lesson is that sometimes even the boring approach of simply trying harder can work.'

The ground visibly flattened ahead. 'You're going to like this,' Chris called back. A moment later the plateau was laid bare: that rubble-strewn wasteland and its ruined observatory, the triangulation pillar on its rock plinth. I could go no higher.

As Glyn Jones descended the Ben, the poetry died. He had returned from the realm of his soul. He was a 'white-haired one' again. I came down in convoy, initially with David and Chris, following the concertina of the tourist track, and from Red Burn, joined by Gordie, Karen and Javi. After arriving in midge-infested Fersit shortly before dawn, I imagined Javi would be crushed with disappointment. After all, I represented what he might have been. But that is not how he sees the world. 'When we finally parted,' Javi said, 'I felt happy – happy because I love being on my own, especially in the wild; happy because of the incredible night we were lucky to have.' Like Angela Mudge, Finlay Wild or Jasmin Paris, Javi's joy comes from the fundamental pleasure of being among mountains. For him, Ramsay's Round was merely a conduit to an emotional state.

In a gentle rain, I was guided down, along the gravel tracks that bypassed the steps, through packs of tourists. 'Show offs,' one walker sneered. It would take more than an hour to get down from the summit, but time was no longer a concern. At last, the track split: one way heading to the walkers' car park at Achintee, the other swinging left to the hostel on a path that eventually levelled in the floor of the glen. The others had dropped back. I cleared the final boulder and stepped onto the wooden bridge over the River Nevis.

I remember hearing a rising cheer. I remember tasting champagne. I remember lurching backwards, as if my body could not comprehend the idea of ceasing motion. I remember running my hand over the black back of Sparky, Mark Hartree's Labrador. I remember shaking my head. I remember thinking that I should feel something – anything, but there was only crushing relief: relief that compulsion had not given way to that devastatingly human trait of weakness. That was it. I did not know then that I would recall these moments forever.

A few hours later, I would be on the list, the 101st Ramsayist. In the days that followed, hundreds of people congratulated me, many of them strangers, many of them non-runners. I was assailed by questions. What did I eat? When did I sleep? Was it hard? What about – *you know* – going to the toilet? People had tracked my journey through the night. John Busby and I had not been alone on Beinn na Lap.

On the Friday morning of my first week as a Ramsayist, Andrew Ramage, a biology teacher and a hillwalker who had 'compleated' the Munros and Corbetts, addressed the school at morning assembly. He was talking about 'achievement'.

Andrew introduced the Munros, then Ramsay's Round, and I knew where this was going. 'Last Friday, at 5pm, one of your teachers set off on Ramsay's Round. Please can we all give Mr Muir of the English Department a huge round of applause for completing Ramsay's Round in 22 hours and eight minutes. Unbelievable.'

I was sitting on the end of a row, next to a teenager in my National 5 English class, a student who had listened to me talk about the poetry of Jackie Kay and the drama of Tennessee Williams for the previous nine months. I sensed her start when Andrew uttered my name. As she glanced to her right, I empathised with her contemplation: *Him? That?*

There was glory, but not in the having done. The adulation was tendered with a genuine warmth that I could only compare to my wedding day or the birth of my children, but, however well-intended, the praise did not seem worthy now it was all over. That person on those mountains on that day was not the person who now stood in front of a classroom of students, or that person who now read bedtime stories to his children. I was a 'white-haired one' too.

From the wall of the hostel, I had looked up at the Ben. The glory was up there, high up there, in the scree and the boulders, in the grass and the heather, in the darkness of Beinn na Lap, in the dawn of Stob Coire Sgriodain, in a blue Frustration barrel, in a hand on a back, in 22 hours and eight minutes of a life, in the mountains that touch the sky, in the mountains that had called, but had now, finally, fallen silent.

21

BEAUTIFUL MADNESS

'The nature of the challenge is very severe and there is a risk of serious injury or death,' cautions the blurb of the Glen Coe Skyline. The warning continues: 'Our route features long and sustained sections of scrambling terrain, which is roughly equivalent to moderate standard rock climbing. Be under no illusions that a slip or trip on these serious sections of the route could result in death.'

Shane Ohly, the race director, was told it could not be done: a contest that ascended the formidable Buachaille Etive Mòr by the fabled rock climb of Curved Ridge, and then passed over the serrated edge of the Aonach Eagach, was simply not viable.

'Is this the most dangerous race in the world?' the *Daily Mirror* asked. Why were runners being hurled into the domain of climbers and mountaineers, into the jaws of unnecessary peril?

But Shane Ohly is a symbol of perseverance. The extraordinary resilience of a 30-hour Ramsay's Round bears testament to that. The Glen Coe Skyline has echoes of that run: a kind of beautiful madness. Moments after winning the inaugural race in 2015, Joe Symonds is bent over in the car park of Glencoe ski centre, hands on his knees, shaking his head. 'I can't believe we thought this was a sensible thing to do,' he says. 'The enemy was the course, not the other competitors.'

So the race was made harder still: the distance increased to 32 miles and the required ascent and descent to 4,800 metres – equivalent to climbing Mont Blanc – by moving the headquarters to sea level in Kinlochleven. Very soon, the race seemed established, as if it had always been part of the Scottish calendar. Also very soon, the Glen Coe Skyline became a race like no other in Scotland, attracting some of the world's best mountain runners to the Highlands.

It is hard to resist such beautiful madness.

With seconds to go before the mass start, Shane shouted across the crowd: 'Bib three, your tracker isn't working.' Bib three belonged to Jonathan Albon, a twenty-seven-year-old Norway-based Londoner and champion obstacle racer. It was just as well the race paused for him.

We followed the twisting, rising curls of the West Highland Way, spilling southwards, then down the sweeping bends of the Devil's Staircase to reach Glen Coe. It would have seemed too easy – running along a benign trail, miles vanishing beneath our feet – had I not known what was ahead.

Geographical features on Buachaille Etive Mòr are not named with irony. We would pass beneath the entrance to Great Gully; further around the mountain was The Chasm. We were here for Curved Ridge, a perilously steep and exposed ladder of rock that ascends to the 1,022-metre summit of Stob Dearg. We climbed in single file silence, nothing mattering but the next handhold, the next foothold, the next ledge. There was a runner just in front. I glanced at the face of her watch. The digits were her heart rate: 175. We were not even running; we were clasping cliff, moving directly to the clouds. For a moment, I put my back to the wall and looked across Rannoch Moor. I laughed aloud, an incredulous laugh that rang out from the cliff.

However many times I find myself in the mountains of Scotland, it is still the scale that overwhelms. It did on that sweltering May afternoon when I looked east from the summit of Mullach nan Coirean, dwelling on incalculable numbers and deeds. These places are bewilderingly vast. As we emerged from mist, a line of racers was strung out ahead, scurrying across the rubbly plateau of Buachaille Etive Mòr, engulfed by unbounded mountain and sky. Nan Shepherd would not have approved: 'To pit oneself against the mountain is necessary for every climber: to pit oneself merely against other players, and make a race of it, is to reduce to the level of a game what is essentially an experience.' She understood all the same. 'Yet what a race-track for these boys to choose!' I had watched runners here twelve months earlier. Then I had been on neighbouring Buachaille Etive Beag, waiting for people like me to appear as distant stick men and women across a gaping glen. There had been one, then two, then dozens of tiny silhouetted figures. It was one of the most beautiful things I had seen. Now I was among them.

Sporting arenas are as renowned as the teams and sportsmen and women who inhabit them: St Andrews, Aintree, Wembley, Lord's, Wimbledon. None could be more exceptional than Glen Coe. 'Glen Coe is no great beauty,' W.H. Murray wrote in his 1968 *Companion Guide to Scotland*, arguing it was incomparable to Glen Affric or Glen Lyon. 'It is bare and bleak, adorned by neither tree nor heather,' he continued, offering a 'wild and ugly majesty. When you lift your eyes from the glen to the mountains towering above, you see an array of rock peaks, packed close, trenched by ravines, of its own kind unrivalled.'

We ran into that 'unrivalled' place: a jumble of crags, ribbons of scree and precipitous drops, over Stob Coire Sgreamhach, along a ridge high above the Lost Valley, immersed in a screen of cloud to Bidean nam Bian. From the summit, a lean finger reached east to Stob Coire an Lochan. We went out and came back, touching the top of Bidean nam Bian for a second time, then snuck along a rocky backbone, sank into a corrie and thereafter a gully of long grass and boulders, descending abruptly to the floor of the glen. I turned my head for a moment, looking back, astounded. Then I looked forward – and up, and up.

Hill running could then have seemed utterly nonsensical.

From the road that dissects Glen Coe, the summit of Sgorr nam Fiannaidh is scarcely a mile away. But this is a prodigiously steep mile, a mile of literal crawling, a mile that climbs higher than any manmade structure on Earth, and at 59 minutes, a mile that might be the slowest I ever 'run'. Yet the climb seemed incidental, for something even more exceptional lay ahead. Looking east from the summit, out there, somewhere, was the saw-edge of the Aonach Eagach, hiding in clag.

In truth, there is little to tax the runner on the Aonach Eagach – a largely horizontal ridge that is classed as a scramble, not a climb. But the exposure...

The words of the race blurb seemed to murmur in the breeze: 'one slip' from oblivion. I could not see what was below, but I knew: wickedly-angled faces of grass and cliffs. There is reputed to be no safe line of descent to the south, even if descent was made willingly. There is no escape. Grant Macdonald, a competitor in the first Skyline race, was not being sarcastic when he summed up the significance of reaching the end of the Aonach Eagach: 'This marks the point when you know you aren't going home in a helicopter.'

As I progressed along the ridge, desperately clinging to wet rock, dangling cramping legs, and hoping, Jonathan Albon was back in Kinlochleven, winning the Glen Coe Skyline. It would be three hours before I reached where he was just then. Albon's exploits belonged in this otherworldly place; his run, a little over six-and-a-half hours, resembled something fantastical.

There was a sublime horror to it all. David Brown's words seemed fitting: 'Best-thing-worst-thing I've ever done.'

The innovative brilliance of a race that includes Curved Ridge, Bidean nam Bian and the Aonach Eagach cannot be underestimated. Shane Ohly had lauded the creator's imagination as he sought to make history on Ramsay's Round, but here was the outcome of Shane's imagination: an ability to bring to reality the incredible. 'When asked what I thought of the race, I could only be honest and say it was the best course

I had ever experienced,' Albon said. 'It truly was a fantastic combination of everything a mountain race should be and trumped every race I have done to date.'

Not everyone agrees, for if this is the trajectory of the sport, some say it is a future at odds with the longstanding tradition of hill running and racing in Scotland. The branding and corporate sponsorship is garish, opponents argue, transforming runners into expectant customers. The consequences of such an event are dire, they fear: small, club-organised and less well-off races will die out. Notably, the Two Inns, a point-to-point contest that ended at the Clachaig Inn, quietly vanished as the Glen Coe Skyline emerged. There is also a question of respect. The Skyline's sister event, the Ring of Steall Skyrace, has clashed with a British and Scottish championship race at Merrick.

Gordon Pryde, the convener of Scottish Hill Runners from 2012 to 2016, began hill racing in the 1980s. He has stood on the start line of races held for the first time; he has stood on the start line of races that no longer exist. He fears the emergence of the Glen Coe Skyline, and its associate races, could be a watershed moment, the thin end of the wedge. 'It has the potential to damage the sport,' he says, 'but I hope that's not the case.'

So what? So what if hill racing in Scotland as we know it dies out? So what if existing races are replaced by events like the Glen Coe Skyline? Gordon looks worried. I am playing devil's advocate, I assure him, and he continues, almost sadly: 'There is something so simple about this sport.'

'Simple.' How many times had I heard that word? What does it actually mean? Certainly not the word's mere dictionary definition. Being 'simple' is paradoxically a complex matter. 'Simple' – when it comes to hill racing – looks something like this: you can enter on the day and – crucially – cheaply; the course will not be marked; the race briefing *will* be brief; there will be no sponsorship and no branding; you must carry a physical map and compass; at the end, you will be fed and watered – probably with soup, cake and tea – but there will be no memento or 'goody bag'; you will chat to the race winner without realising they were the race winner; as for the results, you might never see them.

It is a list that makes even simplicity seem contrived. This is how the sport has always been in Scotland. Even the youngest McGregor was able to enter on the day. Why should it change?

The ex-convener is not a lone voice. His fears are shared by several of the committee members of Scottish Hill Runners, notably the most prominent of them all.

Angela Mudge utters the words like a confession: 'I am a traditionalist.' There is a derogatory undertone to the term, as if a 'traditionalist' is blindly tethered to the past, unable to evolve and adapt. 'I like the way we used to decide on a Friday, I'll do that race tomorrow, turn up, pay £5, and run,' she explains. 'That's what we love. That's the bottom line. We love the simplicity of it.'

The entire route of the Salomon-sponsored Glen Coe Skyline is marked by orange flags with such regularity it should really be impossible to get lost, while the particularly technical sections on the Aonach Eagach are flagged with lines of tape running around and across bands of rock. Even in the thickest cloak on Bidean nam Bian, I had no cause to look at a map. I had challenged some of the leading British runners – Jasmin Paris, Jon Ascroft, Jim Mann – on the course marking. The consensus was it was 'fine because it's different': this is 'skyrunning', not hill running. The former emerged in Italy in the early 1990s as a hybrid of mountaineering and running, featuring various prerequisites: an altitude of more than 2,000 metres, a climbing difficulty up to Grade Two, and slopes of at least 30 per cent. Altitude aside, Scotland just about qualifies, even if the motto of the International Skyrunning Federation, 'less cloud, more sky,' was clearly not inspired by a Highland summer. Cynics would say the difference between the sports is marginal, that skyrunning is a sexed-up, glossy version of hill running, the made-up sister to a dowdy sibling, and that skyrunning is a brand as much as a standalone sport.

'Different is good,' Angela says, 'but does this difference now mean there's going to be a lot more difference? On its own, it's fine. But it won't stay on its own.'

They were prophetic words. Early in 2016, it was announced that two other linked events would be held on the same weekend as the Glen Coe Skyline: a vertical kilometre race – the first to be staged in the UK – to Na Gruagaichean on Friday, and the Ring of Steall Skyrace on Saturday, ahead of the original Skyline on Sunday. When entries opened, 100 people registered for the Skyline in the first seven minutes; the number peaked at 349, each prepared to pay £80, when entries closed. The 2017 'Skyline Scotland' weekend of events then included a fourth race – the Ben Nevis Ultra, costing £150. Ultra Trail Scotland emerged in the same year, offering a programme of three races on Arran that mirrored the format: a 'gruelling' 47-mile headline ultramarathon featuring 5,600 metres of ascent; a shorter, more accessible secondary race; and The Goat, a 'quick dash' to the summit of Goatfell. Entry for The Goat was £25, double the price of the traditional Goatfell race already established in the hill running calendar. If the format succeeded, Casey Morgan, the owner of the Ultra Trail Scotland brand, hoped to 'possibly grow to other islands'.

Traditional races organised by clubs cannot hope to compete, Angela argues. 'Stùc a' Chroin is never going to get media attention because no-one is being paid to stick it on Twitter and Facebook. Big companies aren't going to be behind little hill races, but they will get behind these big corporate events.'

Gordon Pryde tells me he has spent the previous days tangled in the 'bureaucracy' of ensuring a race scheduled to take place in Falkland goes ahead. 'It's a village race; the winner will be done in 20 minutes,' he says. Organisation should be straightforward, but Scottish Hill Runners were having to negotiate a fee with the estate the course passes through.

Landowners are beginning to realise there is money to be

made in the hosting of such events, Gordon explains. 'Perhaps there is a feeling that because someone can make a buck out it, they feel entitled to do so.' Can small races compete in such a market? In the long term, probably not, but surely there is hope?

This is not the end of the hill running world. Salomon might be the name on the branding of the Glen Coe Skyline, but Shane Ohly, a man schooled in the motifs of hill running simplicity and tradition – mountain marathons, classic races, 24-hour rounds – is the catalyst of the change. Shane and Jim Mann would spend 21 hours in the Cairngorms, running a Rigby Round in rain and 80mph gusts, soon after we spoke. Hill running does not get much more classic or traditional than that.

'I love doing that £3 fell race on a Wednesday night; they are brilliant, low-key, community-supported events,' Shane tells me. 'There is also a place in the sports calendar for highly-credible, rich experience events. That is where the Glen Coe Skyline sits.'

I paint a picture of the future – a network of branded races across north-west Scotland: the An Teallach Skyline, the Cuillin Skyline, the Torridon Skyline. Shane admits to having similar thoughts. They would make outstanding races, as 'special and unique' as Glen Coe, he says, but attempting to turn any of the three, or something similar, into a workable race would be fraught with complexity. Not only would there be inevitable opposition to racing in sacrosanct mountains like the Cuillin, the events would need to turn a profit – that is the bottom line. If Skyline Scotland is 'hardly commercially viable' and creates 'eye-watering costs', as Shane admits, it suggests that the prospect of replicating the Skyline model elsewhere in the Highlands and islands would be unachievable. Shane is pragmatic too. While a race that included the Cuillin traverse would be the 'ultimate challenge of ridge running' in Britain, he knows such an event would have to be closed to all but the elite. 'How many people could do it safely? It would be a tiny group – less than 100,' he says.

High profile, high price races also need a high level of logistics. When Skyline Scotland was let down by a company providing crowd control barriers, from where in the Highlands could such things be sourced at late notice? The prospect seemed unlikely, before another supplier was tracked down at a cost of £800.

Kinlochleven – with its relative proximity to Fort William – is positively metropolitan compared to Sligachan or Torridon. Could Shane 'deliver excellence' to customers who expect a significant return for their financial outlay? Can he even guarantee a reliable internet connection? Possibly, but possibly is not adequate – and that alone is probably enough to insulate Scotland from rampant commercialism. An army of midges can be stood down for now.

Shane argues that any negativity towards Skyline Scotland deflects attention from the pressing matter of raising participation in hill running, particularly among young runners. 'Look at the Glen Coe Skyline,' he says. 'How many people are there in their twenties? Very, very few. Young people need a pathway to get into racing, something exciting and challenging. Your average £3 race, where your car gets stuck in a field and there are midges everywhere, does not appeal as it does to the hardened hill runner. Young people need something aspirational.'

Sasha Chepelin is the face of the future: ambitious, talented and intelligent. The twenty-year-old will win a hill race – Clachnaben, by a staggering 12 minutes – in the days after we meet, but Sasha's real excellence is in the discipline of orienteering. A third-year mechanical engineer at the University of Edinburgh, Sasha – wearing a British Talent Squad polo shirt – is part of a golden generation of Scotland-based orienteers, a group of athletes who were also taking hill runners on at their own game, and beating them. Orienteers had won four of the previous five Scottish championship races: Alasdair McLeod at Creag Dhubh, Rhys Findlay-Robinson at Merrick,

Kris Jones at the Pentland Skyline, and Graham Gristwood at Criffel. Finlay Wild would break the streak at Stùc a' Chroin, only for Murray Strain, the coordinator of the Scottish senior orienteering team, to overcome Finlay in the next championship race at Goatfell.

Sasha shares a university home in Edinburgh with Jacob Adkin, a two-time Scottish junior hill running champion. When they run uphill in training, Jacob is 'out of sight', but Sasha finds himself waiting for his housemate at the bottom, 'especially if it's a technical descent'.

Jacob, another third-year engineer, laughs when I repeat Sasha's words. 'He's about right. Orienteers are used to bashing over hardcore terrain. They are just fine going through a big load of bracken.'

The secret is little more than practice. The orienteer is schooled in the punishing terrain of the forest floor, evidenced by the grazes and scratches on Sasha's arms. Orienteers must think swiftly and operate flexibly, utilising a high knee lift to clear debris, continually adapting stride length. The best orienteers have, therefore, phenomenal cardiac strength. Compare that to the hill runner who in training will typically run on paths and trails, deskilling themselves for the rigours of crude, direct and pathless descents that often feature in races.

Murray Strain does not mince his words. Orienteers are simply working harder than hill runners, he insists. Orienteering, Murray explains, is a global sport: essentially, it is the same in every country, every continent. Hill running is not. Nowhere is quite like the Highlands. In Europe, they call what we know to be hill running 'mountain running', but they are utterly different sports. As fell running lives within the parochial borders of northern England, so hill running exists within the national boundary of Scotland; orienteers, meanwhile, look to the world. 'At training camps, orienteers are told how to train, how to recover, how to be fit and fast,' Murray adds. 'Orienteers take their sport that bit more seriously.'

I think of Finlay Wild and Jasmin Paris, the male and female emblems of hill running in Scotland, two uncoached athletes who admit there is 'no plan'. I find it hard to disagree with Murray.

And what of the future of a sport that is dominated – certainly in racing terms – by over-40s?

'Every year there seems to be a new strategy to get kids involved in orienteering,' Sasha says. Schools like the cognitive element of orienteering, with the sport promoting a sense of independence and encouraging decision-making. 'My old school in Banchory has a huge group and they send teams to the World Schools,' he continues. 'I'm not saying orienteering is perfect. Some would say it's not doing enough, but when you compare the two, orienteering has the advantage in terms of what's being done to recruit in primary and secondary schools. It's becoming more and more common.'

What are Scottish Hill Runners doing in schools? 'That's not the sort of thing we talk about at meetings,' Angela Mudge concedes. Hill running would, admittedly, be a harder sell. Should the organisation be encouraging schoolchildren – or anyone for that matter? The brief of Scottish Hill Runners is not to 'actively promote' the sport. That responsibility falls on Scottish Athletics, the governing body. While Scottish Athletics supports 'competitive opportunities' for school-age athletes through junior hill running championships, participation rates are unimpressive. In the first event of 2017, held in conjunction with Cioch Mhòr, there were eight finishers, with just one of those a girl. There was a greater turnout at the individual championships at the more conveniently-located Lomonds of Fife, where 62 runners raced in eight age categories, albeit with race numbers dwindling in the older years.

Perhaps the numbers confirm hill running has no place in schools' games programmes and will forever be marginalised in favour of easier-to-manage athletics and cross-country. But while I would pity the person writing the risk assessment form to take a group of fourteen-year-olds for a run in the mountains, it can be done.

A 'Mini Stùc' race was held the day before Stùc a' Chroin, featuring 51 children from a cluster of schools in the Strathyre area. Off they went, along a forestry track, up a hill, and back down. Eve Hatton, a Primary 7 pupil at Strathyre Primary, might not have appreciated her extended metaphor: 'I set off and it was very steep at first, but it got better. It was harder than I thought. When I crossed the finishing line I was relieved and proud of myself.'

Libby Brydie in Primary 6, meanwhile, already sounds like a hill runner: 'After the race we got sandwiches.'

Where hill running goes from here – like a lot of things in the twenty-first century – ultimately depends on its image, something that might just keep Eve and Libby going to the mountains.

'The viewpoint that hill running is a bit crazy has always been there,' Sasha explains. 'You don't get a parkrun going up a hill; if you get a parkrun with 50 metres of climb it's seen as being "hilly". If there was an equivalent, like racing up and down Arthur's Seat every Saturday morning, maybe it would be different? When I say I run, some people are like, "that's cool, I go running too," but their definition of running is half an hour once a week. Other people ask, "why would you do that? Why not go to the gym and run on a treadmill?"' At least the treadmill runners have some comprehension. 'There's a large group of people who wouldn't consider running, let alone running on hills,' Sasha says.

Jacob agrees. Even he was put off the sport when, in a 'baptism of fire', he ran the Scald Law junior race attached to the Carnethy 5 in deep snow as a twelve-year-old. He did not race in the hills again until he was fourteen. 'People think hill running is a bit weird. Outside the running community, people ask, "why do you do it?" They are shocked you might spend your time running up a hill for pleasure.'

As editor of *Athletics Weekly*, Jason Henderson has an overview of an entire, incomparably varied sport. 'Track athletics has glamour and appeal,' he says. 'Some events are just more popular than others, but hill running isn't some tiny sport at the bottom of the pecking order.' Hill and mountain runners have occasionally featured on *Athletics Weekly*'s coveted front page: Kilian Jornet, unsurprisingly; Jessica Augusto; Lizzy Hawker. 'I reckon we probably had some well-known fell and hill runners from the 1970s and 80s on our covers during that period,' Jason adds. He likens the sport to cross-country, a pursuit that is also 'basic' and 'pure', but they have together been overtaken by more fashionable and marketable pursuits. Perhaps this makes hill running and cross-country stronger? These are sports built on deep, firm foundations that do not need continual reinforcement.

Even then, no sport can stand still. Running is now a market-place, subject to fads and driven by trends, and the sport is booming. The UK's running population is apparently more than 10 million. Even in Scotland, a country overwhelmed by an obesity epidemic – 67 per cent of the population are over-weight, according to a UK Government report – and where children are derided as sedentary social media addicts, adult participation rates are up.

The amateur sport seems to be developing along two lines – the first, accessibility; the second, extremity. The parkrun movement is largely responsible for the former, with some 500 events in the UK, giving people who might never have run a stepping stone into the sport. While some are step-ping, others are taking giant leaps. Ultrarunning – be it on road, track or trail – began as a secretive, niche discipline of, according to Jason, 'anoraks plodding around by themselves'. Not now. The anoraks at the Ultra-Trail du Mont-Blanc cost hundreds of pounds; the event is 'trendy and cool', the Formula 1 of trail running. Like the Glen Coe Skyline, it is a race unafraid to look in the mirror and pout: 'You are the fairest of them all.' The images that accompany the action are spectacular: runners moving across narrow ridges, framed on a background of serrated mountains or – in the case of the Skyline – the wildscape of Rannoch Moor. The photographs and videos, with drone footage heightening the spectacle, are better than the real thing, for when you race along a hairline ridge, you do not pause to look behind. The rhetoric too is crafted to enthral. Shane Ohly has described the Skyline as 'the pinnacle mountain running event in the world'; the Ultra-Trail du Mont-Blanc is characterised as 'mythical'. The words carry a swagger that does not exist in traditional hill racing, a sport that defers to gritty pragmatism. 'Direct descent to lochans impossible due to sheer precipice on north side of Beinn Shiantaidh,' reads one of the typically robust instructions to competitors in the Isle of Jura fell race.

In Britain, ultra races have become harder and longer; interest in events like the Dragon's Back or the Spine Race along the Pennine Way is unprecedented. 'Is 100 miles the new marathon?' *Runner's World* asked in 2015. As the appetite for more extreme undertakings grows, what will be the 'new' 100 miles? What is next?

Even though an astonishing 380,000 people entered the ballot to run the 2018 London Marathon, 'running around a city centre is probably something runners want to do a little less,' says Jason Henderson. 'The pioneers of marathon running in the 1970s couldn't have imagined the London Marathon would come along, then be the huge spectacle it is today.'

It is a view shared by Kilian Jornet. 'More people are living in cities and I think they have a greater need to get out into natural surroundings,' he said in an interview with *Athletics Weekly*.

Could hill running be next? Does the sport hold the untapped potential that marathon running possessed 40 years ago? Does the sport linger at the same junction that faced triathlon and ultrarunning in the early years of the century?

Scottish Hill Runners will not seek to market the sport. That they are happy with the status quo is clear. Nor will the Fell Runners Association. When the organisation asked its members whether its 'passive stance in publicising fell running' should be maintained, the clear majority of more than 2,000 people responded overwhelmingly – only 16 per cent believed the association should 'be more proactive'. There is logic in that. Surely it would be irresponsible to encourage those to the hills who may be ill-equipped and unprepared for the rigours of high, unpredictable British mountains? But it is a view that is merely the tip of a very complex iceberg.

'Where does the sport go from here?' I posed the question on the Fell Runners UK Facebook group, a fast-expanding crowd with numbers of members in five figures. Two themes quickly emerged: hill runners care passionately about the future of their sport; as a result, they will fight to preserve what they perceive to be its culture and tradition. That should not come as a surprise. Running up and down hills is not a pursuit you can afford to be lukewarm about. An only half-joking response from David Johnson epitomised the hands-off-our-sport-at-all-costs sentiment that characterised many of the comments. 'New FRA rule: To be classified as a fell race an event must not provide a T-shirt or medal or goody bag for just finishing or entering. Only pies, cakes, chocolate and alcohol should be provided at the organiser's discretion.'

What else does the future hold? Access to land will become an increasing problem; National Parks will begin to impose tighter restrictions on land use – the Lake District notably became a UNESCO World Heritage Site in 2017; race organisers will need to be determined to cut through the red tape faced by Gordon Pryde and many others; inexperienced runners attracted to the idea of hill running *will* put themselves at risk; the cost of racing will go up. There are some who even envisage hill running becoming an underground sport, with secret races occurring at night. 'The best raves were low-key, word of mouth and illegal,' wrote Gavin Stewart. 'Fell running can follow suit.'

I will stop there, for this is thoroughly depressing.

Of this there is no doubt: hill running will become more popular; there will be more races in the style of Skyline

Scotland and Ultra Trail Scotland; there will be more races billed as 'ultra' or 'tough' or 'trail' that feature elements of running on hills; outdoor companies will increasingly see the sport as a lucrative market; the brilliance of the mountains will have to be shared.

Can hill running ever 'boom'? Can the sport be the 'new' 100 miles? The 'simple' version of hill running could not, for it surely lacks the necessary infrastructure or accessibility. What about trail and ultrarunning that crosses over into hill running? Possibly. The consequences of that growth are what threatens the sport – or at least what is perceived as threatening.

Hill running has been here before. While it is easy to see commercialisation as a vulgar, modern trait, cynics would argue otherwise: fell running was turned into a commercial enterprise as early as the late nineteenth century by guides racers competing for money, while the treeless landscape of the Lake District is a product – to use the words of the environmental activist George Monbiot – of the 'great damage farming has inflicted'.

Nor are we powerless in this. People inspire people, and whatever the brave new world of hill running is, it can be led by us: the runners.

It is already happening. Let us call it the Donnie Campbell effect.

What riled people about *that* 'winter' Ramsay was Donnie's apparent self-promotion, initially on Facebook and Twitter, and then on the news channels that picked up the story. Traditionalists were appalled by the glorification. Stuff tradition, Donnie seemed to say. Let's not keep these things quiet. Let's shout about them. Let's celebrate them. To some, it is an attitude that tarnishes the sport in the same way as the symbolic orange flags of the Glen Coe Skyline on the Aonach Eagach. But Donnie did no harm. To borrow a sentiment written about Skye, his place of birth, Donnie merely brought 'to the notice of the world the glories of these grand mountains'.

Donnie was also at work, representing Salomon, and is one of an increasing number of hill and fell runners sponsored or supported by companies seeking to raid the purses of hill runners. Being a capable athlete is a pre-requisite, but so is the desire to sell. What use is a runner living in a social media black hole? He or she *needs* to share a photograph of their sponsor-branded socks received in the morning post. There is no shortage of volunteers: runners are willingly being turned into marketers. Take Ben Mounsey, a Yorkshire schoolteacher and fell running champion who flies the flag for Inov-8, Mountain Fuel and Suunto. 'Social media platforms have allowed information, photos, results and videos to be shared more freely, and people are beginning to take a bigger interest in the sport,' he says. That is partly down to him. With Ben's followers across three social media platforms numbering several thousands, he is a potentially powerful influence. His words and actions matter.

'Hill running has maintained its traditional values and stayed true to its roots,' Ben says. 'It still remains a very specialist activity, popular only with hardened athletes in the northern parts of Britain. It appeals to those who love it for what it is – a tough, simple and honest sport. The reasons to compete are purely intrinsic.'

Those who already go to the hills will nod furiously in agreement at such statements, but can someone promote 'traditional values' when they are effectively in the pay of corporate enterprises? I would not know; I have never been a sponsored athlete. What I do know is that if I was as accomplished in the mountains as Ben Mounsey, there is no way I could fund myself: the race entries, the shoes, the kit, the travel. Even 'the greatest', Angela Mudge, received sponsorship from Salomon. How else does a top-class runner in an amateur sport do just that – be a top-class runner in an amateur sport? In that context, who can begrudge Ben Mounsey the occasional free pair of shoes from Inov-8? Guides racers expected payment; Ben would probably do it all for nothing.

In their tweets and updates, Donnie and Ben do not need to preach to the converted. As salesmen for their brands and sport, their message is distilled to a wider audience – to those people who might one day be hill runners, those people who have at times been characterised as ill-prepared, disrespecting incomers. These intruders will pour uncontrollably into the mountains, spook the sheep, kick down stone walls, discard gel sachets in bogs, get lost and hypothermic.

We all start somewhere. We cannot all grow up on a sheep farm in a remote Lakeland valley. Where should incomers start? Perhaps that is the role of 'trail' events and the more accessible races of the Skyline Scotland and Ultra Trail Scotland packages: to offer a springboard to pure hill and fell running, a kind of parkrun-on-steroids. Some of those considering the Ultra Trail Scotland races have come from an obstacle racing background, Casey Morgan tells me. 'Our races are a safe middle ground between things like Tough Mudder and traditional hill racing, albeit in a very real and challenging environment.' The runners will soon work out if they belong, for competing in the Ring of Steall Skyrace on a marked course with dozens of others is utterly different from running it alone in clag.

I was a southern intruder. I did not put my spare clothes in a waterproof bag; I blindly relied on others for navigation; I got very cold indeed.

I did all right in the end.

The Bob Graham was thrust into public consciousness as never before, when, within the space of three weeks, Jasmin Paris broke the women's record, and Nicky Spinks became only the second person to run a continuous double round within 48 hours. People suddenly began to get excited about a niche aspect of hill running that is the equivalent of cricket's five-day test match. Nonetheless, with a door left ajar, the masses peeped in.

I was once running with my brother-in-law and two of his

university friends on the paths of Delamere Forest when one of them told me he 'fancied doing the Bob Graham'. To his face, I encouraged. Secretly, I was incredulous. Deano might have watched Salomon Running TV's episode featuring the Bob Graham, starring firefighter-cum-fell runner Ricky Lightfoot that morning. Lightfoot runs across wind-blasted fells, falls in bogs and completes the round in archetypal January weather. It is inspiring, stirring stuff. Or Deano might have seen *Run Forever*, the Inov-8 film of Spinks' extraordinary back-to-back rounds. There is no dialogue for the first 60 seconds, just footage of Spinks trudging up a fell. Then she speaks: 'I'm probably going to push my body to a stage where it just goes enough is enough, and I sit down on the floor. I just want to know what I can do.'

Minutes later, as we climb out of the trees, I could tell Deano – red-faced, breathing hard, taking baby steps – is at his limit, even though the incline is moderate. I try to imagine him on Yewbarrow. Deano will probably never stand at the Moot Hall in the early hours, before hopefully scampering down a Keswick ginnel, torch light showing the way to Skiddaw. That is not the point; sometimes it is enough to dream. Good for Deano. To use Shane Ohly's word, here was 'aspiration' – aspiration inspired by hills and mountains, and by the terribly simple act of running among them.

'I like her because she seems normal,' Fi said after hearing about Jasmin Paris' 15-hour Bob Graham. And that was the point. If a vet from Edinburgh can run faster than any man on Ramsay's Round, and if a farmer who survived breast cancer can run non-stop over 84 fells for 45 hours, surely I can do *something*, goes the thinking. More and more people, from Deano to Nicky Spinks, want to work out what they 'can do', and there are few better places than mountains to find out what exactly that is.

Should that not be the role of our sport. To inspire? To give people a reason to aspire?

Thank goodness then for a personal trainer, a teacher, a

sheep farmer, a vet and a firefighter, telling it like it is. Here is a sport like no other: thrilling, bold, life-affirming, and – dare I say it – 'simple'. These people, these real and in many respects thoroughly normal heroes, inspire ordinary people to do astonishing things, and those examples are infinitely more powerful than a selfie with a shiny medal.

I think our sport is in safe hands.

Ultimately, the future belongs to the young – people like Jacob Adkin. The twenty-one-year-old has raced in Europe, marvelling at mountains four times the height of Munros, buoyed by the roaring enthusiasm of spectators lining the trails. He has trained with the Salomon Running Academy in the Bavarian Alps. He has written – in language young people can understand – about his joy in meeting Kilian Jornet and Emilie Forsberg in the French Pyrenees: 'OMG! Gobsmacked. We were completely speechless! They had seemed to exist only on videos and in pictures through social media, and yet here they were, in the flesh!'

Does Jacob want to move to the Alps, to attempt to 'make it' like Robbie Simpson? Quite simply, no. He wants to live and work and run in Scotland. Running in the Alps or Pyrenees is 'amazing', he says, but so too is running in the Pentlands or the Highlands – in a 'quieter, different way'. And that is the way it should be. Scotland has no need for imitation: hill running is already something special and unique.

After speaking to Jacob, I watched a series of short films posted on his blog. One features himself and Sasha as they ventured across Devil's Ridge to Sgùrr a' Mhaim. The soundtrack is appropriately called *Uplifting*. This sport does not look 'weird'; all I see is beautiful madness.

Richard Askwith's seminal book on fell running, *Feet in the Clouds*, was an attempt to explain the sport to outsiders. It became a classic, inspiring a generation of hill runners and would-be Bob Graham contenders. Capturing a sport that is defined by character and fortitude, not races and records, it ends nonetheless on a pessimistic note. In a book that was published in 2004, the author predicted the near-demise of fell running, envisaging a 'far more marginal' sport, and that it would be 'hard to imagine very many young people being capable of running in the mountains in twenty years' time'.

Twenty years are not yet up, but Richard does not need to wait until 2024 to reassess his view. 'I was completely wrong, wasn't I? It hasn't worked out like that at all.' Richard can be forgiven for not predicting the future. We are speaking on the day after the 2017 general election, after all.

'I wrote that partly because that's what was being said: it's dying out.' Young people at the turn of the century seemed to be more interested in the emerging, trendier sports of triathlon and adventure racing, he says. Similarly, Richard could not have predicted the impact of technology – from what runners wear on their feet and wrists, to the gadgets that have made hill-going far more accessible – or that there would be an influx of people to the sport able to afford such luxuries. Richard was writing in the era of map and compass, when hill running was primarily about 'getting to know mountains'.

'For the people winning a lot of hill and ultra races now, it's really about being a great athlete, rather than being a mountain person.' He tells me about Marcus Scotney, the winner of the 2017 Dragon's Back, who Richard had met a few weeks earlier at the Buxton Mountain Festival. 'Marcus says he goes around with a blue arrow on his wrist and just follows it. The whole idea of, where am I, am I going to get lost? has gone out of the window. It's a question of whose legs and lungs are the strongest. It's still awe-inspiring, but in a different way.'

Does he think the sport has lost its moral compass? 'Not necessarily, but it's changed,' Richard says. 'The thing that impressed me back then was how these guys were just so hard, so tough, really just human beings against the mountains and the elements, and I couldn't understand how people could be that tough because I certainly wasn't.'

He asked me what I thought. I thought of Sasha Chepelin

running efforts on Arthur's Seat, 30 seconds hard, 30 seconds easy – for an hour. I thought of Steph Provan stepping out of her front door after putting her children to bed. I thought of Colin Donnelly moving up Craig Varr, his nose to the floor. I thought of Alan Smith jumping off a cliff.

'I think they are still hard,' I say.

Hill running will always be defined by hard men and women. How could it not? Technology and social media cannot make running up a hill easier.

In a world of change, the greatest obstacle will always be geography, but let's not overcomplicate 'simple' things. Find a hill, do your best to run up, stay high for as long as you can, run down, call yourself a hill runner, and one day, like the monarch of the glen, you might know what it is to fly.

'Why do you run?' I ask Jacob. That question again.

'It's a cliché,' he says. 'It's a massive sense of freedom. Running up a hill, getting to the top, running along a ridge, seeing what you have accomplished. I have gone to places I would never have been.'

This is no cliché. Hill running is a metaphor for human existence. Even an eleven-year-old girl from Strathyre gets that. Dress it up as you will – call it the Glen Coe Skyline, or the Pentland Skyline, or that £3-to-enter race on a weekday evening, or maybe just you, on your own, in the mountains – the sensation, the thrill of being high, is perpetual. That can never, ever change. There is something of Dennisbell McGregor of Ballochbuie in us all – that insatiable desire to touch the sky. There always will be. The future will unravel in ways we could not have foreseen, but there can never be a day when we no longer answer the call of the mountains.

22

ADMIRING THE VIEW

Newtonmore, the first Saturday in August, always the first Saturday in August. We run a lap of the games field, duck under a rail, hurdle a gate, dash across a field of long grass, jump a fence, then another, wade a river, scramble up a bank of earth, find yet another fence, cross a road, fling legs over a crash barrier, follow a rough, twisting track, file along an ever-rising path through birch woods, climb a steepening slope of naked rock, meet a wall of soil, toil along a heather-lined thread, crest a windy summit. There is a sport, synthesised into 2 miles and 23 minutes.

There, on the top of An Torr, we are at the centre of Scotland, at the pulsing heart of beautiful madness, a hill running summer pirouetting about us.

The Cairngorms are a grey pile to the north-west; Jim Mann had made a 'race-track' of them, toppling Jon Broxap's twenty-nine-year-old record for the number of Munros climbed within 24 hours. But imagination was the victor here. So established were the core of the long-distance mountain routes pioneered by Philip Tranter and Blyth Wright, the assumption that a greater concentration of Munros could be found elsewhere had not been seriously considered. A little imagination was all that was required. Not long after meeting Jon to discuss the record, Jim received a note through the mail. Written on an attached post-it were the words: 'An alternative!' Beneath a puzzling title, 'The Phil Clark Round', there was a list of mountains and the distances between them. The names of the Munros, at first, were unfamiliar. These were not peaks in Lochaber or Affric or Shiel; these mountains were the Cairngorms. The overall distance was further than Jon's 29-Munro round, but with less ascent. 'It might just work,' Jim concluded. It did. Starting on Lochnagar and finishing on Bheinn Bhreac, Jim summited 30 Munros in 22 hours, making it back to Invercauld Bridge in time for last orders. The round, named after its innovator Phil Clark, has three provisos: 30 Munros, one pint, no more than 24 hours.

The summits that circle Glen Coe, meanwhile, could only be imagined. In a year in which he had twice climbed Everest without supplementary oxygen and won the Hardrock 100 despite dislocating a shoulder in a fall at mile 13, Kilian Jornet arrived in Lochaber several days ahead of the Glen Coe Skyline. It was his first time in Scotland, but he quickly got into the spirit: climbing wind-blasted Tower Ridge, before finding the summit of Ben Nevis immersed in clag – he probably had a better view from Everest – and later posting a photograph of himself grinning behind a midge net. It was on the Aonach Eagach that Jornet made his break, moving decisively clear of Jonathan Albon. It seemed like a true race, with only six minutes separating the pair at the end, but Albon insisted his rival won 'easily'. In terms of mountain running, Jornet was 'two brackets' above Albon, the latter reckoned. 'Two brackets.' Where does that leave the rest of us?

So, to Ben Nevis. Could the monarch of the glen make it eight in a row? It would be easy to assume so, perhaps to even entertain creeping cynicism about the whole affair. But no-one wins Britain's greatest hill race by luck. To succeed year after year requires a level of commitment and consistency that only man can truly appreciate. Nor did Brice Delsouiller, a sheep farmer from the French Pyrenees, and Rob Jebb, come to Fort William just to make up the numbers. Yet there is nothing they can do. Finlay Wild is first to the top and first to the bottom – finishing six minutes clear of Delsouiller. He leaves Claggan Park by bicycle. Car horns toot; passers-by give him a thumbs-up. Finlay just smiles.

From An Torr, Wigtownshire is as distant as Orkney. Glyn Jones has had a busy summer. While he hoped to return to hill running, he had been 'welded limpet-like to the grind of daily chores on the croft'. He wondered: 'How did I ever find enough time to do those hill challenges?' What he misses most is the inspiration they brought. 'Enthusiasm for anything is so lacking in this insipid grey climate of "cool",' he bemoans.

He does not mean this sport, of course.

The chance for John Hammond to spend 24 hours running up and down Arthur's Seat had not arisen. It had for Lewis Breen. The twenty-five-year-old project engineer from Duntocher had walked Arthur's Seat as a boy, but running to the top was a new experience. 'I couldn't really remember what it looked like,' he said. Lewis would soon be over-familiar, summiting 48 times, fuelled by the bakery aisle of Lidl, climbing a cumulative 7,500 metres.

For others, a single ascent of any hill or mountain will suffice. A figure, bending forward, was on the last of the wall of steps that decorate the western outlook of Blackford Hill. 'Hello, Bill,' I called as I passed. Others on the hill that day would have seen old age and frailty. They would greet the doddering man with a sympathetic smile. I imagined Bill Gauld dancing.

Another who dances is Jasmin Paris. No major races, no rounds, no records. 'What *is* Jasmin up to?' people were asking. She would stand on the start line at Caerketton, finishing sixth woman, two-thirds of the way down the field. But Jasmin had a handicap – she was six months pregnant. I watched the end of her race, a bulge prominent under her shirt, remembering this was the person who ran Ramsay's Round in 16 hours. That did not seem to matter now. Some things are more important – and some things no 'lad' can emulate.

The once-purple heather is brown and frayed as I stand again on the summit of Allermuir. I am facing north, looking across city and forth, when I sense a touch on my back. I turn to look at the Pentlands, bathed in the low pink and yellow of sunset. I am not a 'white-haired one' here. I am untouchable. Glory cradles me. What else is there to do but run on, for the mountains are calling.

ACKNOWLEDGEMENTS & BIBLIOGRAPHY

The 'hearts bursting' opening of *Running Through Time* is inspired by Robert Louis Stevenson's novel *Kidnapped* (1886), which is referenced in more detail in *The Road to Swanston*. An account of the eleventh century race on Creag Choinnich is told in *Legends of the Braes O'Mar* (1876), by John Grant. Although the event is generally accepted as the world's first hill race, Grant's narrative of the event should be treated as romanticised entertainment rather than historical fact. The 'omniscient narrator' nonetheless is Grant. *The Essential Guide to the Highland Games* (1992), by Michael Brander, is a more conservative history of gatherings in Scotland. Queen Victoria's observations in the same chapter are taken from *Leaves from the Journal of Our Life in the Highlands* (1868). The first of several references to Nan Shepherd's *The Living Mountain* (1977) appear in this chapter, while William Forsyth's *In the Shadow of Cairngorm* (1900) also gives an atmospheric insight into the plateau. The closing remarks of *Running Through Time* – and of course the title of this book – are a homage to John Muir's oft-repeated words: 'The mountains are calling and I must go.'

The 72-second Tennent's lager advert that opens *Epiphany* is easily found on YouTube. Alec Keith's long history of endurance running is gleaned from his self-authored essay *Cairngorm Timeline*, published in the *Scottish Hill Runners*

Journal. He thinks the 'misty mountain' might have been Ben Macdui, but he cannot be sure. It is, perhaps, more mysterious in anonymity. The history of the Isle of Jura fell race is told in Donald Booth's *They Come ... and They Go* (2013).

I have inherited a welter of literature about Skye that proved integral in writing *The Monarch of the Glen*. The pick of these are Alasdair Alpin MacGregor's *Over the Sea to Skye* (1926), Ben Humble's *Tramping in Skye* (1949), W.H. Murray's *The Companion Guide to the West Highlands of Scotland* (1969), Derek Cooper's *Skye* glossary (1970), and Norman Newton's *Skye* (2010). For mountain heights and clarification on routes, as in all chapters, I referred to the Scottish Mountaineering Club (SMC) publications, *Munro's Tables* (1997) and *The Munros* (2010). Earlier editions of SMC guidebooks, notably *The Island of Skye* (1954) and J.W. Simpson's *Climbers' Guide to the Cuillin of Skye* (1969) also proved useful. Finlay Wild's typically understated blog was referenced, as were interviews published in *The Fellrunner*, by the John Muir Trust, and *Scotland Outdoors*. For further details on Eric Beard, a biography by Ally Beaven, published on his blog, is excellent. The spelling of mountain names in this chapter and throughout the book mimics the style used by Ordnance Survey.

The accounts in *Imagination* are pieced together from a variety of interviews and sources, including the referenced *Scotsman* article and *Yet Another Yawn (Yarn?)*, by Helene Whitaker (nee Diamantides), which came to me in a wad of notes from Adrian Belton. Richard Askwith's *Feet in the Clouds* (2003) provides further insight into Helene Whitaker, as does Steve Chilton's *The Round: in Bob Graham's footsteps* (2015) in respect of Martin Stone. Information from three further sources – *The Fellrunner*, the long-distance records section of the Scottish Hill Runners website, and the Ramsay's Round website maintained by Charlie Ramsay – are used extensively in this chapter and later in the text. The Carnethy Hill Running Club winter talks series is open to non-club members and is highly recommended, featuring speakers (on subjects not exclusively related to hill running) who would not be out of place at mountain or outdoor festivals.

The full account of Nick Clark's attempt on the Bob Graham, referenced in *An English Distraction*, can be read on his personal website.

Stevenson's real-life and fictional influence in *The Road to Swanston* is obvious. His description of Swanston on the wall of the Brasserie appears in *Edinburgh: Picturesque Notes* (1879). The historical detail of the Ben Nevis Race, in this chapter and more extensively in *Running Forever*, is partly sourced from Hugh Dan MacLennan's exhaustive *The Ben Race* (1994). In the same chapter, Colin Youngson's biographical note on Colin Donnelly on the *Scottish Distance Running History* website was a helpful starting point for research, as was the history section of the Scottish Hill Runners website, and Colin Muskett's interview of Colin on his eponymous climbing website.

As stated in *The Invincibles*, Adrian Belton's notes on his Ramsay's Round, and also his 24-hour Munro round (featured in *Climb Every Mountain*), are from his personal archives. Jez Bragg allowed extracts from his personal blog to be included. The *Catcher in the Rye* quote that concludes *The Invincibles* encapsulates my feelings at the time: utterly inspired by the feat of Jon Ascroft.

Parts of several posts from Jasmin Paris' blog are quoted in *Prosecco, Pizza and Ice Cream*. Comments made by Wendy Dodds and Martin Stone in this chapter originally appeared in *The Fellrunner*. Suse Coon's *Race You to the Top* (1987), which provides a short history of the sport, interviews and a list of races, was a useful source of reference in this and later chapters. Steven Fallon's excellent compendium, *Classic Hill Runs and Races in Scotland* (2009), served a similar purpose throughout the writing and editing process. The footage of Jasmin drinking Coke in the Glen Coe Skyline was captured by Claire Maxted.

Like *The Fellrunner*, the *Scottish Hill Runners Journal* is an esoteric publication, but diligent searching through back issues can uncover gems. *The Art of Descending*, referenced in *Anatomy of the Ramsayist*, is such a find. In the same chapter, I am also indebted to Mark Hartree – whose Ramsay's Round report begins with the opening lyrics to the chorus of the Rolling Stones' *Honky Tonk Women*, 'I met a gin-soaked, bar-room queen in Memphis' – for permission to use extracts from his musically-inspired account. Incidentally, the B-side to the album *Live'r Than You'll Ever Be* is appropriately *You Can't Always Get What You Want*. Similarly, Bill Johnson's *Charlie Ramsay and Me: A Tale of Obsession*, which has also appeared in Calder Valley Fell Runners' marvellously-named newsletter *Sheepsheet*, was enormously useful. Furthermore, in *Anatomy of the Ramsayist*, like a number of other chapters, I referenced Scottish Hill Racing, a website maintained by Chris Upson, providing race details and results dating back to 2005. A more detailed profile of Malcolm Patterson is included in *Running Hard* (2016), by Steve Chilton. I am also obliged to Renee McGregor for her insight into performance nutrition. Her running-specific book, *Fast Fuel: Food for Running Success* (2016), is particularly recommended.

A Way of Death was an especially hard chapter to write. I am grateful, therefore, for the blessing of Lynda Johnston, Alex Brett's partner, and also for the contributions of Alex's friends, notably Ross Bannerman. I am also thankful to Nick Macdonald and Alan Renville, who were prepared to speak frankly about the accidents that befell Peter Brooks and Martin Hulme respectively.

Davy Duncan's *A Journal for all Hill Runners and Other Eccentrics*, as referenced in *A Way of Life*, remains accessible on the Ochil Hill Runners website. Much of the information on Harkabir Thapa stems from my previously-referenced Skye library and a brief history published on the Carnethy website.

The Stevenson quote in *Finding My Way* is taken from his poem *Winter-time*.

In writing *Ambushed by Chno Dearg*, I am particularly indebted to Glyn Jones, initially for allowing me to take copies of 24 pages of writing on his Tranter's and Ramsay's rounds, and later in letters. Glyn is the hero of this book and a source of personal inspiration, as alluded to in my conclusion to *Glory*. Much of the narrative in *Ambushed by Chno Dearg* was also derived from the meticulous reports of John Fleetwood, Shane Ohly, Tom Phillips and Jon Gay, as well as Dan Gay's article in the *Scottish Hill Runners Journal*. I am appreciative also to Al Powell and Martin Moran for their timely input. Shane Ohly's remarks on Donnie Campbell's round were originally published on the *UK Hillwalking* website.

The Robbie Simpson interview referenced in *Answering the Call* is available on the *Tracksmith* website.

Further details of Jon Broxap's 29-Munro round in *Climb Every Mountain* can be found in *The Fellrunner* and an article authored by Martin Moran in *The Scots Magazine*. There is a plethora of literature on various continuous running and walking rounds in Scotland, notably Andrew Dempster's *The Munro Phenomenon* (1996), *Hamish's Mountain Walk* (2010), by Hamish Brown, Hugh Symonds' *Running High* (1991), *Millennial Munros* (2017), by Charlie Campbell, and Manny Gorman's *The Corbett Round* (2014), all referenced in this chapter. Chris Townsend's *The Munros and Tops* (1997) and Mike Cawthorne's *Hell of a Journey* (2004) were also cross-referenced. The websites of Charlie Campbell, Chris Upson and Stephen Pyke offer perspectives into the continuous Munro runs. Interviews with Rob Woodall on the *Munros Scotland* and the *UK Hillwalking* websites offer further insight into his prodigious bagging.

Angela Mudge and Martin Hyman were unwaveringly patient in various interviews for *The Greatest*. Martin's impeccable files of his correspondence with Angela were essential to the narrative. Alex Menarry's interview with Angela Mudge, published in the *Carnethy Journal*, provides additional insight.

In *Glory*, I briefly reference the blogs of Alicia Hudelson and Pete Duggan.

Likewise in *Beautiful Madness* and *Admiring the View*, I refer to blog posts by Jonathan Albon, Sasha Chepelin and Jacob Adkin. For their contributions to *Beautiful Madness*, I am particularly grateful to Shane Ohly, the pupils of Strathyre Primary, Jason Henderson, Gordon Pryde, Richard Askwith, and to Roger Scrutton for his valuable insight into orienteering in Scotland.

Despite the traditionalism of hill running, social media and blogs were invaluable, and numerous titbits have been sourced from the likes of Attackpoint, Facebook, Instagram, Strava and Twitter.

Not all references are mentioned here, but I hope they are otherwise detailed in the text. I can only apologise for any oversights.

Beyond the sources listed above, I have, of course, spoken to hundreds of hill runners, past and present, from the front to the back. Many are not named in the narrative, but every conversation has helped to shape my understanding and appreciation of this wonderful sport. I must single out Ross Christie, however, who combines his love for the mountains with creatively mapping them, and it is his maps that adorn these pages.

It is right that my family are part of this story. It was hearing Arielle chanting 'higher' and wanting to 'touch the sky' as I pushed her on the swings in Morningside Park that inspired the phrase that first appears in the opening paragraph. To run among hills and mountains is to receive a calling; the same can be said of writing a book. So to Fi, Arielle and Aphra, for helping me do that, I am most grateful.

And finally: to the high places.

INDEX